Great American Drives *of the West*

Fodor's Travel Publications
New York Toronto London Sydney Auckland
www.fodors.com

Fodor's Road Guide USA: Great American Drives of the West

Contributors
Editor: Paul Eisenberg
Editorial Contributor: Carissa Bluestone
Editorial Production: Linda K. Schmidt
Maps: Rebecca Baer, Robert Blake, David Lindroth, Todd Pasini
Design: Siobhan O'Hare
Cover Photograph: Craig Aurness/Corbis
Production/Manufacturing: Robert B. Shields

First Edition
ISBN 1–4000–1205–8
ISSN 1538–7615

Special Sales
Fodor's Travel Publications are available at special discounts for bulk purchases for sales
promotions or premiums. Special editions, including personalized covers, excerpts of
existing guides, and corporate imprints, can be created in large quantities for special
needs. For more information, contact your local bookseller or write to Special Markets,
Fodor's Travel Publications, 280 Park Avenue, New York, NY 10017. Inquiries from Canada
should be directed to your local Canadian bookseller or sent to Random House of
Canada, Ltd., Marketing Department, 2775 Matheson Boulevard East, Mississauga,
Ontario L4W 4P7. Inquiries from the United Kingdom should be sent to Fodor's Travel
Publications, 20 Vauxhall Bridge Road, London SW1V 2SA, England.

PRINTED IN THE UNITED STATES OF AMERICA
10 9 8 7 6 5 4 3 2 1

CONTENTS

Great American Drives

For some vacationers, driving is a means to get from one destination to the next as fast as Mother Nature, the roads, and the law will permit. If this is how you drive, you've picked up the wrong book.

If, for you, driving *is* the destination, and you pull over for reasons that don't necessarily involve food, fuel, or driving faster than the law permits, congratulate yourself on finding this guide. Inside are all the tools you'll need to plan perfect road trips in the 22 glorious states west of the Mississippi River.

Every chapter includes one or two easy-to-follow, point-by-point driving tours, corresponding maps, and specific rules of the road. And since this wouldn't be a Fodor's guide without reviews, we harvested our multivolume Road Guide series to give you more than 1,400 listings for attractions, restaurants, and hotels along the way. With all the specific and practical information we provide, you can easily call to confirm the details that matter and study up on what you'll want to see and do before you leave home.

These drives set you on specific paths, but by all means allow yourself a few detours. Because as wonderful as it is to know the correct exit, it can be serendipitous to turn off elsewhere to discover that hole-in-the-wall diner with transcendent tomato soup, or a gallery crammed with dusty local curiosities. After all, it's this sense of adventure that helped shape the Great American Drives you have in your hands.

How to Use This Book

Alphabetical organization should make it a snap to navigate through these pages. Still, in putting them together, we've made certain decisions and used certain terms you need to know about.

ORGANIZATION

Following each tour are alphabetical, town-by-town listings with additional information about many of the sights mentioned in the tours, as well as listings for other attractions in those towns. We've also included information on nearby restaurants and hotels.

Attractions, restaurants, and hotels are listed under the nearest town covered in the tour.

Parks and forests are sometimes listed under the main access point.

Exact street addresses are provided whenever possible; when they are not available or applicable, directions and/or cross-streets are indicated.

FODOR'S CHOICE

Stars denote sights, restaurants, and hotels that are Fodor's Choices—our editors' picks of the best in a given region or price category.

SIGHTS

Admission is charged at many sights listed in this book, but we don't note the cost. If your drive passes a major city with high-profile historical sights or recreation areas, call for fees if this matters to you. Admission charges in most local museums are reasonable, and a fair number of the outdoor attractions we list are free. Also see our guidelines below for visiting national parks.

RESTAURANTS

We have provided restaurant listings for almost every town mentioned in these drives. Restaurants are grouped by price category, from most to least expensive, and arranged alphabetically within each category.

CATEGORY	COST*
$$$$	over $30
$$$	$20–$30
$$	$10–$20
$	under $10

*per person for a dinner entrée (or a lunch entrée if no dinner is served)

Some restaurants are marked with a price range ($$–$$$, for example). This indicates one of two things: either that the average cost straddles two categories, or that if you order strategically you can get out for less than most diners.

All restaurants are air-conditioned unless otherwise noted, and all permit smoking unless they're identified as "no smoking."

Dress: Assume that no jackets or ties are required for men unless specified.

Meals and hours: Assume that restaurants are open for lunch and dinner unless otherwise noted. We always indicate days closed.

Reservations: They are always a good idea. We don't mention them unless they're essential or are not accepted.

HOTELS

Hotels are listed only for towns we suggest as overnight stops. Properties are grouped by price category, from most to least expensive, then arranged alphabetically within each category.

CATEGORY	COST*
$$$$	over $200
$$$	$125–$200
$$	$75–$125
$	under $75

*cost of a double room for two during peak season, excluding tax and service charges.

Some hotels are marked with a price range ($$–$$$, for example). This indicates that the average cost straddles two categories.

Bear in mind that the prices gathered for this book are for standard double hotel or motel rooms, and you may pay more for suites or cabins. If a property we recommend is comprised only of suites, cabins, and other atypical lodgings, assume that the given price category applies.

AP: American Plan. The rate includes all meals. AP may be an option, or it may be the only meal plan available.

Baths: You'll find private bathrooms with bathtubs unless otherwise noted.

Business services: We note these only for properties with significant business amenities.

Exercising: We mention any "exercise equipment" even when there's no designated exercise area; if you want a dedicated facility, look for "gym."

Facilities: We list what's available but don't note charges for use. When pricing accommodations, always ask what's included.

Hot tub: This term denotes hot tubs, Jacuzzis, and whirlpools.

MAP: Modified American Plan. Rates at these properties include two meals.

Opening and closing: Assume that properties are open year-round unless otherwise indicated.

Pets: We note whether or not they're welcome and whether there's a charge.

Pools: Assume they're outdoors; indoor pools are noted.

Telephone and TV: Assume that you'll find them unless otherwise indicated.

NATIONAL PARKS

National parks protect and preserve the treasures of America's heritage, and they're always worth visiting. Many warrant a long detour. If your drive brings you to many national parks, consider purchasing the National Parks Pass ($50), which gets you and your companions free admission to all parks for one year. (Camping and parking are extra.) A percentage of the proceeds from sales of the pass helps fund park projects. Both the Golden Age Passport ($10), for those 62 and older, and the Golden Access Passport (free), for travelers with disabilities, entitle holders to free entry to all national parks, plus 50% off fees for the use of the many park facilities and services. You must show proof of age and of U.S. citizenship or permanent residency (such as a U.S. passport, driver's license, or birth certificate) and, if requesting Golden Access, proof of your disability. You must get your Golden Access or Golden Age passport in person; the former is available at all federal recreation areas, the latter at federal recreation areas that charge fees.

You may purchase the National Parks Pass by mail or through the Internet. For information, contact the National Park Service (Department of the Interior, 1849 C St. NW, Washington, DC 20240-0001, 202/208–4747, www.nps.gov). To buy the National Parks Pass, write to 27540 Ave. Mentry, Valencia, CA 91355, call 888/GO–PARKS, or visit www.nationalparks.org.

IMPORTANT TIP

Although all prices, opening times, and other details in this book are based on information supplied to us at press time, changes occur all the time in the travel world, and Fodor's cannot accept responsibility for facts that become outdated or for inadvertent errors or omissions. So always confirm information when it matters, especially if you're making a detour to visit a specific place.

LET US HEAR FROM YOU

Keeping a travel guide fresh and up-to-date is a big job, and we welcome any and all comments. We'd love to have your thoughts on places we've listed, and we're interested in hearing about your own special finds, even the ones in your own backyard. Our guides are thoroughly updated for each new edition, and we're always adding new information, so your feedback is vital. Contact us via e-mail in care of roadnotes@fodors.com (specifying the name of the book on the subject line) or via snail mail care of Road Guides at Fodor's, 280 Park Avenue, New York, NY 10017. We look forward to hearing from you.

Important Numbers and On-Line Info

LODGINGS

Adam's Mark	800/444—2326	www.adamsmark.com
Baymont Inns	800/428—3438	www.baymontinns.com
Best Western	800/528—1234	www.bestwestern.com
	TDD 800/528—2222	
Budget Host	800/283—4678	www.budgethost.com
Clarion	800/252—7466	www.clarioninn.com
Comfort	800/228—5150	www.comfortinn.com
Courtyard by Marriott	800/321—2211	www.courtyard.com
Days Inn	800/325—2525	www.daysinn.com
Doubletree	800/222—8733	www.doubletreehotels.com
Drury Inns	800/325—8300	www.druryinn.com
Econo Lodge	800/555—2666	www.hotelchoice.com
Embassy Suites	800/362—2779	www.embassysuites.com
Exel Inns of America	800/356—8013	www.exelinns.com
Fairfield Inn by Marriott	800/228—2800	www.fairfieldinn.com
Fairmont Hotels	800/527—4727	www.fairmont.com
Four Seasons	800/332—3442	www.fourseasons.com
Friendship Inns	800/453—4511	www.hotelchoice.com
Hampton Inn	800/426—7866	www.hampton-inn.com
Hilton	800/445—8667	www.hilton.com
	TDD 800/368—1133	
Holiday Inn	800/465—4329	www.holiday-inn.com
	TDD 800/238—5544	
Howard Johnson	800/446—4656	www.hojo.com
	TDD 800/654—8442	
Hyatt & Resorts	800/233—1234	www.hyatt.com
Inns of America	800/826—0778	www.innsofamerica.com
Inter-Continental	800/327—0200	www.interconti.com
La Quinta	800/531—5900	www.laquinta.com
	TDD 800/426—3101	
Loews	800/235—6397	www.loewshotels.com
Marriott	800/228—9290	www.marriott.com
Master Hosts Inns	800/251—1962	www.reservahost.com
Le Meridien	800/225—5843	www.lemeridien.com
Motel 6	800/466—8356	www.motel6.com
Omni	800/843—6664	www.omnihotels.com
Quality Inn	800/228—5151	www.qualityinn.com
Radisson	800/333—3333	www.radisson.com
Ramada	800/228—2828	www.ramada.com
	TDD 800/533—6634	
Red Carpet/Scottish Inns	800/251—1962	www.reservahost.com
Red Lion	800/547—8010	www.redlion.com
Red Roof Inn	800/843—7663	www.redroof.com
Renaissance	800/468—3571	www.renaissancehotels.com
Residence Inn by Marriott	800/331—3131	www.residenceinn.com
Ritz-Carlton	800/241—3333	www.ritzcarlton.com

Rodeway	800/228—2000	www.rodeway.com
Sheraton	800/325—3535	www.sheraton.com
Shilo Inn	800/222—2244	www.shiloinns.com
Signature Inns	800/822—5252	www.signature-inns.com
Sleep Inn	800/221—2222	www.sleepinn.com
Super 8	800/848—8888	www.super8.com
Travelodge/Viscount	800/255—3050	www.travelodge.com
Vagabond	800/522—1555	www.vagabondinns.com
Westin Hotels & Resorts	800/937—8461	www.westin.com
Wyndham Hotels & Resorts	800/996—3426	www.wyndham.com

AIRLINES

Air Canada	888/247—2262	www.aircanada.ca
Alaska	800/426—0333	www.alaska-air.com
American	800/433—7300	www.aa.com
America West	800/235—9292	www.americawest.com
British Airways	800/247—9297	www.british-airways.com
Continental Airlines	800/525—0280	www.continental.com
Delta	800/221—1212	www.delta.com
Northwest	800/225—2525	www.nwa.com
SkyWest	800/453—9417	www.delta.com
Southwest	800/435—9792	www.southwest.com
TWA	800/221—2000	www.twa.com
United	800/241—6522	www.ual.com
USAir	800/428—4322	www.usair.com

BUSES AND TRAINS

Amtrak	800/872—7245	www.amtrak.com
Greyhound	800/231—2222	www.greyhound.com
Trailways	800/343—9999	www.trailways.com

CAR RENTALS

Advantage	800/777—5500	www.arac.com
Alamo	800/327—9633	www.goalamo.com
Allstate	800/634—6186	www.bnm.com/as.htm
Avis	800/331—1212	www.avis.com
Budget	800/527—0700	www.budget.com
Dollar	800/800—4000	www.dollar.com
Enterprise	800/325—8007	www.pickenterprise.com
Hertz	800/654—3131	www.hertz.com
National	800/328—4567	www.nationalcar.com
Payless	800/237—2804	www.paylesscarrental.com
Rent-A-Wreck	800/535—1391	www.rent-a-wreck.com
Thrifty	800/367—2277	www.thrifty.com

Note: Area codes are changing all over the United States as this book goes to press. For the latest updates, check www.areacode-info.com.

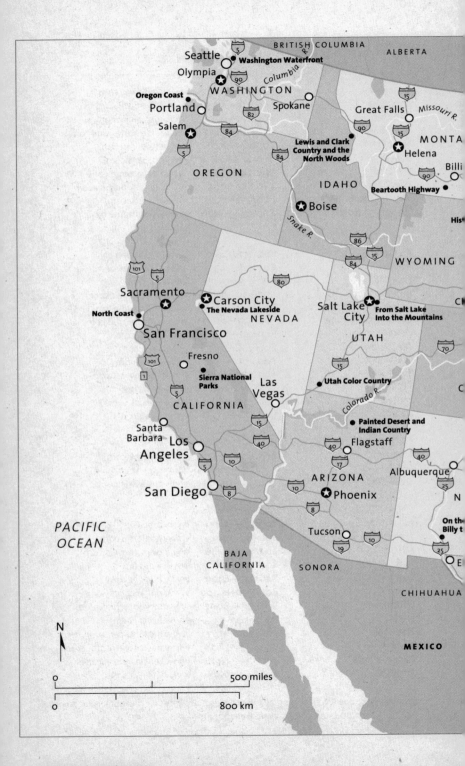

Regina

SASKATCHEWAN

MANITOBA

Winnipeg

ONTARIO

Lake Superior

Missouri R.

MONTANA

Billings

Bozeman Trail

NORTH DAKOTA

North Dakota Frontier

Fargo

Bismarck

MINNESOTA

Duluth

WISCONSIN

Historic Trails Trek

SOUTH DAKOTA

Pierre

Missouri R.

Minneapolis

St. Paul

Green Bay

Lake Michigan

Milwaukee

Black Hills and Badlands

Great River Road Along US 61

Madison

Iowa Great River Road

From the Powder River to the Parks

WYOMING

NEBRASKA

IOWA

Chicago

Cheyenne

Lincoln

Omaha

Des Moines

ILLINOIS

Denver

Lewis and Clark's Journey: Along the Missouri River

Topeka

Kansas City

Missouri Caves

Springfield

Colorado's Heartland

COLORADO

Santa Fe Trail Along US 56

Jefferson City

St. Louis

Mississippi R.

Ohio R.

KANSAS

MISSOURI

Circling Northern New Mexico

OKLAHOMA

Tulsa

ARKANSAS

Memphis

Santa Fe

Oklahoma City

Ouachita National Forest Along U.S. 59

Little Rock

NEW MEXICO

Amarillo

On the Trail of Billy the Kid

Scenic 7 Byway

MISSISSIPPI

El Paso

Dallas

Jackson

Rio Grande

TEXAS

Bandera to New Braunfels

Austin

Baton Rouge

Mississippi River Plantations

New Orleans

CHIHUAHUA

San Antonio

Houston

LOUISIANA

Kingsville to Aransas National Wildlife Refuge

COAHUILA

Gulf of Mexico

PAINTED DESERT AND INDIAN COUNTRY

FROM CAMERON TO THE THIRD MESA

Distance: 430 mi   Time: 3 days
Overnight Breaks: Kayenta, Chinle

While you could probably spend the better part of three days soaking up the beauty of the Painted Desert and the other scenic wonders of northeast Arizona, the main goal of this drive is to immerse you in the culture and history of the Navajo and Hopi tribes. The region is dominated by the 25,000-square-mi Navajo Nation. Although it's the largest reservation in the United States—larger than many eastern states, in fact—the Navajo Nation is sparsely populated—only 175,000 residents call it home.

Etiquette is key when visiting any reservation. In some areas, such as the Navajos' Monument Valley, off-road driving, hiking, and rock climbing are forbidden. Photography and videotaping also are unwelcome in many situations. Hopi villages and ceremonies may not be photographed, sketched, nor their sounds recorded. Navajos, however, do business with photographers, charging a dollar or two for a pose. In general, where anything is prohibited, signs will be abundant.

Summer is the most popular time along this route, so spring or fall (when the weather is cooler) are ideal touring times.

❶ The **Cameron Trading Post** is a good place to get your bearings and pick up maps before you begin your journey. There's a large arts-and-crafts store, where you'll find a wide range of Navajo and Hopi pottery, jewelry, baskets, and rugs. When you're ready, take U.S. 89 north from Cameron. You'll drive through the west end of the Painted Desert. Continue for approximately 15 to 20 mi along this serene landscape of pink-hued vistas until you reach U.S. 160, which will take you to Tuba City. A short detour off U.S. 89 at Milepost 316 will lead you to Dinosaur Tracks, the preserved footprints of what is thought to have been a dilophosaurus.

❷ Back on U.S. 160, you'll come to **Tuba City.** The landscape around the town includes sediments deposited 20 million years ago. There's a small trading post on Main

Street, and it's a good place to stop for gas before heading on. Tuba City is also the home of the administrative center for the **Navajo Indian Reservation.**

❸ From Tuba City, continue east on U.S. 160 to Route 564 and head north for approximately 10 mi to **Navajo National Monument.** Here, in two strikingly spare and beautiful canyons, you'll find two of the largest and best-preserved cliff dwellings in all of the Southwest, Keet Seel and Betatakin, home to ancestral Puebloans, the Anasazi, between AD 1250 and 1300.

❹ Navajo for "broken pottery," **Keet Seel** is a well-preserved 160-room ruin. It's at an elevation of 7,000 ft, and only 20 visitors are allowed per day (between Memorial Day and Labor Day, when a ranger is on duty). The hike to the actual ruins is a vigorous 17 mi round-trip, but it's possible to obtain a permit to camp overnight if you call ahead.

❺ A shorter hike to **Betatakin** (Navajo for "ledge house") is possible, but it, too, is strenuous. Most visitors simply walk the ½-mi trail from the visitor center for a good view of the ruins. Those who hike to the site itself will find a 135-room ruin that seems to hang in midair before a sandstone wall. It was discovered in 1907 by a traveling rancher.

❻ **Kayenta,** about 30 mi to the northeast of Navajo National Monument (just north of U.S. 160 on U.S. 163) is a good base for touring the monument and is also a good place to spend the night.

7 The next morning, head back to U.S. 160 and proceed for approximately 10 mi to Route 59. Take Route 59 southeast for approximately 40 mi to the tiny town of Many Farms. From Many Farms, head south on U.S. 191 to **Chinle**. From here, you can begin your exploration of Canyon de Chelly (pronounced *d'shay*), which is 3 mi east of Chinle on Route 7.

Canyon de Chelly is a magnificent 84,000-acre park, whose two main gorges have dramatic, eroded sandstone walls up to 1,000 ft high. Ancient pictographs adorn many of the cliffs, and the canyon is home to more than 7,000 archaeological sites, some dating back 4,500 years. The bottom of the canyon is lush pasture; you'll see streams, peach orchards, and occupied hogans (Navajo dwellings).

Take the **South Rim Drive,** Route 7 from the visitor center, a 36-mi round-trip that goes through Spider Rock, Tsegi, and Junction overlooks to White House Overlook, where you'll find the trailhead of the only hike to the bottom of the canyon that visitors are permitted to take without a guide. You can hike down this steep but short (1¼ mi) path in just less than an hour (leave a little more time for the uphill return).

Chinle is an ideal place to spend the night after a day of exploring the canyon and its environs.

8 Day 3 begins on U.S. 191 south out of Chinle. Drive for about 30 mi to Route 264 and then head east for a few miles toward **Ganado** and the **Hubbell Trading Post National Historic Site.** In 1878, a 24-year-old by the name of John Lorenzo Hubbell purchased this establishment, where the Navajo and Hopi traded wool and blankets for brass and tin tokens (called "pesh tai") redeemable for goods at the market. Hubbell was an advocate for native peoples, translating their letters, settling family disputes, and caring for the sick. You can take an interesting tour of the Hubbell house, viewing his extensive collection of paintings, rugs, and baskets.

9 Continue west on Route 264 for approximately 60 mi to the **Hopi Indian Reservation.** The Hopi, a Pueblo people, can trace their presence in the region back more than 1,000 years. They live in villages grouped around three plateaus, designated First Mesa, Second Mesa, and Third Mesa, connected by a 37-mi strip of Route 284.

10 The **First Mesa** contains the villages of Walpi, Sichomovi, and Hano, but you must first stop at the **visitor center** to obtain permission to tour the area. To get there, follow the signs to First Mesa villages; you'll see the visitor center at the top of the mesa. Request a guide to help you tour Walpi, a tiny community with fewer than 10 families.

11 Continue west on Route 264 for approximately 6 mi to the **Second Mesa,** the center of which is the **Hopi Cultural Center.** Here you'll find a compelling museum that traces the Hopi people's turbulent history. There's also a restaurant on the premises that serves such traditional Hopi dishes as *nok qui vi* (a lamb hominy and green chili stew), blue corn pancakes, and fry bread.

12 At the **Third Mesa,** the **Office of Public Relations** has a wealth of information on local ceremonies and dances held year-round throughout the Hopi Reservation.

To return to Cameron, continue west on Route 264; at the junction with U.S. 160, make a left. Continue for about 5 mi until you reach U.S. 89 south, which will take you back to Cameron in less than an hour.

Chinle

Attractions

Canyon de Chelly National Monument. In the northeast corner of the state, Canyon de Chelly has two main gorges. The 26-mi-long Canyon de Chelly and 35-mi-long Canyon del Muerto have sandstone walls, though they are only 30 ft at the canyon's entrance. Visitors can drive around the rim of the canyon (about 2 hrs), hike a well-marked trail to the White House Ruin, or take guided tours of the canyon floors. Contemporary Navajo people still live and farm here. The canyon mouth is 3 mi east of Chinle. | Navajo Rte. 7, 86503 | 520/674–5500 | www.nps.gov/cach | Visitor center: May–Sept., daily 8–6; Oct.–Apr., daily 8–5.

South Rim Drive. The 36-mi round-trip around the rim of Canyon de Chelly includes seven overlooks, from which you will be able to see different cliff dwellings and geological formations, including the White House and Spider Rock. Allow at least 2 hours for this drive. | Canyon de Chelly, 86503 | 520/674–5500 visitor center | www.nps.gov/cach | May–Sept., daily 8–6; Oct.–Apr., daily 8–5.

North Rim Drive. You'll drive 34-mi round-trip along the rim of Canyon del Muerto. Among the stops are Antelope House, where you can spy Black Rock Canyon, and Massacre Cave Overlook, where over 100 people were killed by Spanish soldiers in 1805. This drive turns into Highway 64. | Canyon de Chelly, 86503 | 520/674–5500 visitor center | www.nps.gov/cach | May–Sept., daily 8–6; Oct.–Apr., daily 8–5.

ARIZONA RULES OF THE ROAD

License Requirements: To drive in Arizona you must be at least 16 years old and have a valid driver's license.

Right Turn on Red: You may make a right turn on red *after* a full stop, unless there is a sign prohibiting it.

Seat Belt and Helmet Laws: If you are sitting in the front seat of any vehicle, the law requires you to wear your seat belt. Kids weighing between 4 and 40 pounds must be strapped into an approved safety seat. Anyone under the age of 18 is required to wear a helmet while riding on a motorcycle. For more information call 602/223–2000.

Speed Limits: Speed limits in Arizona go as high as 75 mph, but remain at 55 mph in heavily traveled areas. Be sure to check speed limit signs carefully and often.

For More Information: Call the **Department of Public Safety** | 602/223–2000.

White House. Construction of the best known of the canyon's cliff dwellings was probably begun around 1060. It derives its name from a wall in the upper part of the dwelling that is covered in white plaster. Nearby, you'll see some of the unique foot-size steps the Anasazi chipped into canyon walls across the Southwest. The dwelling is reached by a 2½-mi round-trip trail, and it's the only part of the canyon that can be visited unescorted. | Canyon de Chelly, 86503 | 520/674–5500 visitor center | www.nps.gov/cach | May–Sept., daily 8–6; Oct.–Apr., daily 8–5.

Dining

Junction Restaurant. Native American. Both Navajo and American cuisine is served in three dining areas. Try the Navajo beef or ham or Navajo burger. | Navajo Rte. 7 (U.S. 191) | 520/674–8443 | Breakfast also available | AE, D, DC, MC, V | $–$$$

Garcia's Restaurant. American. In the Holiday Inn Canyon de Chelly in Chinle, this is one of the few full-service restaurants in the area. The menu includes burgers, chicken, steaks, and pasta. Kids' menu. | Navajo Rte. 7, 86503 | 520/674–5000 | AE, D, DC, MC, V | $–$$

Pizza Edge. Pizza. If you're in the mood for pizza or just something quick, this is the best place to go in Chinle. The menu also includes sandwiches and hot wings. | Basha's Shopping Center, U.S. 191 | 520/674–3366 | Closed Sun. | AE, D, DC, MC, V | $–$$

Lodging

Thunderbird Lodge. A pink adobe structure at the mouth of Canyon de Chelly in a grove of cottonwoods, this popular stone-and-adobe lodge has motel-style rooms and is as close as you can get to the canyon. A guide service offering Jeep tours of the canyon operates out of the lodge. Restaurant. Cable TV. Business services, airport shuttle. | Navajo Rte. 7, 86503 | 520/674–5841 or 800/679–2473 | fax 520/674–5844 | www.tbirdlodge.com | 72 rooms | AE, D, DC, MC, V | $$–$$$

Coyote Pass Hospitality. About 30 mi northeast of Chinle, this B&B is run by the Coyote Pass clan of the Navajo Nation. Guests sleep on bedding on the dirt floor of a hogan, use an outhouse, and eat a Navajo-style breakfast prepared on a wood-burning stove. Complimentary breakfast. | Box 91-B, Tsaile, 86556 | 520/724–3383 | www.navajocentral.org/cppage.htm | Hogan can accommodate up to 15 people | No credit cards | $$

Holiday Inn Canyon de Chelly. Part of a historic trading post is incorporated into the structure of this motel, ½ mi from the entrance to Canyon de Chelly. Restaurant, room service. Cable TV. Pool. Business services. | Navajo Rte. 7, 86503 | 520/674–5000 | fax 520/674–8264 | www.holiday-inn.com | 108 rooms | AE, D, DC, MC, V | $$

Ganado

Attractions

Hubbell Trading Post National Historic Site. Merchant John Lorenzo Hubbell set up this still active trading post in 1878; during an 1886 smallpox epidemic, he transformed the site into a hospital to care for the sick. | Rte. 264 | 520/755–3475 | www.nps.gov/hutr | Daily 8–5.

Dining

Ramon's Restaurant. Native American. While the main focus of the menu is on Native American food, this small restaurant also serves Mexican and American specialties. The Navajo burger and mutton soup are popular. | Hwy. 264 | 520/755–3404 | Closed Sun. No dinner Sat. | No credit cards | $

Kayenta

Attractions

Kayenta Visitor's Center. Housed in a circular stone structure reminiscent of Navajo hogans (dwellings), the center houses a small museum of Navajo artifacts, plus a gift shop stocked with Navajo crafts. | U.S. 160, ½ mi west of U.S. 163 | 520/697–3572 | Daily 9 AM–6 PM.

Monument Valley Navajo Tribal Park. The attraction here is all of Monument Valley, a sprawling, arid, 30,000-acre expanse once home to the Anasazi, now populated by Navajo farming families. You'll see staunch red buttes, smoothly eroded mesas, deep canyons, and strange sculpted rock formations. The park has a 17-mi self-guided driving tour. | Visitor center: off U.S. 163, 84536 | 435/727–3287 or 435/727–3353 | Daily sunrise–sunset.

Navajo Code Talkers Exhibit. In Kayenta's Burger King restaurant is an exhibit of World War II memorabilia that honors the Navajo code talkers of the Pacific campaign. These Navajo Marines sent and received military orders and dispatches in the Navajo language, a code the Japanese could not break. | U.S. 160, ½ mi west of U.S. 163 | 520/697–3170 | Daily 7 AM–10 PM.

Navajo National Monument. Two unoccupied 13th-century cliff pueblos, Keet Seel and Betatakin, stand under orange and ocher cliffs. The largest ancient dwellings in Arizona, these stone and mortar dwellings were built by the Anasazi. At the visitor center there are also a small museum, exhibits of prehistoric pottery, and a crafts shop (9 mi north of U.S. 160, about 20 mi southeast of Kayenta). | Hwy. 564, 86044 | www.nps.gov/nava | 520/672–2366 | Daily 8–5.

Dining

Anasazi Inn Restaurant. Native American. Ten miles west of Kayenta, this is a good place to go for a quiet, peaceful meal. The Navajo fry-bread sandwiches and tacos are especially tasty. | U.S. 160 | 520/697–3793 | Breakfast also available | AE, D, DC, MC, V | $–$$

Golden Sands Restaurant. American. In this ultracasual place next door to the Best Western Wetherill, you can get Navajo tacos and hamburgers. | U.S. 163 | 520/697–3684 | No credit cards | $–$$

Lodging

Goulding's Monument Valley Trading Post & Lodge. The John Wayne films *Stagecoach* and *Fort Apache* were set here. The original trading post houses a museum with movie memorabilia. The two-story motel offers basic, comfortable rooms with spectacular views of Monument Valley. Goulding's also runs a campground, a grocery store, and a convenience store. Two restaurants. Refrigerators. In-room VCRs (and movies). Pool. Laundry facilities. Pets allowed. | Indian Hwy. 42, 84536 | 435/727–3231 or 800/874–0902 | fax 435/727–3344 | www.gouldings.com | 19 rooms in lodge, 41 motel rooms, 2 cabins | AE, D, DC, MC, V | $$$

Holiday Inn Kayenta. About 25 mi south of Monument Valley, this comfortable chain motel is at the junction of U.S. 160 and U.S. 163 in Kayenta. Restaurant, room service. Cable TV. Pool, wading pool. Laundry facilities. Business services. | U.S. 160 at U.S. 163 | 520/697–3221 | fax 520/697–3349 | www.holiday-inn.com | 155 rooms, 8 suites | AE, D, DC, MC, V | $$–$$$

Best Western Wetherill Inn. Named for John Wetherill, a frontiersman who discovered prehistoric Native American ruins in Arizona, this two-story motel on the north side of Kayenta has southwestern decor. Cable TV. Pool. Business services. | Hwy. 163,

86033 | 520/697–3231 or 800/780–7234 | fax 520/697–3233 | www.bestwestern.com | 54 rooms | AE, D, DC, MC, V | $$

Hampton Inn Navajo Nation. A three-story chain property with immaculate rooms and a friendly staff, it's close to all the local attractions. Room service is available, local phone calls are free, and there are coffeemakers and irons in the rooms. The gift shop sells some Navajo crafts. Restaurant, complimentary Continental breakfast. In-room data ports. Cable TV. Pool. | U.S. 160 | 520/697–3170 or 800/426–7866 | fax 520/697–3189 | www.hamptoninn.com | 73 rooms | AE, D, DC, MC, V | $$

Tuba City

Attractions

Cameron Trading Post. Twenty-nine miles southwest of Tuba City is this historic enterprise, now known as the place to buy authentic Navajo and Hopi crafts. The post also includes a restaurant, cafeteria, post office, grocery store, and butcher shop. | U.S. 89 at AZ 64 | 520/679–2244 or 520/679–2231 | Daily.

Dinosaur Tracks. Some well-preserved dilophosaurus tracks can be viewed at this site about 5½ mi west of Tuba City, between Mileposts 316 and 317 of U.S. 160. | U.S. 160 | No phone | Daily.

Tuba City Trading Post. Founded in the 1880s, this octagonal trading post sells authentic Navajo, Hopi, and Zuni rugs, pottery, baskets, and jewelry as well as groceries. | Main St. and Moenabe Rd. | 520/283–5441 | Daily.

Dining

Kate's Café. American/Casual. Fine, reasonably priced food is the hallmark of this local favorite. You may have to wait a bit for seating. | Edgewater and Main Sts. | 520/283–6773 | Breakfast also available | No credit cards | $–$$

Tuba City Truck Stop Cafe. American. Fast service and hearty home cooking distinguish this stop. Try the Navajo vegetarian taco, a mix of beans, lettuce, sliced tomatoes, shredded cheese, and green chilis served open-face on succulent fry bread. Or you might consider mutton stew served with fry bread and hominy. | Hwy. 264 at U.S. 160 | 520/283–4975 | Breakfast also available | MC, V | $–$$

Hogan Restaurant. Southwestern. Next to the Quality Inn Tuba City, this spot serves mostly southwestern and Mexican dishes like chicken enchiladas and beef tamales. | Main St. (Hwy. 264) | 520/283–5260 | Breakfast also available | AE, D, DC, MC, V | $

ARKANSAS

SCENIC 7 BYWAY
THROUGH THE OUACHITAS AND OZARKS

Distance: 295 mi   Time: 5 hours to several days
Overnight Breaks: Hot Springs, Russellville, Jasper, Harrison

When *Car and Driver* named Arkansas's Scenic 7 Byway (Route 7) one of the country's top 10 driving experiences, the magazine was referring in part to the road's breathtaking vistas.

The route begins at Exit 78 of I–30, about 55 mi southwest of Little Rock, and winds 190 mi north to Harrison, crossing the Arkansas River at its approximate midpoint. The southern portion of Route 7 is a gentle roller-coaster ride across the Ouachita Mountains, whose folds and faults run in a rare east–west pattern rather than the north–south alignment common to most of the world's ranges. North of the Arkansas river town of Russellville, the ride becomes more thrilling thanks to the highway's twists and turns, steep ascents, and low-gear descents. Occasionally, the road rides the tops of mountain ridges for panoramic views before descending to wide valleys and tiny villages.

You should be aware that hills and curves and occasional fog and snow can make the drive difficult, particularly in the northern portion of the journey.

❶ Heading north from Exit 78 of I–30 (just north of Arkadelphia), **DeGray Lake** soon appears to the west. This 13,800-acre lake was formed by damming the Caddo River. Surrounded by the Ouachita Mountains, its shoreline is dotted with campgrounds, rental cabins, and marinas. At **DeGray Lake Resort State Park,** on the lake's northeast shore, is a lodge with a restaurant and pool, a championship golf course, a full-service marina, RV and tent campsites, and numerous outdoor activities, plus interpretive programs by park rangers.

❷ From DeGray, Route 7 winds north through the countryside for approximately 25 mi toward Hot Springs. Just south of Hot Springs is the man-made **Lake Hamilton,** which has long been a favorite spot for vacationers, retirees, and residents desiring a water view. The highway passes the docks of the *Belle of Hot Springs,* an excursion boat that sails Lake Hamilton. You'll find shopping malls near the intersection with

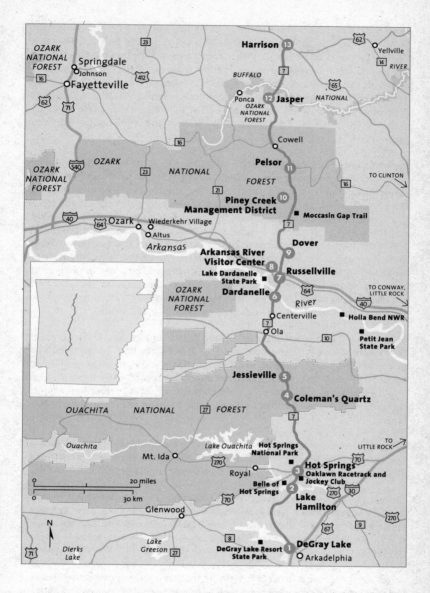

U.S. 270. Farther toward downtown Hot Springs you will pass the **Oaklawn Racetrack and Jockey Club,** Arkansas's only thoroughbred track.

❸ The thermal springs at **Hot Springs** have drawn visitors since prehistoric days. Bathhouse Row—eight turn-of-the-20th-century spa buildings in the heart of town—is the center of **Hot Springs National Park,** where you will find a campground, 30 mi of hiking trails, and picnic areas in mountains and gorges. The visitor center and museum are in the restored Fordyce Bathhouse. Hot Springs has numerous accommodations worthy of an overnight stay, as well as additional sightseeing attractions and scenic drives.

④ From Hot Springs, you'll head north on the byway along U.S. 70 and Route 7 for about 15 mi to Blue Springs. You'll pass Gulfa Gorge, DeSoto Park, the Belvedere Country Club, and, on weekends, the tin-roof stands of Snow Springs Flea Market. Crystal boulders on a weathered, weedy stand mark the edge of Mountain Valley. As you get closer to Blue Springs you'll pass real-estate offices and a full-scale mall across from the gate to the private community of Hot Springs Village. In Blue Springs is **Coleman's Quartz,** where you can buy or just admire gorgeous agate bookends and other pieces largely from Brazil. Only the clear and white crystals are from Arkansas.

⑤ **Jessieville** also lies within Arkansas's crystal-mining region. The town has a handsome native-stone schoolhouse that was established in 1937. Staff at the **Ouachita National Forest Visitors Center,** a mile north of Jessieville, have plenty of information on the forest's trails, scenic drives, sports-utility-vehicle drives, and outdoor activities.

The next 40 mi through the Ouachita National Forest afford the fine views that earned Route 7 its scenic-byway status. Roadside signs point out picnic tables and trail heads. The route makes ear-popping descents and steep climbs as the Ouachitas loom taller and the valleys narrow. Along the way you'll spot a country store at Hollis and pretty crossings of Fourche LaFave River branches, and you can gaze at long vistas south over Nimrod Lake and north across the Arkansas River valley. Past the village of Ola and the Petit Jean River, the environs of Centerville provide bucolic scenes of cattle and horses grazing in rolling, white-fenced pastures.

⑥ Crossing the flat Arkansas River floodplain, Route 7 enters the old river town of **Dardanelle,** where tall, bare Dardanelle Rock at its northern edge served as a landmark for explorers and pioneers. Among cottages and Victorian homes west of Route 7 on Front Street rises the ancient **Council Oak.** Beneath this imposing tree, now surrounded by a low iron fence, Chief Black Fox and other Cherokees reluctantly agreed to hand over part of their treaty-given lands along the river to white settlers in 1820.

⑦ Heading north again on Route 7 you will come to **Russellville,** on the north side of the Arkansas River. Shop, sightsee, and spend the night here. You'll find decent casual dining options as well as grocery stores if you want to stock your cooler.

⑧ Just west of Route 7 and Russellville is the **Arkansas River Visitor Center,** in **Lake Dardanelle State Park.** The visitor center is operated by the U.S. Army Corps of Engineers at Old Post Road Park and sits above **Dardanelle Lock and Dam,** whose 54-ft lift makes it the largest on the river as it forms the 35,300-acre, 50-mi-long Lake Dardanelle.

⑨ Across I–40 heading north out of Russellville, the Scenic 7 Byway passes the lakeside Shiloh Park. Roadside churches, used-car lots, retread tire outlets, homes, and a jerry-built flea market give way to forests and farms. Gradually the hills open into a wide valley where beef cattle graze, and 7 mi from the interstate, a green sign marks the town limits of **Dover,** the Pope County seat before it was moved to Russellville.

Beyond Dover to the north, the landscape returns to pastures and hay barns in a flat valley along Illinois Bayou, which carved cliffs into the limestone layers along its north side. The road runs uphill into mountain terrain, with more cliffs and slopes visible through the leafless trees. The small town of Pleasant Valley is scattered along the highway. A sign warns that the road will be "Crooked and Steep Next 63 Miles" as it snakes uphill through a forest of pine and hardwoods. Vistas reach even greater distances. Road signs mark sharp curves and intersections and are pocked with shotgun holes.

10 Scenic 7 enters the Ozark National Forest's **Piney Creek Management District.** Soon there's a turnoff to Long Pool Campground at a scenic spot with a natural pool in Big Piney Creek. The site has hiking trails, fishing, swimming, picnic areas, and a spot to launch canoes. Signs point out rental cabins and a private campground in the area.

In the forest, the road crosses Church Bell Ridge and passes the old Lane Cemetery. You'll spot another reminder sign: "Crooked and Steep Next 53 Miles." The Moccasin Gap horse trail leads west into the trees. The road, still winding uphill, slices through the limestone. The forest floor is strewn with rocks coated with green and gray lichen and moss. You may want to stop and pick up a ham or a wonderfully tacky souvenir in Booger Hollow—"Pop. 7, Countin' One Coon Dog" boasts the town sign. Scenic 7 curves out of Booger Hollow along the top of a ridge, gaining a bit more altitude, and a metal sign arches over the driveway to "God's Little Half Acre." There are more vistas—one of the finest at a turnoff point called Rotary Ann—plus picnic tables, before the next warning: "Crooked and Steep Next 43 Miles."

11 Continuing downhill on Scenic 7, the road curves toward the crossroads of **Pelsor,** named for Loretta Pelsor who was appointed postmaster in 1923. At the Pelsor intersection, you can pick up picnic supplies, oak baskets, sandwiches, and other good stuff at the **Hankins Country Store,** and after eating your fill you can try the porch swing outside.

Leaving Pelsor, Scenic 7 soon passes into Newton County. A parking lot sits at an access point to the **Ozark Highlands Trail,** which runs 178 mi between Lake Fort Smith State Park and Tyler Bend Campground on the Buffalo River. The rustic Fairview campground is nearby. Continuing north you'll pass through Lurton, then farms carved into the top of a ridge. Soon you'll enter gift-shop country, where baskets, quilts, dolls, crafts of "hillbilly barnwood," honey, and other items are for sale.

12 Closing in on **Jasper,** you'll pass several B&Bs and campgrounds that you might want to explore for an overnight break. A sign announces "Very Crooked and Steep Next 3½ Miles," and a brake-check area and two runaway-truck ramps are at the ready as Scenic 7 curves and plummets downhill into the Newton County seat of Jasper. The small town radiates from its weathered stone courthouse. Close by are churches, gifts and crafts shops, a bakery, cafés, and **Arkansas House Bed and Breakfast**; Coco the bear lives out back.

The journey from Jasper to Harrison is about 25 mi along Scenic 7. You'll cross the Little Buffalo River, then curve past the Ozark National River Visitor Center, RV parks, cottages, cabins, and shops as the road heads through the forests and bluffs lining the **Buffalo National River.** At the river crossing are an information station, a parking lot, and trail heads. Gravel roads lead to historic homesteads and churches, and it's possible to spot elk, which have been reintroduced to the region. On an uphill curve, a marker commemorates the site where stone was quarried in 1836 for Arkansas's contribution to the Washington Monument in Washington, D.C. Soon Scenic 7 passes the derelict Dogpatch theme park, then Mystic Caverns, beautiful despite heavy damage resulting from centuries of human use.

13 The terrain flattens as Scenic 7 heads into **Harrison.** RV camps, a smoked meats store, and fast-food spots begin to appear between the farms. A mule trots across a pasture, a white horse hot on its heels. Harrison's population of 12,000 makes it seem a booming metropolis after the small Ozark communities. Restaurants, motels,

B&Bs, and shops line its highways and circle its courthouse square. You might want to overnight in Harrison before continuing.

From Harrison, Route 7 leads northeast through Bergman to Lead Hill and the shores of Bull Shoals Lake. Other highways lead toward Eureka Springs, Mountain Home, Marshall, and Branson, Missouri. All are scenic, but not as breathtaking—or as challenging a drive—as the Scenic 7 Byway.

Arkadelphia

Attractions

Arkadelphia's Historic Homes Tour. You can view some impressive 19th-century buildings in this self-guided, half-hour driving tour. Some of the well-maintained properties date back to the 1840s and are included in the National Register of Historic Places. Brochures are available from the Chamber of Commerce. | 870/246–5542 | fax 870/246–5543 | www.arkadelphia.org.

DeGray Lake. The man-made lake is a water playground surrounded by the Ouachita Mountains, with cabins, camping, and marinas along its shores. There are 10 Corps of Engineers campsites and day-use areas around this lake. Take Exit 78 off I–30, then drive north on Highway 7 and turn left at Skyline Drive. The visitor center (543 Skyline Dr.) is on the left, before you cross the dam. | 2027 State Park Entrance Rd., Bismarck | 870/246–5501 | Daily.

ARKANSAS RULES OF THE ROAD

License Requirements: In Arkansas, you may apply for a driver's license if you are 14 and can provide a birth certificate, proof of enrollment in school, and proof of grade point average of at least 2.0; a parent or legal guardian must accompany you to the testing site. (For the location of testing sites, call the Arkansas State Police at 501/618–8251.) When driving, an adult with a valid driver's license must be in the car with you. Valid out-of-state and foreign driver's licenses are good in Arkansas.

Right Turn on Red: A right turn on red at a traffic signal is permitted *after* you come to a full stop and yield to pedestrians and other traffic, unless a "No Turn on Red" or similar sign is posted.

Seat Belt and Helmet Laws: State law requires all passengers to wear seat belts. All children under age five must wear safety restraints while the vehicle is in motion. Children under age four or weighing less than 40 pounds must be secured in an approved safety seat.

Speed Limits: Speed limits on major freeways are from 60 to 70 mph.

Other: Vehicle headlights must be turned on when windshield wipers are on.

For More Information: For information about **driver's licenses,** call | 501/682–7059. For information about road conditions, call **Arkansas Highway and Transportation Department** | 501/569–2374.

DeGray Lake Resort State Park. The park has a 98-room island lodge, a lakeside swimming pool, meeting and convention services, a restaurant, and a rent-a-yurt (that's a year-round universal recreational tent). On I–30, take Exit 78, then go north on Highway 7 toward the town of Hot Springs and look for signs. | 2027 State Park Entrance Rd., Bismarck, 71929 | 501/865–2801 for park information and campsite reservations; 800/737–8355 for lodge reservations | www.degray.com | Daily.

Dining

Bowen's. Southern. Casual and cozy, this family restaurant has nightly theme buffets including Tex-Mex on Tuesday and seafood Friday and Saturday. Bowen's is known for its chicken and dumplings, broasted chicken, and chicken-fried steak. Kids' menu. | 104 Malvern Rd. | 870/246–8661 | Breakfast also available | AE, D, MC, V | $

The Honeycomb. American. College students and professors congregate at this small, eat-and-go restaurant near Henderson State and Ouachita Baptist Universities. The menu includes homemade breads, desserts, and chicken on Ritz. Needlepoint pieces done by local artists hang on the walls. | 706 Main St., 71923 | 870/245–2333 | Reservations not accepted | Breakfast also available. Closed weekends. No dinner | No credit cards | $

Kreg's Catfish. American. Inexpensive plate lunches and fried catfish fillets by the pound attract hungry crowds to this modest college-town restaurant. It's popular for the catfish and chicken dish, the salad platter topped with fried chicken, and the homemade rolls, among other items. No smoking. Kids' menu. | 2805 W. Pine St. | 870/246–5327 | AE, D, MC, V | $

Harrison

Attractions

Boone County Heritage Museum. Harrison's past comes alive with this museum's genealogy library, railroad room, Civil War artifacts, and Native American relics. | 110 S. Cherry St., 72601 | 870/741–3312 | Mar.–Nov., weekdays 10–4; Dec.–Feb., Thurs. 10–4.

Mystic Caverns. The upper level has enormous formations; the lower level is pristine. You may find the climb strenuous. There are a mineral museum and gift shop on site. | 870/743–1739 | Mar.–May, Sept.–Dec., Mon.–Sat. 9–4:30, Sun. 1–4:30; June–Aug., Mon.–Sat. 9–5:30, Sun. 1–5:30.

Dining

Ol' Rockhouse. Barbecue. An early 1900s home has been converted to a restaurant filled with local memorabilia, including old school photographs and athletic trophies. Hickory-smoked meats (brisket is most popular) are supplemented by Rick's steak and the Rockhouse burger. You can also try Louisiana-style catfish, fried pickles, and bread pudding with rum sauce. There is a deck for outdoor dining. Kids' menu. | 416 S. Pine St. | 870/741–8047 | MC, V | No dinner Sun. | $$–$$$

Catfish Wharf. American. Deep-fried and grilled catfish and hushpuppies are the specialties at this casual family establishment with speedy service. | 1318 Hwy. 62/65 N, 72601 | 870/741–9200 | fax 870/741–9200 | D, MC, V | Closed Sun. | $–$$

Lodging

Comfort Inn. You'll find this hotel on Highway 65 3 mi from the Boone County Regional Airport and across the street from a golf course, with a free shuttle and discounts on the links. Branson, Missouri, is 35 mi away, and the White River and Buffalo River in the Ozarks are within a 1-hour drive. Complimentary Continental breakfast. In-room data ports. Cable TV. Pool. Laundry facilities. | 1210 U.S. 62/65 N | 870/741–7676 | fax 870/741–0827 | 93 rooms | AE, D, DC, MC, V | $–$$

Executive Inn. Two miles from the Harrison airport, this hotel is close to a movie theater, shopping, restaurants, and the Boone County Fairgrounds. Restaurant, room service. In-room data ports. Cable TV. Indoor pool. Hot tub. Exercise equipment. Laundry facilities. Business services. | 816 N. Main St. | 870/741–2391 | fax 870/741–1181 | 86 rooms | AE, D, DC, MC, V | $

Ozark Mountain Inn. This inn is on a hill overlooking the town of Harrison. Lake Harrison is 2 mi away. The large, spacious lobby has plenty of seating. Complimentary Continental breakfast. Cable TV. Pool, wading pool. Playground. Business services. Pets allowed. | 1222 N. Main St. | 870/743–1949 | fax 870/743–2960 | 100 rooms | AE, D, DC, MC, V | $

Hot Springs

Attractions

Arkansas Alligator Farm and Petting Zoo. You can see more than 300 alligators, some 10 ft long, plus deer, pygmy goats, llamas, lambs, and ostriches, at this small museum. | 847 Whittington Ave. | 501/623–6172 or 800/750–7891 | Labor Day–Apr., daily 9:30–5; May–Labor Day, daily 9–6.

Belle of Hot Springs. The 400-passenger excursion boat sails Lake Hamilton on sightseeing, lunch, dinner, and dance cruises. | 5200 Central Ave. (Rte. 7S) | 501/525–4438 | Feb.–Nov., daily.

Coleman's Crystal Mine & Rock Shop. Dig for crystals and keep what you find, or browse among those already cleaned and polished in this shop, 15 mi north of Hot Springs on Highway 7. | 5837 North Hwy. 7, Jessieville | 501/984–5328 | Daily 8–5.

★ **Fordyce Bathhouse.** The restored bathhouse, the most opulent on Hot Springs National Park's Bathhouse Row, now serves as the park's visitor center and museum; stained-glass windows and an ornate fountain grace the interior along with original facilities. There are also a bookstore and an orientation film. | 369 Central Ave. | 501/624–3383 | Daily 9–5.

Lake Catherine State Park. The Civilian Conservation Corps built the now modernized, fully equipped housekeeping cabins in this park. You'll also find hookups for RV and tent camping, rent-a-camp equipment, swimming, boating, fishing, a playground, and picnic areas. | 1200 Catherine Park Rd. | 501/844–4176 | Daily.

Lake Ouachita State Park. The park is on the eastern tip of the state's largest man-made lake. Swim, ski, scuba dive, rent a boat, fish, hike trails, and take part in interpretive programs. Fully equipped housekeeping cabins, RV and tent campsites, picnic areas, a marina with boat rentals and supplies are also available. | 5451 Mountain Pine Rd., Mountain Pine | 501/767–9366 | Daily.

Ouachita National Forest. The oldest and largest state forest in the United States has 1⁶/₁₀ million acres of woodland dotted with campsites, fishing areas, and picnic sites. Hiking trails include the 223-mi-long Ouachita National Recreation Trail, which runs from Talimina, OK, to Pinnacle Mountain State Park near Little Rock. You can canoe and go white-water rafting on the rivers. Call for directions from Hot Springs. | 501/321–5202 | Daily.

President Bill Clinton's boyhood sites. A self-guided tour passes two of Clinton's boyhood homes, along with his schools, church, and favorite teenage hangouts. A tour brochure and map are available at Fordyce Bathhouse. | 629 Central Ave. | 800/772–2489 | Daily.

Dining

Mollie's. Delicatessens. You can get fried catfish, brisket, and chicken-in-the-pot at this Hot Springs fixture. You'll also find big sandwiches, including corned beef, and grilled chicken. Open-air dining is available. Kids' menu. | 538 W. Grand Ave. | 501/623–6582 | AE, D, DC, MC, V | Closed Sun. | $$–$$$

Bohemia. Eastern European. Take a culinary tour of Europe with bratwurst, herring, German pot roast, and sauerbraten, and even venture into the new world for baked Alaska. The Eastern European heritage of the owner-chef is evident in the menu, collector's plates, and original art that adorn one of the city's oldest restaurants. Kids' menu. | 517 Park Ave. | 501/623–9661 | AE, D, MC, V | Closed Sun. No lunch Mon., Wed., Fri., Sat. | $$

Hot Springs Brauhaus. German. The 110-year-old building wasn't designed with a German beer cellar in mind, but, by happy coincidence, it has a huge selection of imported brews, German fare, lively accordion music, and entertainment on weekends. Kids' menu. | 801 Central Ave. | 501/624–7866 | AE, D, MC, V | Closed Mon. No lunch | $$

McClard's Bar-B-Q. Barbecue. Little has changed since the 1940s at this sparkling clean stucco building, where you nearly always have to wait for a seat. But the waits are short as veteran waitresses speed orders of smoked meat, hot tamales, shakes, and fries to happy diners. The place is known for barbecue ribs. Beer is the only alcoholic beverage served. Kids' menu. | 505 Albert Pike | 501/624–9586 | No credit cards | Closed Sun., Mon. | $$

Lodging

Arlington Resort Hotel and Spa. If you wish to "take the cure," you can do it in this landmark with views of Hot Springs National Park. 3 restaurants, bar (with entertainment). Cable TV. 2 pools. Beauty salon, hot tub, massage. Driving range, putting green, tennis courts. Exercise equipment. Laundry facilities. Business services. | 239 Central Ave., 71901 | 501/623–7771; 800/643–1502 reservations (outside AR) | fax 501/623–2243 | 484 rooms | AE, D, DC, MC, V | $$

Hampton Inn. Family suites are available in this hotel in downtown Hot Springs. Complimentary Continental breakfast. In-room data ports, some microwaves, some refrigerators, some in-room hot tubs. Cable TV. Pool. Laundry facilities. Pets allowed. | 151 Temperance Hill Rd., 71913 | 501/525–7000 | fax 501/525–7626 | 83 rooms, 17 suites | AE, D, DC, MC, V | $$

Downtowner Hotel & Spa. The luxury hotel is one block from Bathhouse Row and 1 mi from the Hot Springs Mountain Tower. Restaurant, complimentary breakfast. Cable TV. Outdoor pool. Beauty salon, hot tub. Shops. | 135 Central Ave., 71901 | 501/624–5521 or 800/251–1962 | 139 rooms | AE, D, DC, MC, V | $–$$

Jasper

Attractions

Ozark Ecotours. Guides take small groups on 1-day and overnight trips into the rugged Buffalo River landscape to learn about Native American, pioneer, Civil War, and outlaw history and explore the area's natural history. Some trips involve easygoing hikes; others include canoeing, caving, and horseback riding. | 870/446–5898 | Apr.–June, Sept.–Nov., call for hrs.

Dining

Point of View Family Dining. American. Enjoy such entrées as chicken-fried steak and catfish with all the trimmings. | 106 W. Hwy. 74, 72641 | 870/446–2992 | MC, V | $–$$

Dairy Diner. American. If you've never been to a truck-stop greasy spoon, this place fits the bill. Comfort foods include hamburgers, meatloaf, and fried chicken. | 217 E. Hwy. 7, 72641 | 870/446–5343 | No credit cards | $

Ozarks Cliff House Inn. Southern. For homemade biscuits, fried catfish, pinto beans with sugar-cured ham, and just plain good Southern food, you've come to the right place. You may find the circa-1932 boat motor hanging in the dining room a bit odd, but the main distraction will undoubtedly be the stunning view into the Grand Canyon of Arkansas, the state's deepest natural valley. | Hwy. Cty. Rte. 31, Jasper, 72641 | 870/446–2292 | Breakfast also available. No dinner | DC, MC, V | $

Riverfront Dairy Diner. American. The family-owned diner is part of the Ozarks Arkansas House, a 19th-century–style B&B. Daily specials include apricot chicken and chicken-fried steak. A former owner used to carve stone animals; you can still spy his lizards and fish in the Rock Garden. | Hwy. 7 at Hwy. 74, Box 325, Jasper, 72641 | 870/446–5179 | AE, D, MC, V | $

Lodging

Ozarks Crawford's Cabins. Two log cabins with full kitchens, bent-willow furniture, and a back porch swing are in the woods adjoining the Ozark National Forest, 3 mi north of Jasper. The old general store makes deli sandwiches, and you can canoe, fish, and enjoy the water at Buffalo National River less than 2 mi away. Microwaves, refrigerators. Cable TV, in-room VCRs (and movies). Hiking. No pets. No smoking. | Hwy. Cty. Rte. 31, Jasper, 72641 | 870/446–2478 | fax 870/446–5824 | www.ozarkcabins.com/crawfords | 2 cabins | AE, D, MC, V | $–$$

Arkansas House Bed and Breakfast. The Little Buffalo River flows behind this two-story house made with native cut limestone. In addition to enjoying a complimentary three-course breakfast, you may visit with Coco, a friendly 500-pound bear, who is trotted out once a day to greet the public. Restaurant. Some microwaves, some refrigerators, some in-room hot tubs. Cable TV, in-room VCRs (and movies). Laundry facilities. | 217 E. Hwy. 7, Box 325, 72641 | 870/446–5179 | www.mcrush.com/arkansashouse | 2 rooms, 3 suites | AE, D, DC, MC, V | $

Cliff House Inn and Restaurant. The rustic country inn and restaurant is perched on Mt. Judea above the Arkansas Grand Canyon—it's the largest valley in Arkansas. Restaurant. No room phones. No smoking. | HCR 31, Jasper, 72641 | 870/446–2292 | 5 rooms | D, MC, V | Closed Oct.–mid-Mar. | $

Russellville

Attractions

Arkansas River Visitor Center. "Renaissance of the River" exhibits explain the river's development, and tours of Dardanelle Lock and Dam are given in the summer. RV camping, a boat ramp, tennis courts, a basketball court, a playground, a ball field, and a soccer–football field are available. | 1590 Lock and Dam Rd. | 501/968–5008 | www.usac.army.mil | Weekdays 8–4.

Holla Bend National Wildlife Refuge. The 7,055-acre refuge 7 mi south of Russellville is a wildlife-rich area that is also a bird-watcher's paradise during the winter; there is seasonal hunting and fishing. | Hwy. 155, Dardanelle | 501/229–4300 | Daily.

Lake Dardanelle. Created by damming the Arkansas River, this 34,000-acre body of water is one of the state's most popular recreational lakes as well as a barge channel. Numerous RV and tent campsites and boat ramps lie along its shoreline, which includes scenic tentacle-like inlets and coves. | 1590 Lock and Dam Rd. | 501/968–5008 | Daily.

Lake Dardanelle State Park. The park has two areas—at Russellville and near Dardanelle. Both have marinas, campsites, picnic areas, and beaches. Interpretive programs are available in Russellville only. The Russellville area park hosts dozens of bass tournaments. It's on Dardanelle–Highway 22, 10 mi southwest of Russellville. | 2428 Marina Rd. | 501/967–5516 | www.cswnet.com/~ldsp | Daily.

Lile Handmade Knives. Lile has crafted knives for actors Jimmy Stewart and Fess Parker (of TV's *Daniel Boone* fame in the 1950s) and President Richard Nixon. The most dangerous-looking blades were made at Sylvester Stallone's request for the movies *First Blood* and *Rambo*. | 2721 S. Arkansas Ave. | 501/968–2011 | www.lileknives.com | fax 501/968–4640 | Mon.–Sat. 9–4:30.

Mount Nebo State Park. Up a steep, zigzag road not recommended for trailers over 24 ft long, the 3,000-acre Mount Nebo State Park offers spectacular views of the Arkansas River valley. The park has 15 cabins with kitchens, campsites, 14 mi of hiking trails, a swimming pool, tennis courts, picnic areas, playgrounds, pavilions, a small store with bicycle rentals, and a visitor center with exhibits. The park is 12 mi south of Russellville. | 1 State Park Dr., Dardanelle | 501/229–3655 | Daily.

Nimrod Lake. Known for its excellent crappie fishing, this 3,700-acre Army Corps of Engineers lake 30 mi south of Russellville also has waterskiing, camping, picnicking, and swimming, with hiking and hunting in season. | 501/272–4324 | Hwy. 60 | Daily.

Ozark–St. Francis National Forests. At scattered sites you will find numerous campsites, picnic areas, float and canoeing streams, horse and bicycle trails, fishing and swimming spots, five wilderness areas, and access to hiking trails, including the 165-mi-long Ozark Highlands Trail. | 605 W. Main St. | 501/968–2354 | www.fs.fed.us/oonf/ozark | Daily.

Dining

Madame Wu's Hunan Restaurant. Chinese. A plethora of Hunan and Szechuan dishes is available here, including sweet and sour, garlic, lo mein, and vegetable-based entrées. | 914 S. Arkansas Ave., 72801 | 501/968–4569 | MC, V | No lunch Sat. | $–$$

Guido's Deli. Delicatessens. A small dining area gives you the option of eating in or taking your purchases elsewhere for a picnic. A variety of meats, cheeses, breads, and daily lunch specials is available. | 113 N. El Paso Ave., 72801 | 501/967–8781 | fax 501/967–3357 | No credit cards | Closed Sun. No dinner Sat. | $

Lodging

Russellville Travelodge. All rooms at this hotel near I–40 and Highway 7 have a refrigerator, and pets are welcome to stay for an extra $10 a night. Guests can take advantage of the outdoor pool and free Continental breakfast. Complimentary Continental breakfast. In-room data ports, refrigerators. Cable TV, room phones. Outdoor pool. Pets allowed (fee). | 2200 N. Arkansas Ave., 72802 | 501/968–4400 | 45 rooms | AE, D, DC, MC, V | $$–$$$

Best Western Inn. You'll find comfortable accommodations at this two-story Best Western Inn on scenic Highway 7 at I–40. Many parks and scenic areas are nearby and there are restaurants within walking distance. Some microwaves, some refrigerators. Cable TV. Pool. Hot tub. | 2326 N. Arkansas Ave. | 501/967–1000 | fax 501/967–3586 | www.bestwestern.com | 99 rooms | AE, D, DC, MC, V | $

Holiday Inn. The two-story modern hotel is 2 mi south of Russellville and 1½ mi from Arkansas Technical University. Fishing, boating, and camping are available at Dardanelle Lake, only one block away. Restaurant, room service. In-room data ports. Cable TV. Pool. Business services, airport shuttle. Pets allowed. | 2407 N. Arkansas St. | 501/968–4300 | 149 rooms | AE, D, DC, MC, V | $

Lakeside Knights Inn. All the rooms at this two-story motel face Lake Dardanelle, and there is a boat ramp on the motel's property. It's easily recognizable from afar because of the neon green doors to all the rooms. Room phones. Cable TV. | 504 W. Birch St., 72801 | 501/968–9715 | 98 rooms | MC, V | $

CALIFORNIA NORTH COAST

FROM SAN FRANCISCO TO REDWOOD NATIONAL PARK

Distance: 250–275 mi   Time: 7 days
Overnight Breaks: Inverness, Mendocino, Eureka

Driving the California coast's Route 1 is a beautiful experience, especially if taken at a leisurely pace. Indeed, there are many portions of the highway along which you won't want to drive faster than 20-40 mph. You can still have a fine trip even if you don't have much time, but be realistic and don't plan to drive too many miles in one day.

The north coast is a year-round travel destination, though the time of your visit determines what you'll see. The migration of the Pacific gray whales is a winter-time phenomenon, roughly from mid-December to early April. In July and August, views are often obstructed by fog.

❶ Depart from San Francisco and head north over the Golden Gate Bridge for approximately 10 mi, then proceed west (take the Mill Valley/Stinson Beach exit off U.S. 101 and follow signs) to **Muir Woods National Monument.** This is the world's most popular grove of old-growth *Sequoia sempervirens* (redwoods). Spend an hour or so hiking around before leaving for Stinson Beach.

❷ **Stinson Beach,** approximately 8 mi north of Muir Woods National Monument on Route 1, has the most expansive sand beach in Marin County. If you're traveling in summer, allow extra time because the roads are often jammed.

❸ **Bolinas,** north on Route 1 about 5 mi, is the southern entry to the **Point Reyes National Seashore,** which borders the northern reaches of the Golden Gate National Recreation Area. It's a great place for hiking and viewing wildlife, full of rugged, rolling grasslands. The ½-mi Earthquake Trail passes by what is believed to be the epicenter of the 1906 quake that destroyed much of San Francisco. Nearby is the late 19th-century Point Reyes Lighthouse, a good spot to watch for whales.

❹ Head north to the town of **Olema,** 15 mi north of Stinson Beach on Route 1, and the Point Reyes National Seashore's **Bear Valley Visitor Center,** which has exhibits of park

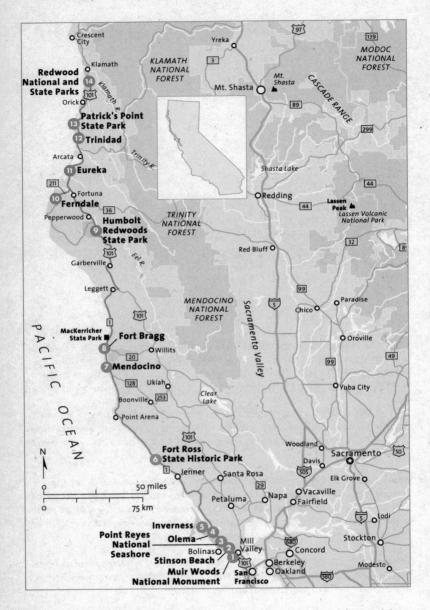

wildlife. The rangers here can advise you on everything from whale-watching to hiking trails and camping. A reconstructed Miwok village, a short walk from the visitor center, provides insight into the daily lives of the region's first human inhabitants.

⑤ From Olema continue north, 5 mi on Route 1 to **Inverness,** a town that boomed after the 1906 earthquake, when wealthy San Franciscans built summer homes in its hills. Today many of the structures serve as full-time residences or small inns. The **Point Reyes Lighthouse Visitors Center** is between 10 and 20 mi southwest, about a 45-minute drive, from Inverness, across rolling hills that resemble Scottish heath.

There are hundreds of steps from the cliff top to the lighthouse below, but the views are worth it. A stay overnight in Inverness is worth your time.

⑥ Next you'll come to **Fort Ross State Historic Park,** 50 mi north of Inverness via Route 1. Completed in 1821, Fort Ross was Russia's major fur-trading outpost in California. By 1841 Russian settlers had depleted the area's population of seals and otters and sold the post to John Sutter, later of Gold Rush fame. The state park service has reconstructed Fort Ross, including its Russian Orthodox chapel, a redwood stockade, the officer's barracks, and a blockhouse.

⑦ Continue 72 mi north on Route 1 to **Mendocino.** Logging created the first boom in this windswept town, which flourished for most of the second half of the 19th century. As the timber industry declined in the early 20th century many residents left, but the town's setting was too beautiful for it to remain neglected for long. Artists and craftspeople flocked here in the 1950s, and in their wake came entrepreneurial types who opened restaurants, cafés, and inns.

The restored **Ford House,** built in 1854, serves as the visitor center for Mendocino Headlands State Park. The house has a scale model of Mendocino as it looked in 1890, when the town had 34 water towers and a 12-seat outhouse. Guided history walks leave from Ford House on Saturday afternoon at 3. The park itself consists of the cliffs that border the town.

The **Mendocino Coast Botanical Gardens** offer something for nature lovers every season. Even in winter, heather and Japanese tulips bloom. Along 2 mi of coastal trails, with ocean views and observation points for whale-watching, is a splendid array of flowers. If time permits, stay two nights in Mendocino.

⑧ **Fort Bragg,** about 5 mi north of the botanical gardens on Route 1, has changed more than any other coastal town in the past few years. The decline in what was the top industry, timber, is being offset in part by a boom in charter-boat excursions and other tourist pursuits. The city is also attracting many artists, some lured from Mendocino, where the cost of living is higher.

MacKerricher State Park includes 10 mi of sandy beach and several square miles of dunes. Canoeing, hiking, jogging, bicycling, camping, harbor-seal watching at Laguna Point, and fishing at two freshwater lakes, one stocked with trout, are popular. You can often spot whales between December and mid-April from the nearby headland.

⑨ **Humbolt Redwoods State Park,** 85 mi north of Fort Bragg on Route 1, is home to the giant redwoods. The Avenue of the Giants begins about 7 mi north of Garberville and winds north, more or less parallel to U.S. 101, toward Pepperwood. Some of the tallest trees on the planet tower over this stretch of two-lane blacktop.

At the Humboldt Redwoods State Park Visitor Center you can pick up information about the redwoods, waterways, and recreational opportunities. Brochures are available for a self-guided auto tour of the park; stops include short and long hikes into redwood groves.

⑩ The town of **Ferndale** (20 mi north on U.S. 101 and 8 mi west on Rte. 211) has some of the best-preserved Victorian homes in California, built by 19th-century Scandinavian, Swiss, and Portuguese dairy farmers who were drawn to the mild climate.

The main building of the **Ferndale Museum** hosts changing exhibitions of Victoriana and has an old-style barbershop and a display of Wiyot Indian baskets.

⑪ From Ferndale, drive north to **Eureka** via Route 211 and U.S. 101 for approximately 10 mi. With a population of 28,500, Eureka is the North Coast's largest city. It has gone through cycles of boom and bust, first with mining and later with timber and fishing. Many of the nearly 100 Victorian buildings here are well preserved.

The most splendid is the **Carson Mansion,** built in 1885 for timber baron William Carson. A private men's club occupies the house. Stay overnight in Eureka.

⑫ The town of **Trinidad,** 23 mi north via U.S. 101, got its name from the Spanish mariners who entered the bay on Trinity Sunday, June 9, 1775. The town became a principal trading post for the mining camps along the Klamath and Trinity rivers. As mining, and then whaling, faded, so did the luster of this former boomtown, but it still has good dining spots and several inns; spend the night at one of them.

⑬ **Patrick's Point State Park,** 5 mi north of Trinidad via U.S. 101, is the ultimate California coastal park. On a forested plateau almost 200 ft above the surf, it has stunning views of the Pacific and hiking trails through old-growth forest.

⑭ **Redwood National and State Parks** are less than 20 mi north of Patrick's Point State Park. After 115 years of intensive logging, this 106,000-acre parcel of tall trees came under government protection in 1968, marking the California environmentalists' greatest victory over the timber industry.

At the **Redwood Information Center** you can get brochures, advice, and a free permit to drive up the steep, 17-mi road (the last 6 mi are gravel) to reach the Tall Trees Grove, where a 3-mi round-trip hiking trail leads to the world's first-, third-, and fifth-tallest redwoods.

Within **Lady Bird Johnson Grove,** off Bald Hills Road, is a short circular trail to a grove of redwoods that was dedicated by, and named for, the former first lady. For additional views, take Davison Road to Fern Canyon.

To reach the entrance to **Prairie Creek Redwoods State Park** take the Prairie Parkway exit off the U.S. 101 bypass. Extra space has been paved alongside the parklands, providing fine vantage points from which to observe an imposing herd of Roosevelt elk grazing in the adjoining meadow.

To return to San Francisco drive south on U.S. 101/Route 1 for approximately 250 mi.

Eureka

Attractions

Sequoia Park and Zoo. You get a taste of nature, both native and exotic, in this 50-acre, redwood-filled zoo, which also has an aviary and municipal garden. | Glatt and W Sts. | 707/442–6552 | www.eurekawebs.com/zoo | Oct.–Apr., Tues.–Sun. 10–5; May–Sept., Tues.–Sun. 10–7.

Dining

Café Waterfront. Seafood. Best known for its bottomless oyster bar and clam chowder, this small eatery also serves fresh fish fillets, steak, and pasta. Windows overlook a bay and marina. | 102 F St. | 707/443–9190 | MC, V | $$–$$$

Restaurant 301. Contemporary. The candlelit restaurant uses vegetables and herbs grown in the adjacent hotel's greenhouse or at a nearby ranch. Impressive fish and game selections are complemented by a wine list considered to be of the finest in northern California. Vegetarian menu available. | 301 L St., 95501 | www.carterhouse.com | 707/444–8062 | No lunch | MC, V | $$–$$$

★ **Samoa Cookhouse.** American. Loggers and miners have chosen to dine at this landmark for over a century. The hearty, family-style menu is pre-set, and consists of soup or salad, an entrée like meatloaf, roast pork, or fried chicken, a side dish like scalloped potatoes or corn, and dessert. | 79 Cookhouse La. | 707/442–1659 | AE, D, MC, V | $$

Sea Grill. Seafood. In a restored Victorian building (ca. 1870) and best known for grilled, poached, and deep-fried fish. Try salmon and halibut fillet, calamari, stuffed sole, Dungeness crab, baked oysters, or beer-battered prawns. There are also Harris Ranch steaks. Salad bar. No smoking. Kids' menu. | 316 E St. | 707/443–7187 | Closed Sun. and early–mid-Nov. | D, DC, MC, V | $–$$

Lodging

★ **Elegant Victorian Mansion.** Victorian furnishings fill each room, and the innkeepers may even greet you in vintage clothing. Entertainment includes croquet, silent movies, old records on a wind-up Victrola, and free tours of downtown in a 1930 model A coup driven by the innkeeper, who will share his knowledge of the town history and architecture. Complimentary Continental breakfast. Sauna. Bicycles. Laundry service. | 1406 C St., 95501 | 707/444–3144 | fax 707/442–3295 | www.eureka-california.com | 3 rooms, 1 suite (2 shared baths) | MC, V | $$–$$$

Eureka Inn. Built in 1922, this large Tudor-style hotel was named to the National Register of Historic Places in 1982. Its vast, high-ceilinged lobby with polished redwood

CALIFORNIA RULES OF THE ROAD

License Requirements: You must be at least 16 years of age to get a driver's license in California. Persons with valid driver's licenses from other U.S. states and foreign countries are permitted to drive in the state.

Right Turn on Red: Unless otherwise posted, right turns on red are permitted *after* a full stop.

Seat Belt and Helmet Laws: All passengers are required to wear safety belts in the state of California. Children under 4 years of age or weighing less than 40 pounds must travel in an approved child safety seat. Motorcyclists must wear helmets.

Speed Limits: The maximum speed limit on California highways is 70 mph, unless otherwise posted. Always follow posted speed limits.

For More Information: California Highway Patrol | 916/657–7202.

beams, crystal chandeliers, and massive brick fireplace plays host to swing dances and a 22-ft Christmas tree. Past guests have included Winston Churchill, Robert F. Kennedy, J. D. Rockefeller, Cornelius Vanderbilt, Jr., Shirley Temple, Ronald Reagan, Bill Cosby, Steven Spielberg, and Mickey Mantle. 2 restaurants, 2 bars (1 with entertainment). Cable TV. Pool. Hot tub, saunas. Business services, airport shuttle. Pets allowed. | 518 7th St., 95501 | 707/442–6441 or 800/862–4906 | fax 707/442–0637 | www.eurekainn.com | 95 rooms, 9 suites | AE, D, DC, MC, V | $$–$$$

Best Western Humbolt Bay Inn. In downtown Eureka, this two-story inn is just four blocks from historic Old Town. It is nicely landscaped with fountains, trees, and flowers. Rooms have standard, modular furniture. Restaurant, room service. In-room data ports, some refrigerators. Cable TV. Pool. Hot tub. Laundry facilities. Business services. | 232 W. 5th St., 95501 | 707/443–2234 | fax 707/443–3489 | www.bestwestern.com | 112 rooms | AE, D, DC, MC, V | $$

Weaver's Inn. In a quiet residential area a few blocks from downtown Eureka and 1 mi east of the Old Town area, this B&B occupies a stately Colonial Revival house built in 1883. Special touches include overstuffed canopied beds and a Japanese Contemplation Garden. Complimentary breakfast. No room phones. TV in common area. Pets allowed. | 1440 B St., 95501 | 707/443–8119 or 800/992–8119 | fax 707/443–7923 | www.aweaversinn.com/weaversinn | 3 rooms, 1 suite | AE, D, DC, MC, V | $$

Fort Bragg

Attractions

California Western Railroad Skunk Train. Following the same coastal "Redwood Route" between Fort Bragg and Willits that it has since 1885, the Skunk Train crosses some 30 bridges and trestles and passes through two deep mountain tunnels. | 100 W. Laurel St., 95437 | 707/964–6371 or 800/777–5865 | fax 707/964–6754 | www.skunktrain.com | July–Nov., 9–2.

Mendocino Coast Botanical Gardens. Formal flower gardens, pine forests, 100 species of birds, and 80 species of mushrooms fill the lush grounds here, the only public garden in the continental United States that is on the ocean. | 18220 N. Rte. 1, 95437 | 707/964–4352 | www.gardenbythesea.org | Mar.–Oct., daily 9–5, Nov.–Feb., daily 9–4.

Dining

The Restaurant. Contemporary. You can see the Skunk Train depot across the street, and the ocean from the window tables. Lemon prawns, razor clams, burgers, and a pasta of the day are among the menu choices. A jazz brunch is held on Sundays. | 418 N. Main St., 95437 | 707/964–9800 | Closed Wed. No lunch Mon., Tues., Sat. | MC, V | $$–$$$

The Wharf. Continental. From the dining room you can enjoy views of fishing boats in the harbor, and there's plenty of fresh seafood on the menu, including Pacific red snapper, prawns, scallops, and Dungeness crab. There's also prime rib. At lunch you can sit out on the patio under a big green umbrella. Kids' menu. Beer and wine only. | 780 N. Harbor Dr. | 707/964–4283 | D, MC, V | $$–$$$

Headlands Coffee House. Café. Musicians perform most nights at this local meeting place and cultural center. Along with pastries, cheesecakes, and biscotti to go with your coffee, you can order lasagna, chicken enchiladas, panini, soups, stews, and sandwiches for lunch or dinner. Belgian waffles are breakfast favorites. Breakfast from 7 AM daily. | 120 E. Laurel St., 95437 | 707/964–1987 | D, MC, V | $–$$

Inverness

Attractions

Heart's Desire Beach. The water at this popular swimming beach is warmer than in less-protected parts of the Point Reyes area. Hiking trails, rest rooms, showers, and a picnic area with grills provide a comfortable site to spend the day.

Johnson's Oyster Company. Drive down the crunchy driveway littered with bleached-white shells at this bustling oyster farm, where workers harvest shellfish from adjacent Tomales Bay. Several sizes of oysters are for sale, shucked or not. The staff is happy to give you a deft demonstration of how to wield a shucking knife. | 17171 Sir Francis Drake Blvd., 94950 | 415/669–1149 | Closed Mon.

★ **Point Reyes National Seashore.** Wild shorelines don't get much better than this: windswept headlands, dunes, tide pools, and secluded beaches on 65,300 acres of protected park land. Inland rolling hills and freshwater lakes link up with more than 140 mi of hiking and horse trails, 35 of which are open to bicycles. There are four hike-in campgrounds. | Sir Francis Drake Blvd. | 415/464–5100 | www.nps.gov/pore | Daily dawn–dusk.

Samuel P. Taylor State Park. A 2,700-acre park with 60 campsites nestled among redwoods, this area has many wilderness activities ranging from a swimming hole to hilly hiking trails with occasional ocean views. Campsites fill rapidly between May and September. | Sir Francis Drake Blvd. | 415/488–9897 | www.parks.ca.gov | Mar.–Oct., daily.

Tomales Bay State Park. Sheltered coves, surf-free beaches, tidal marshes, and Bishop pine forests occupy much of this 2,000-acre park north of Inverness on Point Pierce Road. A popular area for swimming, clamming, picnicking, and boating, you can best explore this area by sea-kayak or hiking. | 415/669–1140 | Daily dawn–dusk.

Dining

Manka's Inverness Lodge Restaurant. American. Candles in three wood-paneled dining rooms lend a romantic touch at dinner in this former hunting lodge. Manka's is known for fresh-caught fish and wild game grilled in a fireplace. You can expect unique daily specials including local king salmon and rabbit. Kids' menu. Beer and wine only. | 30 Calendar Way | 415/669–1034 | Reservations essential | Closed Tues., Wed.; No lunch | MC, V | $$$

Grey Whale. American. Enjoy this casual café overlooking Tomales Bay where you can relax in the salt-scented air, or warm yourself inside on cooler days. They claim to serve the best vegetarian pizza in three counties, and other pizzas, hot and cold sandwiches, and salads complete the menu. Toys are available for kids. Beer and wine only. | 12781 Sir Francis Drake Blvd., 94937 | 415/669–1244 | MC, V | $–$$

Lodging

Blackthorne Inn. Built in 1982 from salvaged railway station doors and timber from the San Francisco wharves, this inn exudes rustic history. Enjoy the solitude of a 3,500-square-ft sundeck elevated above the grounds; descend the deck via a firepole. Complimentary Continental breakfast. Hot tub. Business services. No smoking. | 266 Vallejo Ave., 94937 | 415/663–8621 | www.blackthorneinn.com | 5 rooms (2 with shared bath) | MC, V | $$$–$$$$

Hotel Inverness. With sweeping views of forested parklands, the redwood-shrouded Inverness Ridge, and peaceful Tomales Bay, this 1906 hotel makes a tranquil retreat. Rooms each have their own look, such as the lively chili-red hues of Room 3, or Room 4's Bentwood-style queen canopy bed made from willow trees. That room also has a private deck. Enjoy breakfast in your room, on the main deck, or in the pretty garden. Complimentary breakfast. No room phones. TV in common area. No smoking. | 25 Park Ave., 94937 | 415/435–4343 | fax 415/669–1702 | www.hotelinverness.com | 5 rooms | MC, V | $$$

Ten Inverness Way. Antiques, handmade quilts, and fresh flowers abound in this turn-of-the-20th-century shingle house one block from Tomales Bay. Rooms are painted in warm tones and accented with wicker furniture and quilts. Daily sunroom breakfasts might include warm buttermilk spice coffeecake, cheese and basil scrambled eggs, or banana pancakes. Dining room, complimentary breakfast. No room phones. Hot tub. Library. No smoking. | 10 Inverness Way, 94937 | 415/669–1648 | fax 415/669–7403 | www.teninvernessway.com | 4 rooms | MC, V | $$$

Mendocino

Attractions

Jughandle State Reserve. Five miles of nature trails explore coastal and forest environments. The Ecological Staircase trail leads to a pygmy forest of trees that are over 100 years old but only a few feet tall. | 15700 Rte. 1N, Fort Bragg, 95437 | 707/937–5804 | Daily dawn–dusk.

Kelley House Museum and Library. William Henry Kelley, a Gold Rush pioneer who arrived in 1852 and bought out the holdings of shipwrecked William Kasten, Mendocino's founder, lived here. The restored residence is now used as a research center, museum, and popular wedding spot. | 45007 Albion St. | 707/937–5791 | www.homestead.com/kelleyhousemuseum | Sept.–May, Fri.–Sun. 1–4; June–Aug., daily 1–4.

Mendocino Art Center. Scattered among the landscaped grounds are two galleries and studios for ceramics, textiles, jewelry, and sculpture. The center hosts community theater productions and has arts and crafts fairs in summer and at Thanksgiving. | 45200 Little Lake St. | 707/937–5818 or 800/653–3328 | www.mendocinoartcenter.org | Daily, call for class and exhibit schedules.

Mendocino Headlands State Park. The 347-acre day-use park surrounds Mendocino village. The visitor center has exhibits on local history. You can also hike and explore the beach. | Headrow Dr. and Main St., off Hwy. 1 | 707/937–5804 | Daily dawn–dusk.

Russian Gulch State Park. The craggy wilderness at this 1,162-acre state park with 7,630 ft of ocean frontage is characteristic of the north coast. You can explore heavily forested Russian Gulch Creek Canyon, a headland that includes the Devil's Punch Bowl (a large, collapsed sea cave with churning water), and a beach where you can swim, skin dive, and check out tidal pools. Inland, there is a 36-ft high waterfall. | Hwy. 1 | 707/937–5804 | Apr.–Nov., daily dawn–dusk.

Dining

Hill House Inn and Restaurant. Contemporary. The selling point here is the Pacific Ocean, which you can see from every table in the house. After trying a seafood appetizer or soup, sample a favorite entrée, rack of lamb in a blueberry cabernet reduction sauce. Desserts include blueberry pudding made with locally grown berries and served with whiskey sauce. Sunday brunch includes complimentary champagne. | 10701 Palette Dr. | 800/422–0554 | Breakfast also available. No lunch. Dinner Thurs.–Sat. in restaurant; dinner daily in upstairs lounge | AE, D, MC | $$$–$$$$

★ **Café Beaujolais.** French. Gardens surround this Victorian farmhouse, which has an intimate, woody dining room and an enclosed atrium where you can eat in the summer. Fresh French-inspired food with organic local ingredients are the specialty here. Try braised asparagus, roasted free-range chicken, duck, or lamb loin in herb crust with white beans, accompanied by homemade bread. Beer and wine served. | 961 Ukiah St. | 707/937–5614 | MC, V | $$–$$$

955 Ukiah Street. Contemporary. The daily menu includes brandy prawns and a seafood menagerie, as well as steaks, roast duck, and pasta dishes such as giant ravioli with spinach and red chard and duck-filled cannelloni. | 955 Ukiah St. | 707/937–1955 | No lunch. Closed Tues. | MC, V | $$–$$$

The Ravens. Vegetarian. Sea palm strudel is the signature dish: whole-wheat phyllo dough layered with caramelized julienned carrots, red onions, and sea palm and finished with two sauces—wasabi and Ume plum sauce—with Asian greens and shiitake mushrooms on the side. The menu always includes baked tofu. Also popular is the vegan chocolate torte. The wine list has organic and nonorganic selections. | 44850 Comptche Rd. | 800/331–8884 or 707/937–5615 | AE, D, DC, MC, V | $$–$$$

Lodging

Mendocino Hotel. Stained-glass lamps, Frederic Remington paintings, polished wood and Persian carpets lend a swank 19th-century feeling to this 1875 building overlooking the bay. The location is top-notch, too, since it's across the street from the Mendocino Headlands State Park. Guest rooms are filled with antiques, and some have wood-burning fireplaces and private balconies or patios. 2 restaurants, 2 bars, dining room, room service. Cable TV, no TV in some rooms. Business services. | 45080 Main St. | 707/937–0511 or 800/548–0513 | fax 707/937–0513 | www.mendocinohotel.com | 51 rooms, including 14 with shared bath; 6 suites | AE, MC, V | $$–$$$$

★ **Whitegate Inn.** With a white-picket fence, a latticework gazebo, and a romantic garden, the Whitegate is picture-book Victorian. The wooden house with large bay windows, built in 1883, has 19th-century French and Victorian antiques, including the owner's collection of Civil War memorabilia. Three rooms have ocean views. It is one block west of Mendocino Headlands State Park. Complimentary breakfast. No air-conditioning. | 499 Howard St. | 707/937–4892 or 800/531–7282 | www.whitegateinn.com | 7 rooms | AE, D, DC, MC, V | $$–$$$$

Agate Cove Inn. In a residential area 1 mi south of the Russian Gulch State Park, this 1860 inn is on a half acre garden on a bluff. Your room will have an ocean view. Complimentary breakfast. No air-conditioning. In-room VCRs. | 11201 N. Lansing | 707/937–0551 or 800/527–3111 | fax 707/937–0550 | www.agatecove.com | 10 rooms | AE, MC, V | $$–$$$

Blackberry Inn. Each single-story unit here has a false front, creating the image of a frontier town. There are a bank, a saloon, Belle's Palace, and "offices" for doctors and sheriffs. Most rooms have ocean views and fireplaces. Complimentary Continental breakfast. No air-conditioning, some room phones, some kitchenettes, some refrigerators, in-room hot tubs. Cable TV. | 44951 Larkin Rd. | 707/937–5281 or 800/950–7806 | www.innaccess.com/bbi | MC, V | $$–$$$

McElroy's Cottage Inn. Gardens surround the house, water tower, and cottage that make up this early 1900s Craftsmen Period inn, which faces the ocean at the east end of the village of Mendocino. The beach is about three blocks away (down the cliffside via a staircase with safety railings); the headlands, where you can do some whale watching, are three blocks west. The rooms have radios, books, and games. Kids are welcome. Complimentary Continental breakfast. Pets allowed. | 998 Main St. | 707/937–1734 | 4 rooms | MC, V | $$

Point Reyes Station

Attractions

Point Reyes National Seashore. Bird-watching and hiking are the key activities here. From the broad, white secluded beaches you can watch towering breakers crash on shore during winter storms. Worth investigating are semi-sheltered **Drake's Beach**; **Limantour Beach,** ideal for bird-watching; rocky but beautiful **McClure's Beach,** where swimming is prohibited; and **South Beach,** one of the best winter storm-watching spots in the state. | Sir Francis Drake Blvd. | 415/464–5100 | Daily dawn–dusk.

The visitor center at **Point Reyes Lighthouse** offers exhibits on the region's flora, fauna, geography, and the stories of the many ships that have wrecked in the turbulent ocean below. You may be able to see migrating gray whales from atop the 300-step staircase. | Daily dawn–dusk; visitor center Thurs.–Mon. 10–4:30.

Dining

Rancho Nicasio. American. Dark wood walls adorned with trophy animal heads set the tone for the game-filled menu, which includes prime rib, steak, and rack of lamb. Live music weekends. Sunday brunch. | 1 Old Rancheria Rd., Nicasio, 94946 | 415/662–2219 | Closed Mon., Tues. (Oct.–Apr.) | AE, MC, V | $$–$$$

Olema Farmhouse Restaurant and Bar. Continental. Housing a restaurant since 1890, this building has such mementos as a hand-carved glass wall depicting a scene of what the room—and life—was like a century ago. Outside, sit on the broad deck overlooking rural Route 1. Consider the local Tomales Bay oysters, raw on the half-shell, barbecued, or in oyster stew. Microbrewed beer is available. | 10005 Rte. 1, Olema, 94950 | 415/663–1264 | www.olemafarmhouse.com | Breakfast also available weekends | AE, D, DC, MC, V | $$

Station House Café. Continental. A popular family spot, Station House is known for fresh fish, steak, pasta, and locally harvested mussels. There's live music on weekends, and open-air dining in the garden. | 11180 Main St. | 415/663–1515 | Breakfast also available | D, MC, V | $$

Trinidad

Attractions

North Coast Adventures. Guided tours allow you to explore Trinidad Bay by kayak, from which you might catch sight of seals, sea birds, or whales. Previous kayak experience is required. Call to make reservations and arrange a put-in site. | 707/677–3124 | fax 707/677–0603 | www.northcoastadventures.com | Apr.–Oct., daily 7–7.

Patrick's Point State Park. The 640-acre park, cloaked in fir, hemlock, red alder, and spruce, has trails to cliffs overlooking the Pacific. It's a great spot for whale-watching, rock hunting, or exploring tidepools. A reconstructed Indian village has a bookstore, campgrounds, rental cabins, and several picnic areas. | 4150 Patrick's Point Dr. | 707/677–3570; 800/444–7275 (camping information) | www.cal-parks.ca.gov | Daily.

Telonicher Marine Laboratory. Follow a self-guided tour, observe displays on marine science and environment, and check out the critters in the "touch tanks" at this marine and environmental science lab, part of Humboldt State University. | 570 Ewing St. | 707/826–3671 | www.humboldt.edu/~marinelb | Mid-Aug.–May, weekdays 9–5, weekends 10–5; June–mid-Aug., weekdays 9–5.

Dining

★ **Larrupin' Cafe.** Contemporary. Mesquite-grilled ribs and fresh fish are among the choices in this bright yellow, two-story house on a quiet country road 2 mi north of town. | 1658 Patrick's Point Dr., 95570 | 707/677-0230 | Reservations essential | Closed Tues. No lunch | No credit cards | $$-$$$

SIERRA NATIONAL PARKS

FROM THE YOSEMITE VALLEY TO KINGS CANYON AND SEQUOIA NATIONAL PARKS

Distance: 390 mi   Time: 5 days
Overnight Breaks: Kings Canyon, Yosemite Valley area

Yosemite, Kings Canyon, and Sequoia national parks are famous worldwide for their granite peaks, towering waterfalls, and giant sequoias. Summer is the most crowded season for all the parks, though things never get as hectic at Kings Canyon and Sequoia as they do at Yosemite. During extremely busy periods—when snow closes high-country roads in late spring or on crowded summer weekends—Yosemite Valley may be closed to all vehicles unless their drivers have overnight reservations. Avoid these restrictions by visiting from mid-April through Memorial Day and from Labor Day to mid-October, when the parks are less busy and the weather is usually hospitable.

The waterfalls at Yosemite are at their most spectacular in May and June. By the end of summer, some will have dried up. They begin flowing again in late fall with the first storms, and during winter they may be hung with ice, a dramatic sight. Snow on the floor of Yosemite Valley is never deep, so you can camp there even in winter (January highs are in the mid-40s, lows in the mid-20s). Tioga Road is usually closed from late October through May; unless you ski or snowshoe in, you can't see Tuolumne Meadows then. The road to Glacier Point beyond the turnoff for Badger Pass is not cleared in winter, but it is groomed for cross-country skiing. In parts of Kings Canyon and Sequoia snow may remain on the ground into June; the flowers in the Giant Forest meadows hit their peak in June or July.

❶ Begin your tour in the **Giant Forest** at **Sequoia National Park.** The Giant Forest is known for its trails through a series of sequoia groves. You can get the best views of the big trees from the park's meadows, where flowers are in full bloom by June or July. The most famous sequoia in the area is the General Sherman Tree: weighing in at 2$^{7}/_{10}$ million pounds, it has the greatest volume of any living thing in the world.

Moro Rock, an immense, granite monolith, lies along Moro Rock–Crescent Meadow Road. It rises 6,725 ft from the edge of the Giant Forest. Four hundred steps lead to the top; the trail often climbs along narrow ledges over steep drops. From the top you look southwest toward the Kaweah River to Three Rivers, Lake Kaweah, and—on clear days—the Central Valley and the Coast Range.

Crystal Cave is the best known of Sequoia's many caves, formed from limestone that metamorphosed into marble with stalactites and stalagmites of various shapes, sizes, and colors. To visit the cave, you must first stop at the Lodgepole Visitor Center or the **Foothills Visitor Center** at Ash Mountain to buy tickets. Drive to the end of a narrow, twisting, 7-mi road off the Generals Highway, 2.2 mi south of the old Giant Forest Village. From the parking area it's a 15-minute hike down a steep path to the cave's entrance.

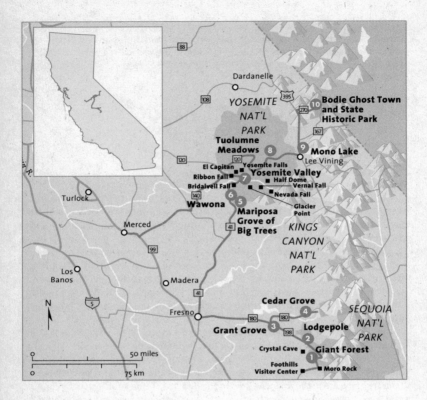

Map labels: 88, Dardanelle, 108, YOSEMITE NAT'L PARK, 395, 270, **10** **Bodie Ghost Town and State Historic Park**, 167, Tuolumne Meadows **8**, **9** **Mono Lake**, Lee Vining, 120, 120, El Capitan, Yosemite Falls, **Yosemite Valley**, Ribbon Fall, **7**, Half Dome, Bridalveil Fall, Vernal Fall, 140, **6**, Nevada Fall, Turlock, **Wawona**, **5**, Glacier Point, **Mariposa Grove of Big Trees**, 41, KINGS CANYON NAT'L PARK, Merced, 99, Los Banos, Madera, 41, 5, Cedar Grove, **4**, SEQUOIA NAT'L PARK, Fresno, 180, 180, **Grant Grove**, **3**, 198, **Lodgepole**, **2**, Crystal Cave, **Giant Forest**, **1**, Foothills Visitor Center, Moro Rock, 50 miles, 75 km, N

2 Within Sequoia National Park, **Lodgepole,** 5 mi north of the Giant Forest via Route 198, is in a canyon on the Marble Fork of the Kaweah River. Lodgepole pines, rather than sequoias, grow here because the U-shape canyon directs air down from the high country that is too cold for the big trees but is just right for lodgepoles.

The **Lodgepole Visitor Center** has the best exhibits in Sequoia or Kings Canyon and a small theater that shows films about the parks. You can buy tickets for the Crystal Cave, get advice from park rangers, and purchase maps and books.

3 From the Lodgepole Visitor Center, continue north on Route 198 for 20 mi to **Kings Canyon National Park** and **Grant Grove,** the original grove that was designated as General Grant National Park in 1890. Here you can pick up several trails and visit the **Gamlin Cabin,** an 1867 pioneer cabin that's listed on the National Register of Historic Places. Also within Grant Grove is the **Centennial Stump,** the remains of a huge sequoia cut for display at the 1876 Philadelphia Centennial Exhibition.

Grant Grove Village has a visitor center, a grocery store, campgrounds, a coffee shop, overnight lodging, and a horse-rental concession.

4 Drive 20 mi east on Route 180 to **Cedar Grove,** which takes its name from the area's plentiful incense cedars; it's at the bottom of King's Canyon. It takes about an hour to travel the spectacular 30-mi length down from Grant Grove along the Kings Canyon Highway (usually closed from mid-October to April). At road's end you can hike, camp, or turn right around for the drive back up. There are amazing views into the deepest gorge in the United States, at the confluence of the two forks, and up the canyons to the High Sierra. Spend a night or two in the Kings Canyon National Park.

⑤ Proceed north from Cedar Grove to **Mariposa Grove of Big Trees.** (It's 58 mi west on Rte. 180 and then 50 mi north on Rte. 41.) Mariposa is Yosemite's largest grove of giant sequoias. They can be visited on foot—trails all lead uphill—or, in summer, on 1-hour tram rides. The Grizzly Giant, the oldest tree here, is estimated to be 2,700 years old. If the road to the grove is closed (which happens when Yosemite is crowded), park in Wawona and take the free shuttle; passengers are picked up near the gas station. The access road to the grove may also be closed by snow for extended periods from November to mid-May. You can still usually walk, snowshoe, or ski in.

⑥ From Mariposa proceed northwest to **Wawona,** approximately 5 mi on Route 41. The historic buildings in **Pioneer Yosemite History Center** were moved to Wawona from their original sites in the park. From Wednesday through Sunday in summer, costumed park employees re-create life in 19th-century Yosemite. Ranger-led walks leave from the covered bridge on Saturday at 10 AM in summer. Near the center are a post office, the Wawona General Stores, and a gas station.

⑦ Continue 22 mi north via Route 41 to the **Yosemite Valley area.** At the Valley Visitor Center you can see exhibits, obtain information, and pick up local maps.

Waterfalls and mountain peaks are scattered liberally throughout this area. Be sure to see **Yosemite Falls**—actually three falls that combine to a height of 2,425 ft—the highest waterfall in North America and the fifth-highest in the world. **Bridalveil Fall,** a filmy fall of 620 ft that is often diverted as much as 20 ft one way or the other by the breeze, is the first view of Yosemite Valley for those who arrive via the Wawona Road. At 1,612 ft, **Ribbon Fall** is the highest single fall in North America, but also the first valley waterfall to dry up in summer; the rainwater and melted snow that create the slender fall evaporate quickly at this height. Fern-covered black rocks frame 317-ft **Vernal Fall,** and rainbows play in the spray at its base. The 594-ft **Nevada Fall** is the first major fall as the Merced River plunges out of the high country toward the eastern end of Yosemite Valley.

El Capitan, rising 3,593 ft above the valley, is the largest exposed granite monolith in the world, almost twice the height of the Rock of Gibraltar. Astounding **Half Dome** rises 4,733 ft from the valley floor to 8,842 ft. **Glacier Point** yields what may be the most spectacular vistas of the valley and the High Sierra—especially at sunset—that you can get without hiking. The Glacier Point Road leaves Wawona Road (Rte. 41) about 23 mi southwest of the valley; then it's a 16-mi drive, with fine views into higher country.

All this exploring is sure to leave you tired and hungry, so plan to spend a night or two in one of the campgrounds or lodges in the park.

⑧ After a good night's rest, start your 55-mi drive to **Tuolumne Meadows**; you'll travel west on Big Oak Flat Road to Route 120 (Tioga Road east). Tioga Road, the scenic route to Tuolumne Meadows, stays open until the first big snow of the year, usually about mid-October. Tuolumne Meadows is the largest subalpine meadow in the Sierra and the trailhead for many backpack trips into the High Sierra. There are campgrounds, a gas station, a store (with limited and expensive provisions), stables, a lodge, and a visitor center.

⑨ Twenty miles east of Tuolumne Meadows on Route 120 to U.S. 395, you'll come to **Mono Lake.** Eerie tufa towers—calcium carbonate formations that often resemble castle turrets—rise from the impressive lake. Stop at the **Scenic Area Visitor Center** for information on trails and activities in the area.

⑩ From Mono Lake and Lee Vining, continue north on U.S. 395, then east on Route 270 for 23 mi to **Bodie Ghost Town and State Historic Park**—the last 3 mi of this drive are on unpaved roads, and snow may close Route 270 in winter and early spring. Odd shacks and shops, abandoned mine shafts, a Methodist church, the mining village of Rattlesnake Gulch, and the remains of a small Chinatown are among the sights at fascinating Bodie Ghost Town, elevation 8,200 ft. There's an excellent museum, and you can tour an old stamp mill (where ore was stamped into fine powder to extract gold and silver) and a ridge that contains many mine sites. Return west on Route 120 through Yosemite to Route 140 west to Merced, approximately 110 mi away.

Sequoia and Kings Canyon National Parks

Attractions

Boyden Cavern. Take a guided tour through this chain of underground formations, at the bottom of Kings Canyon just north of Kings Canyon National Park, in Sequoia National Forest. The caves are on the south side of Route 180, 10 mi west of Cedar Grove Village. | 209/736–2708 | fax 209/736–0330 | www.caverntours.com | Oct.–May, daily 11–4, tours on the hour, last tour starts at 4; June–Sept., daily 10–5, tours on the hour, last tour starts at 5; additional evening tours available.

★ **Cedar Grove.** The best view of this region is from the spectacular 30-mi descent along Kings Canyon Highway from Grant Grove to Roads End, where the highway ends, 6 mi east of Cedar Grove Village. | 559/565–3766 | www.nps.gov/seki | Mid-Apr.–early Nov., daily sunrise–sunset.

Crystal Cave. Buy a ticket at Foothills or Lodgepole visitor centers, in Sequoia National Park, then hike the scenic half mile along Cascade Creek to the cave. It's 9 mi off Generals Highway. The 45-minute tour takes you from room to room on paved and lighted pathways, while water drips and echoes in the eerie subterranean spaces. | End of Crystal Cave Rd. | 559/565–3134 or 559/565–3782 | www.sequoia.national-park.com | June–Sept., daily 11–4.

Foothills, Lodgepole, and Grant Grove Visitor Centers. The visitor centers have displays on park history, birds and beasts, and geology as well as helpful rangers and park volunteers. Talks and walks are offered year-round. Park hours have seasonal variations, so call to confirm. | 559/565–4212 Foothills; 559/565–3782 Lodgepole; 559/565–4307 Grant Grove | www.nps.gov/seki | Daily 9–5.

General Grant Grove. Named for Ulysses S. Grant, this grove of trees on the north end of Generals Highway between the Giant Forest and Cedar Grove was the original grove designated as General Grant National Park in 1890. It's 4 mi from the Big Stump Entrance. | Kings Canyon Hwy./Rte. 180 | 559/565–4307 | www.nps.gov/seki | Daily.

Giant Forest. The grove of giant sequoia, in Sequoia National Park, encircles five meadows speckled with wildflowers mid-May through June. Go 4 mi south of Lodgepole on the Generals Highway. | 559/565–3782 | Daily.

Redwood Mountain Grove. See the world's largest grove of *Sequoia giganteum*, or giant sequoia, the largest living things on earth. As you exit Kings Canyon on Generals Highway, a paved turnout lets you look out over the grove. There are also hiking trails accessing the grove, two 6-mi loops and a 10-mi out-and-bike hike along Redwood Creek. | 559/565–3782.

Dining

Wuksachi Lodge Dining Room. Eclectic. Far from offering predictable park fare, this glass-enclosed restaurant serves creative food to match spectacular views of the giant trees and mountains. Try the rock shrimp flautas. | Sequoia National Park, 93262 | 559/561–3314 | Breakfast also available | D, MC, V | $$–$$$

Lodging

Wuksachi Lodge. You can't beat the rustic chic at this granite-and-cedar hotel, 2 mi south of Lodgepole Visitor Center, 22 mi from the Ash Mountain entrance. Named after a local tribe that used to migrate through this part of the Sierra, it has modern rooms with views of either nearby mountains or forests. Rangers lead programs and guided walks in summer. Restaurant, bar. In-room data ports. Hiking. No smoking. | 64740 Wuksachi Way, Sequoia National Park, 93262 | 888/252–5757 or 559/565–4070 | fax 559/565–4097 | www.visitsequoia.com | 84 rooms, 18 suites | AE, D, DC, MC, V | $$–$$$

Cedar Grove Lodge. Although accommodations are close to the road, Cedar Grove manages to retain a quiet atmosphere. Book far in advance—the lodge has only 18 rooms. Each room is air-conditioned and has two queen-size beds, and three have kitchenettes. You can order trout, hamburgers, hot dogs, and sandwiches at the snack bar and take it to one of the picnic tables along the river's edge. Restaurant, picnic area. No room phones. Laundry facilities. No smoking. | Rte. 180 | 559/335–5500 | fax 559/335–5507 | www.sequoia-kingscanyon.com | 18 rooms | Closed Nov.–Apr. | D, MC, V | $$

John Muir Lodge. The lodge is nestled in a wooded area near Grant Grove Village. The 30 rooms and six suites have queen beds and private baths. There's a comfortable lobby with a stone fireplace, but no restaurant. Picnic area. Air-conditioning. No room phones. Laundry facilities. | Rte. 180 | 559/335–5500 | fax 559/335–5507 | www.sequoia-kingscanyon.com | 21 rooms | Closed Nov.–Apr. | D, MC, V | $$

Stony Creek Lodge. Pine beams and stone make up this lodge, in Sequoia National Forest between Sequoia and Kings Canyon national parks. The lodge is 14 mi southwest of Grant Grove Village. Restaurant. No air-conditioning. No room phones. | Generals Hwy. | 559/335–5500 | fax 559/335–5507 | www.nps.gov/seki | 11 rooms | Closed Nov.–Apr. | D, MC, V | $$

Grant Grove Cabins. Clusters of cabins (some with private baths) and tent cabins (wooden structures with canvas roofs) are scattered through the sugar pines and other conifers at this family-friendly location. There's a central bath and shower facility. Ranger-led walks and talks are held daily in summer, on weekends in winter. Cabins are in Grant Grove Village, 4 mi east of the Big Stump entrance to Kings Canyon National Park. Restaurant, picnic area. No smoking. | Rte. 180 | 559/335–5500 | fax 559/335–5507 | www.sequoia-kingscanyon.com | 15 tent cabins, 24 rustic housekeeping cabins (no running water; 3 with electricity; wood-burning stove on porch for cooking, summer only), 9 housekeeping cabins with bath (heating, electricity; must provide own stove for cooking on outside deck) | D, MC, V | $

Yosemite National Park

Attractions

Forests. Dense stands of incense cedar, Douglas fir, and assorted pines cover much of the park, but the standouts are the giant sequoia.

Mariposa Grove. Self-guided trails lead uphill through the massive cinnamon-red trunks, with interpretive signs explaining the ecology and threats to the sequoia ecosystem. There's also a guided, 1-hour Big Trees Tram Tour; you can ride it all through the grove, or disembark at any point to hike back to the parking lot. | 209/372–0200 | Grove May–early Oct., weather permitting; tram tour late spring–August, daily 9–4.

Several 19th-century buildings have been gathered together in Wawona to create the **Pioneer Yosemite History Center.** Learn about people and events that shaped Yosemite's history. Ranger-led walks leave from the covered bridge, Saturdays at 10 in summer. | Rte. 41 near the South Entrance, Wawona | 209/379–2646 | Daily year-round; hrs change seasonally.

For maps, guides, and information from park rangers, be sure to stop at the helpful **Valley Visitor Center,** which also has exhibits on the history of Yosemite Valley. A 1-mi paved loop trail, "A Changing Yosemite," charts the park's natural evolution. Hours are extended in summer. | Off Northside Dr. | 209/372–0299 | www.yosemitepark.com | Daily 9–5.

Dining

★ **Ahwahnee Dining Room.** American. The dining room's 34-ft tall trestle-beam ceiling is supported by entire tree trunks. Equally grand are the full-length windows, wrought-iron chandeliers, and snappily dressed waitstaff. Specialties include New York steak, broiled swordfish fillet, and prime rib. Sunday brunch. Men are required to wear jackets, and jeans and sneakers are not permitted. | Ahwahnee Rd. | 209/372–1489 | Breakfast also available | Reservations essential | AE, D, DC, MC, V | $$–$$$

Mountain Room Restaurant. American. The food becomes secondary when you see Yosemite Falls, the world's fifth largest waterfall, through the enormous, floor-to-ceiling wall of windows in this dining room in the Yosemite Lodge. Baked shrimp, sautéed blackened Cajun catfish, steak, and pasta are a few of the menu choices. Kids' menu. No smoking. | Northside Dr. | 209/372–1281 | No lunch. Closed weekdays from Thanksgiving–Easter except for holiday periods | D, DC, MC, V | $$–$$$

Sierra Restaurant. Contemporary. A freestanding stone fireplace warms this casually elegant dining room, with open-beam, 30-ft ceilings, and French doors opening onto a heated patio. Try the Rainbow trout with almond-roasted potatoes and caper butter, or the Burgundy-roasted pork tenderloin with cinnamon-apple potatoes. The Sunday brunch is extremely popular. Kids' menu. No smoking. | Tenaya Lodge, 1122 Rte. 41, Fishcamp | 800/635–5807 | www.tenayalodge.com/dining.htm | No lunch | Reservations essential | AE, D, DC, MC, V | $$–$$$

Wawona Dining Room. Contemporary. Watch deer graze on the meadow while dining in the romantic, candlelit dining room of the whitewashed Wawona Hotel, which dates from the late 1800s. The American-style cuisine favors California ingredients and flavors. Trout is a menu staple. Sunday brunch. | Rte. 41, Wawona | 209/375–1425 | Closed weekdays Nov.–Easter, except at holidays | Reservations essential | D, DC, MC, V | $–$$$

Lodging

Tenaya Lodge at Yosemite. Rustic but upscale touches here include iron chandeliers, exposed timbers, and a huge stone fireplace with plenty of soft seating nearby. Native American rugs add warm earth tones to the mix. The main lodge and wing of rooms and suites look out across heavily wooded parklands. In summer, this is a prime spot for families, especially for touring Yosemite's southern sites—the Mariposa Grove and Glacier Point. The hotel is 2 mi south of Yosemite's South Gate entrance. 2 restaurants, bar, room service. In-room data ports. Cable TV. 2 pools (1 indoor). Hot tub. Exercise equipment, hiking, horseback riding. Water sports, boating, bicycles. Cross-country skiing, downhill skiing. Children's programs (ages 3–12). Laundry facilities. Business services. Pets allowed. | 1122 Rte. 41, Fish Camp, 93623 | 559/683–6555 or 800/635–5807 | fax 559/683–8684 | www.tenayalodge.com | 244 rooms, 20 suites | AE, D, DC, MC, V | $$$–$$$$

Yosemite Lodge. On the Valley floor near Yosemite Falls, this lodge was the former headquarters of the U.S. Cavalry when it protected and maintained the park prior to World War II. Built in 1915, it has glass and wood detailing, designed to blend with the surrounding wilderness. Lodge rooms are larger than standard rooms, and have patios or balconies. Restaurant, bar. No air-conditioning. Pool. | Northside Dr. | 559/252–4848 | fax 559/456–0542 | www.yosemitepark.com | 226 rooms | AE, D, DC, MC, V | $$–$$$

Wawona Hotel. At the southern entrance of the park, this 1879 National Historic Landmark is near the Mariposa Grove of Big Trees. It's an old-fashioned Victorian hotel with wraparound verandas. Rooms are small and furnished with antiques. Horseback riding trips through surrounding trails are available. Dining room. No air-conditioning, no room phones. Pool. Golf courses, putting green, tennis courts. Horseback riding. | Rte. 41, Wawona | 209/375–6556 | fax 209/375–6601 | 104 rooms (54 with shared bath) | AE, D, DC, MC, V | $$

Yosemite Valley Tent Cabins and Housekeeping Cabins. More than 400 tent cabins (rough wood frames and canvas walls and roofs) are also available in the valley at Curry Village. Just be forewarned that you'll be cheek-by-jowl with your neighbors and no cooking is allowed. Another option is the rustic—and very popular—housekeeping cabins in the valley. You can book these ahead—up to a year in advance is a good idea. | 559/252–4848 | www.yosemitepark.com | D, DC, MC, V | Late May–early Oct.; reservations office daily 7–7 | $–$$

Camping in Yosemite. There are plenty of campgrounds in Yosemite (nearly 2,000 in summer, 400 year-round), and reservations at most are required. Most of the park's 15 campgrounds are in Yosemite Valley and along the Tioga Road (Rte. 120). Glacier Point and Wawona have one each. None of the campgrounds has water or electric hookups, but there are dump stations and shower facilities in the valley area year-round. On the 15th of each month you can reserve a site up to five months in advance. Pets allowed. | Box 1600, Cumberland, MD 21502 | 800/436–7275 | reservations.nps.gov | D, MC, V | $

COLORADO'S HEARTLAND
GOLD AND SILVER COUNTRY TOUR

Distance: approximately 275 mi   Time: 1 or 2 days
Overnight Break: Breckenridge

In summer you can make this trip in a single day if you leave early and plan on getting back to Colorado Springs late. However, that's too much of a stretch in winter, when an overnight in Breckenridge is in order and would also give ample time for more relaxed driving on potentially hazardous roads. Given the number of attractions to see on this tour, if you have the time, it would be best to make it a 2-day trip, summer or winter.

❶ From **Colorado Springs** proceed northwest on U.S. 24 for 3 mi, then turn right on 30th Avenue and view the absolutely stunning **Garden of the Gods.** Take the time to follow the one-way drive completely though this geological wonderland, which has acres of fantastic, 300-million-year-old red sandstone formations.

❷ Leaving the Garden of the Gods, follow U.S. 24 to **Manitou Springs,** just outside the city limits of Colorado Springs. There, you will want to tour the Miramont Castle Museum, a late 19th-century mansion. If you're up to a brisk walk, you may want to visit the **Cave of the Winds.** A 45-minute underground tour takes you past millions of years of local geology. Bring a light jacket, and by all means, wear comfortable shoes.

❸ From Cave of the Winds, proceed west on U.S. 24 for another 21 mi until you enter the village of Florissant and see the sign pointing southward to **Florissant Fossil Beds National Monument,** where a Oligocene redwood forest and all its inhabitants were perfectly preserved. Enjoy a ranger-led or self-guided walk on one of the well-marked trails. This little-known wonder is a boon for fossil buffs.

❹ Leaving the Fossil Beds, continue westward on U.S. 24 for 30 mi to Hartsel. (On your way you will cross Wilkerson Pass at an elevation of 9,507 ft.) At Hartsel take Route 9 north for 17 mi to **Fairplay.** Here you may wish to visit the **South Park City Museum,** which contains 30 original buildings, mining exhibits, and 60,000 artifacts from the past.

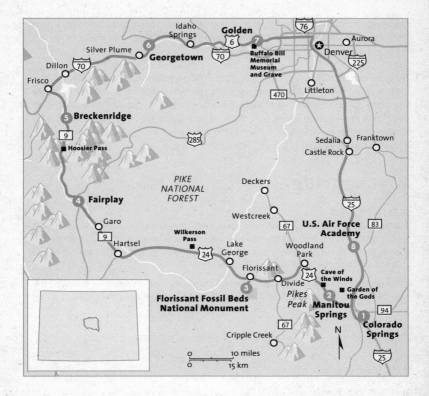

⑤ From Fairplay, proceed north on Route 9 for 22 mi and through the 11,541-ft-high **Hoosier Pass** to **Breckenridge.** You'll marvel at the snowcapped peaks on all sides. There's plenty to do and see in Breckenridge, which had its beginnings in 1859 as a gold-rush boomtown, and which today attracts skiers and other vacationers. If your visit is on a weekday or Saturday, you can take a walking tour of the historic district and some of the outlying gold mines. Spend the night in Breckenridge.

⑥ Leaving Breckenridge, take Route 9 north for 10 mi to its junction with I–70, and proceed east on I–70 for about 38 mi to historic **Georgetown.** Georgetown dates from 1859, when gold was discovered in the area. Since then the area has produced more than $200 million worth of precious metals. If you have the time, try to visit the **Georgetown Loop Historic Mining and Railroad Park,** with reconstructed mining and railroad buildings dating from the town's heyday. Also visit the **Hamill House Museum,** the restored home of Colorado state senator and silver mogul William A. Hamill, and the **Hotel de Paris Museum,** where period furnishings recreate a period of wealth and influence.

⑦ When you leave Georgetown, it's just a straight shot—and 29 mi—east along I–70 into Denver, which is certainly worth a stay. But since you only have a short amount of time on this tour, **Golden** should be your next stop. Take Exit 244, pick up U.S. 6, and proceed the 10 mi or so into the town that Coors beer and the **Colorado School of Mines,** both renowned throughout the world, put on the map. You can tour the **Coors Brewing Company** and watch as the ever-popular Coors beer is being brewed. Mineral and mining history exhibits are on display at the **School of Mines' Geology**

Museum. Learn more about scout and entertainer William F. Cody, better known as Buffalo Bill, at **The Buffalo Bill Memorial Museum and Grave,** 5 mi west of town off U.S. 6.

⑧ Leaving Golden, pick up U.S. 6 eastbound and follow it through Denver (about 12 mi) to its junction with I–25. Turn south on I–25 and proceed 50 mi to the **U.S. Air Force Academy** (take Exit 156B [North Gate] or Exit 150B [South Gate]). This magnificent campus is the Air Force's answer to West Point and Annapolis. Be sure and visit the chapel, which is an architectural wonder in itself. After leaving the Academy, take I–25 again and proceed south back to Colorado Springs.

Breckenridge

Attractions

Breckenridge Golf Club. Dramatically set, the course resembles a nature reserve, with woods and beaver ponds lining the fairways, This is the only municipally owned golf course in the world designed by Jack Nicklaus. | 200 Clubhouse Dr. | 970/453–9104 | May–Aug., daily 7 AM–6 PM; Sept., daily 8 AM–7 PM.

Breckenridge Ski Resort. America's second-most popular ski resort in terms of the number of visitors per year (a sister resort of Vail, Keystone, and Beaver Creek) is 1 mi

COLORADO RULES OF THE ROAD

License Requirements: As a visitor driving an automobile in Colorado, you must have a valid driver's license from your home state.

Right Turn on Red: A driver can legally turn right on a red light *after* coming to a full stop.

Seat Belt and Children's Safety Seat Laws: State law requires automobile drivers and passengers in the front seat of the vehicle to use seat belts. Children under four years old and under 40 pounds, regardless of where in the vehicle they are riding, must use an approved safety seat.

Speed Limits: Individual speed limits are posted along all major thoroughfares and in all municipalities. The interstate system, except where posted for lower rates, maintains a 75-mph speed limit.

For More Information: on highway laws, safety, and the condition of specific roads, call the **Colorado State Patrol** 303/239–4500. For medical emergencies, call 911.

west of Breckenridge off Route 9. The 2,043 skiable acres encompass Peaks 7, 8, 9, and 10 of the Ten Mile Range. This was one of the first resorts in the United States to allow snowboarding. The ski area has 23 lifts, 139 runs (the longest 3½ mi), and a 23-km cross-country ski layout; there's a 3,398-ft vertical drop. More than half the terrain is advanced or expert. Summertime activities include miniature golf, an alpine slide, horseback riding, hiking, and biking. | Ski Hill Rd. | 970/453–5000 or 800/221–1091 | www.snow.com | Year-round, daily 8:30–4.

Summit Historical Society. The society conducts guided walking tours of the historical homes and businesses of Breckenridge. Learn about the Victorian structures and get a chance to tour some of their interiors. | 309 N. Main St. | 970/453–9022 | www.summithistorical.org | Daily; reservations required for tours.

Dining

Pierre's Riverwalk Café. French. Watch the chefs at work through the open kitchen at this elegant café. Try the Rocky Mountain trout, or the Colorado rack of lamb. Dine alfresco on a deck overlooking the Blue River and the Rocky Mountains. | 137 S. Main St. | 970/453–0989 | Closed May and early Nov. | DC, MC, V | $$$

★ **Café Alpine.** Eclectic. Contemporary paintings and ceramics fill the rooms of this late 1880s three-story Victorian House with a tapas bar and fireplace. Kids' menu. No smoking. Private dining also available. | 106 E. Adams St. | 970/453–8218 | AE, D, MC, V | $$–$$$

Hearthstone. Continental. Lace curtains frame fabulous mountain views at this eatery in a late 19th-century house; walls are hung with antique barn wood. Try *tilapia pepita* (pumpkin seed–crusted tilapia fillet) and elk chops. Four large decks overlook the Breckenridge ski mountain. Kids' menu. No air-conditioning. | 130 S. Ridge St. | 970/453–1148 | No lunch | AE, MC, V | $$–$$$

Poirrier's Cajun Café. Cajun/Creole. Green tables and red carpet provide the backdrop for paintings by Louisiana artists, photos of crawfish, and scenes from Louisiana life in this cozy, intimate place known for its catfish, seafood platters, crawfish, and gumbo. Open-air dining on patio. Kids' menu. No smoking. | 224 S. Main St. | 970/453–1877 | AE, D, DC, MC, V | $$–$$$

Horseshoe II. American. An 1890s Brunswick Bar in mahogany and cherry wood anchors this former barbershop in Breckenridge's historic district. Enjoy such hearty fare as sirloin steak, teriyaki salmon, and a half-slab of pork ribs. Open-air dining on patio. Kids' menu. No air-conditioning. | 115 Main St., (Rte. 9) | 970/453–7463 | Breakfast also available | AE, MC, V | $–$$

Lodging

Great Divide. Just 50 yards from the base of Peak 9 and two blocks from Main Street, this is one of the few full-service hotels in Breckenridge. Expect especially large guest rooms, some with private balconies. Bar. In-room data ports, refrigerators. Cable TV. Pool. Hot tub, massage. Gym. Video games. Business services, airport shuttle. Pets allowed. | 550 Village Rd., 80424 | 970/453–4500 or 800/321–8444 | fax 970/453–0212 | www.greatdividelodge.com | 208 rooms | AE, D, DC, MC, V | $$$–$$$$

Village at Breckenridge. The Village stretches from Main Street to the mountains. The centerpiece is a pond that serves as the area's only outdoor ice rink. Reserve a room, a studio with a full kitchen, or a condominium with a fireplace and balcony. 9 restaurants, 3 bars. Some kitchenettes. Cable TV. Indoor-outdoor pool, 2 outdoor pools. 9 hot tubs, sauna. Health club. Ice-skating. Shops. | 535 S. Park | 970/453–2000 or 800/800–7829 | fax 970/453–3116 | www.breckresort.com/village | 347 rooms | AE, D, DC, MC, V | $$$–$$$$

★ **Bed and Breakfasts on North Main Street.** Three buildings—two restored, historic cottages and a converted barn—comprise this unique property. The innkeepers have favorite skiing spots, where they're happy to bring guests. Picnic area, complimentary breakfast. No air-conditioning, some in-room data ports, some room phones, some refrigerators. No TV in some rooms, TV in common area. Hot tubs. No smoking. | 303 N. Main St. | 970/453–2975 or 800/795–2975 | fax 970/453–5258 | www.breckenridge-inn.com | 11 rooms | AE, DC, MC, V | $$–$$$$

Allaire Timbers Inn. There are fabulous views of the Ten Mile Range from the main deck of this stone-and-log B&B. All rooms have a private deck and king-size beds. Complimentary breakfast. Cable TV. Hot tub. Cross-country skiing, downhill skiing. Business services. No kids under 13. No smoking. | 9511 S. Main St., (Rte. 9) | 970/453–7530 or 800/624–4904 | fax 970/453–8699 | www.allairetimbers.com | 8 rooms, 2 suites | AE, D, MC, V | $$$

Evans House. Each of the four guest rooms honors a Breckenridge hero in this B&B, an 1886 house two blocks from Main St. Picnic area, complimentary breakfast. No air-conditioning. Cable TV. Hot tub. Exercise equipment. Business services. No smoking. | 102 S. French St. | 970/453–5509 | fax 970/547–1746 | www.coloradoevanshouse.com | 4 rooms, 2 suites | AE, D, DC, MC, V | $$–$$$

Colorado Springs

Attractions

★ **The Broadmoor.** Even if you're not staying here, it's worth passing by the pink-stucco, Italianate Broadmoor complex, built in 1918 and still one of the world's great luxury resorts. You can also survey original owner Spencer Penrose's collection of antique carriages. | 1 Lake Ave., (I–25, Exit 138) 80901 | 719/634–7711 or 800/634–7711 | fax 719/577–5700 | www.broadmoor.com | Daily.

Cheyenne Mountain Zoological Park. America's highest zoo (6,800 ft) has 800 animals and an antique carousel and "tot train." During the summer, a zoo tram helps you get up and down the mountain. Admission includes the Will Rogers Shrine. | 4250 Cheyenne Mountain Zoo Rd., 80906 | 719/633–9925 | www.cmzoo.org | June–Sept., daily 9–6; Oct.–May, daily 9–5.

★ **Colorado Springs Fine Arts Center.** American Indian art, Latin American textiles, and 19th- and 20th-century western art dominate this excellent museum. | 30 W. Dale St. | 719/634–5581 | Tues.–Fri. 10–5, Sat. 9–5, Sun. 1–5.

Pro Rodeo Hall of Fame and American Cowboy Museum. Become a cowboy for a day at the world's only museum and hall of fame dedicated to the wild world of professional rodeo. The heart of the museum, the Hall of Champions, contains photographs, personal memorabilia, trophies, and the original saddles, ropes, clothing, and hats worn by rodeo contestants. | 101 Pro Rodeo Dr., at Rockrimmon Blvd. (I–25, Exit 147) | 719/528–4764 | fax 719/548–4874 | Daily 9–5.

★ **Seven Falls.** Either walk the 224 steps to the top of this natural wonder, or ride the elevator; you can also hike a 1-mi trail. The view from the top encompasses the entire city of Colorado Springs. At night there is a light show. | S. Cheyenne Canyon Rd. | 719/632–0765 | www.sevenfalls.com | Memorial Day–Labor Day, daily 8 AM–11 PM; Labor Day–Memorial Day, daily 9–4.

U.S. Air Force Academy. Since its establishment in 1954, the academy has graduated thousands of career Air Force men and women; for the Air Force, this is the equivalent of West Point. Though much of the campus is off-limits to civilians, don't miss the beautiful scenery. | I–25, Exit 150B (South Gate) or 156B (North Gate) | 719/333–2025 or 800/955–4438 | www.usafa.af.mil | Memorial Day–Labor Day, daily 9–5; Labor Day–Memorial Day, daily 9–6.

World Figure Skating Hall of Fame and Museum. Exhibits tell the story of figure skating through the years. Featured are a library, art, and skating memorabilia. The museum is adjacent to the U.S. Figure Skating Association headquarters. | 20 1st St. | 719/635–5200 | www.worldskatingmuseum.org | June–Aug., Mon.–Sat. 10–4; Sept.–May, weekdays and 1st Sat. of each month 10–4.

Dining

Penrose Room. French. One of the finest restaurants in the state, the Broadmoor Hotel's famed Penrose Room is a luxurious place with grand chandeliers, rich velvet draperies, and majestic views of the city and mountains. Try the chateaubriand *Bouquetiére*, the grilled duck breast Bigarade, and the restaurant's signature sweet soufflées. Entertainment nightly. | 1 Lake Ave., in the Broadmoor Hotel | 719/634–7711 | Reservations essential | Jacket required | No lunch | AE, D, DC, MC, V | $$$–$$$$

La Petite Maison. Contemporary. In this romantic restaurant in a restored Victorian cottage, Parisian posters hang on pale pink walls, and there are bouquets of fresh flowers on the tables. Try the curried shrimp with banana chutney or the pork chops with Peruvian mashed potatoes. Early bird supper. No smoking. | 1015 W. Colorado Ave. | 719/632–4887 | Reservations essential | Closed Sun., Mon. No lunch | AE, D, DC, MC, V | $$–$$$

★ **El Tesoro.** Southwestern. Enjoy the *posole* (hominy with pork and red chile), the green chili, the mango quesadillas, or a margarita made with fresh-squeezed lime juice and a large selection of tequilas. | 10 N. Sierra Madre | 719/471–0106 | Closed Sun. No dinner Mon. No lunch Sat. | AE, D, MC, V | $$

Fairplay

Attractions

Monument to Prunes, a Burro. Prunes was a faithful burro who hauled supplies to area mines for more than 60 years. | Between 16th and 17th Sts. | 719/836–2622 | Daily.

Pike National Forest. Fairplay is surrounded on three sides by national forest, and by following U.S. 285 in either direction, you'll arrive at the entrance of Pike National Forest. This wilderness wonderland of more than 1 million acres offers hiking, fishing, and other outdoor activities. Stop by the South Park Ranger station for more information. | U.S. 285 at Rte. 9 | 719/836–2031 | www.fs.fed.us/r2/psicc | Daily.

South Park City Museum. A re-creation of an old mining town has 30 buildings and more than 60,000 artifacts dating from 1860 to 1900. | 100 4th St. | 719/836–2387 | Mid-Oct.–mid-May, by appointment only.

Dining

Front Street Café. Contemporary. A casual atmosphere in a bistro-type setting awaits diners at this café. The grilled Portobello mushroom sandwich and sesame-seared salmon are highly recommended. The weekend brunch is very popular. | 435 Front St. | 719/836–7031 | Breakfast also available weekends | D, MC, V | $$

Georgetown

Attractions

Georgetown Energy Museum. The museum provides a thorough look at hydro-electricity. Witness how electricity is created as you stand a few feet from spinning generators. | 600 Main St. | 303/569–3557 | www.historicgeorgetown.org | Mon.–Sat. 10–4, Sun. noon–4.

Georgetown Loop Railroad and Historic Mine. Reconstructed mining and railroad buildings from the late 1800s are highlights of this tour. The railroad travels 6 mi to Silver Plume. | 100 Loop Dr. | 800/691–4386 or 303/569–2403 | fax 303/569–2894 | www.gtownloop.com | Late May–early Oct., daily 9–4; call for schedule.

Hamill House Museum. See the restored home of Colorado state senator William A. Hamill, who made his fortune in silver. Period (1860s–70s) furnishings are displayed. | 305 Argentine St. | 303/569–2840 | www.historicgeorgetown.org | Late May–Sept., daily 10–4; Oct.–Dec., weekends noon–4.

Hotel de Paris Museum. French immigrant Louis Dupuy built this hotel in 1878 and watched it become one of the West's finest hostelries. | 409 6th St. | 303/569–2311 | www.colostate.edu/depts/hist/hdp | Memorial Day–Sept., daily 10–5; Oct.–Memorial Day, weekends noon–4.

Loveland Ski Area. The ski area 12 mi west of Georgetown has 3 quads, 2 triple and 4 double chairlifts, 1 Pomalift, 1 Mighty-mite, 60 runs (the longest is 2 mi), and a vertical drop of 2,410 ft. | I–70, Exit 216 | www.skiloveland.com | 303/569–3203 or 303/571–5580 | Mid-Oct.–May, weekdays 9–4, weekends 8:30–4.

Dining

The Red Ram. American. Serving patrons for five decades, this spot is known for its great hamburgers, ribs, and Mexican dishes. | 606 6th St. | 303/569–2300 | AE, D, DC, MC, V | $–$$

Victorian Lady Restaurant. Contemporary. In a Victorian-era building dating from 1869, this restaurant serves up salads, burgers, and seafood. Known, appropriately, for "Victorian" chicken and also halibut. | 415 Rose St. | 303/569–2208 | Closed Thurs. | MC, V | $–$$

Happy Cooker. American/Casual. Homey and comfortable, this inexpensive spot is famous for its waffles and cinnamon buns. Open-air dining with great views of the Rocky Mountains. Kids' menu. | 412 6th St. | 303/569–3166 | Breakfast also available. No dinner | D, MC, V | $

Golden

Attractions

Astor House Museum. Displaying period furnishings, this was the first stone hotel west of the Mississippi, built in 1867. | 822 12th St. | 303/278–3557 | astorhousemuseum.org | Tues.–Sat. 10–4:30.

Buffalo Bill Memorial Museum and Grave. Buffalo Bill Cody's final resting place is complemented by a small museum and gift shop. It's worth the trip just for the beautiful drive up Lookout Mountain. | 987½ Lookout Mountain Rd., 80401 | 303/526–0747 | www.buffalobill.org | May–Oct., daily 9–5; Nov.–Apr., Tues.–Sun. 9–4.

Colorado Railroad Museum. Located just outside the Golden city limits, this is a must for railroad buffs. A replica of a depot from the 1880s has railroad memorabilia, artifacts, and a working model railroad. | 17155 W. 44th Ave. | 303/279–4591 or 800/365–6263 | www.crrm.org | June–Aug., daily 9–6; Sept.–May, daily 9–5.

Colorado School of Mines. Founded in 1874, this is one of the world's foremost mining engineering schools. More than 3,100 students attend annually. The lovely campus houses an outstanding geology museum, as well as the National Earthquake Information Center. | 16th and Maple Sts. | 303/273–3000 | www.mines.edu | Late Aug.–early May, Mon.–Sat. 9–4, Sun 1–4; early May–late Aug., Mon.–Sat., 9–4.

USGS National Earthquake Information Center. On the campus of the Colorado School of Mines, the center records data gathered and transmitted by the Earthquake Early Alerting Service. Free tours are given by appointment. | 1711 Illinois St. | 303/273–8500 | wwwneic.cr.usgs.gov/ | Tues.–Thurs., by appointment only.

Geology Museum. Minerals, ore, and gemstones from around the world, as well as mining history exhibits are on display. | 16th St. and Maple St. | 303/273–3815 | Late Aug.–early May, Mon.–Sat. 9–4, Sun 1–4; early May–late Aug., Mon.–Sat., 9–4.

Coors Brewing Company. Each year thousands of beer lovers make the pilgrimage to this venerable brewery, founded in 1873 by German immigrant Adolph Coors. It's one of the largest breweries in the world. Output exceeds 1½ million gallons a day. The tour includes an informal tasting for those 21 and over. | 13th and Ford Sts. | 303/277–2337 | Mon.–Sat. 10–4.

Dining

Chart House. Seafood. The Chart House Cut steak is a specialty, but fresh fish and other seafood dishes dominate the menu. Salad bar. Kids' menu. | 25908 Genesee Trail | 303/526–9813 | No lunch | AE, D, DC, MC, V | $$–$$$

Table Mountain Inn Restaurant. Southwestern. Dine in a stucco room warmed by a fireplace in winter. Popular dishes are the buffaloaf (buffalo meatloaf), pan-seared fillets, and smoked pork loin chop. Open-air dining on patio on Main Street. Kids' menu. Sunday brunch. | 1310 Washington Ave. | 303/277–9898 | Breakfast also available | AE, D, DC, MC, V | $$–$$$

Hilltop Café. Mediterranean. In a 1900 Victorian house, the café is known for its five-cheese stuffed chicken breast, ricotta and zucchini fritters, and triple-decker strawberry shortcake. Open-air dining on patio in the garden. No smoking. | 1518 Washington Ave. | 303/279–8151 | fax 303/278–1583 | Closed Sun. | AE, D, DC, MC, V | $$

Manitou Springs

Attractions

Cave of the Winds. Discovered by two boys in 1880, this cave has been a popular regional tourist attraction ever since. | U.S. 24 | 719/685–5444 | www.caveofthewinds.com | May–Labor Day, daily 9–9; Labor Day–Apr., daily 10–5.

Florissant Fossil Beds National Monument. See the remains of a 35-million-year-old lake that was filled in with volcanic ash, which in turn fossilized all of the sealife. Nearby are the remains of a redwood forest that was likewise covered by ash and similarly preserved. The grounds include picnic areas, nature trails, and a restored 19th-century farmstead. The beds are 22 mi west of Manitou Springs on U.S. 24. | County Rd. 1, Florissant, 80816 | 719/748–3253 | www.nps.gov/flfo | June–Sept., daily 8–7; Oct.–May, daily 8–4:30.

Garden of the Gods. Acres of fantastic, 300-million-year-old red sandstone formations are 3 mi northwest of Colorado Springs. | 1805 N. 30th St. | 719/634–6666 or 719/385–5940 | www.gardenofgods.com | Sept.–May, daily 9–5; June–Aug., daily 8–8.

Garden of the Gods Trading Post. At the south end of the park near Balanced Rock, this 100-year-old trading post sells southwestern art, jewelry, pottery, and kachinas. | 324 Beckers La., Manitou Springs, 80829 | 719/685–9045 or 800/874–4515 | Daily.

Manitou Cliff Dwellings Museums. See 40 rooms of prehistoric cliff dwellings dating to AD 1100. In summer (June–August) traditional Native American dance performances are held several times a day. | On U.S. 24 | 719/685–5242 | www.cliffdwellingsmuseum.com | June–Aug., daily 9–8; May and Sept., daily 9–6; Jan.–Apr. and Oct.–Dec., daily 9–5.

Pikes Peak. The best-known landmark in the entire state is this 14,110-ft mountain named after Zebulon Pike; though the peak is named after him, Pike never climbed it. Views from the top are expansive and inspired Katharine Lee Bates to write "America the Beautiful." Go 10 mi west of Colorado Springs on U.S. 24 to Cascade, then 19 mi on a toll road to the summit. | Hwy. 24, Exit 141, Cascade, 80901 | 719/385–7325 or 800/318–9505 | www.pikespeakcolorado.com | May–Sept., daily 7–7; Oct.–Apr., daily 9–3 (weather permitting).

Pikes Peak Cog Railway. Dating from the 1880s, this is the highest railroad in the United States. It makes the round-trip up to the summit in about 3 hours, including some time at the top. The railroad makes up to eight round-trips daily during peak season from its depot in Manitou Springs, 5 mi west of Colorado Springs. | 515 Ruxton Ave., Manitou Springs, 80829 | 719/685–5401 | www.cograilway.com | Daily 8–5; call for exact train schedules.

Dining

Adam's Mountain Café. Contemporary. Notable creations are the shiitaki-crusted tuna with wasabi, potato cakes topped by a miso apricot glaze, or lemon rustic chicken (a lemon- and rosemary-infused leg and thigh that is slow-roasted and garnished with spinach and sun-dried tomatoes). | 1100 Cañon Ave. | 719/685–1430 | MC, V | $–$$

Historic Stagecoach Inn. Steak. Dine by the banks of Fountain Creek in a rustic setting. Try the popular sirloin steak, prime rib, or slow-roasted buffalo. | 702 Manitou Ave. | 719/685–9400 | AE, D, MC, V | $–$$

LEWIS AND CLARK COUNTRY AND THE NORTH WOODS

FROM LOLO PASS TO SANDPOINT

Distance: 367 miles   Time: 4 days
Overnight Breaks: Coeur d'Alene, Lewiston

Deep, cool woods sprinkled with lakes—some of the state's largest and the color of a deep blue winter sky—drape across the folded mountains of north-central Idaho and the slender Panhandle region.

You'll follow the path taken by early explorers as you drive through wilderness mountain ranges and the native lands of the Nez Perce tribe. After a stop at Hell's Canyon—the state's lowest point and the site of an inland seaport—the route heads north through the north woods of Idaho, where the Coeur d'Alene tribe hunted and fished. Avoid this drive in the winter, when snow and wintry conditions can make the roads impassable.

❶ Begin your tour at Lolo Pass (on the Montana–Idaho border on U.S. 12). The **Lolo Pass Visitors Center,** a refurbished log cabin, has exhibits and information on the Lolo Trail, which roughly parallels U.S. 12 and is the trail that Lewis and Clark followed on their epic journey. Originally it was a trail used by the Lolo tribe to travel between the buffalo hunting grounds in Wyoming and the Weippe Prairie of Idaho. Remnants of the trail are still visible today. Roughly halfway to Grangeville, the **Lochsa Historical Ranger Station** recalls how rangers lived and operated one of the state's earliest U.S. Forest Service stations, which you could reach only on foot until the mid-1900s.

❷ Your drive from Lolo Pass to **Grangeville** will run 80 mi on U.S. 12 to Kooksia, then another 16 mi on Route 13. **White Bird Road,** as U.S. 95 is known between Grangeville and White Bird, was an engineering marvel when it was built in the late 1930s, climbing 4,429 ft in elevation. The **White Bird Hill Battlefield Auto Tour** recalls the fascinating story of the first battle of the Nez Perce War in the hills near White Bird. At the **White Bird Interpretive Shelter,** exhibits explain the battle.

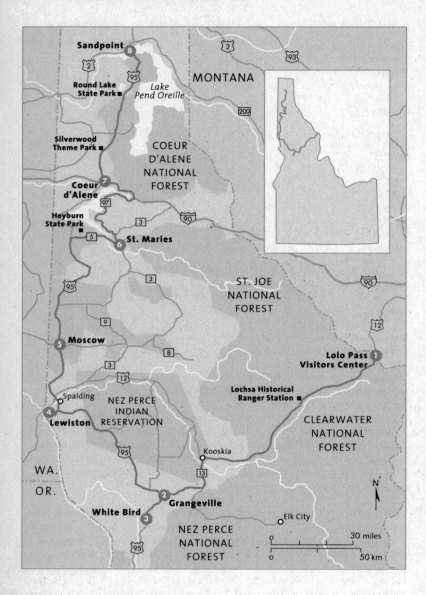

③ At **White Bird** (12 mi south of Grangeville on U.S. 95), a gravel road, Route 493, will take you 12 mi to the northern rim of the continent's deepest gorge, Hells Canyon. At 1 mi deep, it surpasses the Grand Canyon. **Pittsburg Landing** is the only year-round access point to the 71½-mi steep-walled basalt canyon. Picnic at the shady area near the river's edge. Explore the canyon by jet boat and raft on trips from one to six days.

④ When you're finished at White Bird and Pittsburg Landing, backtrack 24 mi north to Grangeville, then 47 mi north on U.S. 95 to Spalding and the **Lewiston** area. Exhibits and artifacts tell the poignant story of the Nee-Me-Poo people or Nez Perce

Indians and their legacy at the **Nez Perce National Historical Park and Museum.** Nez Perce Chief Joseph is known for his words, "My heart is sick and sad. From where the sun now stands, I will fight no more forever." The park encompasses 38 sites in Idaho, Montana, Oregon, and Washington. The **Luna House Historical Museum** has exhibits on the history of Nez Perce County and the surrounding area. Among the displays is a pioneer kitchen in a building that was originally a hotel catering to miners en route to the northern goldfields. Spend a night or two in Lewiston.

⑤ From Lewiston, proceed 26 mi north on U.S. 95 to **Moscow** and the **Appaloosa Museum and Heritage Center.** The museum highlights the history of Appaloosa horses, which the Nez Perce bred centuries ago. The **McConnell Mansion** was built in 1886 and reflects Eastlake, Queen Anne, and Victorian Gothic styles. Period furnished rooms display artifacts and Victorian-style furniture from the early 1900s to 1930s. Changing exhibits also tell the county history. The town is cradled by mountains to the east and the Palouse Hills to the west. Moscow is known as the dry pea and lentil capital of the world—the crops carpet the hills. From Moscow Mountain, a few miles northeast of town via Mountain View Road, you get a panoramic view of the area.

⑥ Leaving Moscow, head 51 mi north on U.S. 95, then 6 mi east on Route 3 to **St. Maries** and **Heyburn State Park,** at the foot of sprawling Lake Coeur d'Alene on a lakelet known as Chatcolet Lake. Herons and ospreys are often seen nesting here. Six hiking trails cover 20 miles.

⑦ From Heyburn State Park, continue 7 mi north on Route 3, 21 mi north on Route 92, and 7 mi west on I–95 to **Coeur d'Alene.** A busy vacation resort area surrounds much of the northern tip of the lake, which includes the world's only floating golf green. The picturesque lake is 2½ mi wide and 25 mi long, and is nestled in a glacially sculpted setting of soft mountains and pine forests. **Lake Coeur d'Alene Cruises, Inc.** takes visitors on two-hour sightseeing tours and sunset dinner cruises, departing from the city dock. In town near the waterfront, the **Museum of North Idaho** has major exhibits on the region's rich history of Native American culture, steamboating, the logging industry, and nearby communities. Fifteen miles north of town on U.S. 95 is **Silverwood Theme Park.** Silverwood is a charming Victorian-style park patterned after an 1880s mining town and the state's only amusement theme park. Supplementing the rides and games is an antique airplane museum. Spend the night in Coeur d'Alene.

⑧ From Coeur d'Alene, proceed 43 mi north on U.S. 95 into **Sandpoint.** The state's largest lake, **Pend Oreille,** is nearby, and dips to an amazing depth of 1,200 ft, making it an angler's paradise for big fish and "fish stories" about the lake's own "Nessie." When asked, locals can spin a tale or two about the fabled lake monster. The 65-mi-long lake has more than 300 mi of shoreline and at the northern end, the resort town of Sandpoint. The city beach features a sweeping stretch of sparkling white sand and a view to the east of Montana's Cabinet Mountains. Also along the lake is a shopper's paradise, the **Cedar St. Bridge,** with dozens of shops lining an enclosed rustic timbered bridge across Sand Creek. On the west side of the lake are tiny **Round Lake** and **Round Lake State Park,** one of the state's smallest. A little more than 140 acres of land surrounds the 58-acre lake. Since the lake is only 37 ft deep, it warms enough for comfortable swimming.

To return to Lolo Pass, leave Sandpoint on U.S. 95 and proceed for about 30 mi to Coeur d'Alene. From there either backtrack, or head east on I–90 for about 130 mi to Missoula, Montana, and then proceed south on U.S. 93 into Lolo and west on U.S. 12 to the pass.

Coeur d'Alene

Attractions

Canefield Mountain Trail System. Thirty miles of trails are available to hikers, motorcyclists, mountain bikers, and equestrians. | Fernan Ranger District, 2502 E. Sherman Ave., east off I–90 | 208/664–2318.

Farragut State Park. One of Idaho's largest state parks at 4,000-acres, it edges Lake Pend Oreille and has several beaches. You might spot whitetail deer, badgers, black bears, coyotes, bobcats, and an occasional elk. Hike, fish, boat, swim, and ride horses. | E. 13400 Ranger Rd., Athol | 208/683–2425 | www.idoc.state.id.us/irti/stateparks | Daily dawn–dusk.

Idaho Panhandle National Forests. The Panhandle Forest administers approximately half the total forested acres in the Panhandle region of Idaho. Notable are the old stands of cedars at Hanna Flats and Roosevelt Grove near Priest Lake, and the Settlers Grove of ancient cedars near Prichard and Hobo Cedar Grove near Clarkia. At the East Fork of Emerald Creek, 8 mi southeast of Route 3 near Clarkia, you can collect gem-quality garnets for a fee. The Idaho Panhandle National Forests include the Coeur d'Alene and portions of the Kaniksu and St. Joe national forests. | 3815 Schreiber Way | 208/765–7223 Forest Supervisor's Office | fax 208/765–7307 | Daily dawn–dusk.

Lake Coeur d'Alene. Glaciers carved out the basin for this lake, elevation 2,152 ft, that extends south of town for about 25 mi. The lake is just 2½ mi wide, tucked in among

IDAHO RULES OF THE ROAD

License Requirements: To drive in Idaho you must be at least 16 years old and have a valid driver's license (15-year-olds may drive during daylight hours only). Residents of Canada and most other countries may drive with valid licenses from their home countries.

Right Turn on Red: Throughout the state, a right turn on red is permitted *after* a full stop, unless otherwise indicated by a no-turn-on-red sign.

Seat Belt and Helmet Laws: Drivers and front-seat passengers must wear seat belts. Children under the age of 5 must use a federally approved child safety seat. Only motorcyclists under the age of 18 are required to wear helmets.

Speed Limits: The speed limit on most interstate highways is 70 mph, except for portions of road that travel through urban or congested areas.

For More Information: Contact the **Idaho Transportation Department** | Office of Public Affairs, Box 7129, Boise, ID 83707 | 208/334–8005.

softly sculpted and forested mountains. Most of its water comes from the Coeur d'Alene, St. Joe, and St. Maries rivers, which rise along the Pend Oreille Divide and the Bitterroot Range. The highly developed shoreline offers lakeside restaurants, marinas, and hotels. | www.idoc.state.id.us | Daily dawn–dusk.

Museum of North Idaho. The museum's major exhibits highlight Native American culture, steamboats, the logging industry, and nearby communities. | 115 Northwest Blvd. | 208/664–3448 | www.coeurdalene.org | Apr.–Oct., Tues.–Sat. 11–5.

Fort Sherman Museum. Within the Museum of North Idaho, the Fort Sherman Powder House contains artifacts and information on Fort Sherman, which was founded in 1878. It also contains an original Forest Service smoke-chaser's cabin. | 208/664–3448 | May–Sept., Tues.–Sat. 1–4:45.

Silverwood Theme Park. The theme of this amusement park is an 1880s mining town. Within it are a narrow-gauge steam train, a wooden roller coaster, a log flume, and 24 other rides, including the newest roller-coaster ride Tremors, which spends much of the time in underground caves. | 26225 U.S. 95 N, Athol | 208/683–3400 | fax 208/683–2268 | www.silverwood4fun.com | Call for hrs.

Tubbs Hill. Come to this 120-acre wooded preserve to find century-old pine and fir trees, as well as hidden coves and beaches. Open to foot traffic only. | Box 7200 | 208/769–2252 | Daily dawn–dusk.

Dining

Beverly's. Contemporary. The inspired Northwest cuisine is made even more enjoyably by the lake views through window walls. The 7th-floor restaurant, part of the Coeur d'Alene Resort, has a contemporary design with copper and dark-wood accents. Try the grilled salmon drizzled with huckleberry salsa or the tenderloin of beef. Kids' menu. | 115 S. 2nd St. | 208/765–4000 | AE, D, MC, V | $$–$$$$

Iron Horse Bar and Grill. Contemporary. Old photographs and local memorabilia offer a slice of Idaho history in this fun family dining spot. The menu includes steaks, prime rib, seafood, and burgers. Weather permitting, you can eat on the patio. | 407 Sherman Ave. | 208/667–7314 | AE, D, DC, MC, V | $$

★ **Jimmy D's.** Contemporary. The work of local artists is showcased on the redbrick walls of this popular spot, where dinner is served by candlelight. The menu includes creative pastas, grilled steaks, and fresh fish. | 320 Sherman Ave. | 208/664–9774 | AE, D, DC, MC, V | $$

Hudson's Hamburgers. American. Double cheeseburgers and sandwiches are among the six items at this local downtown landmark dating to 1907. | 207 Sherman Ave. | 208/664–5444 | No credit cards | Closed Sun., Mon. No dinner | $

Lodging

★ **Clark House on Hayden Lake.** When it was built in 1910 as the summer home of F. Lewis Clark and his wife Winifred, the 15,000-square-ft home was on 1,400 acres and was the most expensive home in Idaho. The guest rooms are furnished with antiques and heavy traditional furniture in ivory, black, and gold. Four rooms have fireplaces, and three overlook the garden or a small cedar forest. A formal, two-course breakfast is served, and six-course candlelight dinners are available by reservation. Dining room, complimentary breakfast. Hot tub. No pets. | E. 4550 S. Hayden Lake Rd. | 208/772–3470 or 800/765–4593 | fax 208/772–6899 | www.clarkhouse.com | 10 rooms | AE, D, DC, MC, V | $$–$$$$

Best Western Templin's Resort. Old but well maintained, this hotel is a good choice if you plan to do a lot of hiking: it's a 5-minute walk from the Centennial Trail, which runs from Couer d'Alene to Spokane. Many rooms overlook the marina and private beach. I–90, Exit 5. Restaurant, bar (with entertainment), picnic area, room service. In-room data ports, some refrigerators. Cable TV. Indoor pool. Hot tub. Tennis courts. Exercise equipment. Beach, dock, boating. Laundry facilities. Business services. Pets allowed (fee). | 414 E. 1st Ave., Post Falls | 208/773–1611 | fax 208/773–4192 | www.bestwestern.com | 167 rooms | AE, D, DC, MC, V | $$–$$$

Fairfield Inn by Marriott. Just ½ mile from Lake Coeur d'Alene, this hotel has easy access to I–90. Designed for business travelers, the spacious rooms have well-lighted work desks and in-room data ports. Complimentary Continental breakfast. In-room data ports, some microwaves, some refrigerators. Cable TV. Indoor pool. Hot tub. Laundry facilities. No pets. | 2303 N. 4th St. | phone/fax 208/664–1649 | www.fairfieldinn.com | 69 rooms | AE, D, DC, MC, V | $–$$

Holiday Inn Express, Post Falls. You can request a microwave or refrigerator if you need one, a nice amenity if you're traveling with a family. The hotel is close to the lake, off the interstate but near downtown. Complimentary Continental breakfast. Some microwaves, some refrigerators. Laundry service. Pets allowed (fee). | 3105 E. Seltice Way, Post Falls | 208/773–8900 or 800/779–7789 | fax 208/773–0890 | 47 rooms | $–$$ | AE, D, DC, MC, V.

Grangeville

Attractions
Hells Canyon National Recreation Area. The deepest canyon in North America, Hells Canyon plunges 7,913 ft. The terrain and wildlife habitats range from desert at the canyon floor to alpine in the mountains. Idaho's Seven Devils Mountains tower above one rim and Oregon's Wallowas on the other. You can see the gorge on a sightseeing cruise, originating in Lewiston, or by raft or dory. Canyon rapids range from Class III to Class IV. Wildflowers bloom in spring, and summers from June to August bring daytime temperatures of 80° to 100°. Summers and fall are ideal for steelhead and sturgeon fishing. | 88401 Rte. 82, Enterprise | 541/426–4978 or 509/758–0616; 509/758–1957 river info | www.fs.fed.us/r6/w-w | Daily.

   Hells Canyon Creek. The primary launch point for float trips on the Snake River, this is also the only place in Hells Canyon where the Snake is accessible by a two-lane paved road. Pick up information at the staffed visitor center. | Forest Rd. 517, west of Riggins and HCNRA office | 208/628–3916 | Daily.

   Cache Creek Ranch. At the very northern end of the area, the ranch was histori-cally part of the Dobbins and Huffman sheep ranch that flourished in the 1930s, and is now a rest stop for river trips. It's reached by water only. The buildings are surrounded by lawns, a fruit orchard and a small visitor center. | 208/628–3916 | Visitor Center: June–Sept., daily dawn–dusk.

   Pittsburg Landing. You reach the area via the only year-round public road leading to the Snake River. There is a concrete boat ramp and float apron for launching or takeout. | North of Riggins on U.S. 95, west on Forest Rd. 493 at White Bird | 208/628–3916 | Daily dawn–dusk.

   Kirkwood Historic Ranch. The historic ranch on Kirkwood Bar offers a glimpse of canyon life from the 1930s. Displays in the old bunkhouse contain historic and prehis-toric artifacts. You can reach it by boat or trail only. Call ahead for road conditions. From the end of the road you hike 6 mi on the Snake River National Recreation Trail. | North of Riggins on U.S. 95, west on Forest Rd. 493 at White Bird, south on Forest Rd. 420, west on Forest Rd. 242, or drive to Pittsburg and hike | 208/628–3916 | Daily dawn–dusk.

★ **Nez Perce National Historical Park.** For thousands of years, the prairies and plateaus of north-central Idaho, northeastern Oregon, and southeastern Washington have been home to the Nez Perce. This park interprets Nez Perce culture and history. It includes 38 sites in Idaho, Montana, Oregon, and Washington. At the visitor center near Spalding, you can enjoy audio-visual programs and, during the summer, attend daily talks. | Headquarters and Visitor Center, Spalding, 1 mi east on U.S. 12 | 208/843–2261 | www.nps.gov/nepe | Spalding Visitor Center, June–Sept., daily 8–5:30; Nov.–May, daily 8–4:30.

White Bird Summit and Road. The Old White Bird Road can be seen en route to the summit on U.S. 95, south of Grangeville. This road was considered an engineering feat in its day, as its zigzags gained 4,429 ft in elevation within 14 mi. Paved in 1938, it is listed on the National Register of Historic Places. | 5 mi south on U.S. 95 | 208/843–2261 | Daily.

White Bird Hill Battlefield Auto Tour. The first battle of the Nez Perce War was fought here on June 17, 1877. Thirty-four soldiers were killed while the Nez Perce lost none. The visitor center in Spalding has maps you can use for a tour of the battlefield. The White Bird Interpretive Shelter has exhibits that explain the sequence of the battle. | 12 mi south on U.S. 95 | 208/843–2261 | Daily dawn–dusk.

Dining

Oscar's Restaurant. American. The memorabilia and photos scattered throughout trace the town's history and make this almost as much a museum as a restaurant. Gourmet burgers, steaks, and other basic fare are available. | 101 E. Main St. | 208/983–2106 | MC, V | $–$$

Lewiston

Attractions

If you're an outdoor adventure lover, give **Beamers Hells Canyon Tours and Excursions** a try. Jet-boat tours include the one-day tour, which takes you 100 mi upriver to Rush Creek, just past the end of navigation on the Snake River. The historic mail-run tour is offered year-round; boaters help deliver the U.S. mail to rugged canyon reaches as it's been done since 1919. The overnight is at Beamers' Copper Creek Lodge, and includes private modern cabin accommodations. It departs at 9 AM every Wednesday year-round for a two-day, one-night tour. | 800/522–6966 | fax 509/758–3643 | www.hellscanyontours.com.

Hells Gate State Park. Grassy open picnic areas are an attraction at this park, which also has a large swimming beach, boating facilities, a volleyball area, trails, and campsites within 100 yards of the Snake River. The park connects with the Lewiston beltway bike path. The marina has more than 100 slips available on a daily to annual basis. If you're an angler, try the famous steelhead runs of the Snake during the fall and winter. Bird-watchers should keep an eye out for pheasants, quail, chukar, hawks, geese, ducks, and owls, as well as eagles, pelicans, herons, and swans. | 3620-A Snake River Ave. | 208/799–5015 | www.idahoparks.org | Marina closed Dec.–Feb.

Nez Perce County Museum. Formerly known as the Luna House, this house-museum is devoted to the history of Nez Perce County and its surrounding area. It contains reproductions of a pioneer kitchen and a typical room setting. | 306 3rd St. | 208/743–2535 | Mar.–mid-Dec., Tues.–Sat. 10–4.

Winchester State Park. More than one-fourth of the park's total area is water, a 103-acre lake. You can camp, hike, and picnic here during the summer, and in winter, if the weather's on your side, you can cross-country ski, ice-skate, or ice-fish. The park has two yurts for rent year-round. You might see white-tailed deer, beavers, raccoons, muskrats, and the painted turtle. Trails ring the lake, and there is an interpretive nature trail next to the park headquarters. | Off I–95 near Winchester, or follow signs from town | 208/924–7563 | www.idahoparks.org | Daily.

Dining

Jonathan's. Contemporary. A solid mahogany bar anchors this spot with a menu strong on Northwest-inspired dishes that draw heavily on fresh seafood and local beef and produce. | 1516 Main St. | 208/746–3438 | AE, MC, V | Closed Sun. | $$–$$$

Zany's. Contemporary. Offbeat, this restaurant has '50s decor with jukeboxes, an old-fashioned soda counter, a carousel horse, a bathtub, and other miscellany hanging from the ceiling. They serve some Mexican dishes, as well as steaks, chicken, burgers, salads, and pasta. | 2006 19th Ave. | 208/746–8131 | AE, D, MC, V | $$

Bojack's Broiler Pit. American. Casual dining and good food are the order of the day at this small restaurant. The house favorites are the prime rib and the shrimp salad. | 311 Main St. | 208/746–9532 | AE, D, DC, MC, V | Closed Sun. | $–$$

Lodging

Red Lion Hotel. Set on a hillside above the Clearwater River 1 mi from I–15, this hotel has a full-service athletic club, a sports bar, and its own microbrewery. Restaurant, bar, room service. Cable TV. 2 pools (1 indoor). Hot tub. Gym. Laundry facilities. Airport shuttle. | 621 21st St. | 208/799–1000 | fax 208/748–1050 | www.redlionlewiston.com | 136 rooms | AE, D, DC, MC, V | $–$$

Riverview Hotel. Two miles from I–95A is this large, multistory hotel. Complimentary Continental breakfast. Cable TV. Pool. Pets allowed. | 1325 Main St. | 208/746–3311 or 800/806–7666 | fax 208/746–7955 | 75 rooms | AE, D, DC, MC, V | $

Sacajawea Select Inn. About two miles from I–15 and near downtown, this older motel with well maintained rooms is in a quiet area. The motel's restaurant, the Helm, serves simple, well-prepared food. Restaurant, bar. Refrigerators. Cable TV. Pool. Hot tub. Exercise equipment. Laundry facilities. Airport shuttle. Pets allowed. | 1824 Main St. | 208/746–1393 or 800/333–1393 | fax 208/746–3625 | 90 rooms | AE, D, DC, MC, V | $

Moscow

Attractions

Appaloosa Museum and Heritage Center. The Nez Perce tribes who lived in the area practiced selective horse breeding and produced large herds of high-quality horses, including Appaloosas. Regalia, saddles, and artifacts associated with the Appaloosa are on display. | 2720 W. Pullman Rd. | 208/882–5578 | www.appaloosamuseum.org | Tues.–Fri. 10–5, Sat. 10–4.

Latah County Historical Society McConnell Mansion. Built in 1886 by Idaho's third governor, the house is a combination of Eastlake, Queen Anne, and Victorian Gothic styles. On display are artifacts and Victorian-style furniture from the early 1900s to 1930s. The Latah County Historical Society, which presents changing exhibits on county history, is based here. | 110 S. Adams St. | 208/882–1004 | users.moscow.com/lchs/mansion.html | Tues.–Sat. 1–4.

University of Idaho. Established in 1889, the college was founded a year before Idaho became a state. As one of the state's largest institutions of higher learning, the school enrolls 10,000 and offers an agricultural extension service that reaches 42 of the state's counties. Colleges include architecture, art, agriculture, business, education, engineering, and forestry. | 208/885–6163 | Daily.

Dining

Bacilio's. Italian. In the Moscow Hotel, this restaurant offers updated Italian cuisine in a bright dining room fitted with artwork from ceiling to floor. The menu has a good variety of pastas. | 313 S. Main St. | 208/892–3848 | MC, V | $–$$

Casa de Oro. Mexican. Massive margaritas and genuine south-of-the-border entrées are reasonably priced here. Eat in the dining room or sit outside. | 415 S. Main St. | 208/883–0536 | AE, DC, MC, V | $

St. Maries

Attractions

Heyburn State Park. One of the more popular state parks, Heyburn spans 5,505 acres near Chatcolet Lake. At the west end of the lake are six hiking trails that at various points pass through stands of 400-year-old ponderosa pines. The Hawleys Landing Amphitheater presents lectures, slide shows, and other naturalist programs. | 7 mi west on Rte. 5 | 208/686–1308 | www.idoc.state.id.us/irti/stateparks | Daily.

St. Joe, Moyie, and Clearwater Rivers. The Moyie, St. Joe, and Clearwater rivers are popular for river trips that take only a single day but still give you a white-water experience. The picturesque St. Joe has blue-green water and its banks are covered with moss and dotted with cedars. Beginning rafters learn to paddle here. The Clearwater is a quiet and scenic river with no rapids and is popular with families. | Just east of town on Rte. 5 | 208/476–4541 | Daily.

IOWA

IOWA GREAT RIVER ROAD
FROM NEW ALBIN TO KEOKUK

Distance: 237 mi   Time: 2–3 days
Overnight Breaks: Dubuque, Burlington

The Great River Road is a 3,000-mi network of federal, state, and county roads that parallels the Mississippi River on both sides, from Canada to the Gulf of Mexico. The upper Mississippi River, dominated by Iowa countryside, offers spectacular scenery, charming communities, and interpretive centers that explain the impact of the Great River. The green paddle-wheel symbol found on maps and road signs is known throughout the region as the symbol of the Great River Road.

❶ Begin on Route 26 in **New Albin,** a quiet little town of dense forests and fertile farmland. From this area, the upper Iowa River flows into the Mississippi River.

❷ Continue 11 mi south on Route 26 to **Lansing,** where you should stop for your first look at the region known locally as Little Switzerland: During the Ice Age, when great glaciers carved out the Mississippi River valley, the hills in northeastern Iowa were not flattened like those in much of the area. From Mt. Hosmer Park, you can see for miles into Wisconsin and Minnesota.

❸ Leaving Lansing, the Great River Road departs Route 26 for a county road, X52, which is clearly marked. Within a few miles, you come to the village of Harper's Ferry, which is home to the 9,000-acre **Yellow River State Forest.** With additional access to approximately 3,000 acres of Mississippi River backwater, the forest is a good bet for hikers and anglers.

❹ Farther south X52 rejoins Route 26, and you'll come to the twin communities of **Marquette** and **McGregor.** Iowa's only National Monument, **Effigy Mounds,** is in this area. Here you'll see some 200 burial and ceremonial mounds created by prehistoric Native Americans between 500 BC and AD 1300. Effigy Mounds also has several hiking trails that provide views of the many tiny islands that comprise the upper Mississippi River valley.

New Albin **1**

Lansing **2**

Harper's
Ferry

9

76

3 Yellow River
State Forest

■ Effigy Mounds

McGregor
52
4 Marquette

Clayton

West
Union
18

Garnavillo
Historical
Museum **5**

Lockmaster's House
Heritage Museum

6

52

13

3

3

52 Dubuque **7**

20

Dyersville

WISCONSIN

18

61

151

Bellevue
State Park **8**

52

218

380

13

Wyoming

61

64

Sabula

Cedar
Rapids

30

Clinton **9**

67

Iowa
City

80

88

Quad Cities **10**

Muscatine **11**

61

Mississippi River

80

1

218

92

Mark Twain
National
Wildlife
Refuge **12**

67

74

78

34

13 Burlington

16

ILLINOIS

2

14 Fort Madison

136

MO.

15 Keokuk

30 miles

50 km

N

Marquette is named for the French Canadian explorer who, along with Louis Joliet, journeyed down the Mississippi River in the 1670s. Marquette is home to **Pikes Peak State Park,** which contains the highest bluff along the 1,100-mi path of the Great River. From the top of this 500-ft bluff, the confluence of the Wisconsin River and the mighty Mississippi may be seen to the south. To the north, there is a breathtaking view of the twin suspension bridges that connect Iowa and Wisconsin.

Adjacent to Marquette is McGregor, a community of historic homes with a business district filled with antiques shops. Here you may wish to divert from the Great River Road for a jaunt around the **River Bluffs Scenic Byway,** which will take you along hilly U.S. 18 through Gunder, Clermont, and West Union. If you think Iowa is all flat farmland, this 40-mi roller-coaster journey will certainly prove you wrong.

⑤ You may continue on Route 26 where your next stop is the historic fishing village of Clayton, followed by Garnavillo, where you'll find numerous Native American artifacts in the **Garnavillo Historical Museum.**

⑥ At Guttenberg, Route 26 becomes one with U.S. 52 for a few miles. Park the car at Guttenberg, take a quick mile-long walk through River Park, and investigate the activities at Lock and Dam 10. The **Lockmaster's House Heritage Museum** is one of the few left along the river, providing a look inside the lives of those who built the lock and dam system. Guttenberg also has an art gallery and microbrewery, as well as several shops and restaurants in its historic downtown square.

⑦ About 20 mi south of Guttenberg along U.S. 52 is **Dubuque.** Depending on the number of stops you've made along the way, Dubuque may be your first overnight stay. You'll find numerous B&Bs and a surprisingly wide variety of restaurants here. There's also plenty to do in Dubuque. The Mississippi River Museum, the Dubuque Art Center, **Crystal Lake Cave,** and trolley and carriage rides are among the city's many offerings. You might also want to drive west on U.S. 20 to **Dyersville** and play baseball at the *Field of Dreams* Movie Site baseball field.

⑧ Leaving Dubuque along U.S. 52, you'll come to the Luxembourger community of St. Donatus. Also on U.S. 52, in nearby Bellevue you can visit the butterfly garden at **Bellevue State Park.** The **Grant Wood Scenic Byway** is another diversion from the river. This 30-mi drive along Route 64 passes through the towns of Andrew, Maquoketa, and Preston. You may, however, decide to just continue driving south from Bellevue along U.S. 52 to Sabula, the only Iowa town on an island.

⑨ At Sabula, the Great River Road becomes U.S. 67, on which you should continue south to **Clinton. Eagle Point Park** is worth a stop, as it provides a view of the widest part of the Mississippi River, an impressive 3-mi span of water. A casino and a showboat are docked in Clinton, but be sure to save time for the arboretum and museum as well.

⑩ From Clinton, continue south on U.S. 67 into the **Quad Cities (Davenport** and **Bettendorf, Iowa,** and **Rock Island** and **Moline, Illinois).** More riverboats and walking trails dominate the riverfront, along with Lock and Dam 15. Take time to drive onto **Arsenal Island** for a visit to the **Rock Island Arsenal Museum** and the **Mississippi River Visitor's Center.** Activities are numerous in the Quad Cities; you could chose to spend several days here or continue south on U.S. 61 to Muscatine, driving through great camping and boating communities such as Buffalo, Montpelier, and Fairport.

⑪ **Muscatine** is at a bend in the river where fresh-water mussel shells accumulate; in the 1850s, German immigrants used the shells to build an enduring business of pearl button manufacturing, which put Muscatine on the map. Muscatine's **Mark Twain Overlook** provides one of the best views of the river during the course of this drive. Have your camera handy for shots of the bald eagles, tugboats, or the immense power of the Mississippi River.

⑫ Just south of Muscatine on U.S. 61 you'll enter Louisa County, with its **Mark Twain National Wildlife Refuge.** The refuge is marshy and filled with wetlands, a place enjoyed in the past by the Native Americans for hunting and fishing. In Toolesboro, you'll find a series of Native American burial mounds and a museum of Oneota culture.

⑬ From Toolesboro, the Great River Road moves inland a few miles until you reach **Burlington,** 25 mi to the south on Route 99. The **Point of Burlington Welcome Center** is on the riverfront in a 1928 building that once served the city and the commercial barge traffic stopping here.

⑭ The Great River Road returns to U.S. 61 at Burlington. Twenty miles south of Burlington on U.S. 61 is **Fort Madison,** the site of a full-scale replica of the old fort and a museum dedicated to the Great Flood of 1993.

SAR Great River Road continues 25 mi south along U.S. 61 to **Keokuk,** the last town in Iowa before the road enters northeast Missouri. Another of the locks and

IOWA RULES OF THE ROAD

License Requirements: To drive in Iowa, you must be at least 17 years old, although an instruction permit is possible at age 14, and an intermediate license may be granted at age 16.

Right Turn on Red: Right turns on red are allowed in Iowa *after* coming to a full and complete stop, unless otherwise posted.

Seat Belt and Helmet Laws: The driver and front seat occupants must wear a seat belt. Children under the age of 3 are required to be in a car safety seat. Children between the ages of 3 and 6 must be in either a car safety seat or a seat belt. Helmets are not required.

Speed Limits: The speed limit on rural Iowa interstates is 65 mph. In urban areas and on secondary roads, the speed limit is 55 mph, unless otherwise posted. Mopeds that operate over 25 mph are illegal in Iowa.

For More Information: Contact the **Iowa Motor Vehicle Information Center** | 800/532–1121.

dams is in Keokuk, as is the George M. Verity Riverboat Museum, a National Cemetery, and Rand Park, which overlooks the river and is the burial site of Chief Keokuk.

To return to New Albin, take U.S. 218 north out of Keokuk. U.S. 218 north becomes I–380 around Iowa City. Take I–380 into Cedar Rapids, then pick up U.S. 151 out of Cedar Rapids to Route 13 north. Take Route 13 north to U.S. 52 and then take U.S. 52 to U.S. 18 east into Marquette. From Marquette you can follow the Great River Road again. Take Route 76 north to Route 364, then Route X52 to Route 26, which you'll pick up around Lansing. Route 26 will bring you back to New Albin.

Burlington

Attractions

Geode State Park. Geodes, with their hollow centers and sparkling quartz crystals, are Iowa's state rock and can be found in abundance in this park 12 mi west of Burlington. If you are not a rockhound you may enjoy the supervised swimming beach that rims Lake Geode, known for excellent bluegill and crappie fishing, or the park's hiking and camping. | Rtes. 79/J20 | 319/392–4601 | www.state.ia.us/parks | Daily.

Heritage Hill National Historic District. Nearly 160 buildings in various architectural styles provide a sense of local history. | North of downtown, between Washington and High Sts. 52601 | 800/827–4837 | Daily.

The original part of the historic home called **Phelps House** was built in 1851. Some original furnishings remain in the six-story Italianate-style structure, as well as other artifacts of local history. | 521 Columbia St., 52601 | 319/753–2449 | May–Oct., weekends 1:30–4:30.

Some people call **Snake Alley,** a shortcut from Heritage Hill to downtown, the crookedest street in the world. | North of downtown, between Washington and High Sts. 52601 | 800/827–4837 | Daily.

Point of Burlington Welcome Center. The center offers tourist information and displays of local history in a historic 1928 building on the Mississippi River. | 400 N. Front St., 52601 | 319/752–8731 | Mon.–Sat. 9–5, Sun. 10–5.

Dining

Big Muddy's. American. Barbecued ribs are a hot item at this converted historic freight depot, which has a stunning view of the river. | 710 N. Front St., 52601 | 319/753–1699 | AE, D, DC, MC, V | $$

Martini's. Eclectic. Your choices range from Thai food to brick-oven pizza in this bustling spot in the Best Western Pizzaz Motor Inn. Sunday brunch. | 3003 Weingard Dr., 52601 | 319/753–2291 | AE, D, DC, MC, V | $$

Lodging

Best Western Pizazz Motor Inn. Burlington's only full-service hotel is in the northwest corner of town, just north of U.S. 34 and U.S. 61. Most guest rooms are either poolside or have balconies overlooking the three-story indoor pool atrium, which encloses a heated swimming pool and two attached hot tubs. There's also a game room. Restaurant, bar (with entertainment), complimentary Continental breakfast, room service. In-room data ports. Cable TV, in-room VCRs (and movies). Pool. Beauty salon, hot tub. Exercise equipment. Laundry facilities. Business services, airport shuttle. Pets allowed. | 3001 Winegard Dr. | 319/753–2223 or 800/528–1234 | fax 319/753–2224 | www.bestwestern.com | 151 rooms | AE, D, DC, MC, V | $

Comfort Inn. On a commercial street only 2 mi east of Snake Alley and the Mississippi River, this quiet, unassuming motel has plenty of shops and restaurants within walking distance. Complimentary Continental breakfast. In-room data ports. Cable TV. Pool. Business services. Pets allowed. | 3051 Kirkwood | 319/753–0000 or 800/221–2222 | fax 319/753–0000 ext. 301 | www.comfortinn.com | 52 rooms | AE, D, DC, MC, V | $

Super 8. Only a ½-mi walk from the river is this stucco building. Guest rooms with king- and queen-size beds also have recliners. Complimentary Continental breakfast. Some microwaves. Cable TV. | 3001 Kirkwood | 319/752–9806 or 800/800–8000 | fax 319/752–9806 | www.super8.com | 62 rooms | AE, D, DC, MC, V | $

Clinton

Attractions

Bickelhaupt Arboretum. Browse 14 acres of labeled trees, shrubs, and perennials, as well as a medicinal plant display. | 340 S. 14th St. | 319/242–4771 | Daily, dawn–dusk.

Eagle Point Park. A scenic road winds through this 205-acre park overlooking the Mississippi River at the northern edge of town, taking you past ball fields and a picnic area to a three-story stone observation tower built in the 1930s. | U.S. 67 | 319/243–1260 | Daily.

Felix Adler Museum. Celebrating the career of Clinton native and longtime Ringling Brothers clown Felix Adler, this museum's numerous attractions for children include a minigolf course, a rabbit house with live bunnies, a giant bubble machine, a dress-up corner, face-painting, and balloon-animal-making demonstrations. | 216 5th Ave. S | 319/243–3356 | Thurs.–Sat. 10–4.

Riverview Park. A band shell and picnic facilities are among the attractions of this 65-acre riverfront park. | 6th Ave. N | 319/243–1260 | Daily.

Named for the actress born here, the **Lillian Russell Theatre** is aboard the *City of Clinton* showboat, a permanently dry-docked paddle wheeler that's home to Clinton's summer-stock theater. | 309 Riverview Dr. | 319/242–6760 | June–Aug.

Also docked at Riverview Park is the ***Mississippi Belle II,*** a 40-ft cruising riverboat with gambling and entertainment aboard. Children are not allowed on the boat but may stay at a day care center on the premises until 4 PM. | 311 Riverview Dr. | 319/243–9000 or 800/457–9975 | Daily 24 hrs.

Valley Oaks Golf Club. *Golf Digest* considers this challenging 18-hole course a particularly good value. | 3330 Harts Mill Rd. | 319/242–7221 | Apr.–Oct.

Dining

The Unicorn. Contemporary. Eclectic items, like the Duke of Earl sandwich with turkey, melted Swiss, asparagus, and curry sauce, are among the menu choices. | 1004 N. 2nd St., 52732 | 319/242–7355 | AE, D, MC, V | $–$$

Upper Mississippi Brewing Company. American. Built in the early 1900s, this historic brewing house serves steak, ribs, and specialty sandwiches. | 132 6th Ave. S, 52732 | 319/241–1275 | AE, D, DC, MC, V | $

Dubuque

Attractions

Bellevue State Park. Tall cliffs in this 700-acre park 26 mi south of the town of Bellevue afford fine views of the Mississippi River. You'll also find wooded walking trails, a butterfly sanctuary, and a nature center. | 24668 Hwy. 52 | 319/872–3243 or 319/872–4019 | www.state.ia.us/parks | Daily.

Crystal Lake Cave. Discovered in 1868, this cave is about 5 mi south of town, off Highway 52. It contains a "chapel room" and unusual geological formations like cave flowers and soda straws. | 7699 Crystal Lake Cave Dr. | 319/556–6451 or 319/872–4111 | Memorial Day–Labor Day, daily 9–6; Labor Day–mid-Oct., weekdays 11–5, weekends 9–5.

Dubuque Art Center. The glass-curtain walls of this art museum look out onto downtown Dubuque's Washington Park. On display are traveling exhibits and regional artwork, including pieces by Iowa native Grant Wood, who captured the state on canvas during the 1930s and '40s. | 701 Locust St. | 319/557–1851 | Tues.–Fri. 10–5, weekends 1–4.

Fenelon Place Elevator. Traveling just 296 ft while elevating passengers 189 ft, this is the world's shortest, steepest railway. Built in 1882 and now providing both transportation and a wonderful view, this lift is also known as the Fourth Street Elevator. | 512 Fenelon Pl | 319/582–6496 | www.mall.mwci.net/fenplco | Apr.–Nov., daily 8 AM–10 PM.

Mississippi River Museum. Float on a simulated log raft, pilot a riverboat, and explore a boatbuilding shop as you learn about 300 years of river history in this riverfront museum complex. You may get a little wet and lost in the fog during *River of Dreams*, an atmospheric film (involving split screens and fog machines) that tells the history of life on the river. While you are at the museum be sure to climb aboard the 277-ft Sidewheeler *William M. Black*, which once served as a dredge boat along the river. | 300 3rd St. | 319/557–9545 | Daily 10–5:30.

Rustic Hills Carriage Tours. See Dubuque's historical treasures on this horse-drawn carriage tour, which includes the Mathias Ham House and Cable Car Square. 4th and Bluff Sts. | 319/556–6341 | Daily 10–5.

Trolleys of Dubuque, Inc. Old-fashioned trolleys depart from the welcome center and go to major Dubuque sights. | 400 E. 3rd St., Ice Harbor | 563/552–2896 | Apr.–Oct., daily departure 12:30.

Dining

Betty Jane's Candies. Café. Family-owned and -operated since 1938, this candy shop is famous for homemade chocolates, particularly the "gremlin," a caramel, pecan, and chocolate confection. You can also choose from 66 flavors of homemade ice cream. | 3049 Ashbury Rd., 52001 | 319/582–4668 | MC, V | $–$$

Dempsey's Steakhouse. Steak. Steak, pasta, and much of the artwork are for sale in this casual, downtown Irish pub–restaurant. Kids' menu. | 395 W. 9th St., at Bluff St. | 319/582–7057 | AE, MC, V | Closed Sun. No lunch Sat. | $–$$

Mario's. Italian. Italian opera and movie posters hang throughout this cozy, downtown eatery. House specialties include rich-but-delicious fettuccine Alfredo, veal scaloppine, and chicken marsala. Kids' menu. | 1298 Main St. | 319/556–9424 | AE, DC, MC, V | Closed Sun. | $–$$

Breitbach's Country Dining. American. Not much has changed in this restaurant since it was founded in 1852. It looks like a rambling farmhouse outside and is equally homey inside with old photos, lace curtains, and checkered tablecloths. Chicken-fried steak, Iowa pork chops with homemade applesauce, and creamy hand-mashed potatoes are on the menu. The restaurant is 20 mi north of town. | 563 Balltown Rd., Balltown | 319/552–2220 | No credit cards | $

Lodging

Hancock House. Perched halfway up a bluff in the 11th Street Historic District is this meticulously restored lavender Victorian home. The large front porch has swings and comfy deck furniture. Some rooms have fireplaces. The inn's second-floor turret has a great view of the river. Complimentary breakfast. Some in-room hot tubs. No TV in some rooms. | 1105 Grove Terr | 319/557–8989 | fax 319/583–0813 | www.thehancockhouse.com | 19 rooms | AE, D, MC, V | $$–$$$

Holiday Inn. A freestanding fireplace dominates the spacious lobby of this downtown hotel. Some rooms have excellent views of the city and the area's surrounding bluffs. Restaurant, bar, room service. Some refrigerators. Cable TV. Pool. Hot tub. Exercise equipment. Business services, airport shuttle. Pets allowed. | 450 Main St. | 319/556–2000 | fax 319/556–2303 | www.basshotels.com/holiday-inn | 173 rooms | AE, D, DC, MC, V | $$–$$$

Comfort Inn. On Dubuque's main drag, this smallish hotel does a brisk business with tourists on weekends and businesspeople during the week. It's only a half mile from the Kennedy Mall and less than 3 mi from the big riverboat casinos. Rooms have large work areas for business travelers. Complimentary Continental breakfast. In-room data ports, some microwaves, some refrigerators. Cable TV. Pool. Hot tub. Business services. Pets allowed. | 4055 Dodge St. | 319/556–3006 | fax 319/556–3006 | www.comfortinn.com | 52 rooms, 14 suites | AE, D, DC, MC, V | $

Days Inn. Built against the limestone cliffs of the Mississippi River, this motel has pleasant, unassuming rooms with great water views. Restaurant, bar, picnic area, complimentary Continental breakfast. Some microwaves, some refrigerators. Some in-room VCRs. Pool. Exercise equipment. Business services, airport shuttle. Pets allowed. | 1111 Dodge St. | 319/583–3297 | fax 319/583–5900 | www.daysinn.com | 154 rooms | AE, D, DC, MC, V | $

Dyersville

Attractions

Field of Dreams **Movie Site.** The 1989 Academy Award–nominated movie was shot here 3 mi northeast of town. Run the bases, play catch, or cheer from the bleachers, just as Kevin Costner did. Bring your own bat and glove. | 29001 Lansing Rd. | 319/875–6012 | Apr.–Nov., daily 9–6.

National Farm Toy Museum. Many of the farm toys you may have played with as a child are displayed on the front porch of this farmhouse, at the intersection of U.S. Highway 20 and State Highway 136. | 1110 16th Ave. SE | 319/875–2727 | www.dyersville.org | Daily 8–7.

St. Francis Xavier Basilica. One of only 33 basilicas in the country, this is one of the finest examples of Gothic architecture in the Midwest. It's at the corner of 3rd and 1st Sts. near the park. | 104 3rd St. SW | 319/875–7325 | Daily 8–5. Tours by appointment or self-guided tour.

Dining

The Palace. American/Casual. Popular for such comfort food as roasted chicken, stews, and soups, this old-fashioned saloon and bar is in the heart of downtown. If the weather is fair on Friday evenings you can grill your own steaks out on the deck. | 149 1st Ave. E, 52040 | 319/875–2284 | No credit cards | $

Fort Madison

Attractions

Flood Museum. Through TV footage, newspaper clippings, and photos, this museum recounts the Mississippi flood of 1993. | 814 10th St. | 319/372–7661 | Memorial Day–Labor Day, Wed.–Sat. noon–4.

River View Park. River access, a marina, and an ice-skating rink are the attractions in this park on the eastern edge of town. | At junction of Hwy. 61 and 6th St. | 319/372–7700 | May–Sept., daily.

Inside the park you'll also find **Old Fort Madison,** a replica of the first military fort west of the Mississippi. There are daily military reenactments in summer and you can participate in such hands-on learning activities as candle making and basketry. | 319/372–6318 | www.fort-madison.net/oldfort/ | Memorial Day–Labor Day, daily; Sept.–Oct., weekends.

Sante Fe Depot Historic Museum and Complex. Donated by the Sante Fe and Burlington Railroad, this museum contains 100 years of railroad history and the world's largest Sheaffer pen collection. | 9th and Ave. H | 319/372–7661 | Apr.–Sept., daily.

Santa Fe Railway Bridge. On the east edge of town, this bridge from the 1830s is the largest doubledeck swingspan bridge in the country. It's still functioning as a railway and an automobile bridge from Iowa into Illinois. | East edge of town | 800/210–8687 | Daily.

Dining

Ivy Bake Shop. Café. Breakfast treats at this gourmet bakery and café include blackberry scones, rhubarb brunch cake, cinnamon and pecan rolls, and a variety of muffins. Lunches include quiches, pasta dishes, and sandwiches. You can sip specialty coffee drinks, homemade lemonade, and brewed teas all day on the screened-in porch along Avenue G. | 622 7th St., 52627 | 319/372–9939 | No credit cards | No dinner | $

Keokuk

Attractions

George M. Verity Riverboat Museum. You can visit the crew quarters or the pilot house of this dry-docked paddle-wheel steamboat in Victory Park, which also has exhibits on old-time life on the river. | 1st St. at Water St. | 319/524–4765 | Memorial Day–Labor Day, daily 9–5.

Grand Avenue. The Keokuk Convention and Tourism Bureau offers a "Walking Tour of Grand Avenue" map that will guide you past the beautiful homes on Grand and Orleans avenues—prestigious addresses for Keokuk's elite during the late 1800s and early 1900s. | Grand and Orleans Aves. | 319/524–5599 | Daily.

Keokuk Dam. At 12,000 ft, lock and dam No. 19 is the longest on the Mississippi. It's a great place to watch barges and other boats navigate a lock system or to watch for eagles in winter. | End of N. Water St. | 319/524–4091 or 319/524–9660 | Memorial Day–Labor Day, tours daily 11 AM.

National Cemetery. Built in the 1860s, this is one of America's 12 original national cemeteries, and the only one in Iowa. There's a large Civil War section. | 1701 J St. | 319/524–5193 | Daily.

Rand Park. Community flower gardens, a fountain, and the burial site of Chief Keokuk, the city's Sauk–Fox namesake, fill this city park overlooking the Mississippi River. | Between N. 14th and N. 17th Sts. | 319/524–5599 | Daily.

Samuel F. Miller House Museum. Samuel Miller, a local attorney appointed to the Supreme Court by Abraham Lincoln, once owned this 1859 Federal-style house. You'll find period antiques and local history exhibits. | 318 N. 5th St. | 319/524–7283 or 800/383–1289 | Fri.–Sun. 1–4:30, or by appointment.

Dining

Hawkeye Restaurant. American. Barbecued ribs, barbecued prime rib, and chops are among the favorites at this eatery 2 mi north of town, but you can also get catfish, shrimp, and lobster. While you wait for your dinner, enjoy microbrews on tap or study the period photos of Keokuk. The lounge is open until 1 AM. | 105 N. Park Dr., 52632 | 319/524-7549 | AE, D, MC, V | Closed Sun. | $-$$$$

Marquette

Attractions

Effigy Mounds National Monument. The 1,481-acre monument 3 mi north of Marquette contains 191 known prehistoric mounds of various shapes built by the Woodland Indians. Numerous scenic hiking trails are in the area. | 151 Hwy. 76 | 319/873-3491 | www.nps.gov/efmo | Daily 8-4:30.

Garnavillo Historical Museum. Prehistoric and Native American artifacts abound in this little museum in Garnavillo, about 12 mi south of Marquette. | Washington and Centre Sts., Garnavillo | 319/964-2191 | Memorial Day-Labor Day, weekends 1-5 or by appointment.

Lockmaster's House Heritage Museum. The only remaining lockmaster's house on the Mississippi is now a museum in Guttenberg about 21 mi southeast of Marquette. It displays period furnishings and photos and provides insight into the lives of those who built the lock and dam system. | Lock and Dam La., Guttenberg | 319/252-1531 | Memorial Day-mid-Oct., Tues.-Sun. noon-4.

Pikes Peak State Park. You'll have a clear view of Wisconsin and Illinois from the park, on the highest bluff of the Mississippi, 5 mi southeast of town. | 15316 Great River Rd. | 319/873-2341 | www.state.ia.us/parks | Daily.

Dining

Alexander Café. American. Oversize chairs and large windows with fine river views set the tone for this comfortable spot 1 mi south of Marquette. It's known for Friday-night fish fries and Saturday steak specials. | 213 Main St., McGregor | 319/873-3838 | No credit cards | $-$$

Muscatine

Attractions

Mark Twain National Wildlife Refuge. Two of the four separate divisions of this refuge are south of Muscatine on County Route X61. Both the Big Timber Division (10 mi south of town) and the Louisa Division (14 mi south of town) are part of one of the most important flyways in the country, and offer wildlife observation, hiking trails, and educational programs. The Louisa Division closes for four and a half months each year so migrating birds will not be disturbed. | Rte. X61 | 319/523-6982 | Big Timber: daily dawn-dusk; Louisa: Feb.-Sept. 15, daily dawn-dusk.

Mark Twain Overlook. A commemorative plaque with a quote from Twain marks an expansive view of the river. | Hwy. 92 and Business U.S. 61 | 319/263-8895 | Daily 24 hrs.

Pearl Button Museum. Pearl button manufacturing put this town on the map in the late 1800s; at the turn of the last century Muscatine produced a third of the world's buttons. | 206 W. 2nd St. | 319/263-8895 | Sat. 1-3 or by appointment.

Saulsbury Bridge Recreation Area. You'll find a nature center, hunting and fishing areas, and a canoe transport service in this 675-acre county park. | 2007 Saulsbury Rd. | 319/649–3379 or 319/264–5922 | Apr.–Oct., daily; Nov.–Mar., Sun.–Fri.

Shady Creek Recreation Area. The Army Corps of Engineers manages this 16-acre area 7 mi east of town on the Mississippi River, where you'll find 53 modern campsites and a boat ramp. | 1611 2nd Ave. | 319/263–7913 | www.mvr.usace.army.mil/missriver/rec.htm | Daily.

Wildcat Den State Park. One of the focal points of this park 12 mi east of Muscatine is the Pine Creek Grist Mill. Built in 1848, the mill is on the National Register of Historic Places. | 1884 Wildcat Den Rd. | 319/263–4337 | www.state.ia.us/parks | Daily.

SANTA FE TRAIL ALONG U.S. 56

A DRIVE FROM EDGERTON TO ELKHART

Distance: 427 mi   Time: 3 days
Overnight Breaks: Council Grove, Dodge City

The Santa Fe Trail was opened in 1821 as a trade route between the United States east of the Missouri and the Mexican provinces. Hundreds of thousands of pioneers took this route, leaving wagon ruts and devastation of plant life that is still visible today. More than half of the Santa Fe Trail lies within the boundaries of Kansas, roughly following U.S. 56, starting near Edgerton, just south of metropolitan Kansas City.

1 U.S. 56 and 183rd Street intersect in **Edgerton,** at about the point where the Santa Fe Trail separated from the Oregon Trail. The trail follows U.S. 56 west through Baldwin City, home of the **Ivan Boyd Prairie Preserve,** a great place to study the native grasses and flowers the pioneers encountered. The preserve is one of several places where wagon ruts are still visible. About 65 mi farther west along U.S. 56, you'll come to the tiny community of Allen, founded in 1854. Here a cemetery holds 150 unmarked graves of pioneers who succumbed early on the journey. A toll bridge across 142 Creek and a mail station also operated here.

2 West of Allen on U.S. 56 is **Council Grove,** a former outpost for wagon freighters. Council Grove is home to 12 registered historic sites along the trail, including a jail, a tree under which peace treaties were signed, and a mission school for Native Americans. Council Grove is another spot where wagon ruts are visible. To see the ruts, take U.S. 56 (Main Street) west to the city limits sign. Drive another 5 mi west, turn left (south) on a gravel road and go a half mile. A sign indicates the ruts, a shallow trough running in a west-southwest direction. (The ruts are on private property.) Spend the night in Council Grove.

3 Continue following U.S. 56 through the towns of Herrington and McPherson to Lyons. The community about 30 mi west of McPherson is where the trail crosses Crow Creek. **Ralph's Ruts,** considered some of the finest examples of the trail, are seven parallel paths on a farm north of U.S. 56 and east of Chase. Watch for signs.

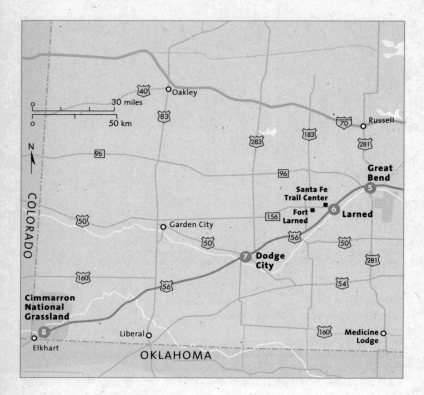

④ The trail continues along U.S. 56 and next passes through Ellinwood, where artifacts from the **Allison Fort Trading Post and Postal Relay Station** are preserved.

⑤ The trail continues along the banks of the Arkansas River to the city of **Great Bend,** where you can see an excellent exhibit of Santa Fe Trail artifacts at the **Barton County Historical Society Museum and Village.** Great Bend is where the trail and U.S. 56 take a dramatic turn to the south, and you (just as pioneers did nearly 200 years ago) will see the Citadel of the Prairie, a huge limestone rock nearly 70 ft high, which is also called Pawnee Rock. A monument on the site tells the significance of the wagon trains' reaching this point.

⑥ Next on the route is the town of **Larned,** a must for those interested in the history of the Santa Fe Trail. Just 2 mi west of Larned on Route 156 is the **Santa Fe Trail Center,** the only research museum specifically designed to study the trail. **Fort Larned** was built to protect commerce along the trail, and ruts are clearly visible for miles near the old fort.

⑦ Next along the trail is **Dodge City,** another must for anyone interested in the "real" Old West. In addition to details of life in "the wickedest city of the west," Dodge City is where you will find the largest continuous stretch of clearly defined tracks along the entire route of the trail. The tracks are 9 mi west of Dodge City on U.S. 50 (watch for the "Historic Marker" signs) and are impressive, even to teenagers and others not easily impressed on family vacations. Before getting out of Dodge, spend the night.

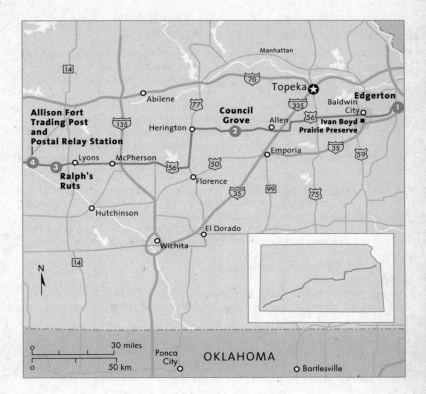

8 The Santa Fe Trail and U.S. 56 leave Kansas, crossing into Oklahoma and New Mexico, at the **Cimarron National Grassland,** near Elkhart (approximately a 2-hour drive along U.S. 56 from Dodge City). The National Forest Service offers a map for a 50-mi self-guided tour through this region, but you can simply continue following U.S. 56 south to continue your journey along the Santa Fe Trail.

Retracing your route on U.S. 56 is the fastest way to return to metropolitan Kansas City.

Council Grove

Attractions

Council Oak Shrine. A sheltered stump is all that remains of a great oak tree where the U.S. government and Osage Tribe signed a peace treaty in August 1825. | 210 E. Main St. | www.councilgrove.com/cou_oak.htm | Daily.

Farmers and Drovers Bank. Built in 1892, this two-story redbrick bank is listed on the National Register of Historic Places and is still in operation. The building's striking architecture combines Romanesque arches, stained-glass windows, and a Byzantine dome. Tours are available by appointment. | 201 W. Main St. | 620/767–5882 | www.councilgrove.com | Weekdays 9–3, Sat. 9–12.

Kaw Mission State Historic Site. Methodist Episcopal missionaries built this school for Kaw children in 1851, but today it showcases the heritage of the Kaw Indians, the Santa

Fe Trail, and early Council Grove. | 500 N. Mission St. | 316/767–5410 | www.councilgrove. com | Tues.–Sat. 10–5, Sun. 1–5.

Old Calaboose. Calaboose is an old-fashioned word for jail, and this old cowboy jail is a replica of the original home for cowboys and homesteaders who got a little out of control during their visits to town. | 502 E. Main St. | 620/767–5882 | Daily.

Dining

Station Restaurant. American/Casual. Soup and made-to-order sandwiches are the staples here. If you want supper, eat early, because they close at 6 PM every day except Friday. Try the Railroad Hoagie (a hero with assorted meats and vegetables), ham and bean soup, strawberry pie, or pound cake. | 219 W. Main St. | 620/767–5619 | No credit cards | $

★ **Hays House 1857.** American. The oldest continuously operating restaurant west of the Mississippi was built in 1857 by Daniel Boone's grandson and is now a National Historic Landmark. Pictures of the building and area line the walls, and there are a few antique church pews that serve as booths. Known for halibut and prime rib. Salad bar. Kids' menu. Sun. brunch. | 112 W. Main St. | 620/767–5911 | Closed Mon. | D, MC, V | $–$$

Lodging

Cottage House. Built in 1867 as a tiny cottage and blacksmith shop, this Prarie Victorian grew into a popular boarding house. Complimentary Continental breakfast. In-

KANSAS RULES OF THE ROAD

License Requirements: Residents of Kansas with a farm permit may drive as early as 14 years of age. However, other drivers must be at least 16 years old, have completed driver's training, and have a valid license from their state of residence.

Right Turn on Red: A right turn on red is allowed in Kansas *after* coming to a full and complete stop.

Seat Belt and Helmet Laws: All front seat passengers, regardless of age, must wear a seat belt. All children under the age of 4 years must be in a safety seat. Motorcycle drivers or passengers are not required, but are encouraged, to wear a helmet.

Speed Limits: Speed limits on the open interstate or any separated multilane highway are 70 mph, on two-lane state highways 65 mph, and on county roads 55 mph.

For More Information: Contact the **Kansas Department of Transportation** | 913/296–1568.

room data ports, some refrigerators, in-room hot tubs. Cable TV. Outdoor hot tub. Business services. Pets allowed (fee). | 25 N. Neosho | 620/767–6828 or 800/727–7903 | fax 620/767–6414 | 38 rooms | AE, D, DC, MC, V | $

Flint Hills Bed and Breakfast. Relax on the porch swing or chat with fellow guests in the sitting room of this 1913 historic American four square house, the childhood home of former Arizona Congressman John J. Rhodes. The B&B has retained its original woodwork and floors. Complimentary breakfast. No pets. No kids under 4. No smoking. | 613 W. Main St., 66846-1712 | 620/767–6655 | 4 rooms | D, MC, V | $

Dodge City

Attractions

Boot Hill Museum. An entire block of downtown has been restored to the way it was when Bat Masterson and Wyatt Earp attempted to bring order here. The museum contains exhibits, documents, and photographs showcasing Dodge City's past, and stagecoach rides, gunfights, and dance hall shows take place all day long. | Front St. | 620/227–8188 | fax 620/227–7673 | www.boothill.org | Memorial Day weekend–Labor Day, daily 8–8; Labor Day–Memorial Day weekend, Mon.–Sat. 9–5, Sun. 1–5.

Dodge City Trolley. Narrated tours spotlight such sites as the Long Branch Saloon, Fort Dodge, and the Santa Fe Trail. | 400 W. Wyatt Earp Blvd. | 620/225–8186 | Memorial Day–Labor Day, daily 8:30–6:30.

Fort Dodge. Several original buildings remain of the fort that supported this area from 1865–1882. | 101 Pershing Ave. | 620/227–2121 | fax 620/225–6331 | Memorial Day–Labor Day, daily 10–4; Labor Day–Memorial Day, daily 1–4.

Mariah Hills Golf Course. Opened in 1975, this 18-hole golf course has great greens and huge fairways. No credit cards. | 1800 Matt Down La. | 620/225–8182 | Year-round.

★ **Santa Fe Trail Tracks.** The wide-open prairie reveals the vastness of the pioneers' undertaking as miles of wagon ruts, found 9 mi west of Dodge City, stretch to the horizon. | On U.S. 50 | 620/227–8188 | Daily.

Dining

Casey's Cowtown Restaurant. American. A brick fireplace, antiques, and local art contribute to this steak house's casual atmosphere. Known for hand-cut black Angus steaks. Kids' menu. | 503 E. Trail | 620/227–5225 | AE, D, MC, V | $$

El Charro. Mexican. Mexican dishes such as "enchilada delights," topped with cheese, lettuce, tomato, and sour cream, make this ranch-like restaurant with wooden tables and flowers a favorite. | 1209 W. Wyatt Earp Blvd. | 620/225–0371 | Closed Sun. | AE, D, MC, V | $

Lodging

Boot Hill Bed and Breakfast. You'll find rooms with such names as the Wild West, Miss Kitty, and Annie Oakley in this 1927 Dutch Colonial home. Most rooms are spacious, and some have cherry-wood four-poster beds, fireplaces, and skylights. Complimentary breakfast. In-room data ports. Cable TV, in-room VCRs. No pets. No smoking. | 603 W. Spruce St., 67801 | 620/225–7600 or 888/225–7655 | fax 620/225–6585 | 6 rooms | AE, MC, V | $$–$$$

Best Western Silver Spur Lodge. Pleasant but undistinguished rooms await you at this sprawling complex, just 5 minutes from Front Street and the downtown district. Restaurant, bar. Cable TV. Pool. Business services, airport shuttle. Free parking. Pets allowed

(fee). | 1510 W. Wyatt Earp Blvd., 67801 | 620/227–2125 | fax 620/227–2030 | www.
bestwestern.com | 120 rooms | AE, D, DC, MC, V | $

Super 8. Basic, economical rooms are available at this chain hotel, 2 mi west of the
Boot Hill Museum. Complimentary Continental breakfast. Cable TV. Pool. Pets allowed.
| 1708 W. Wyatt Earp Blvd. | 620/225–3924 | fax 620/225–5793 | www.super8.com | 64
rooms | AE, D, DC, MC, V | $

Great Bend

Attractions

Allison Fort Trading Post and Postal Relay Station. A historical marker is all that
remains of this significant spot along the Santa Fe Trail. | U.S. 56, 2 mi east of Great
Bend | 620/792–2401 | Daily.

Barton County Historical Society Museum and Village. Nine buildings on a 5-acre tract
of land are vivid reminders of life here nearly 100 years ago. | S. Main St. | 620/793–
5125 | Apr.–mid-Nov., Tues.–Sun. 1–5; mid-Nov.–Mar., by appointment.

Brit Spaugh Park and Zoo. More than 100 animals are sheltered in these 46 acres,
including a pride of lions, bears, and hooved livestock. | N. Main St. | 620/793–4160 |
Daily 9–4:30.

Cheyenne Bottoms. One of the last major wetland systems in Kansas, this stop-over
point for nearly ½ million migrating birds annually is 5 mi north of Great Bend, off
U.S. 281. | 56 N.E. 40 Rd. | 620/793–7730 | Daily.

Quilt Walk. Seven famous quilt patterns are in-laid in the sidewalk around the Barton
County Courthouse. | 1300–1400 Main St. | 620/792–2750 | Daily.

Quivira National Wildlife Refuge. Nearly 22,000 acres of prairie grasses, salt marshes,
sand dunes, and canals are home to hundreds of thousands of water fowl, reptiles,
and mammals. | Rte. 484, 13 mi east from U.S. 281 | 620/486–2393 | fax 620/486–2315 |
quivira.fws.gov | Daily; some seasonal closings for migrations.

★ **Ralph's Ruts.** These seven parallel paths on the farm of Ralph Hathaway (considered
a leading authority on the Santa Fe trail) are thought to be some of the finest examples
on the trail. The ruts are north of U.S. 56 and 4 mi west of Chase. | 4222 Ave. L, Chase,
67524 | 620/938–2504 | By appointment.

Dining

Tenth Street Restaurant. Mexican. The cheerful Southwest-style interior here is
complemented by tasty tacos, burritos, and chalupas. Order the hot made-to-order
chips and the pork enchiladas, both popular with regulars. | 2210 Tenth St. | 620/793–
3786 | Closed weekends | No credit cards | $

Larned

Attractions

Fort Larned National Historic Site. The fort is known as the guardian of the Santa Fe
Trail. Many of its buildings are original military structures. It's 6 mi west of Larned on
U.S. 156. | Rte. 3 | 620/285–6911 | fax 620/285–3571 | www.nps.gov/fols | Daily 8:30–5.

★ **Santa Fe Trail Center.** See a portion of the original wagon ruts made by travelers on
this route, as well as tepees and other artifacts from the 60 years of this commerce
trail. The center is 2 mi west of Larned on U.S. 156. | RR 3 | 620/285–2054 | www.

larned.net/trailctr | Memorial Day–Labor Day, daily 9–5; Labor Day–Memorial Day, Tue.–Sun. 9–5.

Sibley's Camp. These bluffs were the campsite of George C. Sibley's survey team, which in 1825 began to oversee a survey of the Santa Fe Trail. The camp is described in Sibley's journal and diaries as "Cliffs of Soft Rock." | 502 W. Second St., at State St. | 620/285–6916 | Daily.

Dining

Harvest Inn. American. Chicken, steaks, and seafood are on the menu at this family restaurant; pub food is served in the accompanying bar, the Grain Club. | 718 Ft. Larned Ave. | 620/285–3870 | MC, V | $–$$

Papa's Family Restaurant. American. Housed in an old historic train station, this restaurant has a full menu as well as lunch and supper buffets that include up to 20 entrées. Regulars love the barbecue, catfish, and prime rib, and rave about the sweet oatmeal pie made from a secret family recipe. | 320 Broadway | 620/285–0055 | No credit cards | $–$$

Burgerteria. American. As the name implies, you'll find burgers on the menu, along with homemade fries and ice cream. Kids' menu. | 417 W. 14th St. | 620/285–3135 | Breakfast also available | No credit cards | $

LOUISIANA

MISSISSIPPI RIVER PLANTATIONS
NEW ORLEANS TO ST. FRANCISVILLE

Distance: 183 mi; 295 kilometers   Time: 3 days
Overnight Breaks: Baton Rouge, New Roads

Antebellum mansions share the landscape with industrial complexes, making this drive a fascinating view of life along the Mississippi both in the mid-1800s and today. The historic manors are beautiful year-round, but especially when decorated for Christmas and in spring, when azaleas and magnolia trees are in bloom and gardens are splashed with fresh color.

Be aware that because of the many twists and turns as the River Road follows the Mississippi, directions such as "east" or "west" are pointless. Locals go with the flow, indicating either "downriver" (towards New Orleans) or "upriver" (towards Baton Rouge and beyond).

❶ The **Great River Road New Orleans,** a vital trade route for more than a century, is actually two roads tracing both sides of the Mississippi River from **New Orleans** to Baton Rouge. Though many of the historic homes you will pass are private, all of the sites that follow are open for guided tours.

❷ For the first stop at **Destrehan Plantation** in Destrehan, take Exit 6 off I–310 and proceed ¼ mi downriver (back towards New Orleans) on River Road. This French Colonial manor, with hand-hewn cypress timbers and West Indies–style roof, is one of the oldest plantation houses remaining in the Mississippi Valley. It was built in 1787 by planter and legislator Jean Noel Destrehan; a Greek Revival remodeling was completed in 1840. Pirate Jean Lafitte was a frequent visitor, which led to persistent rumors that treasure is buried behind the walls.

❸ Continuing for 25 mi upriver from Destrehan on River Road, between Reserve and Lutcher you'll come to Garyville and the **San Francisco Plantation House.** An ornate and colorful Steamboat Gothic extravaganza, the San Francisco is famous for its hand-painted decorative ceilings and faux marbling. Though it would fit right in with the Bay City's "painted ladies," the name of the 1856 mansion was originally "Sans Frusquin," French slang for "without a penny in my pocket." That rueful claim came

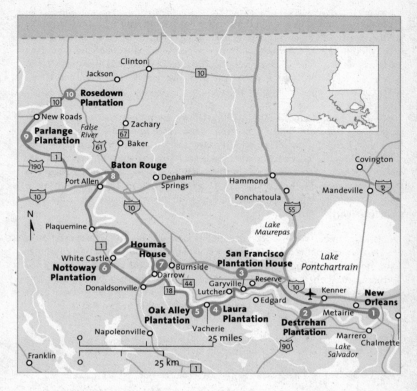

from planter Edmond Bozonier Marmillion, who had spared no expense in the construction of his home.

④ When you're finished exploring the San Francisco, head about 7 mi upriver from Garyville on River Road, cross Gramercy-Lutcher Bridge, then continue 2 mi upriver on Route 18 toward Vacherie. The **Laura Plantation** near Vacherie presents one of the liveliest and best-documented tours in the region, an unusual look at plantation life from the perspective of women, children, and servants. The circa 1805 complex incorporates 12 buildings (two modest manor houses, plus assorted slave quarters and Creole cottages). The folktales of Br'er Rabbit, which originated in West Africa, were first recorded in America on this site in the 1870s.

⑤ From the Laura Plantation, drive 4 mi upriver on Route 18 to the **Oak Alley Plantation,** one of the most famous sights in the South. Twenty-eight live oaks in two rows create a ¼-mi avenue leading all the way from the river to the Greek Revival manor. The trees, planted by an early settler, were already mature when the house was built in 1839 by planter Jacques Telesphore Roman.

⑥ From Oak Alley, follow Route 18 upriver to Darrow, then continue on Route 1 to Route 405 in White Castle. **Nottoway Plantation** in White Castle is the largest surviving antebellum manor in the South, some 53,000 square ft, including a 65-ft Grand White Ballroom. Built in 1859 by planter John Hampden Randolph, the Greek Revival–Italianate house is famous for its intricate plaster friezes, marble fireplaces, and handpainted Dresden doorknobs. You can spend the night at Nottoway or at a hotel closer to Baton Rouge.

7 From White Castle, backtrack to Donaldsonville on Route 1 and cross the Sunshine Bridge, then head upriver on Route 44 to Route 942 in Burnside. **Houmas House** once stood on the largest sugarcane plantation in the U.S., some 20,000 acres producing up to 20 million pounds of sugar per year. The 1840 Greek Revival mansion, built by planter John Preston Smith, is one of the showplaces of the South, with its three-story spiral staircase and formal gardens.

8 Next stop is **Baton Rouge** and the **LSU Rural Life Museum.** The museum incorporates 20 buildings from 19th-century Louisiana, transplanted from plantations and farms statewide, including an overseer's house, slave cabins, a blacksmith shop, a grist mill, and a country church with rustic homemade art. A large barn exhibits a wide variety of artifacts, ranging from an African birthing chair to a horse-drawn hearse. **Magnolia Mound Plantation** stands on a ridge facing the Mississippi River. The 1791 French Creole house is furnished with Federal-style antiques from the 19th century. Spend the night in Baton Rouge.

9 From Baton Rouge, take I–90 west to Route 1N to New Roads. **Parlange Plantation** in New Roads is one of the oldest French Colonial manors in Louisiana, and it continues to command a working plantation (sugar, cattle, pecans). The property is still owned and occupied by 7th- and 8th-generation descendants of the Marquis de Trenant, who built the house in 1750. It is open for tours by appointment only. Parlange doesn't take overnight guests, but consider spending your second night in New Roads.

LOUISIANA RULES OF THE ROAD

License Requirements: To drive in Louisiana, you must be at least 15 years old with a learner's permit or 16 years old with a valid driver's license. Residents of Canada and most other countries may drive as long as they have a valid driver's license from their home countries.

Right Turn on Red: Everywhere in the state you may make a right turn at a red light *after* a full stop, unless a sign is posted prohibiting it.

Seat Belt and Helmet Laws: All drivers and front-seat passengers must wear seat belts. Children under age 13 must wear a seat belt at all times, whether seated in front or back; children under age 4 must ride in a federally approved child safety seat. Motorcyclists may choose to ride without a helmet only if they are at least 21 years of age and carry a medical insurance policy with at least $10,000 in coverage. They are also required to keep their headlights and taillights on at all times.

Speed Limits: 70 mph on interstate highways, 65 mph on controlled-access highways, 55 mph on state highways, and lower where posted.

For More Information: Contact the **Louisiana State Police** | 225/925–6325, 225/754–8510, or 800/469–4828 | www.dps.state.la.us./lsp.

(10) From New Roads, drive east on Route 10 for approximately 8 mi to St. Francisville. **Rosedown Plantation** in St. Francisville is one of the country's most distinguished house museums, set on 1,000 acres with 28 acres of historic gardens and 14 restored outbuildings, including the original hothouse, detached kitchen, barn, and doctor's office. The 1835 Greek Revival manor has been painstakingly restored with all of its original furnishings. **Audubon State Historic Site** once attracted naturalist John James Audubon, who painted 32 of his Birds of America while living here at Oakley Plantation House in the 1820s. The 1799 manor is now furnished in the style of the late Federal period, as it would have been when the artist was in residence. Hikers can follow his tracks through 100 acres of nature trails and woodlands. **Butler Greenwood Plantation** is still owned by members of its founding family, who often act as tour guides. The antebellum mansion, circa 1790, has a formal Victorian parlor. **Catalpa Plantation** is also owned and operated by descendants of the original family. Ancient oaks shade 30 acres of gardens and a Victorian manor filled with antique furnishings, silver, and other treasures.

From St. Francisville, take U.S. 61 south for approximately 20 mi to I–110 S towards Baton Rouge. Exit onto I–10 E and proceed for 75 mi back to New Orleans.

Baton Rouge

Attractions

Enchanted Mansion: A Doll Museum. Only several hundred of this museum's collection of more than 2,000 dolls are on display at any given time. You can also see 19th-century antiques, Victorian doll houses, and works by such modern artists as Marilyn Radzat, Edna Hibel, and Jack Johnson. | 190 Lee Dr., Bldg. 2 70808 | 225/769–0005 | fax 225/766–6822 | Mon. and Wed.–Sat. 10–5, Sun. 1–4.

Houmas House. One of the most beautiful antebellum manors on the Mississippi is set in well-tended formal gardens on the River Road. The Greek Revival showplace is flanked by two octagonal wings, shaded by wide verandas and massive old oaks. It was built by Colonel John Preston, once master of a 20,000-acre plantation. Today tours are led by docents in period gowns. | 40136 Hwy. 942, Burnside Darrow, 70725 | 225/473–7841 or 888/323–8314 | fax 225/474–0480 | www.houmashouse.com | Daily 10–5.

LSU Rural Life Museum. A cluster of 19th-century buildings depicts pre-industrial Louisiana life. The compound includes a plantation commissary, schoolhouse, sickhouse, gristmill, overseer's house, blacksmith's shop, open-kettle sugar mill, and church. Typical homes are represented by a dog-trot cabin (with its two wings connected by a covered porch), Victorian cottage, slave quarters, and other residential architecture. Vintage vehicles are housed in a large barn. Classical statuary graces the 25-acre Windrush Gardens. | Essen La. at I–10 S | 225/765–2437 | fax 225/765–2639 | www.rulise1.lsu.edu | Daily 8:30–5.

Magnolia Mound Plantation. On 16 acres of formal gardens, this 1791 French Creole manor has been restored as a house museum. The main attraction is a major collection of Louisiana and Federal furnishings. Open-hearth cooking demonstrations are held on Tuesdays and Thursdays from October through May. Self-guided walking tours of the slave cabins and grounds are included in tour admission. If you'd like a guided tour that focuses on the servants' perspective, call ahead to join one of the "Beyond the Big House" tours. | 2161 Nicholson Dr., 70802 | 225/343–4955 | fax 225/343–6739 | www.brec.org/museums/magnoliamound | Tues.–Sat. 10–4, Sun. 1–4.

Nottoway Plantation. The tiny riverfront community of White Castle is named for this 53,000-square-ft "white castle," the largest remaining antebellum mansion in the south. It was built in 1859 by sugar planter John Hampden Randolph, and was later spared during the Civil War by a Union gunboat officer who had once been a houseguest. | 30970 U.S. 405, White Castle, 70788 | 225/545–2730 or 225/545–2409 | fax 225/545–8632 | www.nottoway.com | Daily. Tours 9–5.

Port Hudson State Historic Site. From May 23 to July 9, 1863, 6,800 Confederate soldiers defended this site against a Union force of 30,000. It was the longest siege in U.S. history and one of the first battles in which freed slaves fought alongside Union troops. Today interpretive displays tell the story as you walk through a portion of the battlefield, viewing towers, trenches, artillery, and a cemetery for more than 3,000 Union soldiers, most unknown. | 756 W. Plains–Port Hudson Rd., Zachary, 70791 | 225/654–3775 or 888/677–3400 | fax 225/654–1048 | www.crt.state.la.us | Daily 9–5.

U.S.S. _Kidd._ Volunteer war veterans staff this World War II destroyer, which has been restored to its VJ Day configuration. Tours of the 369-ft ship include admission to the adjoining nautical museum with a submarine exhibit, ship models, and Veterans' Memorial Wall. Mock air-and-sea battles are staged every year during riverfront Fourth of July celebrations. The ship also hosts overnight groups ranging from Naval reunions to scout troops. | 305 S. River Rd., 70802 | 225/342–1942 | fax 225/342–2039 | www.premier.net/uss-kidd/home | Daily 9–5.

Dining

Randolph Hall. Cajun/Creole. A sunny atrium restaurant built on the grounds of Nottoway Plantation in 1984 echoes the grand manor's style with white pillars, stone floors, and pastel hues. Cajun two-step—turkey and sausage with shrimp creole—and jambalaya, a rice dish with meat, spices, and green onions, are popular. Pianist weekends. Kids' menu. | 30970 U.S. 405 | 225/545–2730 | www.nottoway.com | AE, D, MC, V | $$–$$$

Mike Anderson's. Seafood. Generous seafood platters and a rustic bayou atmosphere are the selling points for this comfortable and casual family restaurant. Specialties include broiled Guitreau (grilled fish sautéed in white wine and topped with crawfish, mushrooms, and shrimp), shrimp Norman (six jumbo shrimp deep-fried with crabmeat étouffée), and joliet rouge (broiled filet of snapper topped with lump crabmeat and mushrooms). Open-air dining on the side porch. Raw bar. Kids' menu. Reservations not accepted for supper or weekends | 1031 W. Lee Dr., 70820 | 225/766–7823 | www. mikeandersonsseafoodbr.com | AE, D, DC, MC, V | $$

Albasha. Middle Eastern. The savory chicken shawarma (thinly sliced marinated chicken served with hummus, salad, and rice) is a favorite in this bustling restaurant. It's popular and far from intimate, with seating for 90 people. The music and aromas of the Mediterranean and the Middle East pervade the room while you dine by the running waters of the indoor fountain. | 5454 Bluebonnet Rd., 70809 | 225/292–7988 | AE, D, MC, V | $–$$

The Cabin. Cajun/Creole. The restaurant and the surrounding shops are in what were once slave quarters. Domestic artifacts, advertising paraphernalia, and farm implements adorn the rooms and grounds. Popular dishes include crawfish and red beans with rice. Kids' menu. | Hwys. 44 and 22 | 225/473–3007 | www.thecajunvillage.com | No dinner Mon. | AE, D, MC, V | $–$$

Lodging

Nottoway Plantation. Overnight guests may stay in original bedrooms in the main house or in the boys' wing or the overseer's cottage. The Master Bedroom Suite has original pieces that belonged to John Hampton Randolph, the owner. Tours are available. Restaurant, complimentary breakfast. Cable TV. Pool. Library. Business services. | 225/545–2730 | fax 225/545–8632 | www.nottoway.com | 13 rooms, 3 suites | AE, D, MC, V | $$$

Best Western Richmond Suites. Five brick buildings comprise this hotel just off I–10. The River Road plantations are 15 mi east. Cortana Mall (more than 70 stores and restaurants) is about 3 mi away. Complimentary breakfast. In-room data ports, some kitchenettes, refrigerators. Cable TV. Pool. Hot tub. Tennis courts. Exercise equipment. Business services. | 5668 Hilton Ave., 70808 | 225/924–6500, 800/528–1234, or 800/332–2582 | fax 225/924–3074 | www.bestwestern.com/richmondsuiteshotel | 74 rooms, 71 suites | AE, D, DC, MC, V | $–$$

Hampton Inn. Louisiana State University is just 3 mi south of this upscale, modern high-rise favored by business travelers. The Belle of Baton Rouge Casino and Casino Rouge are a few minutes west on the Mississippi River. There's a wide selection of restaurants within two to three blocks. Complimentary Continental breakfast. In-room data ports. Cable TV. Pool. Business services, free parking. | 4646 Constitution Ave., 70808 | 225/926–9990 or 800/426–7866 | fax 225/923–3007 | www.hamptoninn-suites.com | 141 rooms, 1 suite | AE, D, DC, MC, V | $–$$

New Orleans

Attractions

★ **Aquarium of the Americas.** One of the top U.S. aquariums showcases the aquatic life of the Gulf of Mexico and South America. Exhibits include an offshore rig, Amazon rainforest, underwater tunnel, sharks, penguins, and the world's largest collection of jellyfish. River cruises connect the downtown aquarium with the uptown Audubon Zoo. Combination tickets are available. | 1 Canal St., 70130 | 504/581–4629 | fax 504/565–3865 | www.auduboninstitute.org | Sun.–Thurs. 9:30–6, Fri.–Sat. 9:30–7.

Audubon Zoological Garden. Set in oak-shaded Audubon Park on the former estate of artist John James Audubon, one of the top five zoos in the U.S. is a lavish tropical garden with more than 1,500 animals. Major attractions include the Louisiana Swamp Exhibit, the art-filled tropical bird house, an exotic walk through "Butterflies in Flight," and rides along an African-style savannah aboard the Mombassa Train. | 6500 Magazine St., 70118 | 504/581–4629 or 800/774–7394 | fax 504/565–3865 | www. auduboninstitute.org | Sept.–Mar., daily 9:30–5; Apr.–Aug., weekends 9:30–6.

Destrehan Plantation. Destrehan was built in 1787 in French Colonial style by Robin de Logny, who passed it on to his son-in-law Jean Noel Destrehan in 1802. It's a lovely example of French Colonial architecture, with its broad verandas and deep West Indies–style roof supported by fat round columns. It was a filming site for the movie "*Interview with the Vampire*," based on the novel by local author Anne Rice. | 13034 River Rd., Destrehan, 70047 | 504/764–9315 | fax 504/725–1929 | www.destrehanplantation.org | Daily 9–4.

French Market. The oldest open-air market in the United States rambles along the riverfront from Jackson Square to Esplanade Avenue. Built on the site of an ancient Native American trading post, the series of colonnaded structures dates to 1813. Today they house upscale shops and restaurants near the Jackson Square end. The daily flea market provides an entertaining rummage for handmade masks, ethnic jewelry, and leather goods. The farmers' market is open 24 hours and sells produce, hot sauces, and Cajun/Creole food products. | 1008 N. Peters, 70116 | 504/522–2621 | fax 504/596–3410 | Daily.

★ **Hermann–Grima Historic House.** Built in 1831, this is one of the earliest examples of American architecture in the French Quarter. The house was built for wealthy merchant Samuel Hermann and was occupied after 1844 by the family of Judge Felix Grima. It has been restored to represent the gracious life enjoyed by the upper middle classes of that period. You can tour the courtyard and stables, and open-hearth cooking demonstrations are held in the original kitchen every Thursday, October through May. | 820 St. Louis St., 70112 | 504/525–5661 | fax 504/525–9735 | Mon.–Sat. 10–4.

New Orleans Museum of Art. The original Neoclassical building (circa 1910) in City Park has been updated and vastly expanded over the years and is now home to some 35,000 works in 46 galleries including Asian, African, and Oceanic art. An impressive collection of European and American decorative arts includes a room dedicated to Fabergé and one of the largest glass collections in the country. | 1 Collins Diboll Circle, 70179 | 504/488–2631 | fax 504/484–6662 | www.noma.org | Tues.–Sun. 10–5.

★ **Old Ursuline Convent.** The only example of true French colonial architecture in the French Quarter (which is primarily Spanish in style) is also believed by many historians to be the oldest remaining structure in the Mississippi Valley. Built in 1745, the three-story masonry building is graced by a steep roof with dormer windows. In addition to holding classes for wealthy Creole children, it was also the first school on American soil to teach children of Native American and African heritage. | 1100 Chartres St., 70116 | 504/529–3040 | fax 504/529–2001 | www.accesscom.net/ursuline | Weekdays 10–3, weekends 11:15–2.

Preservation Hall. Living legends perform traditional jazz every night before standing-room-only audiences. The only seating is on hard wooden benches, but the musty 1920s atmosphere and Jazz Age sounds are the real stuff. You can't buy tickets in advance, so join the line at least 30 minutes before doors open at 8 PM if you hope to claim a seat. The musicians play 20-minute sets until midnight. No minimum age for entry. | 726 St. Peter St., 70116 | 504/522–2841; 504/523–8939 after 8 PM; 800/785–5772 | fax 504/558–9192 | www.preservationhall.com | Daily.

San Francisco Plantation. Built in 1856 by planter Edmond Bozonier Marmillon, this Steamboat Gothic mansion is an architectural confection lavished with gingerbread trim and bright pastels. The interior is just as ornate, with lofty rooms and famous ceiling frescoes. | River Rd., 34 mi west of New Orleans, between Reserve and Garyville Reserve, 70084 | 504/535–2341 | fax 504/535–5450 | www.sanfranciscoplantation.org | Daily 10–4:30.

St. Charles Avenue Streetcar. If there is one must-see attraction in New Orleans, this is it. The electric cars, installed in 1923, are part of the oldest street railway system in the world, first powered by steam locomotives in 1835. The 13-mi round trip takes about 90 min, if you can resist the temptation to hop off and on every few blocks. | Along St. Charles and Carrollton Aves., from Canal St. to Palmer Park | 504/248–3900 | Daily 24 hrs.

Dining

★ **Commander's Palace.** Cajun/Creole. A flagship local restaurant set in a turreted turquoise mansion in the Garden District provides open-air dining in its famous courtyard. The upstairs Garden Room has glass walls that provide a wonderful view of the oak trees and outside patio. The restaurant is famous for its Bloody Marys and bread pudding, but the menu also includes roasted quail, poached oysters in cream sauce with caviar, trout with pecans, veal chop, and filet mignon. Dixieland band at Sat. and Sun. brunch. Jacket required for dinner and brunch. | 1403 Washington Ave., 70130 | 504/899–8221 | www.commanderspalace.com | AE, D, DC, MC, V | $$$–$$$$

Nola. Contemporary. The furnishings and fanciful modern art transform this 19th-century town house into a trendy stage for owner Emeril Lagasse and his crew of chefs. The dining room has two floors, accessible by a glass elevator. Try the hickory-roasted duck with a whiskey caramel glaze. The dinnertime tasting menu is a boon for the indecisive. Service is very attentive. No smoking. | 534 St. Louis St., 70130 | 504/522–6652 | www.emerils.com | Reservations essential | No lunch Sun. | AE, D, DC, MC, V | $$$

★ **Court of Two Sisters.** Creole. The more-than-80-item brunch buffet and large dining courtyard are the stars of this famous spot. You'll find traditional breakfast items and seafood grits on the weekday menu; weekend brunch includes eggs Benedict and an omelet station. Sit under the canopy of wisteria and enjoy the fountains and jazz band. The Royal Court Room has more formal dining. Kids' menu. | 613 Royal St., 70130 | 504/522–7261 | www.courtoftwosisters | AE, D, DC, MC, V | $$–$$$

Acme Oyster and Seafood Restaurant. Seafood. A rough-edge classic in every way, this no-nonsense eatery at the entrance to the French Quarter is a prime source of cool and salty raw oysters on the half shell, shrimp, oyster, and hot roast beef po'boys, and red beans and rice. There's table service in the front dining room. Expect a rather lengthy line at the marble-top oyster bar and cafeteria-style sandwich counter during peak lunch and dinner hours. Crowds are sparser in the late afternoon. Take out also available. | 724 Iberville St., 70130 | 504/522–5973 | fax 504/524–1595 | Reservations not accepted | AE, D, DC, MC, V | $–$$

★ **Café Du Monde.** Café. Savoring chicory coffee and *beignets* (hot French doughnuts) served around the clock at the city's most famous sidewalk café has been a local tradition since the 1860s. Both residents and tourists flock to this café across from Jackson Square near the river. There's open-air seating on the covered patio under ceiling fans. Early morning hours are the best time to avoid lines, though they generally move quickly. | 813 Decatur St., 70112 | 504/525–4544 | www.cafedumonde.com | Open 24 hrs | No credit cards | $

New Roads

Attractions

Parlange Plantation. One of the oldest examples of French Colonial architecture in Louisiana, this National Historic Landmark house is surrounded by wide verandas and ancient oaks. Built in 1750 of native materials, it was framed by cypress beams and bricks made on the grounds, then plastered with *bousillage*, a traditional mixture of mud, moss, and deer hair. The beautifully maintained manor is set on a working plantation that is still owned and operated by seventh- and eighth-generation members of the Parlange family. | 8211 False River Rd., 70760 | 225/638–8410 | fax 225/638–3453 | Daily, by appointment.

Pointe Coupee Parish Museum. There's no shortage of grand manors in the heart of plantation country, but here is a rare look at a typical middle-class home. The 1760 cottage is furnished with period antiques appropriate to a family of modest means. Authentically restored in its original location on the banks of False River, this small museum also has a general information center. | 8348 False River Rd., 70760 | 225/638–7788 | fax 225/638–3915 | Daily 10–3.

Dining

Satterfield's Riverwalk. Seafood. Choose the dining room that has a fireplace and glass wall overlooking False River, or dine on the outdoor deck. The building, a former Ford Motor Company dealership built in 1917, is on the National Register of Historic Places. Memorabilia includes a 1927 Ford Model A and vintage photos of the dealership and town. Try catfish Satterfield, seafood angel hair pasta, chicken Florentine, or Satterfield rib eye. | 108 E. Main St., 70760 | 225/638–5027 | AE, D, DC, MC, V | $$–$$$

Lodging

Mon Rêve. Joe and Cathi Hinckley opened Mon Rêve—"My Dream" in French—in 1992. The three-story French Creole plantation home was originally built by Joe's great-grandfather in 1820. Like many Creole homes of that time, the house is constructed of cypress wood, brick, and bousillage. All bedrooms are rented with private baths unless a suite is requested, in which case two bedrooms share a connecting bath. Rooms are furnished with period antiques, including armoires, and have hardwood floors. You can fish, boat, or swim from a nearby pier in False River. The B&B is 2 mi southwest of New Roads on Louisiana Highway 1. Complimentary breakfast. No room phones. Cable TV. Dock, fishing. No smoking. | 9825 False River Rd., 70760 | 225/638–7848 or 800/324–2738 | www.monreve-mydream.com | 4 rooms | D, MC, V | $$

Pointe Coupee Bed and Breakfast, the Samson House. In the historic district, this 1835 plantation cottage is listed on the National Register of Historic Places. It has antiques, gardens, courtyards, and an outdoor fireplace. Candlelight suppers are available by reservation. Complimentary breakfast. Cable TV. Library. | 405 Richey St., 70760 | 225/638–6254 | fax 225/638–6254 | 2 rooms | MC, V | $$

St. Francisville

Attractions

Audubon State Historic Site–Oakley House. John James Audubon painted 32 of his Birds of America at Oakley House. A fine example of Colonial architecture with West Indies influences, the house was built in 1799 but is furnished in the style of the 1820s, when the artist lived here. You can also explore the detached plantation and weaving room, formal and kitchen gardens, two slave cabins, a barn, and 100 acres of forested grounds with a nature trail and picnic area. | 11788 Hwy. 965 | 225/635–3739 or 888/677–2838 | fax 225/635–3739 | www.crt.state.la.us | Daily 9–5.

Butler Greenwood Plantation. Members of the founding family guide tours at this National Register of Historic Places property, a 1790s plantation set in oak-shaded gardens. Rooms in the antebellum manor are furnished with original antiques, and there's a formal Victorian parlor. | 8345 U.S. 61, 70775 | 225/635–6312 | fax 225/635–6370 | www.butlergreenwood.com | Mon.–Sat. 9–5, Sun. 1–5.

Catalpa Plantation. Descendents of the original family still live in this National Register of Historic Places plantation home, set in 30 manicured acres abloom with azaleas, camellias, and hydrangeas. The four-bedroom, raised Victorian cottage was built in the 1890s to replace a plantation-style house that burned down after the Civil War. Furnishings from the original house were saved and can be seen here. The house is filled with opulent antiques, including silver, china, and portraiture. | 9508 U.S. 61 | 225/635–3372 | Daily.

Rosedown Plantation. An oak alley leads to an 1835 manor on a 1,000-acre plantation. More than a dozen restored outbuildings include the original hot house, barn, detached kitchen, doctor's office, and milk shed. You'll find formal parterres, classical landscapes, and fine statuary in some of the gardens. Tours are self guided, with audio recordings set up along the way to provide details (eight presentations that total about 1 hour). You can also view a 30-minute video. | 12501 Rte. 10, 70775 | 225/635–3332 | Daily 9–5, tours by curator by appointment only.

Dining

Steamboat Charley's Sports Bar and Grill. American/Casual. You can't miss the large neon sign out front after sunset. Once inside, belly up to the 100-year-old pine bar or shoot pool in one of the side rooms. The menu includes real root beer, burgers, rib-eye steaks, chicken-fried steak, fried or grilled shrimp, crawfish and oyster plates, po'boy sandwiches, club sandwiches, buffalo wings, and salads, as well as daily specials. Live music Friday and Saturday. Thursday is karaoke night. Charley's is on Highway 61 across from the Rosedown Plantation. Reservations recommended for parties of 10 or more. | 7193 Hwy. 61, 70775 | 225/635–0203 | AE, MC, V | $–$$

GREAT RIVER ROAD ALONG U.S. 61

FROM RED WING TO LA CRESCENT

Distance: 107 miles   Time: 1–2 days
Overnight Break: Wabasha

On this portion of the Great River Road you'll follow the bluffs that hug the Mississippi River between Red Wing and La Crescent; some of Minnesota's oldest communities are here, river towns that came into their own during the steamboat era. This is a year-round tour, but the sights are especially beautiful in fall. In late winter you might see bald eagles.

① Begin in downtown **Red Wing,** near the intersection of U.S. 61 and U.S. 63. The town's most distinctive feature is **Barn Bluff,** a huge sandstone and dolomite formation that towers above town. You can park at the end of East 5th Street and climb trails to the top. Well-preserved Victorian architecture is one of Red Wing's biggest attractions. The **St. James Hotel** was built in 1875. The **Pottery District** (north of downtown off U.S. 61) surrounds the old Red Wing Stoneware Company factory and is now home to outlet stores, specialty shops, and galleries of local artisans.

② Your next stop is **Frontenac,** about 10 mi southeast of Red Wing on U.S. 61. Actually, Frontenac consists of two unincorporated communities: Old Frontenac and Frontenac Station. Old Frontenac was founded in 1839 and is a historic district. It includes the **Lakeside Hotel,** which is now part of a larger resort complex. In **Frontenac State Park** more than 200 animal species pass through during the spring and fall. In winter there's cross-country skiing on 6 mi of trails and snowmobiling on 8 mi of trails.

③ Leaving Frontenac State Park, head 5 mi southeast on U.S. 61 into **Lake City.** The Great River Road follows the Mississippi shoreline closely here and provides panoramic views of Lake Pepin, which is actually a bulge in the river created by sediment downstream. The town's 2½-mile Riverwalk is a great place to enjoy the lake's scenery. This is the birthplace of waterskiing.

④ After you've explored Lake City, head southeast on U.S. 61 for approximately 11 mi to **Reads Landing.** It's hard to believe this was once a bustling staging area for rafts of

sawmill-bound northern pine. One of the few reminders of Reads Landing's glory days is the 1870 brick schoolhouse that now houses the **Wabasha County Historical Society,** with displays of Mississippi River artifacts and Laura Ingalls Wilder memorabilia. Reads Landing also marks the northern boundary of the **Upper Mississippi River National Wildlife and Fish Refuge,** a huge, protected floodplain stretching south to Rock Island, Illinois.

⑤ **Wabasha** is 3 mi southeast of Reads Landing on U.S. 61. Here people boast that their home is both the oldest town in Minnesota and the setting for the movie *Grumpy Old Men* and its sequel. The **Anderson House,** built in 1856, is the oldest operating hotel in the state. Life in Wabasha is so tranquil that bald eagles build their nests along the river, sometimes within the city limits. The people at the **Eagle Watch Observatory** can help you spot the great birds. Spend the night in Wabasha.

⑥ Continue southeast out of Wabasha on U.S. 61 for 5 mi and you'll come to **Kellogg.** Try as you might, you'll find few signs that this was a turn-of-the-20th-century transportation hub. Among the remaining attractions is the **L.A.R.K. Toy Factory,** where woodcarvers create toys and carousel animals. **The Kellogg-Weaver Dunes Scientific and Natural Area** is home to one of the largest populations of the rare Blanding's turtle.

⑦ The mighty Mississippi goes in and out of view as you leave Kellogg and wind 31 mi southeast on U.S. 61 to **Winona.** Once there, your gaze will immediately rise to **Sugar Loaf Bluff,** a huge chunk of limestone overlooking town that is reflected in **Lake Winona,** 500 ft below. More than two dozen downtown structures are listed on the National

Register of Historic Places. Among them are the **Church of Saint Stanislaus Kostka** and the Egyptian Revival–style **Winona National and Savings Bank.**

Leaving Winona, travel another 22 mi southeast on U.S. 61 to **La Crescent,** the self-proclaimed apple capital of Minnesota. Harvest time is a great time to follow **Apple Blossom Drive** (Rte. 29). From there you can enjoy a panoramic view of the Mississippi and choose from among the two dozen or so varieties of apples available at the orchards along the way.

Retrace your route along U.S. 61 to return to Red Wing.

Lake City

Attractions

Hok-Si-La Municipal Park. Part of a major migratory flyway, these 160 acres (by far the city's largest park grounds) are among southeastern Minnesota's best bird-watching spots, particularly in early spring and late fall. You might see bald eagles, tundra swans, Canada geese, and Iceland gulls. Besides nature trails and a playground, the park has campsites, picnic areas, and a swimming beach. Most of the city's 500 mi of snowmobile trails, and all 40 mi of its ski trails, are part of this park. It's ½ mi northeast of downtown. | Rte. 61, 55041 | 877/525–3249 | www.lakecity.org | Year-round.

MINNESOTA RULES OF THE ROAD

License Requirements: To drive in Minnesota, you must be at least 16 years old and have a valid driver's license. Visitors to the state may drive in Minnesota as long as they have a valid license from their home state or country.

Right Turn on Red: Unless otherwise posted, you are permitted to make right turns on red *after* your vehicle has come to a complete stop. You must also be in the correct turn lane and your path must be clear.

Seat Belt and Helmet Laws: All drivers, front-seat passengers, and any other passengers aged 4 to 10 must wear seat belts. Children younger than four must ride in a federally approved safety seat. Motorcyclists must wear helmets.

Speed Limits: 65 mph is the speed limit on all interstate highways inside urban areas and on non-interstate freeways and expressways. The limit rises to 70 mph on interstates outside urban areas. In most other locations, the limit remains 55 mph.

For More Information: Contact the **Minnesota Department of Public Safety** | 651/282–6565.

McCahill Park. Playground equipment and a fishing pier are the highlights of this park. | Rte. 61, 3 blocks south of Rte. 63, 55041 | 877/525–3249 | www.lakecity.org | Year-round.

Ohuta Park. Playground facilities, picnic areas, and a swimming beach are all directly on the lakefront. | Lyon Ave., 3 blocks east of Rte. 61, 55041 | 877/525–3249 | www.lakecity.org | Year-round.

Patton Park. One square block in size, the park has a central fountain, a quaint gazebo, and paved walking paths. | Rte. 61, 1 block south of Rte. 63, 55041 | 877/525–3249 | www.lakecity.org | Year-round.

Roshen Park. Besides picnic areas for large and small groups, this park at the south end of town has tennis courts, playground equipment, and fine lake views. | Rte. 61, south end of town, 55041 | 877/525–3249 | www.lakecity.org | Year-round.

Dining

The Galley. American. Burgers and sandwiches are the mainstays at this family-style restaurant, which also serves breakfast. | 110 Lyon Ave., 55041 | 651/345–9991 | AE, D, MC, V | $–$$

Rouletti's. American. The pizza here has won several regional awards. Other favorites are ribs and chicken. | 214 S. Lakeshore Dr., 55041 | 651/345–5333 | AE, D, MC, V | $–$$

Waterman's. American. The menu emphasizes the freshest possible ingredients, from meat to produce; locals favor the filet mignon and Porterhouse steak. Dining room windows face Lake Pepin and the surrounding bluffs. | 1702 N. Lakeshore Dr., 55041 | 651/345–5353 | AE, D, DC, MC, V | $–$$

Red Wing

Attractions

Cannon Valley Trail. Bikers and hikers fill this 21-mi trail along the old Chicago Great Western railroad line, connecting Cannon Falls, Welch, and Red Wing. The main trail head is about ½ mi east of Red Wing, off Route 52S on Route 19. | City Hall, 306 W. Mill Street, Cannon Falls, 55009 | 507/263–0508 | www.cannonvalley.com | Year-round.

Colvill Park. Beside the Mississippi on the south side of town, this is one of several river parks in Red Wing. An outdoor pool is open summers only. | Between 7th St. and Rte. 61 | 800/498–3444 | Daily.

Goodhue County Historical Museum. Among the permanent exhibits are displays on local and regional history, Red Wing ceramics, and Prairie Island Native American artifacts. An extensive library, with more than 15,000 photos and 5,000 books, is used for historical and genealogical research. | 1166 Oak St. | 651/388–6024 | Tues.–Fri. 10–5, Sat.–Sun. 1–5.

Red Wing Pottery. The showroom of the original Red Wing Pottery factory, which opened in the late 1800s and closed in 1967, continues to sell what's left of the famous salt-glazed brown dinnerware, crocks, and jugs, as well as modern stoneware and gifts. The shop hosts local potters who work while visitors look on. | 1995 W. Main St., 55066 | 651/388–3562 or 800/228–0174 | Mon.–Sat. 8–6, Sun. 11–5.

Soldiers Memorial Park–East End Recreation Area. The park has hiking trails, picnic areas, explorable caves, and a spectacular view. | E. 7th St., 1 mi south of downtown | 800/498–3444 | Daily.

Dining

Port of Red Wing. Contemporary. Forest green table cloths, exposed brick, and dark-stained furniture accent this dining room in the downtown St. James Hotel. The menu changes seasonally, but summer dishes might include roasted rack of lamb with garlic whipped potatoes and bourbon-rhubarb glaze, or creole-style chicken with onions, peppers, and mushrooms in a spiced, red-wine tomato sauce. | 406 Main St., 55066 | 651/388–2846 or 800/252–1875 | No lunch | AE, D, DC, MC, V | $$–$$$

Staghead. Contemporary. Exposed brick walls, oak tables, and a pressed-tin ceiling complement the historic maps and paintings of Red Wing on the walls of this dining room. Specialties include beef tenderloin, free-range chicken, and a grilled pork tenderloin with applewood-smoked bacon and sun-dried cherries in a sage demi-glaze. Thursday is all-Italian night. | 219 Bush St., 55066 | 651/388–6581 | No dinner Mon., closed Sun. | MC, V | $–$$$

Liberty's. Continental. Over the years, this 1872 corner building has served as a saloon, shoe store, clothing store, pool hall, and (legend has it) a speakeasy and house of ill repute. Today, the kitchen serves three meals a day; a dinner special is slow-cooked prime rib au jus with horseradish sauce. Sunday brunch. | 303 W. 3rd St. | 651/388–8877 | AE, D, DC, MC, V | $–$$

Marie's Casual Dining & Lounge. American. In a 1901 armory building, this restaurant serves everything from grilled cheese sandwiches to boiled lobster. Fridays bring a fish fry and buffet, Saturdays an all-you-can-eat prime rib buffet. | 217 Plum St., 55066 | 651/388–1896 | AE, D, MC, V | $–$$

Randy's Restaurant. American. After ordering your fried chicken and mashed potatoes (or your sandwich and salad) at the counter, take in the nostalgic advertisements as you wait for a server to bring your food. | 709 Main St., 55066 | 651/388–1551 | Breakfast also available | No credit cards | $

Wabasha

Attractions

Eagle Watch. Wabasha's eagle population soars during fall and spring migrations, and this Audubon group is dedicated to fostering environmental stewardship and celebrating eagles. You can visit the eagle observation deck on the Mississippi River in downtown Wabasha, where volunteers explain eagle activity. | 152 Main St., 55981 | www.eaglewatch.org | Year-round.

Historic Commercial District. Downtown Wabasha is listed on the National Register of Historic Places. Visit the city library for information on walking tours or to see a slide show. | 168 Alleghany Ave. | 651/565–3927 | Year-round.

Dining

★ **Slippery's.** American. Originally just a shack for beer, bait, and burgers, Slippery's was made famous by the movies *Grumpy Old Men* and *Grumpier Old Men*. The land where Slippery's stands used to be the site of the old Wabasha Boat Yard and Marina. The existing building dates back to 1979 when the shack burned down, and Slippery and his wife, Gladys, rebuilt it as a resort, with boat rentals and a gas dock. Next to the Mississippi River, the place attracts boaters, snowmobilers, and eagle watchers. The menu is extensive and, in honor of the "Grumpy" movies, includes such items as "morons chicken" and the "putz burger." | 10 Church Ave., 55981 | 651/565–4748 | AE, D, MC, V | $$–$$$

Grandma Anderson's Dutch Kitchen. American. Fresh homemade breads, chicken noodle soup, baked raisin beans, stuffed beef rolls, and apple brandy pie are served family style in a relaxed atmosphere. The Sunday breakfast buffet has a good variety of eggs, meats, fruits, and breads. | 333 W. Main St., 55981 | 651/565–4524 or 800/535–5467 | MC, V | $$

Papa Tronnio's. American. In the local bowling alley, this eatery serves up generous portions of chicken, spaghetti, and shrimp. Pizza and burgers are also available. | 218 2nd St. W, 55981 | 651/565–3911 | MC, V | $–$$

Lodging

Bridgewaters B & B. One block off the Mississippi River and in town, this 1903 inn has a wraparound porch with wicker seating. The rooms, named for local bridges, have such nice touches as spoon-carved headboards; some have hot tubs or fireplaces. Three rooms have private baths, two rooms share. Complimentary breakfast. No smoking. No pets. | 136 Bridge Ave., 55981 | 651/565–4208 | www.bridgewatersbandb.com | 5 rooms | MC, V | $$–$$$

Eagles on the River B&B. Overlooking the Mississippi River ³⁄₄ mi southeast of town, this B&B has CDs and CD players in all rooms, and fireplaces and whirlpools in some. Complimentary breakfast. Some in-room hot tubs. | 1000 E. Marina Dr., 55981 | 800/684–6813 or 651/565–3417 | www.eaglesontheriver.com | 4 rooms | AE, D, MC, V | $$–$$$

Eagles on the River InnTEL & Suites. On two secluded acres at the base of Coffee Mill Bluff, this establishment has both standard and deluxe rooms. Standard rooms have two double beds. Some rooms have fireplaces and hot tubs. Cable TV. | Rte. 60 W, 55981 | 800/482–8188 | www.eaglesontheriver.com | 21 rooms | MC, V | $–$$$

Winona

Attractions

Julius C. Wilkie Steamboat Center. A museum and a collection of miniature steamboats are aboard this full-size steamboat replica. It's at Levee Park, between Walnut and Johnson Sts. on the Mississippi River. | 507/454–1254 | www.winonanet.com/visitors/welcome.html | June–Oct., Tues.–Sun. 10–4.

Prairie Island Park and Nature Trail. Half of this municipal park is maintained in near-pristine condition, and has a 1-mi interpretive nature trail that stops by an enclosed deer park, a flood-plain forest, and an observation deck overlooking a Mississippi River backwater slough. Also in the park are a visitor center, boat launches, picnic and camping areas, and playgrounds. | 1120 Curry Island Rd. | 507/452–8550 | Daily.

Upper Mississippi River National Wildlife and Fish Refuge. Extending 261 mi along the Mississippi River, from the Chippewa River in Wisconsin almost to Rock Island, Illinois, this is the longest wildlife refuge in the continental United States, providing a habitat for plants, fish, migratory birds, and other animals. | 51 E. 4th St. | 507/452–4232 | www.emtc.nbs.gov/umr_refuge.html | Daily.

Winona County Historical Society Museum. In a former armory, the museum has extensive historical archives, plus exhibits on Native Americans, logging and lumbering, steamboats, transportation, and pioneer life. | 160 Johnson St. | 507/454–2723 | www.winona.msus.edu/historicalsociety | Daily.

Maintained by the Historical Society, **Bunnell House** is an example of rural Gothic architecture. It's built of northern white pine and contains furniture and objects from the mid- to late 1800s. Guides walk you through three floors of pioneer life, describing the era when Native American canoes gave way to steamboats and game-trails became roads and highways for Euro-Americans. Bunnell House is 5 mi downriver from Winona, off Highway 61, in Homer. | 507/452–7575 | www.winona. msus.edu/historicalsociety/sites/bunnell.asp | Memorial Day–Labor Day, Wed.–Sat. 10–5, Sun. 1–5.

Dining

Beier's Family Food and Cocktails. American. On the west end of town, this casual spot serves breakfast until 3 PM and has a daily soup and salad bar, plus a popular prime rib sandwich. | 405 Cottonwood Rd., 55987 | 507/452–3390 | Breakfast also available | AE, D, DC, MC, V | $–$$

MISSOURI

MISSOURI CAVES
FROM HANNIBAL TO BRANSON

Distance: 275 mi   Time: 2–4 days
Overnight Breaks: Camdenton, Branson

Jesse James used Missouri's caves for hiding stolen treasure. More recently, some young couples have chosen to marry under their dripping stalactites. But even if you don't have such dramatic plans you shouldn't overlook Missouri's 5,000 caves.

Missouri's caves are accessible by foot, boat, or car. Some caves offer true wilderness experiences, while others have been developed for tourism, or as storage facilities, office space, and even restaurants and schools. When visiting any cave, remember to bring a light jacket, a pair of pants to change into if necessary, and your most comfortable shoes. The average temperature of the caves is a constant 55°F.

❶ The first cave to open for public tours was the **Mark Twain Cave** in 1886. Tom Sawyer and Becky Thatcher were lost in this cave, which is now a National Historic Landmark. "No man knew the cave; that was an impossible thing. Most of the young men knew a portion of it, and it was not customary to venture beyond the known portion. Tom Sawyer knew as much of the cave as anyone," Twain wrote. An experienced guide will escort you on a 1-hour tour with points of interest mentioned in Twain's writings. Walkways are level and smooth, and there are no steps.

While in **Hannibal,** also visit **Cameron Cave.** Cameron is Missouri's newest cave, first discovered in 1925 and opened to the public in 1976. The tour lasts 1¼ hours, and you might be given a lantern to carry while exploring.

❷ Many consider the entrance to **Boone Cave,** about 9 mi west of Columbia, to be the most picturesque of any cave in the state. The two-story opening is in a valley with streams running out of the entrance through the valley. The cave is named after pioneer Daniel Boone, who came to Missouri in 1799 and lived there until his death in 1820.

❸ While vacationing at the Lake of the Ozarks, thousands of boaters choose to visit **Bridal Cave** in their boats. If you don't have aquatic transportation, you can use the footpath taken by the Osage Indians and see a wedding chapel, mystery lake, and massive onyx formations. Don't be surprised if you happen upon a wedding in progress. A hundred

or more are held here each year and uninvited guests are welcomed and expected. Rated as one of the three most scenic caverns in America, Bridal Cave contains more onyx formations per square foot than any other show cave. Spend the night in **Camdenton,** 2 mi south of Bridal Cave.

④ The Springfield area has two worthy caves. **Crystal Cave** is renowned for Indian symbols and fossils. It's been open to the public for more than 100 years, but the owners have worked hard to keep the cave looking as natural as possible. Although some lighting has been added, the one-hour tour is mostly flashlight and lantern lit.

Fantastic Caverns is an all-riding tour. Jeeps follow the route cut by rivers. Lower levels not accessible to visitors are home to such creatures as the Ozark cavefish, bristly cave crayfish, and grotto salamander, all of which are blind after countless generations of living in darkness. A hydrologist explains these and other facts on a 50-minute tour.

⑤ **Marvel Cave** is a part of Branson's Silver Dollar City theme park, and is Missouri's deepest cave at more than 500 ft. The Cathedral Room is 20 stories high, but you don't have to walk back to the top. A tram car will take you. This cave is a National Historic Landmark.

Silver Dollar City also once held claim to **Talking Rocks Cave,** but after a failed attempt to jazz it up with loudspeakers and echo effects, the cave reverted to private ownership. It's a cave for walkers, however—265 steps up and 265 steps down. There's a beautiful 400-acre nature area above ground. And if you're afraid of bats, Talking Rocks is one of the few caves devoid of the flying creatures.

⑥ To return to Hannibal, retrace your steps north on U.S. 65 to I–44 and travel northeast to Sullivan and a final stop at the **Meramec Caverns,** the first major cave discovery in the state and a hideout for the Jesse James gang. Continue on I–44 into St. Louis, following U.S. 61 back to Hannibal.

MISSOURI RULES OF THE ROAD

License Requirements: To drive in Missouri, you must be at least 16 years old and have a valid driver's license.

Right Turn on Red: You may turn right on red anywhere in the state, *after* a full and complete stop, unless otherwise posted.

Seat Belt and Helmet Laws: Missouri requires all front-seat occupants in cars and persons under 18 years of age operating or riding in a truck to wear safety belts. Children ages 4 to 16 must be secured in a safety belt. All kids under age 4 must be in a child safety seat. These laws include passengers in cars, trucks, vans, and buses manufactured with safety belts. They do not include taxi cabs and commercial buses. Missouri does not require motorcycle and bicycle riders to wear a helmet.

Speed Limits: The speed limit on most Missouri interstates is 70 mph, except where posted in and around large cities. The speed limit on state highways is 65 mph, except where posted. Be sure to check speed limit signs carefully.

For More Information: Contact the **State Department of Motor Vehicles** | 573/526–3669.

Branson

Attractions

Baldknobbers Hillbilly Jamboree. Comedy, gospel, and country music abound at this popular spectacle. | 2835 W. Rte. 76 | 417/334–4528 | Mar.–mid-Dec., Mon.–Sat.

Branson Scenic Railway. A restored depot is the launching point for a railroad ride through the Ozark Mountains. | 206 E. Main St., 65616 | 417/334–6110 or 800/287–2462 | www.bransontrain.com | Mid-Mar.–Dec., Mon.–Sat. 9, 11:30, and 2; June–July and October, also at 5.

Silver Dollar City. The 1880s-style park 5 mi west of Branson on Route 76 offers train and wagon rides, water rides, hands-on crafts, and music shows. | Rte. 76, 65616 | 417/338–2611 or 800/952–6626 | www.silverdollarcity.com | Apr.–May, Tues.–Sun. 9–7; June–Aug., daily 9–7; Sept.–Oct., Tues.–Sun. 9:30–6; Nov.–Dec., Wed.–Sun. 1–10.

Missouri's deepest cave, **Marvel Cave** is within Silver Dollar City. Admission to the cave is included in park admission.

Table Rock Dam and Lake. On the main stream of the White River, about 6 mi southwest of Branson, the dam was built as part of an effort to generate electricity, decrease flooding, and provide recreation opportunities. Construction was completed in 1958 at a cost of $66 million. | 5272 Rte. 165 | 417/334–4101 | www.tablerocklake.org | Visitors center: Apr.–Oct., daily 9–5; Mar., Nov.–Dec., weekends 9–5. Tours: Apr.–Oct., daily hourly except noon; Mar., Nov.–Dec., weekends hourly except noon.

Talking Rocks Cave. Guided tours through this cave, considered one of Missouri's most beautiful, reveal the unusual auditory phenomenon that inspired its name. | Rte. 13, past Hwy. 76 | 417/272–3366 | Hrs vary; closed Jan.

Dining

Buckingham's Restaurant and Oasis. American. Buckingham's is perfect for special occasions; it serves steak, seafood, and pasta, and the staff will prepare some dishes tableside. The restaurant's big-game motif includes a mural of safari animals and a hand-carved cherry bar in the lounge. | 2820 W. Rte. 76 | 417/337–7777 | AE, D, MC, V | $$–$$$

Contrary Mary's. American. Bright and airy, this restaurant resembles a country garden, right down to the live plants. It serves freshly prepared home-style food, including chicken-fried steak, baked ham, pork chops, pasta, and fresh-baked desserts. | 3292 Shepherd of the Hills Expressway | 417/334–7700 | AE, D, MC, V | $–$$

Home Cannery. American. Home-canned goods decorate the walls and shelves of this family-friendly restaurant just a few blocks from Branson's theaters. Specialties include beef dishes and a marinated chicken breast served with mushrooms, peppers, onions, and mozzarella cheese. Kids' menu. No smoking. | 1810 W. Rte. 76 | 417/334–5756 | AE, MC, V | Closed late Dec.–Mar. | $–$$

Sadie's Sideboard and Smokehouse. American. Choose from a menu known for its barbecue or sample the ample buffet at this spacious and friendly-family restaurant. The buffet is available for breakfast, lunch, and dinner, and includes turkey, catfish, and ham. Kids' menu. | 2230 W. Rte. 76, 65615 | 417/334–3619 | AE, D, MC, V | Closed mid-Dec.–Feb. | $–$$

Two Sisters Midtown Diner. American. The breakfast, lunch, and dinner buffet at this retro diner includes baked fish, chicken, and ham. Sandwiches, soups, and other home-style fare are also available. Kids' menu. | 1580 W. Rte. 76 | 417/334–1206 | AE, D, MC, V | $–$$

Lodging

Days Inn. In the heart of Branson's Theater District, this inn is within 1 mi of 15 theaters and is convenient to area shopping, dining, and attractions. Restaurant, complimentary Continental breakfast. Cable TV. Pool, wading pool. Hot tub. Playground. Business services. Pets allowed (fee). | 3524 Keeter St. | 417/334–5544 or 800/329–7466 | fax 417/334–2935 | www.daysinn.com | 425 rooms | AE, D, DC, MC, V | $–$$$

Lodge of the Ozarks. Home to the Celebrity Theatre, this lodge aims for an upscale English feel, with wood trim and decorative tile throughout. Restaurant, bar (with entertainment), complimentary Continental breakfast. Some refrigerators. Cable TV. Pool. Beauty salon, hot tub, massage. Business services. | 3431 W. Hwy. 76, 65616 | 417/334–7535 or 800/655–7330 | fax 417/334–6861 | www.bransonlodging.net | 190 rooms | AE, D, MC, V | $$

Radisson. You can easily walk to several theaters including the Grand Palace and the Andy Williams Moon River Theatre from this upscale chain hotel. Restaurant, bar. In-room data ports. Cable TV. 2 pools. Beauty salon, hot tub. Gym. Business services. | 120 Wildwood Dr. S | 417/335–5767 | fax 417/335–7979 | 500 rooms, 26 suites | AE, D, DC, MC, V | $$

Best Western Mountain Oak Lodge. A shuttle to the Silver Dollar City amusement park runs from this hotel just ½ mi away from the site. It's also convenient to other area attractions. The game room has a pool table and video games. Restaurant, complimentary Continental breakfast, room service. Cable TV. Pool, wading pool. Hot tub. Video games. Laundry facilities. | Rte. 76 at Notch, Box 1059, Branson West, 65737 | 417/338–2141 or 800/528–1234 | fax 417/338–8320 | www.bestwestern.com | 146 rooms | AE, D, DC, MC, V | Closed Jan.–Feb. | $

Southern Oaks Inn. Across from the Shoji Tabuchi Theater and close by the IMAX theater and Country Tonite, this motor inn prides itself on its friendly staff. Complimentary Continental breakfast. Some refrigerators, some in-room hot tubs. Cable TV. 2 pools. Hot tub. Laundry facilities. Business services. | 3295 Shepherd of the Hills Expressway | 417/335–8108 or 800/324–8752 | fax 417/335–8861 | www.southernoaksinn.com | AE, D, MC, V | $

Camdenton

Attractions

Bridal Cave. Weddings are conducted year-round in this cave 2 mi north of town. | Lake Rd. 5-88, 65020 | 573/346–2676 | Daily 9–6.

Camden County Museum. A small collection focusing on the lives of early county residents is in a building that once served as the Linn Creek School. The town of Linn Creek was relocated when the Bagley Dam was built. Classrooms contain themed exhibits on weaving, vintage and antique household furnishings, tools, and banking. | Box 19, N. U.S. 54, Linn Creek, 65052 | 573/346–7191 | May–Oct., Tues.–Fri. 10–4.

Ha Ha Tonka State Park. The remains of a 60-year-old castle, a natural bridge, springs, and caves invite exploration in this 2,993-acre park on limestone bluffs overlooking the Lake of the Ozarks. Among the amenities are a 7-mi hiking trail, 2 docks, and fishing facilities. Take U.S. 54 to D Road to reach the park. | D Rd. 65020 | 573/346–2986 | www.dnr.state.mo.us/dsp | Daily 8–dusk.

Pomme de Terre State Park. Camp, swim, hike, or fish for muskie in one of the many coves of Pomme de Terre Lake. Reach the park by taking U.S. 64, Exit 64B. | Pittsburg, 65724 | 417/852–4291 | www.dnr.state.mo.us/dsp | Daily.

Dining

Barons Bistro. Contemporary. Barons specializes in American and European cuisine. Prime rib, steaks, and seafood top the menu, and some dishes are prepared tableside. | 5-88 Lake Rd. | 573/346–6369 | AE, DC, MC, V | No lunch | $–$$

Lodging

Old Kinderhook Resort. The lake's only gated community, this 638-acre resort has an 18-hole Tom Weiskopf golf course as well as lake access. 3 restaurants. Cable TV. Pool. Dock, boating, fishing. Playground. | 5480 Lake Rd. | 573/346–3952 | fax 573/346–3958 | 38 cottages | AE, D, MC, V | $$$–$$$$

Castleview Bed and Breakfast. Four-poster beds and marble-top tables accent this Victorian-style clapboard home next to the Ha Ha Tonka State Park. All rooms have private baths. Complimentary breakfast. TV in common area. | Rural Route 1, Box 183M, Hwy. D 65020 | 573/346–9818 or 877/346–9818 | www.lakelinks.com/castleview | 4 rooms | MC, V | $$

Rippling Waters Resort. If you looking for a rustic, lakefront cottage at a reasonable rate, consider this resort. Call to confirm when it closes for the season. Picnic area. Kitchenettes. Cable TV. Dock, boating. Video games. Playground. Laundry facilities. | Rte. 80, Box 123 | 573/346–2642 | 15 cottages | MC, V | Closed Nov.–Feb. | $–$$

Columbia

Attractions

Boone Cave. You'll find picturesque picnic facilities outside this small cave, named after explorer Daniel Boone. | 1307 S. Roby Farm Rd. | 573/874–7460 | Daily.

Nifong Park. The park includes walking trails, the 1855 Maple Wood home, and a fine arts gallery, all operated by the Boone County Historical Society. | Off U.S. 63 at Nifong Blvd. and Ponderosa Dr. | 573/874–7460 | Daily.

Shelter Gardens. Roses, cacti, and conifers are among the flora in this 6-acre public garden on the grounds of Shelter Insurance Company. It's a popular choice for weddings and is the site for free summer concerts. | 1817 W. Broadway | 573/214–4715 | Daily, dawn–dusk.

Dining

Boone Tavern. Continental. In the heart of town, this tavern is decorated with historical photos of Columbia. Try the chicken cordon bleu or steak. There's open-air dining in a gazebo. Kids' menu. Sunday brunch. | 811 E. Walnut St. | 573/442–5123 | AE, D, DC, MC, V | $$–$$$

Flat Branch Pub and Brewing. American/Casual. Sample many different beers, pizzas, and such special dishes as chicken *fuente* (chicken, onions, and peppers rolled in a flour tortilla with a spicy enchilada sauce, cheddar and jack cheese, olives, tomatoes, and scallions). Dine out on the pub's grounds. Kids' menu. | 115 S. 5th St. | 573/499–0400 | AE, D, DC, MC, V | $–$$

Springfield

Attractions

Crystal Cave. A great variety of formations, including black stalactites and crystals, awaits you at this cave, which occasionally holds tours lit by flashlights and lanterns. | 7225 N. Crystal Cave La. | 417/833–9599 | Daily 9–1:15.

Fantastic Caverns. You need to stay in the car for this tour, which takes you along the path of an ancient underground river. | 4872 N. Farm Rd. 125 | 417/833–2010 | www. fantastic-caverns.com | May–Oct., daily 8–6.

Laura Ingalls Wilder–Rose Wilder Lane Museum and Home. East of Springfield in nearby Mansfield, this house is where the "Little House" books were written and where Laura, Almonzo, and Rose made their home. | 3068 Hwy. A, Mansfield | 417/924–3626 | Mar.–Oct., Mon.–Sat. 9–5, Sun. 12:30–5:30.

Dining

Catfish House. Southern. Farm-raised catfish, smoked ribs, steaks, crab legs, and even frogs' legs are available here. If you can't decide what to order, graze the 55-item food bar. | 930 N. Glenstone Ave., 65802 | 417/865–3700 | AE, D, MC, V. | $–$$

Aunt Martha's Pancake House. American. Pancakes are always available at this Springfield institution that has been serving stacks for more than a quarter-century; local residents swear by them. Burgers and sandwiches round out the menu. | 1700 E. Cherokee St., 65804 | 417/881–3505 | No credit cards | Breakfast also available; no dinner Sun. | $

Sullivan

Attractions

Meramec Caverns. A hideout of the Jesse James gang, this was the first major cave discovery in the state. | I–44 West, Exit 230 Stanton, 63079 | 573/468–3166 | www.americascave.com | Nov.–Jan., daily 9–4; Mar. and Oct., daily 9–5; Apr. and Sept., daily 9–6; May–June, daily 9–7; July–Labor Day, daily 9–7:30.

Meramec State Park. More than 30 caves and many miles of river await canoers and spelunkers in this 6,896-acre park. | 2800 S. Hwy. 185, (Exit 226 off I–44), Sullivan, 63080 | 573/468–6072 | www.dnr.state.mo.us/dsp | Daily.

Dining

Du Kum In. American. The lacey linen window curtains and wall-mounted plate collection give this restaurant a country feel, as do the fried chicken and homemade pies. | 101 Grande Center | 573/468–6114 | MC, V | Closed Mon., Tues. | $–$$

Homer's Bar-B-Que. Barbecue. Pork steaks are the specialty at Homer's, a small restaurant with a rustic interior. Ribs, chicken, and beef brisket are also available. | 639 Fisher Dr., 63080 | 573/468–4393 | No credit cards | Closed Sun., Mon. | $–$$

Country Market Restaurant. American. Order from the menu or sample the buffet at this diner just off I–44. The fried chicken is particularly popular, but steaks, pasta, and sandwiches are also available. | 825 N. Loop Dr., 63080 | 573/860–8900 | AE, D, MC, V | Breakfast also available | $

BEARTOOTH HIGHWAY
A DRIVE ALONG THE ROOF OF THE ROCKIES

Distance: 69 mi (111 km)   Time: 3 hours
Overnight Break: Cooke City

With mountain switchbacks and high-altitude views of Montana and Wyoming's snowcapped peaks, giant glaciers, and sprawling valleys with deep-blue alpine lakes, the Beartooth Highway ranks among North America's premier scenic byways. The route is impassable and closed to traffic for much of the year, open only from approximately June to September (depending on weather conditions).

Driving from east to west means you'll have a long, steep uphill climb, but you'll save your brakes. To avoid glare, you may want to drive east to west in the morning and west to east in the afternoon. The towns of Red Lodge and Cooke City, at the east and west starting points, respectively, have full services, including lodging, gasoline, and food. The Beartooth Highway passes 10 National Forest campgrounds with picnic tables, fire grates, drinking water, and toilets, but no hookups. Daytime summer temperatures generally average in the 70s, but sudden snowstorms have been reported in every month of the year.

Montana's snowy winters can make for hazardous driving, when sudden storms commonly block highways. You should prepare for the unexpected with winter survival kits of snow tires or chains, a shovel and window scraper, flares or a reflector, a blanket or sleeping bag, a first-aid kit, sand, gravel or traction mats, a flashlight with extra batteries, matches, a lighter and candles, paper, non-perishable foods, and a tow chain or rope.

1 **Red Lodge** (U.S. 212 and Rte. 78) is a historic mining town in Rock Creek Valley at the base of the Beartooth Mountains. In winter it is a magnet for skiers; in summer you can hike, bike, golf, fish, and just look around. The **Beartooth Nature Center** has native North American animals and a children's petting zoo. Directly out of Red Lodge, the Beartooth Highway enters Custer National Forest, one of the three national forests it bisects as it skirts the Montana–Wyoming border adjacent to the eastern edge of Yellowstone National Park; the others are the Gallatin and Shoshone national forests.

2 Continuing on U.S. 212, you'll enter the Beartooth Loop National Recreation Trail, which begins at **Gardner Lake** and traverses 10 mi of rolling alpine landscape typically found

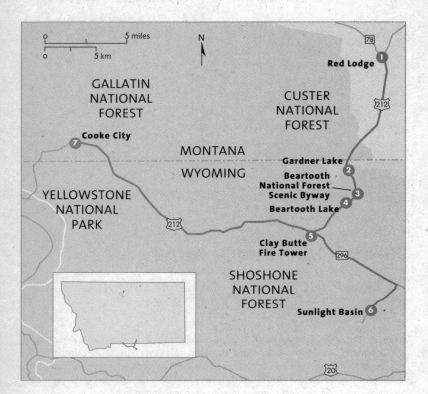

in the Arctic. Note how plants have adapted to this severe climate. View Sawtooth Mountain to the southwest; across the valley to the north, a black fang known locally as the Bear's Tooth juts up from the surrounding forest.

❸ From **Beartooth National Forest Scenic Byway** you get incredible vistas to the south and west—snowcapped peaks, glaciers and alpine lakes, colorful wildflowers, and far-reaching plateaus. Tiny patches of snow and ice remain up here much of the year, often tinted pink from algae. Winter can last into July.

❹ **Beartooth Lake** is at the base of Beartooth Butte. Summer fishermen like its 21-site campground and boat launch. You'll find lots of good hiking and can reach the 100-ft Beartooth Falls on an easy ½-mi trail along a creek.

❺ **Clay Butte Fire Tower** is a beautiful 3-mi detour from the Beartooth. Its visitor information center is open in summer, and from the top of the tower you get a spectacular view of Granite Peak (Montana's highest at 12,799 ft) to the northwest, the North Absaroka Wilderness and Yellowstone National Park to the west, the Clarks Fork Valley and Absaroka Mountains to the southwest, and the Bighorn Mountains to the east.

❻ West of Beartooth Pass you leave the alpine vegetation and descend through a forest of spruce, fir, and lodgepole pine mixed with stands of aspen. To the south and west is the North Absaroka Wilderness; with the Beartooth Wilderness it blankets nearly a million acres. At the junction with Route 296 (also known as Chief Joseph

Scenic Highway) you can take a side trip into the remote **Sunlight Basin** to sightsee, camp, hike, and fish.

The byway continues west, skirts the Clarks Fork of the Yellowstone River, climbs over the summit of Colter Pass, then travels through some of the burn areas from raging 1988 fires. You can see steady regrowth, as well as new flowers, shrubs, and birds, including hawks, falcons, and eagles, and, at times, grizzly and black bears, bighorn sheep, mountain goats, moose, and marmots.

⑦ Head back to the intersection of Route 296 and U.S. 212 and proceed west on U.S. 212, which will take you straight into **Cooke City** on the Montana–Wyoming border. This mining town with a colorful past is now a friendly, small resort community where you can hike, horseback ride, fish, climb, and ski in winter. After Cooke City (where you can spend the night if you're inspired to linger), the byway drops through Silver Gate and ends at the Northeast Gate to Yellowstone National Park.

Cooke City

Lodging

High Country. Some of the rooms in this Beartooth mountains hotel have kitchens and fireplaces. No air-conditioning, some refrigerators. Pets allowed. | U.S. 212, 59020 | 406/838–2272 | 15 rooms, 4 kitchenettes | AE, D, DC, MC, V | $

MONTANA RULES OF THE ROAD

License Requirements: Montana recognizes valid driver's licenses from other states and countries. The minimum driving age is 15 with driver training or 16 without.

Right Turn on Red: Right turns on red are allowed, unless otherwise posted.

Seat Belt and Helmet Laws: The driver and all passengers in motor vehicles on Montana roadways must wear seat belts. Law-enforcement officers will not pull you over if you're not wearing a seat belt, but they will ticket you if you commit other infractions while unbelted. Children two and younger must be in a federally approved child restraint device. Children ages two to four who weigh no more than 40 pounds must also be secured in a child restraint device. All motorcycle riders under 18 years of age must wear a helmet in Montana. Those over 18 may choose whether or not to wear a helmet.

Speed Limits: The maximum speed on the state's interstate highways is 75 mph; non-interstate roadway limits are 70 mph daytime and 65 mph at night. Trucks over one-ton capacity have interstate speed limits of 65 mph and non-interstate limits of 60 mph daytime and 55 mph at night.

For More Information: Contact the **Montana Highway Patrol** | 406/444–3780.

Soda Butte Lodge. You'll find rooms of varying sizes, a sunken lobby with a large fireplace, and spectacular views at this lodge. Restaurant, bar. Cable TV. Pool. Hot tub. Pets allowed. | 209 U.S. 212 | 406/838–2251 or 800/527–6462 | fax 406/838–2253 | 32 rooms | AE, D, MC, V | $

Red Lodge

Attractions

Beartooth Nature Center. Animals that have been injured and cannot be released into the wild again live at this nonprofit educational organization. You might see bears, elk, mountain lions, and deer, and a variety of birds. They have year-round educational programs and a summer camp for children. | 2nd Ave. E, in Coal Miner's Park | 406/446–1133 | June–Sept., daily 10–5:30; Oct.–May, daily 10–2, weather permitting.

Cooney Reservoir State Park. You'll find great walleye and rainbow trout fishing in the reservoir here. The campground has 75 sites, with hiking trails, a boat ramp, and a swimming beach. Pets restricted. | Off U.S. 212 | 406/445–2326 | www.fwp.state.mt.us/parks/parks.htm | Daily.

Custer National Forest. The forest sprawls across Montana, South Dakota, and North Dakota, and is home to Montana's highest mountain, Granite Peak, about 10 mi north of Cooke City off the northeast corner of Yellowstone National Park. | South on U.S. 212 | 406/446–2103 | www.fs.fed.us/r1/custer/main.html | Daily dawn–dusk.

Peaks to Plains Museum. See the family heirlooms of two lady bronc riders, the Greenough sisters, and their brother, Turk, who was married to famous fan dancer Sally Rand. Exhibits on fur trading, a Finnish kitchen, and a coal-mine replica are among the highlights. | 224 S. Broadway | 406/446–3667 | Weekdays 8–5, weekends 1–5.

Red Lodge Historic District. Built during the coal-mining boom between 1883 and 1910, Red Lodge still has many traces of its ethnic roots. Neighborhoods bear names like Finn Town, Little Italy, and "Hi Bug"—a schoolyard tag invented by kids to describe where the English-speaking upper class lived. In August, the nine-day Festival of Nations takes over town. | Main St. | 406/446–1718 or 406/446–3914 | Daily.

Red Lodge Mountain Ski Area. Licensed day care and 30 acres of extreme chute skiing are selling points of this facility, one of the Northern Rockies' top ski areas. It also has 70 trails and groomed slopes and 60 acres of tree skiing, plus rentals and a ski school. You can eat at two full-service restaurants and a cafeteria. | Off U.S. 212, in Custer National Forest | 800/444–8977 or 406/446–2610 | Early Nov.–Apr., daily 9–4.

Dining

Greenlee's at the Pollard. American. Fresh flowers enhance the elegance of this spot, in a beautiful, restored 19th-century hotel. It has an excellent import and domestic wine cellar, microbrews, and bottled beers, as well as a full bar. Try sage-smoked chicken, grilled gulf shrimp, and garlic mashed potatoes. Kids' menu. No smoking. | 102 N. Broadway | 406/446–0001 | AE, D, MC, V | $$–$$$

Old Piney Dell. American. Good Sunday brunch specials await you at this small restaurant with Western style and design. Kids' menu. It's part of the Rock Creek Resort. | Rock Creek Rd. | 406/446–1196 | AE, D, DC, MC, V | No lunch Mon.–Sat. | $$–$$$

BOZEMAN TRAIL
FROM LITTLE BIGHORN NATIONAL BATTLEFIELD TO BOZEMAN

Distance: 200 mi (322 km)   Time: 2 days
Overnight Break: Billings

After a double dose of Bighorn in the southeast, you'll move northwest to Montana's largest city, then west to Bozeman, one of the state's most attractive communities. Weather permitting, you can drive through the Crow and Northern Cheyenne reservations and entrances to Yellowstone National Park, skirt the bank of the Yellowstone River and the fringes of the Gallatin National Forest, climb Bozeman Pass, and descend into Gallatin Valley.

1 At the junction of I–90 and U.S. 212 near Crow Agency, **Little Bighorn Battlefield National Monument** memorializes one of the last armed efforts of the Northern Plains people to preserve their way of life. You'll learn the significance of June 25–26, 1876, when an overconfident lieutenant colonel named George A. Custer and his 7th Cavalry came face to face with the fiercest warriors of the Sioux, Cheyenne, and Arapaho. Programs, films, tours, and interpretive exhibits help paint the picture.

2 **Bighorn Canyon National Recreation Area** has stunning canyon scenery and trails where you can hike, boat, fish, and camp. On Route 313 south of Hardin, 525-ft-high **Yellowtail Dam** creates picturesque, 71-mi-long **Bighorn Lake,** surrounded by the canyon's spectacular limestone walls. Below the dam, the **Bighorn River** is one of Montana's best year-round trout streams.

3 In **Hardin** you'll find a full range of visitor services, restored buildings, picnic areas, and shops. Off I–90 at Exit 497 is the Big Horn County Historical Museum and Visitor Information Center for regional history and interpretation.

4 **Pompeys Pillar National Historic Landmark** is 28 mi east of Billings off I–94. In 1806, Captain William Clark carved his name on the sandstone butte—the only remaining physical evidence along the trail of the Lewis and Clark Expedition. In season, you can take interpretive tours along the Yellowstone River.

5 **Billings** is eastern Montana's cultural, commercial, and educational center with many museums, art galleries, theaters, colleges, and stores. Billings Trolley Tours gives historic tours of town and Pompeys Pillar. The Visitor Center and Cattle Drive Monument on South 27th Street near I–90 commemorate Montana's centennial cattle drive. Spend the night in Billings.

6 **Columbus,** in the foothills of the scenic Beartooths, is good for outdoor recreation, fine shops, and cafés, and has three city parks, a public swimming pool, and tennis, basketball, and a walking path. You can camp and picnic for free at Itch-Ke-Pe, near the Yellowstone River.

7 **Big Timber** is off I–90 40 mi west of Columbus. There you get an impressive view of the Crazy Mountains, and can visit museums, galleries, antiques shops, historic sites, and the **Yellowstone River Fish Hatchery.** On Route 298, 27 mi south of Big Timber, and worth a detour, is the **Natural Bridge,** a spectacular falls and creek-carved canyon along the Boulder River.

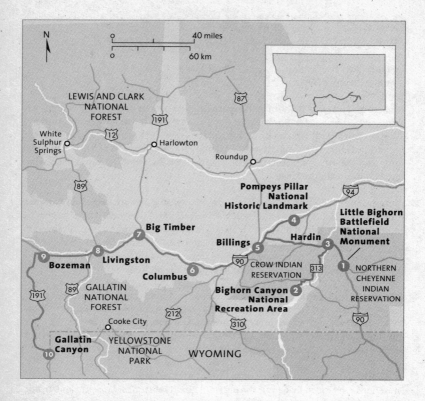

8 Continue roughly 32 mi west on I–90 to **Livingston.** This is the original gateway to Yellowstone National Park; surrounded by the Gallatin National Forest and granite peaks, Livingston is built on the banks of the scenic Yellowstone River, the longest free-flowing river in the United States and one of America's top trout streams.

9 Nestled in the green cradle of the Gallatin Valley and surrounded by a half-dozen mountain ranges, **Bozeman** is a small town with big-city amenities. At the base of the Bridger Range, it is an ideal place from which to start exploring Yellowstone National Park, Big Sky, and numerous Lewis and Clark historic sites. Walk through the campus of Montana State University or the **South Wilson Historic District,** a residential area where houses range from stately mansions to small cottages.

10 **Gallatin Canyon** is an 80-mi drive south of Bozeman on Route 191, following the Gallatin River as it skirts the snowcapped Spanish Peaks then enters the northeast corner of Yellowstone National Park. Along the route, you can fish, camp, watch wildlife, and go white-water rafting.

Big Timber

Attractions

Box Canyon Trailhead. Part of the 1-million-acre Absaroka Beartooth wilderness, this trailhead has miles of spectacular hiking. Be aware that the area is grizzly territory, so overnight stays require either a bear-proof food canister or that all food be hung at least 10 ft off the ground. Phone for current trail conditions. | 50 mi south on Rte. 298 | 406/932–5155.

Crazy Mountain Museum. Exhibits represent Big Timber's history, people, and the Crazy Mountains. Highlights include the Cramer Rodeo and a room dedicated to pioneers, with artifacts dating to the late 1890s. Other exhibits include a detailed miniature of Big Timber in 1907, the restored Sour Dough School House, and the "stabbur"—a reconstruction of an early Norwegian grain storehouse. | Cemetery Rd., I–90 Exit 367 | 406/932–5126 | www.bigtimber.com/html/local_attractions.html | Memorial Day– Labor Day, Tues.–Sun. 1–4, or by appointment.

Greycliff Prairie Dog Town State Park. Ranchers don't like prairie dogs, but the animals are undeniably fascinating to observe. At this large prairie dog town, a preserved habitat, you can wander the trails for easy viewing. Watch for snakes. | Greycliff, I–90 Exit 377 | 406/247–2940 | www.bigtimber.com/html/local_attractions.html | May–Sept., daily dawn–dusk.

Natural Bridge State Park. The view of the 70-ft waterfall is spectacular from this river canyon along the Boulder River. The interpretive signs and trails are helpful, and you need good walking shoes. You can fish here and enter the Absaroka-Beartooth Wilderness. | 27 mi south of Big Timber via Rte. 298 | 406/247–2940 | www.lewisclark.org/m/mtparks.htm | Daily dawn–dusk.

Yellowstone River Fish Hatchery. A biologist is usually on hand to explain the life cycle of the Yellowstone cutthroat trout. You can see all stages of the fish's development, from fingerlings to mature breeding stock. The hatchery is just a short stroll from downtown Big Timber. | ½ mi north on Fairgrounds Rd. | 406/932–4434 | www.bigtimber.com/html/local_attractions.html | Daily 8–4:30.

Dining

The Grand. Continental. Built in 1890, this restaurant within a hotel has an elegant dark-green color scheme and antique paintings. The dining is casual, with a popular prime rib special on weekends and occasional exotic specials of antelope, ostrich, or buffalo. Locally raised lamb and beef are also popular, and the seafood is flown in fresh daily. Sun. brunch. Kids' menu. | 139 McLeod St. | 406/932–4459 | D, MC, V | $$–$$$

Prospector Pizza. Italian. Casual and inexpensive, this local favorite serves up good pizza and other Italian fare. | 139 McLeod St. | 406/932–4846 | No credit cards | $

Billings

Attractions

Alberta Bair Theater. The community fought to save this historic theater from demolition more than a decade ago. Now it is a cultural center, home to the Billings Symphony Orchestra and host to many other events. | 2801 3rd Ave. N | 406/256–6052 | www.albertabairtheater.org/.

Billings Area Visitor Center and Cattle Drive Monument. A heroic-size bronze sculpture of a cattle drover commemorates the "Great Montana Centennial Cattle Drive" of 1989 (which commemorated the drive of 1889). You can take guided tours of the center, study the exhibits, and gather all the information you'll need on area attractions. | 815 S. 27th St. | 406/252–4016 or 800/735–2635 | Weekdays 8–5.

Billings Trolley. Ride on a replica of a 1930 trolley for a historic tour of Billings. You travel from Rimrock to the Yellowstone Valley with stops at local museums. On Wednesday evening ride ZooMontana and get a 3-hour expert tour with the zoo's director as your guide. The tour begins at 5:30, and you'll need reservations. | 888/618–4386 | www.montana.net/funadventures/everything.html | Memorial Day–Labor Day.

Lake Elmo State Park. Around a 64-acre reservoir in Billings Heights, the park is popular for hiking, swimming, fishing, and non-motorized boating. Concerts are occasionally held in the park. Site of the Beach Olympics. | U.S. 87 north to Pemberton La., then ½ mi west | 406/247–2940 | www.state.mt.us | Daily.

Pictograph Cave State Park. People who hunted woolly mammoths in the Yellowstone Valley documented their lives with paintings in caves that you can still explore. The pictographs, ¼ mi in from the park center, are almost 5,000 years old. Bring binoculars for the best view. Special workshops and events are conducted in the 23-acre park. Picnic area and hiking trails. | From Lockwood Exit off I–90, 6 mi south on Coburn Rd. | 406/247–2940 | www.state.mt.us | May–Sept., daily.

ZooMontana. These zoological and botanical gardens specialize in northern-latitude temperate species. You can visit the children's zoo and see exotic and native animals and gardens. | 2100 S. Shiloh Rd. | 406/652–8100 | Daily 10–7.

Dining

Golden Belle. American. Billings's most elegant restaurant is downtown in the Radisson Northern Hotel. Try the beef, specially aged in-house, or one of the fresh catch specials. Reservations essential for dinner. | 19 N. 28th St. | 406/245–2232 | AE, D, MC, V | $$$

Rex. American. Built in 1910 by Buffalo Bill Cody's chef, this restaurant was saved from the wrecking ball and restored in 1975. Now it's a black Angus–certified steak house with plenty of seafood specials nightly. You can also try the Rex Patio Bar and Grill. Kids' menu. No smoking. | 2401 Montana Ave. | 406/245–7477 | AE, D, DC, MC, V | $$–$$$

Walkers Grill. American/Casual. Walkers has a casual and contemporary feel, despite the fact that it's in the 100-year-old Chamber Building. Fresh fish and mountain lamb are favorites on a menu that also has pastas, salads, and Mediterranean pizza. Kids' menu. | 301 N. 27th St. | 406/245–9291 | AE, D, MC, V | Closed Sun. No lunch | $$–$$$

The Windmill. American. Chicken, steak, and shrimp are the specialties at this popular spot. Reservations advised. | 3921 1st Ave. S, Billings | 406/252–8100 | AE, D, MC, V | $$–$$$

Lodging

Josphine B & B. A lovely historic home within walking distance of downtown, this B&B has five themed rooms and a guest parlor with library and a piano. Each room has a private bath. You get free guest passes to a local health club. TV in common area. | 514 N. 29th St., Billings | 406/248–5898 or 800/552–5898 | www.thejosephine.com | 5 rooms, all with private bath | $–$$$

C'Mon Inn. The rooms are contemporary, spacious, and comfortable. Consider splurging on a suite with an in-room Jacuzzi. Complimentary Continental breakfast. Minibars, some refrigerators. Cable TV. Indoor pool. Hot tub. Exercise equipment. Video games. Business services. | 2020 Overland Ave. | 406/655–1100 or 800/655–1170 | fax 406/652–7672 | 80 rooms, 8 suites | AE, D, MC, V | $–$$

Holiday Inn Billings Plaza. Convenient to a mall, water park, and the airport, the hotel has a lobby lounge and traditional rooms, some with whirlpools. Restaurant. Some microwaves, some refrigerators. Cable TV, in-room VCRs. Indoor pool. Hot tub, sauna. Exercise equipment. Video games. | 5500 Midland Rd., I–90 Exit 446 | 406/248–7701 | fax 406/248–8954 | www.holiday-inn.com | 315 rooms and suites | AE, D, DC, MC, V | $

Rimview Inn. Montana's largest saltwater aquarium—a 1,000-gallon tank—is in the lobby of this convenient motel. Some rooms have hot tubs and full kitchens. Complimentary Continental breakfast. | 1025 N. 27th St. | 406/248–2622 | fax 406/248–2622 | 34 rooms, 20 suites | AE, D, DC, MC, V | $

Sleep Inn. Standard modern design characterizes the rooms, and in-room data ports are a nice convenience for those who like to stay connected. The bathrooms have showers only, no bathtubs. Complimentary Continental breakfast. In-room data ports. Cable TV. | 4904 Southgate Dr. | 406/254–0013 or 800/627–5337 | fax 406/254–9878 | www.hotelchoice.com | 75 rooms, shower only | AE, D, DC, MC, V | $

Bozeman

Attractions

American Computer Museum. Geared for all ages, this is only the second museum in the world dedicated entirely to the history of the computer. | 234 E. Babcock St. | 406/587–7545 | www.compustory.com | June–Aug., daily 10–4; May and Sept., Tues.–Wed., Fri.–Sat. noon–4; Oct.–Apr., Tues.–Sat. noon–4.

Bridger Bowl Ski Area. You will find everything a skier could want here, 16 mi northeast of Bozeman. More than 60 runs cover 2,000 acres of Gallatin National Forest. There are 2,000 vertical ft of lift-served terrain, with 500 additional vertical ft on nearly 400 acres. Other amenities include skiing instruction, two cafeterias, a full-service bar, and day care. | 15795 Bridger Canyon Rd. | 406/586–1518 or 800/223–9609 | fax 406/587–1069 | www.bridgerbowl.com | Dec. 12–Apr. 4, daily 9–4.

Gallatin County Pioneer Museum. The building served as the county jail for 70 years and the site for a hanging in 1924. The gallows and several jail cells remain. You'll find hundreds of artifacts, automobiles, Northern Plains crafts, and a model of nearby Fort Ellis. | 317 W. Main St. | 406/522–8122 | www.pioneermuseum.org | Oct.–May, Tues.–Fri. 11–4, Sat. 1–4; June–Sept., weekdays 10–4:30, Sat. 1–4.

Gallatin National Forest. The national forest includes the Absaroka Wilderness and part of the Beartooth Wilderness, and has 37 campgrounds. Tour scenic Gallatin Canyon, an 80-mi drive south of Bozeman on U.S. 191 along the Gallatin River. The road skirts the Spanish Peaks and enters the northwest corner of Yellowstone Park. You can fish, go white-water rafting, and watch wildlife. Additional ranger stations are in Big Timber, Gardiner, Hebgen, and Livingston. | Forest Supervisor's Office: 10 E. Babcock Ave. | Bozeman Ranger Station: 3710 Fallon St. | 406/587–6701 or 406/932–5155 | www.fs.fed.us/r1/gallatin | Daily.

Montana State University. Founded in 1893 as Montana's land-grant institution, Montana State University–Bozeman is a comprehensive research university with approximately 12,000 students. | W. Kagy Blvd. | 406/994–6617 | www.montana.edu | Weekdays 8–5.

The university's **Museum of the Rockies** at the south edge of campus has lifelike displays and rooms full of flora and fauna, as well as the Kirk Hill Nature Trail, a world-class dinosaur display, and a planetarium. The interactive exhibits provide a kid-friendly education. You can participate in dinosaur digs on museum-sponsored summer field trips. | 600 W. Kagy Blvd. | 406/994–3466 | www.montana.edu/wwwmor | Memorial Day–Labor Day, daily 8–8; Labor Day–Memorial Day, Mon.–Sat. 9–5, Sun. 12:30–5.

Dining

Gallatin Gateway Inn. Continental. Succulent and elegantly presented dishes complement the mountain views. Try the prime rib or salmon. Kids' menu. Sun. brunch. | U.S. 191 | 406/763–4672 | Reservations essential | AE, D, MC, V | No lunch | $$$–$$$$

John Bozeman Bistro. Eclectic. The menu is small, but one of the best in the state. Fresh seafood specials are flown in daily. You'll find Pacific Rim, Asian, and classical French entrées on the menu. The restaurant is downtown in the oldest brick building on the Historical Register. Kids' menu. No smoking. Reservations essential for dinner. | 242 E. Main St. | 406/587–4100 | AE, D, MC, V | Closed Mon. No dinner Sun. | $$$

Spanish Peaks Brewery and Italian Cafe. Italian. A large circular bar and spacious dining room distinguish this brewpub and restaurant. The beer is good, as are the desserts and breads. The pasta is made fresh daily. Chef's specials include black pepper fettuccine with sausage and rotisserie chicken. No smoking. | 120 N. 19th St. | 406/585–2296 | D, MC, V | $–$$$

Bacchus Pub. American. Burgers, soups, salads, and daily specials are available in this downtown old German-style pub. Try the smoked chicken fettuccini. Kids' menu. | 105 W. Main St. | 406/586–1314 | AE, D, MC, V | $$

Leaf and Bean Coffee House. American. Stop here when you need a break from exploring downtown, and have a light meal or a homemade pastry with coffee or tea. You can also buy coffee in bulk. Thursday, Friday, and Saturday you can hear live music. No smoking. | 35 W. Main St. | 406/587–1580 | MC, V | $–$$

Hardin

Attractions

Bighorn Canyon National Recreation Area. Straddling the Montana–Wyoming border, Bighorn Canyon gives you stunning canyon scenery and a lake that stretches almost 75 mi. You can boat, swim, fish, hike trails, take naturalist-guided trips, and camp. At the Yellowtail visitor center, rangers present programs about the Bighorn Canyon area and its spectacular limestone canyon walls. | 25 mi south on Rte. 313 | 406/666–2412 | www.nps.gov | Daily dawn–dusk.

Bighorn County Historical Museum and Visitor Information Center. The complex sits on 24 acres and includes 20 permanent buildings. The museum focuses on Native American and early homestead settlement. It also serves as an official Montana State Visitor Center. | I–90 Exit 497 | 406/665–1671 | May–Sept., daily 8–8; Oct.–Apr., weekdays 9–5.

Little Bighorn Battlefield National Monument and Custer National Cemetery. General George A. Custer's 7th Cavalry was defeated by leaders Sitting Bull, Crazy Horse, and Gall and their Sioux and Cheyenne warriors at this site, named a national cemetery in 1879 to protect the graves of cavalry buried there. In 1886, it was proclaimed a National Cemetery of Custer's Battlefield Reservation. It was redesignated Custer Battlefield National Monument in 1946 and renamed December 10, 1991. Guided tours are available. | U.S. 212 | 406/638–2622 | www.nps.gov/libi/ | Memorial Day–Labor Day, daily 8 AM–9 PM; Labor Day–Nov., daily 8–6; Dec.–Apr., daily 8–4:30.

Pompeys Pillar National Historic Landmark. Captain William Clark carved his name on this sandstone butte in 1806. Stop at the visitor center or take interpretive tours. | Off I–94, along Yellowstone River | 406/896–5013 | www.mt.blm.gov/pompeys/index.html | May–Sept., daily 8–8.

Rosebud Battlefield State Park. The site of the 1876 battle between the Sioux and General Crook's infantry set the stage for an Indian victory eight days later at the Battle of the Little Bighorn. The displays explain the battle. You can hike, but watch for rattlesnakes. | 20 mi south, off Rte. 314 | 406/232–0900 | www.state.mt.us | Daily.

Tongue River Reservoir State Park. Summer is the time to camp at one of the 106 campsites at this recreational area on the Tongue Reservoir. Rent boats (there's a boat ramp), fish and swim, and buy groceries from May through August. | Off Rte. 314, 6 mi north of Decker | 406/232–0900 | www.state.mt.us | Daily dawn–dusk.

Dining

Purple Cow. American. The shakes and steaks are good at this family restaurant, or try the chicken or salads: Kids' menu. | Rte. 1, off U.S. 212 at the north end of town | 406/665–3601 | MC, V | $–$$

Livingston

Attractions

Depot Center. A restored Northern Pacific Railroad station, the museum has railroad and Western history displays and artwork. | 200 W. Park St., (U.S. 89) | 406/222–2300 | May–Sept., Mon.–Sat. 9–5, Sun. 1–4.

Firehouse 5 Playhouse. The playhouse presents vaudeville and comedy during the summer and musical productions during the fall and winter. | U.S. 89 S | 406/222–1420 | Call for performance schedule.

Park County Museum. In a turn-of-the-20th-century schoolhouse, this museum has displays on early settlers, Yellowstone National Park, and area railroad history. | 118 W. Chinook St. | 406/222–4184 | June–Labor Day, daily 10–5:30; Labor Day–May, by appointment only.

Dining

Livingston Bar and Grille. Continental. Homey and rustic, this restaurant displays art depicting local history. The menu changes weekly and could include buffalo burgers, chicken sandwiches, seafood, and a large selection of desserts. Kids' menu. | 130 N. Main St. | 406/222–7909 | AE, D, MC, V | No lunch | $$–$$$

LEWIS AND CLARK'S JOURNEY: ALONG THE MISSOURI RIVER

FROM BROWNVILLE TO CROFTON

Distance: 404 mi   Time: 5 days
Overnight Breaks: Nebraska City, Omaha, Crofton

As you drive along the Missouri River you'll essentially follow the same route that Lewis and Clark took in 1804. You will visit such river towns as Brownville and Nebraska City, and the state's major metropolitan area, Omaha. You'll begin to appreciate the agricultural prosperity of the Midwest as you head north to South Sioux City and Crofton.

❶ Begin in **Brownville,** a town that is proud of its heritage as a riverboat community, one of the first established when Congress created the Nebraska Territory. The **Brownville Historic District** includes many buildings dating to the 1860s and 1870s, such as the Captain Bailey House, site of the **Brownville Museum,** the **Carson House,** and the **Governor Furnas Home.** Once you've explored the historic district, stroll down to the waterfront and visit the *Meriwether Lewis,* a former Missouri River dredge that's now a riverboat museum. Several local companies offer cruises on the river.

❷ From Brownville, pick up Route 64E and head south for approximately 9 mi until you reach **Indian Cave State Park.** The park, which sprawls over 3,000 acres along the Missouri River, takes its name from a sandstone overhang with Native American rock carvings. Stop for a quick hike—you'll probably see (and hear) many species of birds, ranging from wild turkeys to bright red cardinals.

❸ When you're ready to leave the park, head north on U.S. 75 to **Nebraska City,** which is also known as the City of Seven Hills. The National Arbor Day holiday was born here. The best places to appreciate the importance of trees are the **Arbor Lodge State Historical Park and Arboretum** and the **Arbor Day Farm.** Historical attractions include **John Brown's Cave,** where fleeing slaves were hidden during the Civil War era, and the **Old Freighter's Museum.** Spend the night in Nebraska City.

④ From Nebraska City, continue north on Highway 75 to **Bellevue,** the site of a fur-trading post established in the early 1800s, making this one of the oldest European American communities in the state of Nebraska. At **The Sarpy County Historical Museum,** learn about Native Americans who knew this area as their homeland for generations.

⑤ Leaving Bellevue, head north on U.S. 75 to **Omaha.** You can spend one or several days and nights here exploring the museums and parks, nature centers, recreation areas, and shops. Some of the top attractions include the **Durham Western Heritage Museum** in the historic Union Station and the **Joslyn Art Museum.** In the **Old Market,** 12 blocks of 19th-century buildings, you'll find shopping galore—from antiques and books to Persian rugs. You can travel through this area by horse-drawn carriage or tandem bicycle if you like. **Father Flanagan's Boys Town** is a national historic landmark, and the **Mormon Trail Visitors Center** is the site of a cemetery that's the final resting place for some 700 Mormons who died during the winter of 1846–47, when the group had stopped en route to Utah.

For the kids, spend a day at the **Henry Doorly Zoo,** which includes the world's largest indoor rain forest, an aquarium, and North America's largest "Cat Complex."

⑥ When you're done with Omaha, head north on U.S. 75 to Fort Calhoun, near Blair. **Fort Atkinson State Historical Park** is a re-creation of the first U.S. military fort built west of the Missouri River and is close to the site where Lewis and Clark met with local Native Americans in 1804.

⑦ When you exit the park, pick up U.S. 75 and head north. After approximately 9 mi, you'll come to **Blair** at the intersection of U.S. 75, Route 133, Route 131, and Route 91. **Black Elk/Neihardt Park** is dedicated to the Oglala Sioux holy man Black Elk and Nebraska poet laureate John G. Neihardt, who helped spread Black Elk's vision to the world. Three miles east of the park, you'll find **DeSoto National Wildlife Refuge,** where the steamboat *Bertrand* sank in the Missouri River in 1865 en route to Fort Benton, Montana. The refuge attracts half-a-million geese, mallards, and bald eagles as they migrate south in the fall and is a year-round home for deer, birds, beaver, and muskrats.

NEBRASKA RULES OF THE ROAD

License Requirements: General driver's licenses are available at age 16, though some special permits for resident youth are allowed.

Right Turn on Red: Unless otherwise posted, right turns on red are permitted *after* a full stop. Left turns on red are allowed where such a turn would not cross an oncoming traffic lane.

Seat Belt and Helmet Laws: Seat belts are required of the driver and all front-seat passengers. Children under age five, or weighing less than 40 pounds, must be secured in a car seat that meets federal guidelines. All motorcycle operators and passengers must wear approved motorcycle helmets.

Speed Limits: Interstate: 75 mph except in metropolitan areas around Lincoln and Omaha. State highways: generally 60 mph; some stretches are 55 mph. City and town streets: 25 mph in residential districts, 20 mph in business districts unless otherwise posted. County roads: 55 mph; 50 mph on unpaved county roads, unless otherwise posted.

For More Information: Contact the **Nebraska State Patrol** | 402/471–4545, the **Emergency Highway Help Line** | 800/525–5555, or the **Department of Motor Vehicles** | 402/471–2281.

⑧ Continue north on U.S. 75 and turn west onto U.S. 20, then north on Route 12 to **Ponca** and **Ponca State Park.** The 892-acre park has impressive views of the Missouri River and attracts hikers and equestrians.

⑨ From Ponca, continue west on Route 12 to **Crofton,** which is a good place to stop for the night and enjoy the recreational activities in the northeastern corner of Nebraska. **Lewis and Clark Lake** was formed by **Gavins Point Dam,** which has a hatchery, aquarium, power plant, and a visitor center.

⑩ Leaving Crofton, head west on Route 12 for approximately 28 mi until you come to **Niobrara State Park,** a 1,640-acre preserve about a mile from the town of Neeligh. The Niobrara and Missouri rivers converge here, and you can hike along a stretch of the Lewis and Clark National Historical Trail and explore Basile Creek Wildlife Area, a wetland used by migratory birds.

Bellevue

Attractions

Bellevue Little Theater. Around since 1968, this small community theater produces about five plays a year, drawing cast and production crews from the Bellevue area. Theater group volunteers also run a thrift shop next door to help fund productions. | 203 Mission St., 68005 | 402/291–1554.

Fontenelle Forest Nature Center. More than 1,300 acres of hilly woodlands, wetlands, and land fronting the Missouri River on the northern edge of town are laced with 25 mi of trails, including about a mile of boardwalk accessible to travelers using wheelchairs. The Nature Center has nature and historical displays and a variety of programs, including guided hikes. | 1111 Bellevue Blvd. N, 68005 | 402/731–3140 | Daily 8–5, weekends 8–6.

Historic Bellevue. Guides lead visitors on 90-minute tours through the state's oldest train depot, church, bank, and cemetery, plus an original log cabin. | 112 W. Mission Ave., 68005 | 402/293–3080 or 800/467–2779 | Daily.

The Sarpy County Historical Museum. Exhibits cover the early history of Sarpy County, home to some of the state's first settlements. On display are Native American artifacts as well as items used by early explorers, fur traders, and trappers. Period rooms recreate the home styles of the turn of the 20th century. | 2402 Clay St. | 402/292–1880 | Mon.–Fri. 9–5.

Dining

Amarillo Barbecue. Barbecue. The quiet dining room has a mix of antiques and "Texas-like" touches, such as metal signs. You can opt for a booth or a table, but the country music is standard with either choice. Favorites include stuffed baked potatoes, smoked meat sandwiches, corn bread with jalapeño peppers, and cobblers. | 303 Fort Crook Rd. N, 68005 | 402/291–7495 | AE, MC, V | $–$$

Nettie's Fine Mexican Food. Mexican. The name says it all—good Mexican food, in an easy-going setting with a range of beef, chicken, and other specialties, all served south-of-the-border style. There's a separate lounge for socializing. | 7110 Railroad Ave., 68005 | 402/733–3359 | Closed Sun., Mon. | No credit cards | $

Stella's. American. A lunchtime institution, this neighborhood bar and lounge is frequented by personnel from nearby Offutt Air Force Base. Pictures of the owner's relatives and friends adorn the walls. The TV's always on, but the volume's rarely up—except during Nebraska football games. Sandwiches and burgers are served on napkins, the fries in a bowl. No forks and knives needed here. | 106 Galvin Rd. S | 402/291–6088 | Closed Sun. | No credit cards | $

Blair

Attractions

Black Elk/Neihardt Park. The 80-acre park includes a pavilion and picnic shelters as well as a monument depicting the visions of the Oglala Sioux seer Black Elk. | 31st St. and College St. | 402/426–5025 | Daily.

Boyer Chute National Wildlife Refuge. A preserve 10 mi southeast of Blair on County Road 34 alongside the Missouri River, the Boyer Chute is a restored river channel surrounded by 2,000 acres of grassland, woodland, and wetlands, with two short nature trails and a 4-mi hiking loop. | 712/642–4121 | Daily dawn–dusk.

DeSoto National Wildlife Refuge. Up to half-a-million snow geese pause here for a few weeks during their southbound migration each fall. You can view them from an outdoor area or from within the glass-walled galleries of the visitor center, 3 mi east of Blair. Besides displays about the flora and fauna of the refuge, which is partially in Iowa, the center has more than 200,000 well-preserved articles recovered from the steamboat *Bertrand,* which sank in the region in 1865. No-wake boating and fishing are permitted on the lake, but you'll find plenty of hiking trails on the grounds. | 1434 316th Lane, Missouri Valley, IA | 712/642–4121 | Daily except winter holidays.

Fort Atkinson State Historical Park. The original fort, for some years the only military presence west of the Missouri, was built in 1820 close to the site where Lewis and Clark met with local Native Americans in 1804. A re-created fort with barracks and log walls is now on the grounds, which are 10 mi south of Blair. Living-history programs are offered the first weekend of every month from May through October. | 7th and Madison, Fort Calhoun | 402/468–5611 | ngp.ngpc.state.ne.us/parks/ftatkin.html | Grounds: daily 8–7. Visitor Center: Memorial Day–Labor Day, daily 9–5 PM.

Dining

Jake's Bar and Grill. American. A big-screen TV and other televisions throughout the dining area drive home that this is a sports bar. Fan favorites are the ground-steak burgers and loaded nachos. | 218 S. 8th St., 68008 | 402/426–9928 | AE, D, MC, V | $

Brownville

Attractions

Brownville Historic District. The buildings are authentically *antebellum,* but with a Midwestern sensibility. Many are red brick, with a spare, squared-off shape, yet their ornately carved accents and the size of the surrounding lots underscore the prosperity of the homes' mid-1800s owners. The area, which covers most of downtown, is a popular tourist attraction and the site of town events. | 116 Main St., 68321 | 402/825–6001 or 402/825–4131 | June–Labor Day, daily 10–5; Labor Day–June, weekends 10–5.

In a gabled brick building in the historic area, the **Brownville Museum** displays day-to-day objects from when Brownville was a bustling port on the Missouri. | 4th and Main Sts. | 402/825–6178 | June–Aug., daily 1–5; Sept.–mid-Oct., weekends and by appointment.

Another popular attraction is the **Carson House.** It was built in 1860 by Brownville's founder, Richard Brown, who then sold it to John Carson, southeast Nebraska's leading banker. The home is filled with original furnishings left by the Carson family. | 3rd St. at Main St. | 402/825–6001 | Memorial Day–Labor Day, daily 1–5.

Governor Furnas Home, home to Robert Furnas, Nebraska's second elected governor, is a 2½-story structure with Italianate and Gothic Revival influences. | 6th St. at Water St. | 402/825–6001 or 402/825–4131 | Weekends 1–5.

Indian Cave State Park. Named after an overhanging sandstone bluff with Nebraska's only known examples of petroglyphs—Native American rock carvings—the park also includes ruins and reconstructed buildings of the old river community of St. Deroin. You'll find areas for hiking, camping, cross-country skiing, and sledding, as well as a modern RV campground. It's about 9 mi south of Brownville on Route 64E. | 402/883–2575 | ngp.ngpc.state.ne.us/parks/icave.html | Daily; camping Mar.–Nov.

Meriwether Lewis **Dredge and Missouri River History Museum.** Brownville's past as a riverboat town is memorialized in the museum on the *Captain Meriwether Lewis,* a retired steam-powered, sidewheel vessel used to dredge the Missouri River for more than 30 years. | 402/825–3341 | May–mid-Oct., daily 10–6.

Crofton

Attractions

Lewis and Clark State Recreation Area. Six recreation areas on the Nebraska side of this dammed portion of the Missouri have picnicking, camping, fishing, swimming, and boating facilities, plus rental cabins and a marina that has gas available for boats 24/7. Ice-fishing, snowmobiling, and other winter sports continue through the cold months. The park entrance is 21 mi from Crofton, off Highway 54C. | 402/388–4169 | ngp.ngpc.state.ne.us/parks/lewclark.html | Year-round; camping, May–mid-Sept.; cabins, Apr.–Dec.

The **Lewis and Clark Lake Visitor Center,** maintained by the U.S. Army Corps of Engineers, is on a bluff 10 mi north of Crofton on Route 121. Inside, you can see exhibits about the upper Missouri from the days of Lewis and Clark to the advent of hydro-electric dams. Outside, the Dorian Prairie Garden is lush with nature's exhibits of grasses and wildflowers.

Dining

Argo Hotel. American. The menu in this candle-lit restaurant includes seafood and steaks, as well as a "chocolate temptation" with homemade cream sauce. Stop by the two cocktail lounges to have a look at the cigar room and a 100-year-old oak bar scarred with bullet holes. | 211 W. Kansas St. | 800/607–2746 or 402/388–2400 | AE, D, MC, V | Daily 5–10 | $–$$$

Lodging

Historic Argo Hotel Bed and Breakfast. Meant to emulate *Titanic*-era luxury, this small brick 1912 building has early 20th-century decorative details and furnishings, such as brass beds in the guest rooms. Restaurant, bar (with entertainment), complimentary breakfast. Cable TV. Free parking. No kids under 12. No smoking. | 211 W. Kansas St. | 402/388–2400 or 800/607–2746 | fax 402/388–2525 | 17 rooms, 1 suite | AE, D, MC, V | $–$$

Nebraska City

Attractions

Old Freighter's Museum. Exhibits in this three-story house—used as the headquarters for the company that founded the Pony Express—has exhibits explaining how freight companies supplied the Army on the Oxbow and Cutoff trails from 1855 to 1863. | 407 N. 14th St., 68410 | 402/873–9360 | By appointment only.

Arbor Day Farm. Originally part of the land owned by J. Sterling Morton, this apple orchard is also a National Historic Landmark. You can't pick apples on your own, but you can walk the trails and buy fresh-pressed cider made from "antique" recipes no longer used by other orchards. | 100 Arbor Ave., 68410 | 402/873–8710 | Mon.–Sat. 9–5, Sun. 12–5.

★ **Arbor Lodge State Historical Park and Arboretum.** What began as a four-room frame home grew into a 52-room neo-Colonial mansion. You can see all the furnishings and a one-lane bowling alley used by the family of J. Sterling Morton, a territorial governor and U.S. Secretary of Agriculture. | 2600 Arbor Ave., 68410 | 402/873–7222 | ngp.ngpc.state.ne.us/parks/arbor.html | Apr.–Memorial Day and Labor Day–Nov. 1, daily 11–5; Memorial Day–Labor Day, daily 9–5; Nov. 2–Dec., daily 1–4.

John Brown's Cave. Allen Mahew's cabin has been certified as the oldest building in Nebraska still standing. The westernmost stop on the Underground Railroad of the Civil War days, it has a trap door leading to underground chambers and a tunnel that was used by slaves. A small village of authentic early 20th-century buildings has been assembled around the grassy commons. | 20th St. and 4th Corso, 68410 | 402/873–3115 | Late Apr.–late Nov., daily 10–5, Sun. 12–5.

Lodging

Arbor Day Farm Lied Conference Center. The sprawling four-story white structure overlooks 260 acres of oak and hickory trees across the creek from the Arbor Lodge grounds. Highlights are the skylighted indoor pool and soaring lobby with a 50-ft-tall fireplace. Meals are included in most rate plans. Restaurant, bar. In-room data ports. Cable TV. Indoor pool. Hot tub. Exercise equipment. Laundry facilities. Airport shuttle. | 2700 Sylvan Rd., 68410 | 800/546–5433 | www.adflcc.com | 144 rooms | AE, D, DC, MC, V | $$–$$$

Apple Inn. What began as one building in 1950 has grown to four prairie-colored structures around a swimming pool. Almost everything in town is within a few miles of this motel, including a nine-hole public golf course ½ mi away and the Factory Stores of America outlet mall at the junction of Highway 75 and Route 2. The town trolley, which circles among various attractions, stops at the lobby. Complimentary Continental breakfast. Some refrigerators. Cable TV. Pool. Laundry facilities. Business services. | 502 S. 11th, 68410 | 402/873–5959 or 800/659–4446 | fax 402/873–6640 | appleinn.net | 65 rooms | AE, D, DC, MC, V | $

Days Inn. There's a relaxed country feeling inside this neatly landscaped two-floor motel. Complimentary Continental breakfast. Refrigerators. Cable TV. | www.daysinn.com | 29 rooms | 1715 S. 11th St., 68410 | 402/873–6656 | fax 402/873–6676 | AE, D, DC, MC | $

Whispering Pines Bed and Breakfast. Built in 1883, this family-owned B&B is on 6½ acres of oaks and pine trees. It has a goldfish pond, a stream, a waterfall, an old-time porch swing and large deck, and a spa enclosed within a gazebo. Two rooms share a bath. Picnic area, complimentary breakfast. Some room phones, no TV in some rooms. Hot tub. No smoking. | 2018 6th Ave., 68410 | 402/873–5850 | 5 rooms | D, MC, V | $

Omaha

Attractions

Botanical Gardens. Divided into several specialty areas, the 75-acre Gardens overlooking the Missouri River include rose, herb, children's, and spring flowering gardens. | 5th and Cedar Sts. | 402/346–4002 | Apr.–Oct., Tues.–Sun. 9–4.

Durham Western Heritage Museum. In Omaha's restored Union Station, the museum's exhibits detail various facets of Omaha's history. There are railroad cars and a steam engine, as well as the Byron Reed Coin and Document Collection. An old-time soda fountain still operates on the main level, its frothy concoctions illuminated by light streaming through salmon-colored windows. | 801 S. 10th St. | 402/444–5071 | www.dwhm.org | Tues.–Sat. 10–5, Sun. 1–5.

Girls and Boys Town. In 1917 Father Edward J. Flanagan founded this refuge for boys as Father Flanagan's Boys' Home. On this large campus in west Omaha, you can tour Father Flanagan's House, gardens, a chapel, and other facilities. On display is the Academy Award won by Spencer Tracy for his portrayal of Flanagan in the 1938 movie "Boy's Town." | 13628 Flanagan Blvd., Boy's Town, 68010 | 402/498–1140 | www.girlsand-boystown.org | May–Aug., daily 8–5:30; Sept.–Apr., daily 8–4:30.

Freedom Park. Paying tribute to some of the nation's wartime vessels, this park along the Missouri River is now the berth of the U.S.S. *Hazard,* a decorated World War II minesweeper; the training submarine U.S.S. *Marlin;* the landing craft LSM-45, and a Coast Guard helicopter and naval aircraft. | 2497 Freedom Park Rd. | 402/345–1959 | www.freedomparknavy.org | Apr.–Oct., daily 9–6.

Gerald Ford Birth Site. A rose garden and colonnade similar to those at the White House commemorate the site where the childhood home of former President Ford once stood. An adjacent structure, the Gerald R. Ford Conservation Center, has a permanent display of exhibits on the 38th president. | 32nd St. and Woolworth Ave., 68105 | 402/444–5955 | Daily 7:30–dusk.

Henry Doorly Zoo. The zoo's Lied Jungle is the world's largest indoor rain forest, displaying some of the flora and fauna found in Africa, South America, and Asia. It has North America's largest cat complex, with rare white tigers as well as more familiar big beasts. The fish in the Scott Aquarium swim in waters that duplicate the conditions of habitats from the tropics to the Antarctic—and you can walk through a 70-ft glass tunnel with sharks swimming around you. There's also an IMAX theater and a petting zoo. | 3701 S. 10th St., 68107 | 402/733–8400 | www.omahazoo/com | Daily 9:30–5.

Joslyn Art Museum. A modern addition to the original Art Deco structure has greatly expanded space for the Joslyn's respected American West collection and 19th- and 20th-century art from Europe and America. The original building has a courtyard and concert hall. | 2200 Dodge St. | 402/342–3300 | www.joslyn.org | Tues.–Sat. 10–4, Sun. 12–4.

Mormon Trail Visitors Center at Winter Quarters. In a building near the cemetery established when the Mormons paused here en route in the late 1840s, you can learn about the history of the Mormon Trail. On a less serious note, you will find up to 300 gingerbread creations displayed here each Christmas, which are given to charitable institutions after the show. | 3215 State St. | 402/453–9372 | Daily 9–9.

Neale Woods Nature Center. In the northern section of Fontenelle Forest in Bellevue, this 550-acre nature center has 9 mi of trails through forested hills, prairie, and wetlands near the Missouri River. | 14323 Edith Marie Ave., 68112 | 402/731–3140.

Old Market. A historic district of early 20th-century brick warehouses, the Old Market is a blend of trendy boutiques, galleries, restaurants, lounges with live music, and loft apartments. Most of the shops along the cobblestone streets are open from 10 to 9, and you can take Old Market's horse-drawn carriages to see the waterfalls and lagoons of the 10-acre Gene Leahy Mall. | 402/341–7151 or 402/346–4445 | Daily.

Dining

V. Mertz. Continental. Despite its out-of-the-way location in the Passageway, V. Mertz is still one of the more sought-after restaurants in Omaha. Soft lights illuminate the tables in the otherwise dark dining room. Specialties are pepper steak, tuna, and salmon. The restaurant's wine selection earned *Wine Spectator*'s Award of Excellence in 2000. | 1022 Howard St., 68102 | 402/345–8980 | AE, D, DC, MC, V | $$$–$$$$

French Café. French. An institution within the Old Market area, this restaurant kick-started the rebirth of the old warehouse district. Black-and-white photos of French scenes adorn the interior, and the patio is open in fair weather. It's known for fresh fish, including salmon piccata, as well as pasta and pepper steak. | 1017 Howard St., 68102 | 402/341–3547 | AE, D, DC, MC, V | $$–$$$

Farm House Café. American. At the end of a small mall, this spacious, quiet restaurant with rich woodwork and private booths serves hamburgers, generous deli sandwiches, barbecued ribs, and fried chicken. | 3461 S. 84th St., 68124 | 402/393–0640 | AE, D, DC, MC, V | $–$$

Joe Tess'. Seafood. Joe Tess' is all about fish, from the albino catfish in its fountain to stuffed fish on the walls and posters and neon beer signs showing still more fish. The menu includes fresh carp, catfish, homemade chowder, shrimp, oysters, farm-raised coho salmon, and rainbow trout. | 5424 S. 24th St., 68107 | 402/731–7278 | AE, MC, V | $–$$

Johnny's Cafe. American. An Omaha institution, this family-owned steakhouse opened in 1922 and is now run by the family's third generation. Casual dining and elaborate meals are available. Try the filet mignon or the prime rib. Kids menu. | 4702 S. 27th St., 68107 | 402/731–4774 | Closed Sun. | AE, D, DC, MC, V | $–$$

Lodging

Embassy Suites. Although this seven-story building is next to the Old Market, it has an atrium and a courtyard for quiet moments away from the busy downtown scene, plus outdoor decks. Each suite has a separate bedroom and living room. Restaurant, bar, complimentary breakfast, room service. Cable TV. Microwaves, refrigerators, in-room data ports. Indoor pool. Hot tub. Gym. Business services, airport shuttle. Pets allowed. | 555 S. 10th St., 68183 | 402/346–9000 or 800/362–2779 | fax 402/346–4236 | 249 suites | AE, D, DC, MC, V | $$$

★ **Hotel Alfredo.** At 19 stories, this is the largest and tallest of downtown Omaha's hotels, and its top-floor restaurant has views of the city and the valley of the Missouri River. It is within walking distance of the Joslyn Art Museum. Restaurant, bar (with entertainment). In-room data ports, some refrigerators. Cable TV. Indoor pool. Beauty salon, hot tub. Exercise equipment. Business services, airport shuttle. | 1616 Dodge St. | 402/346–7600 | fax 402/346–5722 | 413 rooms | AE, D, DC, MC, V | $$–$$$

Four Points Hotel Omaha. With a red roof topping its classically styled six stories, this hotel in southwest Omaha has minibars and coffemakers in each room, as well as complimentary weekday newspapers. About 8 mi from Nebraska Crossroads Mall, it runs complimentary shuttles to the corporate–charter facilities at Millard Airport. Restaurant, room service. Cable TV. Wading pool. Hot tub, sauna. Gym. Laundry facilities. Business services. Pets allowed. | 4888 S. 118th St., 68137 | 402/895–1000 | fax 402/895–9247 | 163 rooms | AE, D, DC, MC, V | $–$$$

Hotel Clarion. Just off I–80, this five-story white building is just down the street from the sports events at Aksarben Coliseum and has in-room movies. Truck parking is available. Restaurant, bar, room service. In-room data ports. Cable TV. Indoor pool. Hot tub, sauna. Laundry facilities. Business services, airport shuttle. Pets allowed. | 3650 S. 72nd St., 68124 | 402/397–3700 or 800/446–6242 | fax 402/397–8362 | 212 rooms | AE, D, DC, MC, V | $$

Holiday Inn Express. A six-story brick building on the west edge of downtown, this hotel is less than 1½ mi from the Great Plains Black History Museum and the Children's Museum and within 5 mi of three casinos in Council Bluffs, Iowa. Rooms have two-line phones, a sauna, and a hot tub. Complimentary Continental breakfast. In-room data ports, refrigerators, in-room hot tubs. Cable TV. Exercise equipment. Laundry facilities. Business services, airport shuttle, free parking. | 3001 Chicago St., 68131 | 402/345–2222 or 800/465–4329 | fax 402/345–2501 | 122 rooms, 10 suites | AE, D, DC, MC, V | $–$$

NEVADA

THE NEVADA LAKESIDE
STATELINE TO CRYSTAL BAY

Distance: 27 mi   Time: 1 day
Overnight Break: Incline Village

An exhilarating drive up the east shore of Lake Tahoe begins at the high-rise casinos of Stateline, but quickly leaves behind the neon and noise. Unlike the California shore of the lake, which is lined with more than a dozen towns, this side is mostly undeveloped, with forested mountainsides, rocky coves, sandy beaches, alpine lakes, and small marinas. And just about the time you're ready for civilization again, the glittering casinos of Crystal Bay appear.

❶ Begin the drive north on U.S. 50 in **Stateline.** Four major and two minor casinos make up the action, clustered on the flats a short hike from the lake. A small residential area hugs the hills above the high-rises, chalets, and condos, close to the sprawling Heavenly Valley Ski Resort.

❷ Head 3 mi north on U.S. 50 and turn left onto Elk Point Road to reach **Nevada Beach.** The nearest public lake access to Stateline on the Nevada side, this large Forest Service facility has a sandy beach, picnic areas, and a 54-site campground.

❸ Four miles north on U.S. 50 is **Zephyr Cove.** Although it's the largest settlement between Stateline and Incline Village, it's a relatively tiny resort, with a beach, marina, campground and RV park, riding stables, and lodge. The 550-passenger sternwheeler MS *Dixie II* and the 20-passenger trimaran *Woodwind* sail from Zephyr Cove.

❹ **Cave Rock,** 4 mi north on U.S. 50, is 25 yards of solid stone; U.S. 50 passes through it via one of Nevada's few tunnels. This monolith towers over a parking lot, a lakefront picnic area, and a boat launch.

❺ Drive 8 mi northeast on U.S. 50, then 2 mi north on Route 28 to reach **Lake Tahoe–Nevada State Park,** which preserves 3 mi of shoreline and a 10-mi by 5-mi clump of the Carson Range rising from the lake. Spooner Lake (just north of the junction) has

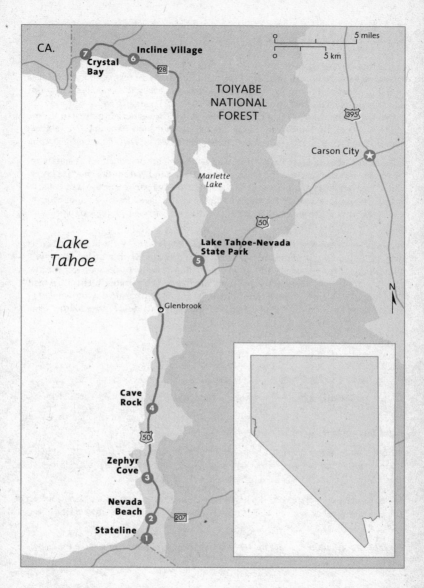

a nature trail and the trailhead for a 5-mi hike through North Canyon to Marlette Lake. Sand Harbor (8 mi north on Rte. 28) is the focal point of the park; it has a beach, rocky cove, and nature trail, and in summer gets very crowded by noon.

6 Go 4 mi farther north on Route 28 to find **Incline Village,** one of Nevada's few master-planned towns, dating back to the early 1960s; it's still privately owned. Check out Lakeshore Drive to see some of the most expensive real estate in Nevada. If you're tempted to linger, spend the night in Incline Village.

7 Just 3 mi more on Route 28 will take you to the end of the tour, **Crystal Bay,** which has a cluster of low-rise casinos. The historic Cal-Neva is bisected by the state line.

Incline Village

Attractions

Diamond Peak Ski Resort. Diamond Peak has a fun family atmosphere, and is smaller and less crowded than many of the super ski resorts nearby. The 1-mi Crystal chairlift rewards you with the best views of the lake of any local ski area. There's a half-pipe run for snowboarders and 22 mi of cross-country skiing. The vertical drop is 1,840 ft. Free shuttles run continuously from the ski area around Incline Village and Crystal Bay. | 1210 Ski Way | 775/831–3211 (24-hr snow phone); 775/832–1177 | www.diamondpeak.com.

Lake Tahoe–Nevada State Park. Preserving a full 3 mi of shoreline and 22 square mi of prime Sierra wilderness, the focus of the park is Sand Harbor Beach State Recreation Area, one of the largest and most popular sandy beaches on the lake. You can follow the short nature trail to explore Sandy Point and have a lesson in Tahoe ecology. The park runs along most of Route 28, near Sand Harbor. | 775/831–0494 | www.state.nv.us/stparks/ | Daily.

Mount Rose Ski Area. With a vertical drop of 1,440 ft, this is one of the highest ski areas around Tahoe. It's geared toward intermediate and advanced (though beginners will find plenty of gentle slopes and an excellent first-timer ski package). It's also the closest skiing to Reno, so it's a popular resort and the parking lots fill up fast. Snowboarders have their own terrain park. Ski shuttles run from downtown Reno. | 22222 Mount Rose Hwy. | 775/849–0704; 800/754–7673 outside NV | www.skirose.com.

NEVADA RULES OF THE ROAD

License Requirements: To drive in Nevada you must be at least 16 and have a valid driver's license.

Right Turn on Red: Permitted everywhere.

Seat Belt and Helmet Laws: All drivers and front-seat passengers must wear seat belts. Children under 10 must wear a seat belt at all times; children under 4 must ride in child seats. Motorcyclists are required to wear helmets at all times.

Speed Limits: Some places on I–80 and I–15 you can drive 75 mph. Other places, and on the U.S. highways, the speed limit is 70. It's a quick 65 mph on the interstates in the heart of Las Vegas and Reno.

For More Information: Contact the **Nevada Department of Motor Vehicles** at | 702/486–4368.

Ponderosa Ranch and Western Theme Park. No, the popular 1960s television series *Bonanza* was not based on this ranch at the south end of town off Route 28. It's the other way around: the Ponderosa is a theme park based on the television show. It centers on the Cartwright ranch house; you'll also find a petting zoo and a collection of antique vehicles. Have a chuck-wagon breakfast, take a wagon ride, and watch a melodramatic shoot-out. The Ponderosa is one of Tahoe's top commercial attractions. | 100 Ponderosa Ranch Rd. | 775/831–0691 | www.ponderosaranch.com/ | May–Oct., daily 9:30–6.

Dining

Lone Eagle Grille. American. A cozy place that's great for pre- or après-ski drinking or dining, the restaurant is a cabin with two fireplaces; open-air dining is right on the beach. Dungeness crab cakes, spit-roasted duck, and braised lamb shank are among the favorites. Entertainment weekends. Kids' menu. Sun. brunch. No smoking. | Country Club Dr. at Lakeshore | 775/832–3250 | AE, D, DC, MC, V | $$$–$$$$

Lodging

Hyatt Regency Lake Tahoe. A self-contained resort half a block from its own beach, this place has virtually everything. The large rooms are both rustic and sophisticated, and you can also relax in the spa. The children's programs are a nice extra. No-smoking floors. 3 restaurants, bars. Minibars, some microwaves, some refrigerators. Cable TV. Pool. Hot tub, massage. Tennis courts. Gym. Beach, bicycles. Children's programs (3–12). Business services. | 458 rooms | 111 Country Club Dr. | 775/832–1234 | fax 775/831–7508 | AE, D, DC, MC, V | $$–$$$$

Inn at Incline. Book early here. It's one of the few motels in a town full of condos. No-smoking rooms. Complimentary Continental breakfast. No air-conditioning. Cable TV. Indoor pool. Hot tub, sauna. Business services. | 38 rooms | 1003 Tahoe Blvd. | 775/831–1052 or 800/824–6391 | fax 775/831–3016 | AE, D, MC, V | $–$$$

Stateline

Attractions

Cave Rock. A towering slab of solid granite, this rock is sacred to the Washoe Indians. A picnic area and boat launch are among the attractions. | 11 mi north on U.S. 50 | Daily 10:30–5.

Nevada Beach. Beach, picnic areas, and a 54-site campground are the big draws of this large Forest Service facility. Make camping reservations as far ahead as possible (up to 120 days in advance). | Left on Elk Point Rd. | 530/573–2600 or 800/280–2267 | May–Oct.

Dining

Summit. Continental. Harrah's Lake Tahoe's crown jewel overlooks the landscape from the 16th floor. The chef has a nightly special, but regular entrées include roasted rack of lamb, wild mushroom saute with fettuccine, grilled New Zealand venison, and many beef and seafood dishes. No smoking. | U.S. 50 | 775/588–6611 ext. 2196 | AE, D, DC, MC, V | No lunch | $$$–$$$$

Llewellyn's. Continental. High atop Harveys on the 19th floor, Llewellyn's offers a spectacular view and a beautiful presentation. Lunch, dinner, and Sunday champagne brunch year-round. No smoking. | In Harvey's Hotel & Casino | 775/588–2411 | AE, D, DC, MC, V | $$–$$$$

Sage Room. American. Steak and other beef cuts top the menu. Opened in 1947, the place retains its Old West furnishings and style. The favorite dessert is bananas Foster. | 775/588–2411 | AE, D, DC, MC, V | No lunch | $$–$$$$

Chart House. Steak. A lake view and nautical decor now match the menu, which has added a lot of fresh fish and seafood. Sesame-crusted salmon, seared, peppered ahi tuna, and grilled swordfish are specialties. Steaks are served as well. Kids' menu. | 392 Kingsbury Grade (Rte. 28), 2 mi east off U.S. 50 | 775/588–6276 | www.chart-house.com | AE, D, DC, MC, V | No lunch | $$–$$$

CIRCLING NORTHERN NEW MEXICO
SANTA FE, TAOS, AND THE FRONTIERS OF NEW SPAIN

Distance: Approximately 500 mi   Time: 4 days
Overnight Breaks: Santa Fe, Taos, and Raton

Spanish conquistadors covered a lot of ground during the 16th and 17th centuries, crossing hundreds of miles of present-day Mexico and southern New Mexico. Along the way, they settled this remote northern section of the state. Attractions on this drive tell the story of these Spanish settlers, as well as early Mexican and American travelers.

Much of the trip is on two-lane state highways. Snow and ice likely will temper your speed if you take this tour during the winter; spring and fall are ideal times to travel, from the standpoints of both temperature and the beauty of the scenery.

① Arrive in **Santa Fe** early and spend the day sightseeing. Shops, museums, art galleries, and other attractions abound. Spend the night in a Santa Fe hotel or bed and breakfast.

② Enjoy a leisurely breakfast and leave Santa Fe around 10 AM, which will give you plenty of time to get to Chimayó. Take U.S. 84/U.S. 285 north out of Santa Fe. When you reach Pojoaque, turn right and take Route 503 to its junction with Route 98. Turn left and follow Route 98 to **Chimayó.** After lunch, save enough time to visit the **Santuario de Chimayó Church** and **Ortega's Weaving Shop,** within walking distance of each other. Eight generations of the Ortega family have been weaving here, and their works of textile art are breathtaking.

③ Pick up Route 98 again to Route 76, turn right, and proceed through the ageless Hispanic towns of Truchas and Las Trampas to the road's junction with Route 75. The scenery through here is stunning. Turn left and follow Route 75 through Dixon to Route 68. Turn right (north) and follow Route 68 to **Ranchos de Taos,** with much-photographed **San Francisco de Asís Mission Church** on your right.

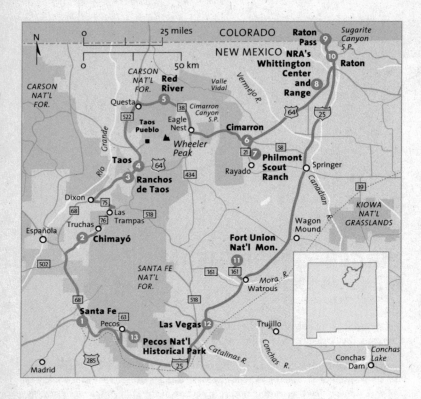

④ Follow Route 68 into **Taos** and the town Plaza. With the Plaza as your base of operations, tour this sleepy Spanish town with its many museums, historic residences, and art galleries.

Taos was famous for many years during the early part of the 20th century as an artists' colony, and the village is full of references to those noted painters (Ernest Blumenschein, Bert Phillips, Irving Couse, Joseph H. Sharp, Oscar Berninghaus, among others) and writers (D. H. Lawrence, Frank Waters, and Mabel Dodge Luhan) who made their homes here. Famed mountain man Kit Carson lived in Taos for several years, and today the **Kit Carson Home and Museum** has been preserved much as it was during his lifetime.

The **Bent House** is where Mexicans and Taos Indians, protesting the U.S. annexation of New Mexico, murdered Governor Charles Bent in January 1847.

Don't miss **Taos Pueblo,** where Governor Bent's attackers were confronted by an American army several weeks later under the command of Colonel Sterling Price. The original church (the ruin of which is a cemetery today) was destroyed in the battle that followed. Spend the night in Taos.

⑤ Leave Taos and travel north on U.S. 64. At the split of U.S. 64 and Route 522, take U.S. 64 to the bridge crossing the Rio Grande. This view is a spectacular one of the wild Rio Grande Gorge, and parking the car and strolling across the bridge on foot is well worth the time (if you're wearing a hat, hold onto it; the winds are brisk on the bridge). Return on U.S. 64 the way you came to Route 522, turn north and continue to the town of Questa. Take Route 38 east to **Red River,** a resort town known primarily for its nearby ski slopes.

⑥ Continuing on Route 38 brings you to the village of **Eagle Nest,** where you will pick up U.S. 64 East and proceed through the beautiful Cimarron Canyon to **Cimarron.** The town was once the administrative seat for the gigantic Maxwell Land Grant, which spread over 2 million acres of northern New Mexico and southern Colorado. Take a look at the historic **St. James Hotel,** which was started in 1880 as a saloon by Henri Lambert, onetime personal chef to both President Abraham Lincoln and General Ulysses S. Grant. Over the next several years, legend has it that as many as 26 men were killed within its walls. See the **Old Aztec Mill Museum** (across the street from the hotel) and other nearby attractions.

⑦ If you have ever been a Boy Scout, you'll want to make a short side trip to see the historic **Philmont Scout Ranch.** The original land in Philmont Ranch (nearly 36,000 acres) was given to the Boy Scouts in 1938 by Waite Phillips, an Oklahoma oilman. Three years later, more acreage was donated, and today the ranch consists of around 140,000 acres. After visiting Philmont, return to Cimarron and proceed back to U.S. 64 toward Raton.

⑧ Just before reaching Raton, on your left, is the **National Rifle Association's Whittington Center and Range.** The range, on 52 square mi, offers hunting in season, an impressive variety of fully equipped shooting ranges, camping and recreational facilities, and a training center.

NEW MEXICO RULES OF THE ROAD

License Requirements: As a visitor driving an automobile in New Mexico you must have a valid driver's license from your home state.

Right Turn on Red: A driver can turn right on a red light *after* coming to a full stop.

Seat Belt and Helmet Laws: A state law requires automobile drivers and passengers to use seat belts. Although bikers are not required by law to wear helmets, they are strongly urged to do so. Children riding in automobiles must be restrained in the back seat, and if they are age four or under, they must be restrained in a children's car seat secured in the back seat.

Speed Limits: Individual speed limits are posted in all municipalities. Most interstates maintain a 75-mph speed limit, depending on location.

For More Information: Contact the **New Mexico Highway Hotline** | 800/432–4269.

⑨ Pick up I–25 at Raton and head toward the Colorado border and through historic and beautiful **Raton Pass.** Turn around on the other side of the Pass and proceed back along I–25 to Raton.

⑩ You should allow yourself some time to visit historic downtown **Raton** and its sights. The town offers an impressive walking tour that highlights the **Santa Fe Railroad Depot,** one of the few remaining vestiges of Raton's once thriving rail facilities, as well as a number of commercial buildings, theaters, hotels, and saloons, dating from the mid- to late 19th century and all remarkably well preserved. There are a number of fine hotel–motel facilities in Raton, so plan on dining and spending the night there.

⑪ Leave Raton early and proceed south on I–25 through Maxwell and Springer until you arrive at Exit 366. Follow Route 161 to **Fort Union National Monument.** Fort Union is an impressive sight; after stopping by the visitor center, walk among its ruins for a sense of what military life was like on the southwestern frontier.

⑫ Leaving Fort Union, follow Route 161 back to I–25 and continue southwest to **Las Vegas.** Visit the many shops clustered around the town Plaza. Return to I–25 and continue toward Santa Fe.

⑬ At Route 63 (Exit 307), leave the interstate and head north to **Pecos National Historical Park.** As in the case of Fort Union, you will want to hike the short trail to fully appreciate this deeply moving and spiritual place. The visitor center maintains a theater, a fine museum, a well-stocked bookstore, and squeaky-clean rest rooms.

Leaving Pecos, return south on Route 63 to I–25 and proceed to **Santa Fe.**

Chimayó

Attractions

Galeria Ortega. The premier gallery in the region features art, gifts, music, southwestern books, and foods of New Mexico. It's next door to Ortega's Weaving Shop. | County Rd. 98 at Hwy. 76 | 505/351–2288 | Mon.–Sat. 9–5:30 (late Mar.–late Oct., also Sun. 11–5).

Ortega's Weaving Shop. The Ortega family of Chimayó has been weaving outstanding products for eight generations; their shop displays samples of their best wares, and there are daily demonstrations of the weaving process. | County Rd. 98 at Hwy. 76 | 505/351–4215 | Mon.–Sat. 9–5.

★ **Santuario de Chimayó.** Legend states that a mysterious light came from the ground on Good Friday in 1810, giving the site of this small frontier adobe church healing properties. The shrine is a National Historic Landmark and is pleasantly free of crass commercialism. Thousands come here each Holy Week. | County Rd. 98 87522 | 505/351–4889 | Daily 9–5:30.

Chapel of Santo Niño de Atocha. Just 200 feet away from the main church, this small chapel built in 1857 is said to have miraculous healing powers. It's named after a boy saint brought from New Mexico who, it is said, lost one of his shoes as he wandered the countryside helping people; it is tradition to place shoes at the foot of his statue as an offering. | Daily 9–5:30.

Dining

★ **Rancho De Chimayó.** Mexican. In a century-old adobe hacienda tucked into the mountains, with whitewashed walls and hand-stripped vigas, this restaurant is still owned and operated by the family that first occupied the house. There's a roaring fireplace in winter and, in summer, a terraced patio shaded by catalpa trees. You can take an after-dinner stroll on the grounds' paths. | Hwy. 98, Chimayó, 87522 | 505/351–4444 | Closed Mon. and Nov.–May | AE, D, DC, MC, V | $$

Leona's de Chimayó. Mexican. Flavored tortillas—from jalapeño to blueberry–chocolate to pesto—are the specialty of this fast-food burrito-and-chili stand at one end of the Santuario de Chimayó parking lot. Anticipate summer crowds. | 4 Medina La., 87522 | 505/351–4569 | Closed Nov.–Apr. No dinner | AE, D, DC, MC, V | $

Cimarron

Attractions

Cimarron Canyon State Park. Palisades Sills, a 400-ft granite formation, dominates this state park 12 mi west of Cimarron on U.S. 64. There's superb rainbow and brown trout fishing here. It's a good place to stop for a morning or afternoon hike. | U.S. 64 | 505/377–6271 | www.emnrd.state.nm.us/nmparks | Daily.

Old Aztec Mill Museum. First operated in 1864, this Old Town mill was built by Lucien Maxwell for $50,000. Today the mill houses four floors of vintage photos, clothing, tools, and memorabilia depicting life in Colfax County from the 1860s forward. | Hwy. 21 | 505/376–2913 | May–Sept., Mon.–Wed. and Fri.–Sat. 9–5, Sun. 1–5. Closed Thurs.

Philmont Scout Ranch. The 140,000-acre Philmont Ranch, 4 mi south of Cimarron on Route 21, is the world's largest private youth camp and was a gift to the Boy Scouts of America by Texas oilman Waite Phillips. If you visit the ranch, you can see the Kit Carson Museum and the Philmont Museum, as well as the Villa Philmonte, Waite Phillips's original summer home. | Hwy. 21 | 505/376–2281 | Weekdays 9–4; June–Aug., weekends 9–4.

Kit Carson Museum. Built on a portion of the original fort founded by Kit Carson and Lucien Maxwell, which is 2 mi south of the main Philmont offices, this interpretive museum has both hands-on exhibits and displays that demonstrate turn-of-the-last-century mountain man life. Hosts, dressed in 1880s period costumes, talk about the history and legends of the area, and you can try your hand at blacksmithing or black powder rifle shooting. | Hwy. 21 | 505/376–2281 | June–Aug., daily 8–5. Closed Sept.–May.

The Philmont Museum and Seton Memorial Library. Across the street from Philmont's main offices and base camp, this museum exhibits photographs, artifacts, and information about the history of the area and the ranch; it also has the extensive book collection of Ernest Thompson Seton, famed naturalist and founder of the Boy Scouts. A gift shop sells Native American jewelry, books, and area memorabilia. | Rte. 21 | 505/376–2281 | June–Aug., daily 8–6; Sept.–May, weekdays 8–5.

Villa Philmonte. Built in 1927, this lavish Mediterranean-style villa was the summer home of oil tycoon Waite Phillips until 1941. The collection here includes brilliantly colored oriental rugs, intricate tilework, antique furnishings, and numerous works of art, as well as photographs of regular guests like Theodore Roosevelt. Reservations for tours must be made at the Philmont Museum and Seton Memorial Library next door. | Rte. 21 | 505/376–2281 | June–Aug., daily 8–5, tours every ½ hour; Sept.–May, tours by appointment only.

St. James Hotel. Dating back to 1872, this still active hotel has sheltered such luminaries as Zane Grey, Wyatt Earp, Doc Holliday, Annie Oakley, Clay Allison, and Buffalo Bill. Sightseeing in the lobby is free if you have dinner or drinks at the hotel; ask about the ghost in Room 18. | 17th and Collinson Sts., 87714 | 505/376–2664 | Daily.

Dining

Colfax Tavern. American/Casual. Also known as Cold Beer, New Mexico, this tavern 11 mi east of Cimarron has been open since Prohibition. In addition to an ongoing card

Shiner Bock on tap, there are Saturday-night dances and a winter *Jeopardy!* ment. The menu includes green-chili burgers, pizza, spaghetti on Monday, and brisket on Wednesday. | U.S. 64 | 505/376–2229 | No credit cards | $

Las Vegas

Attractions

Fort Union National Monument. During its heyday, Fort Union—at a critical point along the Santa Fe Trail about 30 mi north of Las Vegas—was the largest U.S. military establishment in the entire Southwest. Completed in 1869, it served as a supply center for smaller installations across the region. The arrival of the Santa Fe Railroad in the 1880s put the fort out of business, as trains began to bypass the fort and speed much-needed army equipment directly to its destinations. | Hwy. 161 | 505/425–8025 | Memorial Day–Labor Day, daily 8–6; Labor Day–Memorial Day, daily 8–5.

Las Vegas National Wildlife Refuge. Observe American eagles, waterfowl, and a large variety of other wildlife species from your vantage point in this refuge 6½ mi southeast of Las Vegas. It's one of the premier birding sites in the Southwest. | Hwy. 281 | 505/425–3581 | Daily.

Storrie Lake State Park. The lake 6 mi north of Las Vegas has a visitor center and offers windsurfing, fishing, boating, waterskiing, camping, and picnicking facilities. It's a favorite place to catch rainbow and German brown trout. | Hwy. 518 | 505/425–7278 | Daily.

Theodore Roosevelt Rough Riders' Memorial and City Museum. Teddy Roosevelt recruited many members of his Rough Rider regiment from New Mexico and the surrounding territory. After the Spanish–American War, Roosevelt's veterans chose Las Vegas as their reunion site, and over the years the town became the repository for many Rough Rider artifacts. | 727 Grand Ave., 87701 | 505/454–1401 | Weekdays 9–noon and 1–4, Sat. 10–3.

Dining

Blackjack's Grill. Italian. The steaks here are the best in town, and the Old Mexico pork tenderloins, seafood enchiladas, flan and New York cheesecake are also worthy. Both the romantic, old-world dining room or patio by the garden are pleasant places to eat. | 1133 Grand Ave., 87701 | 505/425–6791 or 888/448–8438 | fax 505/425–0417 | Closed Mon. | AE, D, MC, V | $$

El Rialto Restaurant & Lounge. Mexican. In an historic 1890s building packed with antiques, this popular restaurant offers perfectly blended margaritas to set the mood for fajitas, enchiladas, and chiles rellenos. A salad bar and kids menu are available. | 141 Bridge St. | 505/454–0037 | Closed Sun. | AE, D, MC, V | $–$$

Estella's Restaurant. Mexican. Smothering burritos in green chili since 1950, Estrella's is one of the best places to stop for a bite. Don't be put off by the eatery's modest appearance. | 148 Bridge St., 87701 | 505/454–0048 | Closed Sun. No dinner Mon.–Wed. | AE, D, MC, V | $–$$

Landmark Grill at the Plaza Hotel. American. Off the lobby of the landmark Plaza Hotel, the Grill serves New Mexican cuisine with Mexican influences. Try the quail, green chili posole, or *arroz con pollo,* and avail yourself of the large wine selection. | 230 Old Town Plaza | 505/425–3591 | AE, D, DC, MC, V | $–$$

Raton

Attractions

Capulin Volcano National Monument. Walking along the rim of Capulin Mountain, you'll see parts of five states. The volcano is young—only about 60,000 years old—but it has been dormant long enough for you to descend into its crater for a look around. It's 29 mi east of Raton on U.S. 64/U.S. 87 to Capulin, then 3½ mi north. | Off Hwy. 325 88414 | 505/278–2201 | www.nps.gov/cavo | Memorial–Labor Day, daily 7:30–6:30; Labor Day–Memorial Day, daily 8–4:30.

Folsom Museum. Life in eastern New Mexico during the late 19th and early 20th centuries is documented here. Nearby, but on private property, is the site of the discovery of flint points belonging to Folsom Man, one of the earliest humans known to occupy North America. Folsom is 7 mi north of Capulin. | Main St., Folsom | 505/278–2122 or 505/278–3616 | Memorial Day–Labor Day, daily 10–5; May, Sept., weekends 10–5 or by appointment; Oct.–Apr., by appointment only.

Maxwell National Wildlife Refuge. Home to dozens of species of waterfowl, plus bald eagles and deer, this is the site of some of the best trout fishing in northern New Mexico. It's 23 mi south of Raton, 4 mi northwest of Maxwell. | Off Hwy. 505 87728 | 505/375–2331 | southwest.fws.gov/refuges/newmex/maxwell.html | Daily.

National Rifle Association Whittington Center. The country's largest and most complete shooting facility, with ranges for pistols, large- and small-bore rifles, and shotguns, is 10 mi southwest of Raton. | U.S. 64 | 505/445–3615 | www.nrawc.org | Daily; call for range times.

Raton Museum. Artifacts from Raton's past, a fine photo collection, regional artwork, and old musical instruments are just a few of the varied items in this museum. | 218 S. 1st St. | 505/445–8979 | Memorial Day–Labor Day, Tues.–Sat. 9–5; Labor Day–Memorial Day, Wed.–Sat. 10–4.

Sugarite Canyon State Park. The site of an early coal mining camp that drew miners from all over the world, this park is 10 mi northeast of Raton. | Hwy. 526 | 505/445–5607 | Daily.

Dining

Pappas' Sweet Shop. American. Collectibles and antiques give a sense of history and pleasant nostalgia at this spot known for steaks, pasta, and seafood. Kids' menu. | 1201 S. 2nd St., 87740 | 505/445–9811 | Closed Sun. | AE, D, MC, V | $–$$$

Hot Dog Depot. American/Casual. Cute, and smoke-free, this café inside a bright turquoise vintage house serves hearty, homemade chili, soup, and salads. The fresh coffee is a bargain and an eye-opener. | 100 S. 3rd St., 87740 | 505/445–9090 | Closed Sun. No dinner | MC, V | $

Lodging

Best Western Sands. A renovated, late-1950s motel with southwestern decor, the rooms here are a good size and comfortable. Restaurant. In-room data ports, some refrigerators. Cable TV. Pool. Hot tub. Playground. Business services. | 300 Clayton Rd. | 505/445–2737 or 800/518–2581 | fax 505/445–4053 | www.bestwestern.com | 50 rooms | AE, D, DC, MC, V | $–$$

Budget Host Melody Lane Motel. Affordable and unpretentious, this motel is a good choice for a quick stopover. Complimentary Continental breakfast. Refrigerators. Cable TV. Pets allowed. | 136 Canyon Dr. | 505/445–3655 or 800/421–5210 | fax 505/445–3461 | www.budgethost.com | 27 rooms | AE, D, DC, MC, V | $

El Portal. An eccentric hostelry in a restored 1885 downtown building, El Portal exudes personality. The antiques-filled lobby has a working fireplace and a vintage Royal typewriter. Many rooms have themes, such as the Holiday Room, with autographed photos of Hollywood stars. The room amenities are not modern, but the price is right. Adjoining the hotel are 39 apartments leased both short- and long-term. Restaurant. Some kitchenettes. Cable TV. Pets allowed. | 101 N. 3rd St., 87740 | 505/445–3631 or 888/362–7345 | 15 rooms, 39 apartments | MC, V | $

Oasis. A basic old-fashioned roadside motel off I–25, this is a no-frills choice, but comfortable. Restaurant. Cable TV. | 1445 S. 2nd St., 87740 | 505/445–2221 | 14 rooms | Closed late Jan.–early Feb. | AE, D, MC, V | $

Red River

Attractions

Pioneer Canyon Trail. Take this 3-mi-long auto trek and go back more than 100 years to the days when gold and copper were mined in the surrounding mountains. The trip is 2–3 hours long if you stop at all of the marked sites. The trail starts behind the Arrowhead Lodge at the end of Pioneer Road. | Pioneer Rd. 87758 | 505/754–2366 | Daily.

Red River Ski Area. Fifty-eight trails and a 1,600-ft vertical drop are the highpoints of this ski area, a big winter draw for tourists. | Pioneer Rd. | 505/754–2223 or 800/348–6444 | taoswebb.com/redriver | Thanksgiving–Apr. for skiing.

Dining

Sundance. Mexican. Fajitas or burritos are good bets in this southwestern-style restaurant with a large fireplace in the dining room. Kids' menu. Beer and wine only. | 401 High St. | 505/754–2971 | Closed Apr.–mid-May. No lunch | AE, D, DC, MC, V | $–$$

Redwood Café. American/Casual. You can start your day with fresh biscuits, French toast, or an omelet at this restaurant on Main Street. The lunch menu includes barbecued beef brisket sandwiches, chili dogs, and hamburgers. Kids' menu. | 210 Main St. | 505/754–2951 | Breakfast also available; no dinner | MC, V | $

Shotgun Willie's. Barbecue. The meat here is smoked over hickory and mesquite and then served with Willie's own barbecue sauce. Try the barbecued chicken sandwich, the sliced brisket, or the charbroiled burger. The all-you-can eat breakfast is popular. | Main and Pioneer Sts. | 505/754–6505 | Breakfast also available | No credit cards | $

Santa Fe

Attractions

Cristo Rey Church. The largest adobe structure in the United States, this church is considered by many to be the finest example of pueblo-style architecture anywhere. It was completed in 1940 to commemorate the 400th anniversary of Francisco Vásquez de Coronado's exploration of the Southwest. | Canyon Rd. and Christo Rey St., 87501 | 505/983–8528 | Daily 8–7.

La Fonda. A *fonda* (inn) has stood on this site facing the southeast corner of the Plaza since 1610, though the current structure dates to 1922. Architect Isaac Hamilton Rapp, whose Rio Grande–Pueblo Revival structures put Santa Fe style on the map, was the original architect; it was remodeled in 1926 by architect John Gaw Meem. Because of its proximity to the Plaza, La Fonda has been a gathering place for actors, politicos, and cowboys. It is appropriately referred to as "The Inn at the End of the Trail." | 100

E. San Francisco St., 87501 | 505/982–5511 or 800/523–5002 | fax 505/988–2952 | www.lafondasantafe.com | Daily.

Museum of Fine Arts. Santa Fe's oldest art museum opened in 1917 and contains one of the finest regional collections in the United States, displaying the work of many early New Mexico artists who settled and worked around Santa Fe and Taos. | 107 W. Palace Ave. | 505/476–5072 | www.nmculture.org | Tues.–Sun. 10–5.

Institute of American Indian Arts Museum. Native American art from a range of tribes, including those from Alaska and the Southwest, are displayed at this handsomely renovated former post office. You'll find paintings, photography, sculptures, prints, and other crafts. | 108 Cathedral Pl | 505/983–8900 | www.iaiancad.org | Daily 9–5.

New Mexico State Capitol. Sometimes called the Roundhouse, New Mexico's capitol building is built in the shape of a Zia sun symbol. Artwork by regional artists adorns the lobby. | Paseo de Peralta and Old Santa Fe Trail | 505/986–4589 | Weekdays 8–5.

Georgia O'Keeffe Museum. One of many painters who moved to Santa Fe in the early part of the 20th century, Georgia O'Keeffe settled near Santa Fe and focused some of her most famous paintings on southwestern themes. This private museum devoted to her art opened in 1997 and contains 120 of her works. O'Keeffe's favorite foods are for sale in the café. | 217 Johnson St. | 505/995–0785 | www.okeeffemuseum.org | Nov.–July, Mon., Tues., Thurs., Sat. 10–5, Fri. 10–8; Aug.–Oct., also open Wed. noon–8.

★ **Palace of the Governors.** The oldest public building in continuous use in the United States, this humble-looking one-story adobe structure is the headquarters of the Museum of New Mexico. Part of the fun in visiting Santa Fe is to walk under the portals of the palace and view all the wonderful handmade jewelry, the work of native New Mexicans, for sale on blankets lining the street. The museum, bookstore, and printing shop on the premises are all must-sees. | Palace Ave. (north side of the Plaza) | 505/476–5100 | www.nmculture.org | Tues.–Sun. 10–5.

Pecos National Historical Park. On land donated by actress Greer Garson, 2 mi south of Pecos and 26 mi southeast of Santa Fe, this park presents the fascinating story of one of the largest prehistoric pueblos in the Southwest. Take the walking tour and visit the museum and bookstore. | Hwy. 63 (I–25, exit 299), Pecos | 505/757–6414 | Memorial Day–Labor Day, daily 8–6; Labor Day–Memorial Day, daily 8–5.

★ **San Miguel Mission.** Originally built in 1610, the roof of this church was burned during the Pueblo Revolt of 1680; the church was restored and enlarged in 1710. The mission served as a place of worship for Spanish soldiers and settlers and Native American converts. Mass is held on Sunday only. | 401 Old Santa Fe Trail | 505/983–3974 | Weekdays 9–4:30.

Sena Plaza. In the heart of downtown, this plant- and tree-filled plaza, complete with songbirds, is filled with modern shops and eateries. | Between E. Palace Ave. and Nusbaum St., and between Washington and Otero Sts.

Dining

★ **Cafe Pasqual's.** Southwestern. Regional and Latin American specialties such as huevos Motuleños (black beans and eggs over a blue corn tortilla with tomatillo sauce and goat cheese) and chili-rubbed, pan-roasted salmon are the stars here. Murals are by Oaxacan artist Leo Uigildo-Martinez. Sunday brunch. Beer and wine only. No smoking. | 121 Don Gaspar Ave. | 505/983–9340 | Breakfast also available | AE, MC, V | $$–$$$

Blue Corn Cafe. Mexican. In the heart of historic downtown, this second-floor eatery may very well be the best restaurant for the money in Santa Fe. Try the tortilla burger or Portobello fajitas. Kids' menu. | 133 Water St. | 505/984–1800 | AE, D, DC, MC, V | $–$$

★ **Plaza Café.** American/Casual. At this diner, operating since 1918, walls are hung with vintage photos. The eclectic American diner menu includes spicy pasta, blue corn enchiladas, and New Mexico meat loaf. Kids' menu. Beer and wine only. | 54 Lincoln Ave. | 505/982–1664 | Reservations not accepted | AE, D, MC, V | $–$$

Zia Diner. American. Try one of the weeknight blue-plate specials at this upscale diner, or just enjoy a thick slice of strawberry-rhubarb pie. Service is fast and friendly, and the food is fresher and more imaginative than most diner fare. Patio dining is also available. | 326 S. Guadalupe St., 87501 | 505/988–7008 | fax 505/820–7677 | AE, MC, V | $–$$

Lodging

★ **Hotel Santa Fe.** Run by the Indians of Picurís Pueblo, this three-story downtown hotel (about a 10-minute walk from the Plaza) has locally made furnishings and pueblo paintings, many by Gerald Nailor. Regular rooms are fairly small. Restaurant, bar (with entertainment). Minibars. Cable TV. Pool. Hot tub. Laundry facilities, laundry service. Business services, airport shuttle. | 1501 Paseo de Peralta, 87501 | 505/982–1200 or 800/825–9876 | fax 505/984–2211 | www.hotelsantafe.com | 40 rooms, 89 suites | AE, D, DC, MC, V | $$$–$$$$

Adobe Abode. Rooms in this B&B near the Georgia O'Keeffe Museum contain objects the owner has gathered from around the world. Some rooms have fireplaces and/or private patios. Complimentary breakfast. Cable TV. | 202 Chapelle St., 87501 | 505/983–3133 | fax 505/424–3027 | www.adobeabode.com | 6 rooms (3 with shower only) | D, MC, V | $$$

Santa Fe Motel and Inn. Five blocks from the Plaza, this motor hotel is an unusually successful upgrade of a standard motel. Some rooms have fireplaces, and there are an outdoor deck and patio. Complimentary Continental breakfast. Some kitchenettes, some microwaves, some refrigerators. Cable TV, some in-room VCRs. Business services. | 510 Cerrillos Rd., 87501 | 505/982–1039 or 800/999–1039 | fax 505/986–1275 | www.santafemotelinn.com | 13 rooms, 8 casitas | AE, D, DC, MC, V | $$–$$$

Spencer House. Four blocks from the Plaza and around the corner from the Georgia O'Keeffe Museum, this 1920s adobe is furnished with English and American Colonial antiques. Bathrooms are spacious; some rooms have fireplaces. Complimentary breakfast. Some in-room hot tubs. Cable TV. No kids under 12. | 222 McKenzie, 87501 | 505/988–3024 or 800/647–0530 | fax 505/984–9862 | www.spencerhse-santafe.com | 6 rooms | AE, MC, V | $$–$$$

Stage Coach Inn. Quiet rooms done in southwestern pastels and larger than average tile-floor bathrooms are selling points of this small, basic Santa Fe–style adobe motel, which provides a free 10-minute shuttle to the plaza. Picnic area. Cable TV. | 3360 Cerrillos Rd., 87505 | 505/471–0707 | fax 505/471–0707 | 14 rooms | AE, MC, V | $$–$$$

Taos

Attractions

Carson National Forest. Surrounding Taos and spanning almost 1½ million acres across northern New Mexico, the forest has over 50 recreation sites, including lakes, the Wheeler Peak Wilderness Area, and Pecos Wilderness Area. You can hike, bike, fish, or ski, or just look at the wildflowers. | Headquarters: 208 Cruz Alta Rd., 87571 | 505/758–6200 | www.fs.fed.us | Headquarters weekdays 8–4:30.

D. H. Lawrence Ranch and Memorial. The author of *Lady Chatterley's Lover* was one of the first writers to come to the region. The ranch where Lawrence lived for almost two years, 15 mi north of Taos, is now an education and conference center. The house is not open to the public, but you can visit the memorial where Lawrence's ashes were scattered and where his wife Frieda is buried. | Hwy. 522, San Cristobal | 505/776–2245 | Daily 8:30–5.

Fechin Institute. Built between 1927 and 1933 by artist Nicolai Fechin (who died in 1955), this adobe house is a showcase of daring colorful portraits and landscapes. | 227 Paseo del Pueblo Norte, 87571 | 505/758–1710 | Wed.–Sun. 10–2.

Governor Bent Home and Museum. Newly appointed New Mexico governor Charles Bent was killed in this house during the Taos Revolt of January 1847 by a mob protesting the U.S. annexation of New Mexico. See the hole in the wall through which Bent's wife and children tried to escape. | 117A Bent St., 87571 | 505/758–2376 | Daily 10–5.

Kit Carson Home and Museum. Mountain man Kit Carson lived here with his New Mexican wife, Josefa Jaramillo. Exhibits include 19th-century lifestyle artifacts and an herb and flower garden. The bookstore is well stocked with regional titles. | Kit Carson Rd. at U.S. 64, 87571 | 505/758–4741 | Daily 9–5.

Rio Grande Gorge Bridge. A spectacular view greets you as you walk across this bridge, high above the Rio Grande. | U.S. 64, 11 mi northwest of Taos | No phone | Daily.

San Francisco de Asís Church. Restored in 1979, this Spanish Mission–style church dates to the 18th century. It is most famous for the painting *Shadow of the Cross,* by Henri Ault, on which each evening the shadow of a cross appears over Christ's shoulder. The phenomenon is unexplained. | Hwy. 68, 500 yards south of Hwy. 518, Rancho de Taos | 505/758–2754 | Mon.–Sat. 9–4; masses on Sun. at 7, 9, and 11:30.

Taos Plaza. At the heart of the Taos downtown area, the Plaza is one of the oldest parts of the city. By a special act of Congress, the U.S. flag flies 24 hours a day here in honor of Kit Carson's stand against the Confederacy during the Civil War. | Don Fernando Rd. 85751 | No phone | Daily.

★ **Taos Pueblo.** For nearly 1,000 years the mud-and-straw adobe walls of Taos Pueblo have sheltered Tiwa-speaking Native Americans. A United Nations World Heritage Site, this is the largest multistory pueblo structure in the United States. The pueblo today appears much as it did when the first Spanish explorers arrived in New Mexico in 1540. Bread is still baked in *hornos* (outdoor domed ovens) and artisans of the Taos Pueblo produce and sell (tax-free) traditionally handcrafted wares. The public is invited to certain ceremonial dances held throughout the year. Respect the RESTRICTED AREA signs that protect the privacy of residents and native religious sites. | 505/758–9593 or 505/758–1028 | taosvacationguide.com/history/pueblo.html | Daily 8–5; closed during certain ceremonies and funerals.

Taos Ski Valley. Included in many top-10 ski resort lists in the United States and Canada, this resort is 18 mi northeast of Taos. It has a world-class ski school and 72 runs, though there is no snowboarding permitted. | Taos Ski Valley Rd. (County Rd. 150) | 505/776–2291; 800/776–1111 (accommodations) | www.skitaos.org | Late Nov.–early Apr.

Dining

★ **Trading Post Café.** Contemporary. The imaginative menu offers such appetizers as marinated salmon gravlax and paella. For dessert try the homemade raspberry sorbet or the flan. | 4178 Paseo del Pueblo Sur, Ranchos de Taos | 505/758–5089 | Closed Sun. | D, DC, MC, V | $–$$$

Apple Tree. Contemporary. Some say this is the best restaurant in Taos. Dine indoors, surrounded by original art, or sit out in a courtyard, where you can watch the sparrows come to beg crumbs. Try the grilled lamb or chicken fajitas. The restaurant is one block north of the Plaza and a block south of the convention center. Sunday brunch. Beer and wine only. | 123 Bent St. | 505/758–1900 | AE, D, DC, MC, V | $–$$

Orlando's. Southwestern. Frequented by locals, this family-run restaurant serves chicken enchiladas, blue-corn enchiladas, and shrimp burritos. The intimate dining room is casual, and take-out service is popular. Off Paseo del Pueblo Norte. | 114 Don Juan Valdez La. | 505/751–1450 | Closed Sun. | No credit cards | $

Lodging

★ **Hacienda del Sol.** Mabel Dodge Luhan, an heiress who drew literati to the region, owned this pueblo-style house. Most rooms have kiva-style fireplaces, southwestern handcrafted furnishings, and original artwork. This has been named one of the most romantic places to stay in Taos. Picnic area, complimentary breakfast. No air-conditioning, refrigerators. TV in common area. Business services. No smoking. | 109 Mabel Dodge La. | 505/758–0287 | fax 505/751–0319 | www.taoshaciendadelsol.com | 11 rooms (2 with shower only), 2 suites | MC, V | $$–$$$$

Casa Benavides Bed & Breakfast Inn. One block from the Plaza, this B&B combines the charm of an old Taos adobe with modern luxuries. Rooms are furnished with antiques and original artwork, and there is a lovely courtyard in the main building. Many rooms have fireplaces and skylights. Complimentary breakfast. Some room phones, some kitchenettes, some refrigerators. Cable TV, some in-room VCRs, no TV in some rooms. 2 hot tubs. | 137 Kit Carson Rd., 87571 | 505/758–1772 or 800/552–1772 | fax 505/758–5738 | www.taosnet.com/casabena | 33 rooms | AE, D, MC, V | $$–$$$

Best Western Kenicha Lodge de Taos. In a pueblo-style adobe, the large rooms are actually separate casitas and are positioned around the "Dance Circle," where a troupe from Taos Pueblo perform nightly ritual dances from May through October. The handmade and hand-painted furnishings are wonderful accents. Kids under 12 stay free. 2 restaurants, bar, complimentary Continental breakfast. In-room data ports, some microwaves, some refrigerators. Cable TV. Pool. Hair salon, hot tub. Shops. Laundry facilities. Business services. No pets. | 413 N. Pueblo Rd. | 505/758–2275 or 800/522–4462 | fax 505/758–9207 | www.kachinalodge.com | 118 rooms | AE, D, DC, MC, V | $–$$

Hotel La Fonda de Taos. On Taos Plaza, this adobe hotel has many antiques and a collection of erotic paintings by D. H. Lawrence (which can be viewed for a small fee). The hotel is just steps away from the town's shops, galleries, and restaurants. No TV in some rooms, TV in common area. No smoking. | 108 S. Plaza | 505/758–2211 or 800/833–2211 | fax 505/758–8508 | www.silverhawk.com/taos/lafonda.html | 24 rooms | AE, MC, V | $–$$

Old Taos Guesthouse. Once an adobe hacienda, this B&B is on 7½ acres of land. All rooms have private entrances, private baths, and either a king, queen, or twin bed. Some rooms have skylights or fireplaces, and you'll get a magnificent view from the outdoor hot tub. Complimentary Continental breakfast. No room phones, some kitchenettes. TV in common area. Hot tub. No smoking. | 1028 Witt Rd. | 505/758–5448 or 800/758–5448 | fax 505/758–5448 | www.oldtaos.com | 9 rooms | MC, V | $–$$

ON THE TRAIL OF BILLY THE KID
FROM LAS CRUCES TO THREE RIVERS

Distance: Approximately 500 mi   Time: 4–5 days
Overnight Breaks: Las Cruces, Alamogordo, Ruidoso

Of all the outlaws associated with the history of New Mexico, the one who stands out is Billy the Kid. This tour of the south-central section of the state passes through

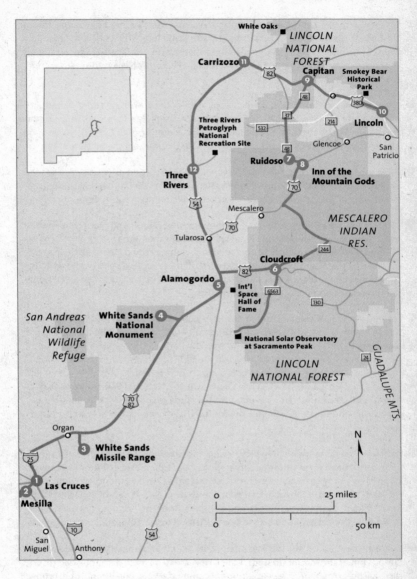

sites with links to the Kid, including the towns of Mesilla, Lincoln, and White Oaks. Along the way you'll also see the White Sands National Monument, the Space Hall of Fame, and the natural beauty of the state. Weather conditions in this region are mild year-round, except for parts of winter in the highlands.

1 The tour begins in the morning in **Las Cruces,** New Mexico's second-largest city. Las Cruces was established in 1848, when the U.S. Army placed a small military post there. Five years later, when the Gadsden Purchase was ratified, the entire region became American territory. There's plenty to see and a good place to get your bearings is the **Las Cruces Museum of Natural History.** Consider spending the night here before continuing.

➋ On the outskirts of Las Cruces is the historic village of **Mesilla.** For a brief period during the Civil War, it was the unofficial capital of the Confederate Territory of Arizona. Billy the Kid was once incarcerated for murder in Mesilla, but escaped. Today the cluster of shops and restaurants lining the **Old Mesilla Plaza** offers everything from crafts to fine food.

➌ Leaving Las Cruces, take U.S. 70 northeast out of town and drive the 25 mi to the entrance of the **White Sands Missile Range.** You will pass through a security station, and if you happen to be there on the first Saturday in either April or October, you will be able to tour the Trinity Site, where America's first atomic bomb was detonated.

➍ After you leave the range, turn back northeast on U.S. 70 and drive until you see the entrance (about 30 mi) to **White Sands National Monument** on your left. This natural wonder encompasses nearly 200,000 acres of glistening gypsum dunes.

➎ After viewing the dunes, follow U.S. 70 into **Alamogordo,** a good place to spend the night. A must-see is the **International Space Hall of Fame,** a four-story cube perched on the side of a mountain. It honors men and women who have made their marks on space research and exploration, and even offers simulated space walks on Mars. **The Alameda Park Zoo** is one of the oldest animal parks in the Southwest and is home to hundreds of domestic and foreign species.

➏ Leaving Alamogordo northward on U.S. 54, proceed until you arrive at the highway's junction with U.S. 82, which you will take to the town of **Cloudcroft.** In the early 1900s surveyors gave the romantic name to the town after spying a single white cloud hovering over a nearby meadow, which in the Old English vernacular is "croft." Today it's a mountain retreat that has great year-round temperatures and one of the nation's highest golf courses. While there, visit the **National Solar Observatory at Sacramento Peak,** the national center for the study of the sun. Pick up Route 244 at Cloudcroft and follow it through the Mescalero Apache Indian Reservation to its junction with U.S. 70.

➐ Follow U.S. 70 eastward into the picturesque Sacramento Mountain town of **Ruidoso** and spend the night. If you tour between May and Labor Day, visit **Ruidoso Downs,** claimed by many to be the premier horse-racing facility in America. Nearby is the **Hubbard Museum of the American West,** which displays a variety of Indian artifacts, horse-drawn vehicles, original art, and antiques. Brush up on your Billy the Kid lore at the **Billy the Kid National Scenic Byway Visitor Center,** adjacent to the museum.

➑ Just outside Ruidoso, on the Mescalero Apache Indian Reservation, is the world-famous **Inn of the Mountain Gods.** Called New Mexico's most distinguished resort, the Apache-owned inn offers luxurious accommodations, fine dining, golf, tennis, boating, fishing, and gambling, including poker and bingo.

➒ Leave Ruidoso on Route 48 and drive north to **Capitan,** the home of the **Smokey Bear Historical Park.** Smokey, the survivor of a 1950 forest fire near town, was the inspiration for the cartoon mascot adopted by the National Council for Forest Fire Prevention. You'll see Smokey's gravesite here, as well as the **Smokey Bear Museum,** which contains an exhibit of Smokey memorabilia.

➓ Proceed east on U.S. 380 to **Lincoln.** Billy the Kid reportedly spent the night at the Ellis Store Country Inn at Mile Marker 98. Prepare to spend at least half a day in Lincoln. Tour the restored frontier town and site of Billy's last escape from the law: he met his end at the hand of Sheriff Pat Garrett near Lincoln in the town of Fort Sumner. The Kid is buried at Fort Sumner Military Cemetery.

⑪ Backtrack on U.S. 380 to Capitan and then continue until you reach **Carrizozo.** Twelve miles northeast of here, via U.S. 54 and Route 349, lies the legendary ghost town of **White Oaks**—an old haunt (no pun intended) of Billy the Kid—which once boasted a population of 4,000, supporting three churches, two hotels, four newspapers, and many saloons.

⑫ Returning to Carrizozo, continue southward along U.S. 54 through the village of Oscuro to the community of **Three Rivers** and the turnoff to **Three Rivers Petroglyph National Recreation Site** on your left. Here, more than 500 ancient drawings and rock carvings grace the cliffs overlooking the Tularosa basin. Spend as much time as you can spare here to enjoy the interpretive trail and other outdoor activities.
Return to U.S. 54 and proceed southward on your way back to **Las Cruces.**

Alamogordo

Attractions
Alameda Park Zoo. More than 90 displays highlight domestic and foreign wildlife in natural settings. | 1021 N. White Sands Blvd., (U.S. 54/70) | 505/439–4290 or 505/437–1292 | Daily 9–5.

Eagle Ranch. You'll find the largest grove of pistachio trees in New Mexico here—some 12,000 trees—4 mi north of the White Sands Mall. Tour the farm, linger in the art gallery, and buy some nuts to take home. | 7288 Hwy. 54, at Hwy. 70 88310 | 505/434–0035 or 800/432–0999 | www.eagleranchpistachios.com | Sept.–May, weekdays at 1:30; June–Aug., weekdays at 10 and 1:30.

Space Center–International Space Hall of Fame. Space and early rocketry exhibits, a planetarium, and outdoor displays and parks are among the attractions at this facility 2 mi east of downtown Alamogordo. | Top of NM Hwy. 2001 | 505/437–2840 or 877–333–6589 | Weekdays 9–5.

Three Rivers Petroglyph National Recreation Site. Ancient Indians, who lived in the area between AD 1000 and 1350, carved thousands of pictures on the surrounding rocks here about 35 mi north of Alamogordo. It's one of the largest petroglyph sites in the United States. 27 RV hookups. | County Rd. B30 | 505/525–4300 | Daily.

★ **White Sands National Monument.** Encompassing 275 square mi, this is the largest deposit of gypsum in the world. It's 15 mi southwest of Alamogordo, between the San Andre and Sacramento mountains. | Off I–70 | 505/679–2599 or 505/479–6124 | Memorial Day–mid-Aug., daily 7–10; mid-Aug.–Memorial Day, daily 7–5.

Dining
Margo's Mexican Food. Mexican. *Chalupas* (beans, meat, and cheese served on crisp tortillas) are the specialty at this casual, family-owned spot. In winter try *menudo*, steaming hot hominy and tripe. | 504 1st St., 88310 | 505/434–0689 | AE, D, MC, V | $–$$

Palm Side Restaurant. Chinese. Popular lunch and dinner buffets include dumplings, chow mein, and chicken wings. | 905 S. White Sands Blvd. | 505/437–8644 | D, MC, V | $–$$

Ramona's Restaurant. Mexican. Locals like this casual family eatery. Try the chimichangas or huevos rancheros. | 2913 White Sands Blvd., 88310 | 505/437–7616 | AE, MC, V | $–$$

Compass Rose. Continental. Patterned after a European-style pub, this unusual establishment has wooden bench seating. Try the salads and hot sandwiches, including Reubens, pepper steaks, and the "ultimate ham and cheese." | 2203 E. 1st St., 88310 | 505/434–9633 | AE, D, MC, V | $

Lodging

Best Western Desert Aire. You'll find larger than average rooms in this attractive adobe-and-brick building. Complimentary Continental breakfast. Some microwaves. Cable TV. Pool. Hot tub, sauna. Laundry facilities. Pets allowed. | 1021 S. White Sands Blvd. | 505/437–2110 | fax 505/437–1898 | www.bestwestern.com | 100 rooms | AE, D, DC, MC, V | $–$$

Holiday Inn Express. Rooms at this comfortable, two-story motel are accessible from an interior hallway, which reduces ambient noise. It's two blocks from the junction of highways 54 and 70. Complimentary Continental breakfast. In-room data ports. Cable TV. Pool. Beauty salon. Laundry facilities, laundry service. Business services. Pets allowed. | 1401 S. White Sands Blvd., 88310 | 505/437–7100 or 800/465–4329 | fax 505/437–7100 | www.hiexpress.com | 108 rooms | AE, D, DC, MC, V | $–$$

White Sands Inn. On Alamogordo's main street, this lovely two-story motel is within walking distance of three restaurants. It's a favorite of business travelers, who appreciate its proximity to the downtown area. Complimentary Continental breakfast. Some microwaves, refrigerators. Cable TV. Pool. Hot tub. Laundry facilities. Business services. | 1020 S. White Sands Blvd. | 505/434–4200 or 800/255–5061 | fax 505/437–8872 | 96 rooms | AE, D, DC, MC, V | $

Carrizozo

Attractions

Sierra Blanca Brewing Co. New Mexico's largest microbrewery offers samples and free tours. | 503 12th St., 88301 | 505/648–6606 | fax 505/648–6607 | Daily 9–4.

Valley of Fires Recreation Area. After the lava from an erupting volcano flowed here 1,500 years ago, it cooled and formed a jagged black landscape called the Malpais, now home to bald and golden eagles and many varieties of cactus. Hiking is permitted on the nature trail. The area is 4 mi west of Carrizozo. | U.S. 380 88301 | 505/648–2241 | Visitor center daily 8–4.

Dining

Four Winds Restaurant. American/Casual. Made-from-scratch cinnamon rolls, soups, hefty steaks, and burgers draw truckers, bikers, and travelers to this family-run diner. | U.S. 54/U.S. 380 | 505/648–2964 | fax 505/648–0028 | AE, D, MC, V | $–$$

Outpost Bar & Grill. American. One of New Mexico's venerable green chili hamburger joints, the Outpost is a well-weathered bar decorated with elk racks and the mounted heads of many critters. Enjoy some hand-cut french fries while watching the big-screen TVs or playing billiards and pinball. | 415 Central | 505/648–9994 | No credit cards | $–$$

Gift Gallery. Café. Known locally as "Roy's," named for the owner, Roy Dow, this old-fashioned ice-cream parlor dishes out malts and sundaes at a 1935 working soda fountain. Store fixtures date to the 1880s. | 1200 Ave. E | 505/648–2921 | Closed Sun. | No credit cards | $

Cloudcroft

Attractions

Lincoln National Forest, Sacramento Ranger District. Hiking, backpacking, and fishing are among the activities at this large reserve. | 61 Curlew St., 88317 | 505/682–2551 | www.fs.fed.us/links/forests.shtml | Daily.

National Solar Observatory. At an altitude of 9,200 ft, the National Solar Observatory hosts research scientists from around the world. During the day you can take a self-guided tour, wander the grounds, or peek through one of the telescopes. | Hwy. 6563 | 505/434–7000 | www.sunspot.noao.edu | Visitor center daily 10–4; observatory daily dawn–dusk.

Sacramento Mountains Historical Museum. In a restored log cabin, this small museum displays pioneer and railroad artifacts from the region. | U.S. 82 | 505/682–2932 | Mon.–Tues. and Fri.–Sat. 10–4, Sun. 1–4.

Dining

Rebecca's. Continental. Dine in a turn-of-the-20th-century atmosphere with a mountain view in The Lodge's restaurant. Try the shrimp, steak, or chateaubriand for two. Pianist nightly. Kids' menu. Sunday brunch. | 1 Corona Pl | 505/682–2566 | AE, D, DC, MC, V | $$–$$$$

The Western Bar and Café. American. Alleged to have the best omelets in New Mexico (try the Mexico omelet with green chili, cheese, tomatoes, and ham), this local landmark has served locals and visitors for half a century. Bring the family for a hearty meal, or come for karaoke night on a Thursday and get to know the locals. | 86 Burro St., 88317 | 505/682–2445 | No credit cards | $–$$

Las Cruces

Attractions

Historical Museum of Lawmen. In the front lobby of the Sheriff's Office you'll find displays of weapons used by law-enforcement officers and criminals. Nifty vehicles out front include an 1865 horse buggy, an 1880s hay wagon, and a 1949 classic Ford police car. | 1725 Marquess St., 88005 | 505/525–1911 | Weekdays 8–5.

Las Cruces Museum of Natural History. Hands-on nature exhibits and flora and fauna from the Chihuahuan desert highlight this museum in the Mesilla Valley Mall. | 700 S. Telshor | 505/522–3120 | Mon.–Thurs. 10–5, Fri. 10–8, Sat. 10–5, Sun. noon–5.

New Mexico Farm and Ranch Museum. Agricultural and ranching exhibits cover the history, heritage, and science of farming and ranching in New Mexico in this museum that opened in 1998, 1½ mi east of Las Cruces. | 4100 Dripping Springs Rd., 88011 | 505/522–4100 | Tues.–Sat. 9–5, Sun. noon–5.

White Sands Missile Range. The Range Museum displays historical exhibits and outside, missiles and rockets. Twice a year you can tour the Trinity Site, where the first atomic bomb in the United States was detonated. | U.S. 70, 25 mi east of Las Cruces | 505/678–1134 | www.wsmr.army.mil | Museum: weekdays 8–4:30, Sat. 10–3. Trinity site: 1st Sat. in Apr. and 1st Sat. in Oct., 8–2.

Dining

My Brother's Place. Mexican. Try the *tostadas compuestos*—a concoction of red or green chili, meat, pinto beans, and cheese in a crispy tortilla cup— and wash it down with wine by the pitcher or several varieties of Mexican beer. For dessert, try an *empanada*

(Mexican pastry) or the crème caramel. | 334 S. Main St., 88001 | 505/523–7681 | Closed Sun. | AE, D, DC, MC, V | $–$$

Si Señor. Mexican. A popular business lunch and dinner spot, this restaurant has pleasant and spacious southwestern-style rooms. Entrées emphasize three distinct chili sauces—Las Cruces green (mild and flavorful), Deming red, and a variety described as "smoke," also known as Hatch green. | 1551 E. Amador Ave., 88001 | 505/527–0817 | Reservations not accepted | AE, D, MC, V | $–$$

Nellie's. Mexican. Its tough to find seating in this tiny, diner-style restaurant, but that's because the food is incredible. You wouldn't give this place a second look if you judged it only by its appearance, but the locals eat here in droves. The restaurant has gained national recognition for its mouthwatering dishes, such as chiles rellenos and a combination of enchiladas and tacos. | 1226 Hadley Ave., 88005 | 505/524–9982 | No dinner | No credit cards | $

Lodging

★ **Inn of the Arts.** Built in 1890, this adobe hotel is furnished with antiques, and there's an art gallery on the property; each room is named for an artist. There are fireplaces in the suites. Picnic area, complimentary breakfast. Some kitchenettes, some microwaves, some refrigerators. Cable TV, some in-room VCRs, TV in common area. Gym. Library. Business services. Pets allowed. | 618 S. Alameda, 88005 | 505/526–3326 | fax 505/647–1334 | www.innofthearts.com | 21 rooms, 7 suites | AE, D, DC, MC, V | $$

Hilltop Hacienda B&B. Just minutes from downtown Las Cruces, this inn with mountain views and lovely gardens sits on 20 acres. Rooms are furnished with family heirlooms, and an extra private kitchen is available for guests. Complimentary breakfast. TV in common area. Library. No kids under 12. No smoking. | 2600 Westmoreland, 88012 | 505/382–3556 | fax 505/382–3556 | www.zianet.com/hilltop | 3 rooms | AE, D, MC, V | $–$$

T.R.H. Smith Mansion Bed and Breakfast. In the center of Las Cruces, this historic B&B is a quiet, elegant, and spacious retreat. Each room has a regional theme, reflecting the travels of the owner. Relax on the porch or enjoy a game of billiards. Complimentary Continental breakfast. In-room data ports. TV in common area. Pets allowed. No smoking. | 909 N. Alameda Blvd., 88005 | 505/525–2525 or 800/526–1914 | fax 505/524–8227 | www.smithmansion.com | 4 rooms | AE, D, MC, V | $–$$

Day's End Lodge. Well priced and conveniently located, this local two-story motel with southwestern-style rooms is less than 1 mi from both I–10 and the downtown area. Complimentary Continental breakfast. Cable TV. Pool. Business services. | 755 N. Valley Dr., 88005 | 505/524–7753 | fax 505/523–2127 | 32 rooms | AE, D, MC, V | $

Lincoln

Attractions

Lincoln State Monument. Eleven individual sites around town comprise the monument, including the San Juan Mission, the Tunstall Mercantile Store Museum, and the Lincoln County Courthouse Museum. | Lincoln, 88338 | 505/653–4372 | www.museumofnewmexico.org | Daily 8:30–5.

Historic Lincoln Visitors Center. Native Americans, buffalo soldiers, and the history of the "Five Day Battle"—as the Lincoln County War is known locally—are the subjects of some of the exhibits here. | 88338 | 505/653–4025 | fax 505/653–4627 | www.museumofnewmexico.org | Daily 8:30–5.

Lincoln County Courthouse Museum. Billy the Kid escaped from this building while he was awaiting his execution. Exhibits contain historical documents, including a letter from Billy to Governor Lew Wallace. | Main St. | 505/653–4372 | www.museumofnewmexico.org | Daily 8:30–5.

Tunstall Store Museum. When the state of New Mexico purchased this store in the 1950s, boxes of old inventory—some dating back to the 19th century—were discovered and are now on display. John Chisum and Alexander McSween had their law offices here as well. | Main St. | 505/653–4049 | www.museumofnewmexico.org | Daily 8:30–5.

Dining

Ellis Store Country Inn. Contemporary. Wild game is the specialty here, but a choice of 10 entrées and several delicious desserts are available nightly. The fare is complemented by fine china and crystal and the intimacy of the oldest house in Lincoln County. The prix fixe dinner is six courses. | U.S. 380, Milepost 98 | 800/653–6460 | fax 505/653–4610 | Reservations essential | AE, D, DC, MC, V | $$$$

Wortley Pat Garrett Hotel. American. Pot roast and mashed potatoes are the main attraction here, but you might also want to sample the green-chili stew. Desserts include cobblers and a pineapple upside-down cake. | U.S. 380 88338 | 505/653–4300 | Closed Nov. 1–Apr. 27. No dinner | No credit cards | $

Mesilla

Attractions

Gadsden Museum. Three blocks from the Mesilla Plaza, this museum displays a variety of Native American and early Spanish artifacts. A painting commemorating the Gadsden Purchase is a highlight. | W. Barker Rd. at Hwy. 28 | 505/526–6293 | Mon.–Sat. 9–11 and 1–5.

Stahmann Farms. With over 4,000 acres, this is the largest family-owned pecan orchard in the world, 6 mi south of Mesilla. You can drive through the orchard on Highway 28 or stop by the farm store to sample and buy products made from pecans. | 22505 Hwy. 28 S, La Mesa, 88044 | 505/526–8974 or 800/654–6887 | Store: Mon.–Sat. 9–6, Sun. 11–5.

Dining

★ **Mesón de Mesilla.** Continental. People drive from all over southern New Mexico and even west Texas to dine in this restaurant—in the Mesón de Mesilla B&B—known for seared sturgeon in pesto, chateaubriand for two, and filet mignon. If you stay in the inn, you'll enjoy the restaurant's gourmet breakfasts. Guitarist on weekends. | 1803 Avenida de Mesilla, 88046 | 505/525–2380 | AE, D, DC, MC, V | $$$

Double Eagle. Continental. On the east side of Mesilla Plaza, this restored Territorial-style hacienda still has its century-old wall coverings. The Sunday champagne brunch is worth the trip. Eat in the skylight-covered courtyard. | 308 Calle Guadalupe, 88046 | 505/523–6700 | AE, D, DC, MC, V | $$–$$$

★ **La Posta de Mesilla.** Mexican. A former stagecoach stop for the Butterfield Overland Mail and Wells Fargo stages, this restaurant serves up southwestern favorites. Chiles rellenos and red or green enchiladas are among the offerings; the chefs follow recipes dating back more than 100 years. | 2410 Calle de San Albino, 88046 | 505/524–3524 | Closed Mon. | AE, D, DC, MC, V | $–$$

Lorenzo's. Italian. Try any of the pizzas or pastas, based on old Sicilian recipes, at this intimate spot. | Mesilla Plaza, 2000 Hwy. 292, 88046 | 505/525–3170 | AE, D, MC, V | $–$$

★ **Old Mesilla Pastry Cafe.** Café. Known for delicious baked goods as well as specialty foods such as buffalo and ostrich meat and delicious pizzas, this café is a good stop for breakfast or lunch. | 2790 Avenida de Mesilla, 88046 | 505/525–2636 | Closed Mon., Tues. No dinner | AE, MC, V | $

Ruidoso

Attractions

Billy the Kid National Scenic Byway Visitor Center. Adjacent to the Hubbard Museum of the American West, this is the headquarters for information about Lincoln County, Billy the Kid, and the Scenic Byway. | Hwy. 70 E, Ruidoso Downs | 505/378–5318 | www. byways.org | Memorial Day–Labor Day, daily 9–5:30; Labor Day–Memorial Day, daily 10–5.

Hubbard Museum of the American West. The heritage of the horse is celebrated at this modern museum at Ruidoso Downs. Browse more than 10,000 horse-related artifacts, as well as exhibits documenting the history of the American West. Note one of the world's largest equine sculptures, 255 ft long, by local artist Dave McGary. | 841 U.S. 70 W, Ruidoso Downs | 505/378–4142 or 800/263–5929 | Labor Day–Memorial Day, daily 10–5.

Lincoln National Forest, Smokey Bear Ranger District. The Smokey Bear Ranger District Headquarters in Ruidoso manages approximately 375,000 acres of the more than 1 million acres of pristine Lincoln National Forest. Semi-desert plants, piñon pine, and juniper mingle with high-elevation grasses and flowering plants for a spectacular four-season display of colors. The forest covers four New Mexico counties and is popular for hiking, camping, and fishing. There are many access points around town. | Ruidoso Headquarters: 901 Mecham Dr., 88345 | 505/257–4095 | Daily.

Ruidoso Downs Racetrack and Casino. Each Labor Day, this historic quarter-horse track holds one of the richest races in the world, for $2½ million. The races run from afternoon to early evening, wrapping up by 7 most nights. | 1461 U.S. 70 W, Ruidoso Downs, 88346 | 505/378–4431 | www.ruidownsracing.com | Mid-May–Labor Day, Fri.–Sun., Thurs.–Fri. 3:30–end of last race, Sat.–Sun. 1:30–end of last race.

  Billy the Kid Casino. The casino offers simulcast horse racing from around the country. | U.S. 70, Ruidoso Downs | 505/378–4431 | Sun.–Thurs. 11–11, Fri.–Sat. noon–12.

Smokey Bear Historical State Park. Dedicated to real forest fire survivor Smokey Bear, this park 22 mi north of Ruidoso in Capitan has a picnic area and a museum documenting the life and times of the bear cub, whose grave is nearby. Smokey lived out his life in the National Zoo in Washington, DC, and died in 1976. | 118 Smokey Bear Blvd., Capitan, 88316 | 505/354–2748; 505/354–2298 (museum) | www.emnrd.state.nm.us/forestry/smokey.htm | Daily 9–5.

Dining

Victoria's Romantic Hideaway. Italian. Reserve a table for the entire evening at this intimate place, which accommodates only 14 people, and is geared towards couples. Each diner is served a seven-course meal from a set menu. Known for traditional Sicilian cuisine. Beer and wine only. | 2117 Sudderth Dr. | 505/257–5440 | Reservations essential | MC, V | $$$$

La Lorraine. French. A French Colonial interior with flower arrangements and chandeliers sets the perfect mood for traditional French cuisine, including chateaubriand, beef bourguignonne, and sausage-stuffed quail. Select your favorite wine from a comprehensive list. | 2523 Sudderth Dr., 88355 | 505/257–2954 | Closed Sun. | AE, MC, V | $$–$$$

Lincoln County Grill. American/Casual. The locals come here for quick service and good, inexpensive food. Step up to the counter to order hearty Texas chili, old-fashioned hamburgers, or chicken-fried steak. At breakfast you can have eggs served with fluffy, homemade "Lincoln County" biscuits. Vinyl-covered tables are covered with old coffee, tea, and tobacco tin images. | 2717 Sudderth Dr., 88345 | 505/257–7669 | fax 505/630–8012 | Breakfast also available | AE, D, MC, V | $–$$

Pub 48. American/Casual. Opened by the Sierra Blanca Brewing Company, this pub, with an adobe brick fireplace and wood ceiling, has a cozy, mountain-cabin feel. Try such microbrews as nut-brown ale while sampling pizzas or barbecued brisket. | 441 Mechem Dr., 88345 | 505/257–9559 | Reservations not accepted | Closed Tues. | AE, D, MC, V | $–$$

Lodging

★ **Inn of the Mountain Gods.** On the shores of Lake Mescalero, this sprawling resort, 3½ mi southwest of Ruidoso, has its own casino and a variety of recreational activities. Rooms are attractive and large. 2 restaurants, bars (with entertainment), room service. Cable TV. Pool, lake, wading pool. Sauna. 18-hole golf course, putting green. Hiking, horseback riding. Fishing, bicycles. Business services, airport shuttle. | Carrizo Canyon Rd., Mescalero, 88340 | 505/257–5141 or 800/545–9011 | fax 505/257–6173 | 252 rooms | www.innofthemountaingods.com | AE, D, DC, MC, V | $$–$$$

Best Western Swiss Chalet Inn. In the mountains 3 mi north of Ruidoso, this charming, simple resort hotel looks like a Swiss chalet. It's a 16-minute drive from Ski Apache slopes. The on-premises restaurant serves German and American food. Restaurant, bar, complimentary breakfast, room service. Cable TV, some in-room VCRs. Pool. Hot tub, sauna. Laundry facilities. Business services. Pets allowed. | 1451 Mechem Dr. | 505/258–3333 or 800/477–9477 | fax 505/258–5325 | www.ruidoso.net/swisschalet | 82 rooms | AE, D, DC, MC, V | $–$$$

High Country Lodge. Tucked beside a quiet mountain lake 5 mi north of Ruidoso, this mountain resort has large two-bedroom cabins, all with fully equipped kitchens and front porches, some with fireplaces. Picnic area. No air-conditioning, kitchenettes. Cable TV. Pool. Hot tub, sauna. Tennis courts. Video games. Playground. Business services. Pets allowed (fee). | Hwy. 48, Alto, 88312 | 505/336–4321 or 800/845–7265 | www.ruidoso.net/hcl | 32 2-bedroom cabins | AE, D, DC, MC, V | $$

Innsbruck Lodge. Across from the city park, this motel in Ruidoso offers small, no-frills rooms. No air-conditioning in some rooms. Cable TV. Business services. | 601 Sudderth Dr. | 505/257–4071 or 800/680–4447 | fax 505/257–7536 | www.ruidosonm.com/innsbruck | 47 rooms (17 with shower only) | AE, D, DC, MC, V | $–$$

Shadow Mountain Lodge. In Upper Canyon, this is a couples-oriented resort hotel with views of the forest and fieldstone fireplaces. Some rooms have full kitchens. Some kitchenettes, microwaves, refrigerators. Cable TV. Hot tub. Business services. No kids under 15. | 107 Main St., 88345 | 505/257–4886 or 800/441–4331 | fax 505/257–2000 | www.smlruidoso.com | 19 suites | AE, D, DC, MC, V | $–$$

NORTH DAKOTA FRONTIER

FROM BISMARCK TO WILLISTON TO MEDORA

Distance: 475 mi   Time: 4 days
Overnight Breaks: Bismarck, Williston, Medora

Native American history, frontier exploration, and early cowboy living are the headlines of this tour. You'll travel from the bluffs overlooking the Missouri River to the open prairie, wind through the majestic Badlands, and finish in the cow town of Medora. At the height of summer, ripening grain fields bow to the ever-present wind, the "big lake"—Lake Sakakawea—glistens, and the rugged terrain of the Badlands wears deep hues of sandy browns and taupes. Spring and fall seasons release sudden splashes of color in this otherwise subtle landscape. Don't forget that the Missouri River forms the dividing line between the Central and Mountain time zones. This tour is not recommended for winter; many of the sights will be closed, and the roads may be covered with snow or ice.

❶ As capital city, **Bismarck** prides itself on its well-maintained residential areas, bustling downtown and shopping districts, and its many sights. Across the Missouri River, sister city **Mandan** was once called the Gateway to the West by novelist John Steinbeck. Mandan is a logical starting place for a busy day of sightseeing. Start with **Fort Abraham Lincoln State Park,** the headquarters for General Custer and the 7th Cavalry. On the fort grounds, the Custer House has been reconstructed and hosts tours. Also at the park is **On-A-Slant Indian Village,** with recreated dwellings called earthlodges from the Mandan people, who lived there from 1650 to 1750. After visiting the park and exhibits, head to Mandan and the **Five Nations Arts** for one-of-a-kind gifts—including quillwork, beadwork, star quilts, and sculptures—made by Native American artists. Just across the street and down a block is **Mandan Drug,** where you can get a sandwich, some homemade soup, and old-fashioned hard ice cream. After lunch, head for Bismarck and the **State Capitol,** where you can enjoy a free tour of the 19-story Art Deco building. Across the street is the **North Dakota Heritage Center,** home to a museum with numerous period exhibits, from a wooly mammoth to a 1940s tractor. For an evening of entertainment, consider dinner and gaming at **Prairie Knights Casino.** Spend the night in Bismarck.

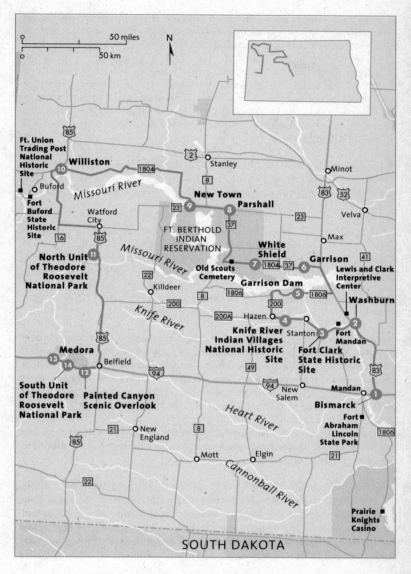

❷ Begin day two with a pleasant drive north to **Washburn,** where you can visit the **Lewis and Clark Interpretive Center.** Exhibits include artifacts from nearly every major tribe encountered by the 19th century explorers. From the center, turn west on Route 200A and watch for signs for **Fort Mandan,** only 1½ mi away on Route 17. Fort Mandan is a replica of the 1804–05 winter quarters used by Lewis and Clark and their expedition.

❸ Return to Route 200A and travel west, past rolling ranchlands and farm fields to **Fort Clark State Historic Site,** the spot of a former fur-trading post. While nothing remains, plaques tell the history of commerce and tragedy: during the summer of 1837, a passenger steamboat brought smallpox to the nearby Mandan Indian village, wiping out 90 percent of its people.

4 Continue west on Route 200A about 8 mi to Stanton and **Knife River Indian Villages National Historic Site,** which was inhabited for thousands of years. Enjoy the exhibits and a visit to a full-size reconstructed earthlodge.

5 Get back on Route 200A and travel west 3 mi to Hazen, then north 19 mi on Route 200 to Pick City, and then east on Route 1806. Enjoy the panoramic rolling farmland along the route, and then prepare to drive over the jaw-dropping **Garrison Dam** from Pick City to Riverdale. The mile-long dam, built between 1947 and 1954, created Lake Sakakawea from the Missouri River and generates hydroelectric power. Free tours are available weekdays.

6 From Garrison Dam, continue on Route 1806 and connect with U.S. 83. Travel north 12 mi on U.S. 83, and turn west on to Route 37, which will take you to **Garrison.** A fun stop here is the **North Dakota Fishing Hall of Fame,** where the state's best anglers are honored.

7 Traveling west from Garrison, Route 37 becomes Route 1804. Continue on 1804 as you enter the Fort Berthold Indian Reservation, home of the Three Affiliated Tribes— Mandan, Hidatsa, and Arikara. About 1 mi into the reservation is **White Shield,** named for a famous Arikara chief who at one time served as a scout for Gen. George A. Custer. Just 3 mi west of White Shield is the **Old Scouts Cemetery.** This small, serene cemetery is the final resting place for war veterans and some of Custer's Arikara scouts.

8 Continue on Route 1804 as it veers north and becomes Route 37 once again; continue on to **Parshall,** about 25 mi. Houses and pastures dot the reservation's hills, interspersed with the occasional gorgeous gully dotted with juneberry bushes. Parshall is home to the **Paul Broste Rock Museum,** a must-see collection of specimens from around the world. After you've visited the museum, turn west on Route 23 and travel along the north edge of the reservation.

9 Just 17 mi west of Parshall, **New Town** is the seat of tribal government. Here you can find the **Three Affiliated Tribes Museum.** Continue west on Route 1804 to **Williston,** and make this your stopping place for the evening.

10 Begin day three of your tour with a jaunt to two forts just west of **Williston** on Route 1804. The first stop is **Fort Buford State Historic Site,** just 21 mi from Williston. A military post established in 1866, Fort Buford is noted for its famous prisoners, Sitting Bull and Chief Joseph. Drive 2 mi west, again on Route 1804, and you'll see **Fort Union Trading Post National Historic Site** clearly from the road. Between 1828 and 1867 this post dominated the fur trade along the upper Missouri River.

11 From Williston, travel south on U.S. 85 about 60 mi and take in the beauty of the prairie, dotted with ranches and an occasional tree. Then prepare for a startling change of scenery, as the dramatic buttes that make up the Badlands begin to appear. The **North Unit of Theodore Roosevelt National Park** is a primitive area where you might spot the buffalo and deer roaming, eagles and hawks soaring, and prairie dogs scampering. After touring this portion of the park, continue south on U.S. 85 about 50 mi and connect with I-94, traveling west.

12 **Painted Canyon Scenic Overlook** is your next breathtaking stop. The visitor center overlooks a panoramic view of the Badlands, called Mako Shika ("land bad") by the Sioux.

⑬ Just off I–94 is the very walkable frontier town of **Medora,** founded by a French nobleman and named for his American wife. Have a look at their 26-room mansion, the **Chateau de Mores State Historic Site.** Depending on the hour and your energy level you can begin to explore the park described at the next stop, or you can knock off for the day and have dinner in Medora, where you'll also want to spend the night.

⑭ After breakfast, head over to the **South Unit of Theodore Roosevelt National Park,** the entrance of which is a mile across from the Chateau de Mores. The visitor center has a film and exhibits, and just a short walk away is the **Maltese Cross Ranch Cabin,** from one of Theodore Roosevelt's two North Dakota ranches. The drive through the South Unit shows off more of the Badlands' incredible terrain. After having lunch in Medora, check out the many museums, including the **Medora Doll House, Museum of the Badlands, and Harold Schafer Heritage Center.** If you'd like to purchase something special, travel to Beach just 26 mi west and visit **Prairie Fire Pottery.** The owner supplies the world's zoos with animal-print tiles and handcrafts exquisite pottery with a unique, shimmery glaze.

To return to Bismarck, travel east along I–94 from Beach (about a 2½-hour trip) or Medora (about a 2-hour trip).

NORTH DAKOTA RULES OF THE ROAD

License Requirements: The minimum driving age in North Dakota is 16. You may not drive in North Dakota if you are under 16, even if you are licensed in another state.

Right Turn on Red: You may turn right on a red light *after* stopping when the intersection is clear of both pedestrians and vehicles, unless otherwise posted.

Safety Belt and Helmet Laws: North Dakota law requires all front-seat occupants to wear safety belts. Children under age 3 must be properly secured in an approved child restraint seat, and children age 3 to 10 must be properly secured in either an approved child restraint seat or a safety belt. North Dakota does not have a motorcycle helmet law.

Speed Limits: The speed limit is 70 mi per hour on interstate highways, except when otherwise posted around major cities. On all other primary and secondary highways, the speed limit is 65 mi per hour unless otherwise posted.

For More Information: Contact the **North Dakota Department of Transportation.** | 608 East Boulevard Ave., Bismarck, 58505–0700 | 701/328–2500 general information; 701/328–7623 road reports; 800/472–2121 emergency assistance | www.state.nd.us/dot/.

Bismarck

Attractions

North Dakota Heritage Center. The state's largest museum and archive has permanent exhibits covering Native Americans, immigrants, dinosaurs, and tractors. | 612 E. Boulevard Ave., 58505 | 701/328–2666 | fax 701/328–3710 | www.state.nd.us/hist | Weekdays 8–5, Sat. 9–5, Sun. 11–5.

Prairie Knights Casino and Lodge. Blackjack, slots, video poker, keno, and poker tables await you at this Vegas-style casino. The fanciest of five reservation casinos, Prairie Knights has wall murals and a large outdoor sculpture of horses. No tipping is allowed in the casino and restaurants. A 69-room lodge is adjacent to the casino. Nearby, the Marina at Prairie Nights on Lake Oahe has ramps, slips, a picnic area, and RV sites. | 3932 Rte. 24, Bismarck, 58502 | 701/854–7777; 800/425–8277 (within ND) | fax 701/854–3795 | www.prairieknights.com | Daily.

State Capitol. The 19-story building is one of only two U.S. state capitols without a traditional dome. The structure, with a Moderne-style exterior and Art Deco interior, was built in the early 1930s after a Christmas fire destroyed the building from the territorial days. | 600 E. Boulevard Ave. | 701/328–2480 | fax 701/328–3710 | Memorial Day–Labor Day, weekdays 8–5, Sat. 9–4, Sun. 1–4; Labor Day–Memorial Day, weekdays 8–5.

Dining

Bistro 1100, An American Café. Eclectic. Ostrich, wood-fired burgers, and Greek pizza are among the choices at this relaxed eatery. In nice weather, you can eat outside on a deck overlooking downtown and the railroad tracks. | 1103 E. Front Ave. | 701/224–8800 | Closed Sun. | AE, MC, V | $$–$$$

★ **Peacock Alley Bar and Grill.** American/Casual. In what was once the historic Patterson Hotel, this restaurant was the scene of countless political deals, captured in period photographs. Choices might include pasta salads, soups, sandwiches, Cajun firecracker shrimp, and pan-blackened prime rib. Kids' menu. Sun. brunch. | 422 E. Main Ave. | 701/255–7917 | No lunch or dinner Sun. | AE, D, DC, MC, V | $$

Los Amigos. Mexican. Expect authentic and homemade food—such as traditional tamales and chile relleno—with mouth-watering hot sauce and the right dash of cilantro. Kids' menu. | 431 S. 3rd St. | 701/223–7580 | Closed Sun. | AE, D, DC, MC, V | $–$$

North American Steak Buffet. Steak. All-you-can-eat is the key phrase here, and you'll choose from salad and hot-foods bars and a variety of desserts. No alcohol. | 2000 N. 12th St. | 701/223–1107 | AE, D, MC, V | $

Lodging

Comfort Suites. A 92-ft water slide at its pool makes this hotel, 2 mi from downtown, popular with families. Complimentary Continental breakfast. In-room data ports, some in-room hot tubs. Cable TV. Indoor pool. Hot tub. Exercise equipment, gym. Laundry service. Business services, airport shuttle, free parking. Pets allowed. | 929 Gateway Ave. | 701/223–4009 or 800/228–5150 | fax 701/223–9119 | www.comfortsuites.com | 60 suites | AE, D, MC, V | $–$$

Holiday Inn. The hotel's downtown location makes it the base for many concert artists and performers at the Bismarck Civic Center, 1 mi away. Restaurant, bar, room service. In-room data ports. Cable TV, in-room VCRs (and movies). Indoor pool. Beauty salon, hot tub. Gym. Laundry service. Business services, airport shuttle. | 605 E. Broadway | 701/255–6000 or 800/465–4329 | fax 701/223–0400 | www.basshotels.com/holiday-inn | 215 rooms, 35 suites | AE, D, DC, MC, V | $–$$

Best Western Doublewood Inn. At I–94 and Highway 83, this two-story motel is ¼ mi from the State Capitol. Restaurant, bar, room service. In-room data ports, microwaves, refrigerators. Cable TV, some in-room VCRs. Indoor pool. Hot tub, sauna. Video games. Playground. Laundry service. Business services, airport shuttle, free parking. Pets allowed (fee). | 1400 E. Interchange Ave., 58501 | 701/258–7000 or 800/554–7077 | fax 701/258–2001 | www.bestwestern.com | 143 rooms | AE, D, DC, MC, V | $

Select Inn of Bismarck. At I–94 in a service strip, this two-story motel, built in 1976, is 3 mi from Kirkwood Mall and 1 mi from Heritage Center at the State Capitol. Complimentary Continental breakfast. In-room data ports, in-room safes, some kitchenettes, some microwaves, some refrigerators, some in-room hot tubs. Cable TV. Laundry facilities. | 1505 Interchange Ave., 58501 | 701/223–8060 or 800/641–1000 | fax 701/223–8293 | www.selectinn.com | 99 rooms, 1 suite | AE, D, DC, MC, V | $

Garrison

Attractions

Audubon National Wildlife Refuge. More than 200 bird species live in this 14,300-acre refuge. On a 7½-mi driving tour you might see Canada geese and white-tailed deer. Stop by the visitor center to see the exhibits and collect information. | 3275 11th St. NW, Coleharbor, 58531 | 701/442–5474 | www.fws.gov | Daily dawn to dusk.

Garrison Dam. The fifth largest in the United States, the mile-long dam controls flooding on the Missouri River and generates electricity. Finished in 1954, the dam also created Lake Sakakawea and a recreation industry. The powerhouse includes a vast network of power stanchions, high-voltage lines, and transformers. Tours of the power plant are conducted by the U.S. Army Corps of Engineers. From Garrison, go 6 mi east on Route 37 to Route 83; go 10 mi south on 83 to junction 48; go west on Route 200 for 14 mi; follow signs to Garrison Dam. | Box 517, Riverdale, 58565 | 701/654–7411 | Memorial Day–Labor Day, noon–4.

Lake Sakakawea. The third largest man-made lake in the United States starts just south of Williston and extends more than 10 mi to the southeast, where it stops at the Garrison Dam. Access to the lake is fairly easy, with more than 1,600 mi of publicly owned shoreline. Walleye, northern pike, and salmon create exceptional sport fishing. From Garrison, go 25 mi south on Route 200; 1 mi north of Pick City; follow signs. | U.S. Army Corps of Engineers, Garrison Project, Box 527, Riverdale, 58565-0527 | 701/654–7411 | cenwo.nwo.usace.army.mil/html/Lake_Proj/garrison.htm.

Lake Sakakawea State Park. Next to the Garrison Dam, this park has a full-service marina with 80 slips, two large boat ramps, and camp sites. About 220,000 people visit the park each year. From Garrison, 25 mi south on Route 200; 1 mi north of Pick City; follow signs. | Box 732, Riverdale, 58565 | 701/487–3315 | www.state.nd.us/ndparks | Daily; campgrounds mid-May–early Oct.

North Dakota Fishing Hall of Fame. In the city park beside a sculpture named Wally the Walleye, this log house museum documents anglers and whoppers of North Dakota. N. Main St. | 701/463–2600 or 800/799–4242 | Memorial Day–Labor Day, Fri.–Sun.

Dining

Stoney End. Steak. Originally built as a WPA project in the 1930s, the restaurant has fieldstone inside and out, two stone fireplaces—one in the dining room and one in the Cabin Fever lounge—and art throughout the building. The menu has certified Black Angus beef, prime rib (only on Saturday) with secret seasoning. Kids' menu. | On Rte. 37, 1 mi east of Garrison | 701/337–5590 | Closed Sun. No lunch | DC, MC, V | $$–$$$

Four Seasons Restaurant and Ice Cream Parlor. American/Casual. In a plain concrete block building you can find an assortment of sandwiches such as chili cheeseburgers and turkey clubs, and buffalo steak. Try the grilled chicken bacon melt. Kids' menu. Sunday brunch. No alcohol. | 182 N. Main St. | 701/463–2044 | No credit cards | $–$$

Lake Road Restaurant. American/Casual. The restaurant is known for hamburgers and a few German dishes such as *knoephle* soup. Kids' menu. Sun. brunch. On Route 37, 6 mi west off Route 83. | Rte. 37 | 701/463–2569 | MC, V | $–$$

Totten Trail Lounge. American/Casual. Stuffed and mounted hunting trophies—from fish to deer—adorn the walls at this roadside café and lounge. The supreme pizza—with sausage, pepperoni, onions, peas, and mushrooms—and the burgers are popular. | 1412A U.S. 83 NW, Coleharbor | 701/337–5513 | AE, MC, V | $–$$

Mandan

Attractions

Five Nations Arts. In an old railroad depot, this shop sells traditional and contemporary arts and crafts from 200 regional Native American artists. Several weekends every year, Native American artists come and work in-house. | 401 W. Main St. | 701/663–4663 | fax 701/663–4751 | www.5nationsarts.com | May–Sept., Mon.–Sat. 9–7, Sun. 12–5; Oct.–Dec., Mon.–Sat. 10–6, Sun. 12–5; Jan.–Apr., Mon.–Sat. 10–5.

Fort Abraham Lincoln State Park. Rich in Native American and military history, this 1870s fort began as a fur-trading post in the 1780s. By 1872 it had been renamed for Lincoln, and it soon became the home of the 7th Cavalry and General George A. Custer. The officers' quarters that Custer shared with his wife, Libby, have been restored to their 1876 appearance, when the doomed general left on his expedition to the Little Big Horn. Also in the 75-acre park are reconstructed barracks, a commissary store, and infantry blockhouses. You'll also find trails and a campground in the park. | 4480 Fort Lincoln Rd. | 701/663–9571 or 701/663–1464 | fax 701/663–4751 | www.state.nd.us/ndparks | Memorial Day–Labor Day, daily dawn to dusk.

On-A-Slant Indian Village was inhabited by Mandan Native Americans between 1650 and 1750. About 1,000 people lived in the village, but by the early 1800s, most had been wiped out by smallpox. Four reconstructed earth lodges give a sense of the Mandan people's world. The village is listed on the National Register of Historic Places..

Dining

★ **Mandan Drug.** American. The pharmacy and other original pieces of this former drugstore are still intact, including the stools, a jukebox with 1960s songs, and a player-piano. Try the Sakakawea sandwich with turkey breast, cream cheese, and cranberry sauce. Follow up with an old-fashioned cherry soda or a brown cow—a root beer float with chocolate syrup—and then take home some delicious hand-made candy. No alcohol. | 316 W. Main St. | 701/663–5900 | Closed Sun. No dinner | MC, V | $

Medora

Attractions

Burning Hills Amphitheatre. Built into a bluff, the seven-story amphitheater hosts nightly performances of the Medora Musical every summer. If you sit near the top, you can enjoy a panoramic view of the Badlands and, if you're lucky, you'll see bison grazing in the distance. The amphitheater seats almost 3,000 people. | Box 198 | 701/

When you pack your MCI Calling Card, it's like packing your loved ones along too.

Your MCI Calling Card is the easy way to stay in touch when you travel. Use it to call to and from over 125 countries. Plus, every time you call, you can earn frequent flier miles. So wherever your travels take you, call home with your MCI Calling Card. It's even easy to get one. Just visit **www.mci.com/worldphone**.

EASY TO CALL WORLDWIDE

1 Just enter the WorldPhone® access number of the country you're calling from.

2 Enter or give the operator your MCI Calling Card number.

3 Enter or give the number you're calling.

Aruba ❖	800-888-8
Bahamas ❖	1-800-888-8000
Barbados ❖	1-800-888-8000
Bermuda ❖	1-800-888-8000
British Virgin Islands ❖	1-800-888-8000
Canada	1-800-888-8000
Mexico	01-800-021-8000
Puerto Rico	1-800-888-8000
United States	1-800-888-8000
U.S. Virgin Islands	1-800-888-8000

❖ Limited availability.

EARN FREQUENT FLIER MILES

AmericanAirlines AAdvantage

MIDWEST EXPRESS AIRLINES
PROGRAM PARTNER

SEE THE WORLD
IN FULL COLOR

Fodor's Exploring Guides bring all the great sights vividly to life with hundreds of photographs, fascinating historical background, and colorful anecdotes. Detailed maps and practical information keep you headed in the right direction.

Pair a **Fodor's** Exploring Guide with your trusted Gold Guide for a complete planning package.

Fodor's EXPLORING GUIDES

At bookstores everywhere.

623–4444 or 800/633–6721 | fax 701/623–4494 | www.medora.com | Memorial Day–Labor Day.

Chateau De Mores State Historic Site. A French nobleman and his wife, Medora, constructed this 26-room mansion in 1883. The couple entertained Theodore Roosevelt during his Dakota ranching days and hosted extravagant hunting parties. The chateau is restored to its glory days and offers interpretive tours during the summer. About 1 mi from the chateau is the De Mores Memorial Park, the spot indicated by a lone-standing brick chimney, all that remains of the beef-packing plant. | 1 Chateau La., (Box 106) 58645 | 701/623–4355 | fax 701/623–4921 | www.state.nd.us/hist | Mid-May–mid-Sept., daily 8:30–6, rest of year by appointment only.

Harold Schafer Heritage Center. Besides housing a modern art gallery, this center salutes the man who saved Medora from obscurity, using money he earned through his Gold Seal Co., manufacturer of Mr. Bubble and other products. | 335 4th St. | 701/623–4444 or 800/633–6721 | fax 701/623–4494 | www.medora.com | Memorial Day–Labor Day, daily 10–6.

Medora Doll House. Antique dolls and toys fill almost every inch of this small house, built by the Marquis de Mores in 1884. Also known as the von Hoffman House, it's listed on the National Register of Historic Places. | 485 Broadway | 701/623–4444 or 800/633–6721 | fax 701/623–4494 | www.medora.com | Memorial Day–Labor Day, daily 10–6.

Museum of the Badlands. In this collection is one of the region's most extensive exhibits of Plains Native American artifacts, along with personal items of Apache chief Geronimo. | 195 3rd Ave. | 701/623–4444 or 800/633–6721 | fax 701/623–4494 | www.medora.com | Memorial Day–Labor Day, daily 10–6.

Prairie Fire Pottery. Handmade stoneware pottery and terra-cotta tiles with wildlife tracks are displayed in a studio and showroom. The studio supplies 27 different animal-track tiles to zoos and parks worldwide. | 127 Main St. E | 701/872–3855 | Mon.–Sat. 9–6, or by appointment.

Dining

Rough Rider Hotel Dining Room. American. Barbecued buffalo ribs, prime rib, and huge hamburgers are the big draw here, but you can also see photos of Theodore Roosevelt hanging on the rustic walls. | 301 3rd Ave., at Main St. | 701/623–4444 | Closed Sun. | AE, D, MC, V | $$–$$$

Chuckwagon Cafeteria. American. Known for ribs, chicken, and steaks, this restaurant also has a sandwich shop and bakery. Note the photographs of the early days of Medora and an extensive collection of Indian arrowheads. Umbrellas shade the outdoor patio. Sun. brunch. No alcohol. | 250 3rd Ave. | 701/623–4444 | Closed Labor Day–Memorial Day | AE, D, MC, V | $–$$

Trapper's Kettle. American. You'll see plenty of traps and kettles here, though perhaps the most unusual aspect of the decor is the salad bar, which is a canoe. The chili topped with cheese is a favorite; also popular are the hearty frontier-style scones. Salad bar. | 83 U.S. 85 N, Hwy. 94, Belfield | 701/575–8585 | Breakfast also available | AE, D, DC, MC, V | $–$$

Lodging

Dahkotah Lodge and Guest Ranch. A real working cattle ranch, the Dahkotah offers you a true life-style change, if only for a few days. Located in a residential area 19 mi outside of town, the single-story cedar-sided ranch was built in 1991. No room phones, TV in common area. Horseback riding. Free parking. | 4456 W. River Rd., 58645 | 701/623–4897; 800/508–4897 (in ND) | www.dahkotahlodge.com | 4 cabins | AP | AE, D, MC, V | $$$$

★ **Rough Riders Hotel.** Built in 1883, this downtown hotel is operated by the Theodore Roosevelt Medora Foundation, a nonprofit organization that restores historic Medora. Rooms on the second floor have country-western antiques, brass beds, patchwork quilts, and red velvet drapes. There's a restaurant on the first floor. Parking is on the street. Guests have pool privileges at Badlands Hotel, four blocks away. Cable TV. No pets. No smoking. | 301 3rd Ave., 58645 | 701/623–4444 or 800/633–6721 | fax 701/623–4494 | www. medora.com | 9 rooms (7 with shower only) | AE, D, MC, V | $$

AmericInn Motel and Suites. Glowing wood, stuffed animals, and western themes accentuate this motel. The two-story cement-block building is in a commercial area three blocks from downtown; restaurants and stores are nearby. Complimentary Continental breakfast Cable TV. Indoor pool. Hot tub, sauna. Laundry facilities. Business services, free parking. Pets allowed. | 75 E. River Rd. S | 701/623–4800 or 800/634–3444 | fax 701/623–4890 | www.americinn.com | 56 rooms, 8 suites | AE, D, DC, MC, V | $

Sully Inn and Book Corral. Built in the 1970s, this downtown motel has a bookstore in the reception area called Book Corral. Rooms have oak furnishings, with shades of brown and beige and colorful quilts on each bed. There is plenty of parking. Some kitchenettes, some microwaves, some refrigerators. Cable TV. Laundry facilities. No smoking. | 425 Broadway, 58645 | 701/623–4455 or 877/800–4992 | fax 701/623–4992 | 19 rooms (showers only) | AE, D, MC, V | $

New Town

Attractions

Crow Flies High Observation Point. Overlooking Lake Sakakawea and 3 mi west of New Town, this spot has a spectacular view of sparkling water and rolling hills. | 701/627–4477.

Four Bears Bridge. Named for Mandan Indian Chief Four Bears, this narrow bridge spans a mile of Lake Sakakawea, making this the longest bridge in the state. It's 4 mi west of New Town. | 701/627–4477.

4 Bears Casino and Lodge. An economic force for the reservation, this Las Vegas–style casino offers slots, blackjack, poker, bingo, and craps. It also has 85 full-service hookups for RVs and special events, including concerts, rodeos, car shows, and boxing. This spot is 4 mi west of New Town, off Highway 23 just across the Four Bears Bridge. | HC3 Box 2A 58763 | 701/627–4018 or 800/294–5454 | fax 701/627–4012 | Sun.–Thurs. 8 AM–2 AM, Fri.–Sat. 24 hours.

Four Bears Memorial Park. Four miles west of New Town, the park honors the Mandan chief and all local Native Americans who died in conflicts from World War I to Vietnam. | 701/627–4477 | Daily.

Old Scouts Cemetery. You'll see headstones for some of Custer's Arikara scouts, though they aren't buried here; it is the actual resting place of military personnel and war veterans from later conflicts. Note that all headstones face east into the rising sun. | 701/627–4477 | Daily.

★ **Paul Broste Rock Museum.** Natural granite from the area was used to create the stone building with a private collection of 5,000 rocks, agates, minerals, and crystals. | N. Main St., Parshall, 58770 | 701/862–3264 | tradecorridor.com/parshall/rockmuseum | Mid-Apr.–mid-Oct., daily 10–6, or by appointment.

Three Affiliated Tribes Museum. The history of the Mandan, Hidatsa, and Arikara cultures are explored at this diverse museum through artifacts and crafts. Take note of the dresses with elk teeth. Four miles west of New Town next to Four Bears Casino, off Highway 23. | New Town 58763 | 701/627–4477 | Memorial Day–Labor Day, daily 10–6.

Van Hook Marina. Known locally as "fisherman's paradise" for its walleye, this little resort area has campgrounds, guide and fish cleaning services, a boat ramp, and a bait shop, whose owners are world-class walleye anglers. | 1801 Van Hook | 701/627–3811 | May–Aug., daily 6:30 AM–10 PM; Sept.–early Oct., daily 6:30 AM–8 PM.

Dining

Lucky's Café at 4 Bears Casino. American. Try the walleye dinner or the T-bone steak at this casino's "sit-down" restaurant. Four miles west of New Town, off Highway 23. | 701/627–4018 | Breakfast also available | AE, D, MC, V | $–$$

Riverside. American. The restaurant is popular for its prime rib feasts on weekends. Kids' menu. | 358 Main St. | 701/627–4403 | No lunch Sat., Sun. | AE, MC, V | $–$$

Scenic 23. American. Families and summer anglers enjoy tucking into steak, lobster, or the prime rib. Kids' menu. | 1803 Van Hook | 701/627–3949 | Closed Sun. No lunch | AE, D, MC, V | $–$$

Lodging

4 Bears Casino and Lodge. You'll have a wonderful view of Lake Sakakawea from this small, two-story brick motel next door to the casino, 4 mi west of downtown, off Highway 23. You can go fishing in a nearby park. Restaurant, bar In-room data ports. Cable TV. Video games. Laundry facilities. Business services, free parking. Pets allowed. | HC3 Box 2A 58763 | 701/627–4018 or 800/294–5454 | fax 701/627–4012 | 40 rooms | AE, D, MC, V | $

Theodore Roosevelt National Park

Attractions

Maah Daah Hey Trail. Hike and ride horses or mountain bikes on this 120-mi trail. Its name means "grandfather" or "be here long" in the Mandan language. The trail passes through the rugged Badlands and the Little Missouri National Grasslands. Maps are available through the U.S. Forest Service. | USDA Forest Service, 1511 E. Interstate Ave., Bismarck, 58501 | 701/225–5151 | Daily.

North Unit. More rugged than the South Unit, the North Unit has spectacular views and may permit chance meetings with bison, mule deer, and elk. You can take a 14-mi loop trail to the Oxbow Overlook, or other self-guided trails that wind in and out of ravines. At the Visitor Center, 15 mi south of Watford on Route 85, you can see a slide show about the park before making your visit. | HC02 Box 35, Watford, 58854 | 701/842–2333 | fax 701/842–3101 | www.nps.gov/thro | Daily. Visitor Center: Memorial Day–Sept., daily 9–5:30.

Painted Canyon Scenic Overlook. Catch your first glimpse of Badlands majesty here and learn more about the Badlands from the wildlife and geology exhibits in the Visitor Interpretive Center. | 201 E. River Rd., Medora | 701/623–4466 | fax 701/623–4840 | www.nps.gov/thro | Daily. Visitor Center: mid-June–Labor Day, daily 8–6; Apr.–mid-June, daily 8:30–4:30; Sept.–mid-Nov., daily 8:30–4:30.

South Unit. A 36-mi scenic loop takes you by prairie dog towns, coal veins, and panoramic views of the Badlands. Self-guided trails, most under 1 mi long, introduce you to the area's geology, ecology, and history. At the Visitor Center, a 13-minute film describes the park. | 315 2nd Ave., Medora, 58645 | 701/623–4466 | fax 701/623–4840 | www.nps.gov/thro | Daily. Visitor Center: mid-June–Labor Day, daily 8–8; Labor Day–mid-June, daily 8–4:30.

When Theodore Roosevelt came to the Badlands in the 1880s, he became a cattle rancher. The **Elkhorn Ranch Site** was one of his ventures and is in the National Register of Historic Places. Today there are no buildings or signs here. Make sure to check at the South Unit Visitor Center for road and river fording conditions. The ranch is 35 mi north of the Visitor Center on gravel roads. | Off Rte. 94 at Medora | 701/623–4466 | fax 701/623–4840 | www.nps.gov/thro | Daily.

Next door to the Visitor Center in the South Unit is Theodore Roosevelt's **Maltese Cross Ranch Cabin,** which was moved from its original site during Roosevelt's day.

The **Peaceful Valley Ranch Horse Rides** are one way to see the South Unit as cowboys and frontiersmen might have seen it a century ago. Guides lead you on some of the park's 80 mi of marked horse trails. | 7 mi north from South Unit Visitor Center | 701/623–4568 | Memorial Day–Labor Day, daily.

Washburn

Attractions

Fort Clark State Historic Site. A fur-trading post built in 1830 near the Missouri River, 15 mi west of Washburn off Highway 83, the fort burned down in 1860. Today, you can reconstruct its history with the help of markers along a walking trail. The site is on the National Register of Historic Places. | State Historical Society of North Dakota, 612 E. Boulevard Ave., Bismarck, 58505 | 701/328–2666 | fax 701/328–3710 | www.state.nd. us/hist | Daily.

Fort Mandan. Built in the shape of a triangle on the banks of the Missouri River just west of Washburn, this fort was Lewis and Clark's home through the winter of 1804–05. It's fully restored and on the National Register of Historic Places. | Lewis and Clark Interpretive Center, 2576 8th St. SW, 58523 | 701/462–8535 | www.ndlewisandclark.com | Daily dawn–dusk.

Freedom Mine. Freedom Mine is one of the 10 largest coal mines in the United States. Its lignite feeds three power stations and a gas plant within an hour of the mine. You can arrange a tour by calling 24 hours ahead. | 204 County Rd. 15, Beulah, 58523 | 701/873–2281 | Weekdays by appointment.

Knife River Indian Villages National Historic Site. Sakakawea met Lewis and Clark here and became their guide and translator in the early 1800s. But community life at this site goes back at least 8,000 years, and flourished until the mid-19th century, when disease started taking its toll on the Native American people in the region. At the interpretive center you can see artifacts as old as 9,000 years, and visit a reconstructed earthlodge, 50 ft across by 12 ft high. | County Rd. 37, Stanton | 701/745–3309 | fax 701/745–3708 | www.nps.gov/knri | Mid-May–Labor Day, daily 7:30–6; Labor Day–mid-May, daily 8–4.

Lewis and Clark Interpretive Center. Lewis and Clark's voyage of discovery to this area in 1804–06 is the focus of this center, where you can see a hand-carved replica of the 4-ton canoes the explorers used. All the Native American groups Lewis and Clark met are represented by objects and artifacts, and there are 1830s illustrations by Karl Bodmer. | 2576 8th St. SW, Washburn | 701/462–8535 | www.ndlewisandclark.com | Memorial Day–Labor Day, daily 9–7; Labor Day–Memorial Day, daily 9–5.

Dining

Dakota Farms Family Restaurant. American. Sit at a booth by the front window and watch the highway traffic while breakfasting on ham and eggs, or retire to the dining area in the back to enjoy a rib steak. Kids' menu. No alcohol. | 1317 Border La. | 701/462–8175 | D, DC, MC, V | $

Lewis and Clark Café. American. Antique wagon wheels and old photos help this small-town café serve up history with its meals. Try the burger or steak named for Lewis and Clark. Kids' menu. No alcohol. | 602 Main St. Between 6th and Maine | 701/462–3668 | Breakfast also available. No dinner Sun. | No credit cards | $

Williston

Attractions

Buffalo Trails Museum. Epping, 22 mi northeast, is a small town with a big museum. In seven buildings you will find antiques, geospheres, and fossils, but the most unusual items are the re-created dentist's office, sickroom, and parlor with lifesize papier-mâché figures. From Williston, head east on Highway 2. Turn right on County Highway 42; follow signs to the museum. | Epping, 58843 | 701/859–4361 | June–Aug., Mon.–Sat. 9–5, Sun. 1:30–5:30; Sept.–Oct., Sun. 1:30–5:30, or by appointment.

Fort Buford State Historic Site. Built in 1866 near the concourse of the Missouri and Yellowstone rivers, this military post was the site of Sitting Bull's surrender in 1881. The officers' quarters are now a museum, and in the soldiers' cemetery you can hunt for unusual, humorous headstones. | 15349 39th La. NW | 701/572–9034 | Mid-May–mid-Sept., daily 9–6; mid-Sept.–mid-May by appointment only.

Fort Union Trading Post National Historic Site. Admire the impressive palisade and three-story bastions of Fort Union from the highway. John Jacob Astor's American Fur Company built the fort, which dominated trade on the upper Missouri River from 1828 to 1867. | 15550 Hwy. 1804, 58801 | 701/572–9083 | www.nps.gov/fous | Memorial Day–Labor Day, daily 8–8; Labor Day–Memorial Day, daily 9–5:30.

Lake Park Drive-In. See a movie at one of the few drive-in theaters still running in the country. The show goes on at dusk, but come early so the kids can enjoy the outdoor playground. | Hwy. 2N | 701/572–9137 | Apr.–Sept., Fri., Sat. 9 PM.

Dining

Airport International Inn. American. The soft lighting and candles help set the mood for a romantic dinner. Try the steamed Tork, a fish entrée served with salad or baked potato. Or try the steak. Kids' menu. Sun. brunch. | 3601 2nd Ave. W | 701/774–0241 | Breakfast also available | AE, D, DC, MC, V | $$–$$$

El Rancho Restaurant. Eclectic. American, Mexican, and Asian foods share the menu. Favorites are the prime rib dinner and the chicken stir fry. Kids' menu. Sun. brunch. | 1623 2nd Ave. W | 701/572–6321 | No lunch Sun. | AE, D, DC, MC, V. | $$–$$$

Dakota Farms Family Restaurant. American. The Dakota Farms serves breakfast all day, and has a reputation for fair prices and good service. Come in for all-you-can-eat fish on Fridays. Kids' menu. No alcohol. | 1906 2nd Ave. W | 701/572–4480 | Breakfast also available | D, MC, V | $–$$

Gramma Sharon's Cafe. American. For home-cooked, inexpensive meals, try Gramma's, but don't come here for the atmosphere: it's attached to a gas station. Known for omelets. Kids' menu. No alcohol. Open 24 hours. | Junction Hwy. 2 and Hwy. 85 N | 701/572–1412 | No credit cards | $–$$

Lunch Box. American/Casual. New and old lunch boxes are everywhere in this café where the menu lists soups, salads, and sandwiches. Try the almond chicken salad or the roast beef on a fresh pita, homemade chili, and pies. No alcohol. Closes at 6:30. | 20 W. Broadway | 701/572–8559 | Closed Sun. | No credit cards | $

Lodging

Airport International Inn. Six blocks from the airport and 4 mi from downtown, this two-story hotel has a conference center. Restaurant, bar. Indoor pool. Hot tub. | 3601 2nd Ave. W | 701/774–0241 | fax 701/774–0318 | 140 rooms, 4 suites | AE, D, DC, MC, V | $

El Rancho Motor Hotel. Six blocks from downtown, this Southwestern-style motel is well known for its restaurant. Restaurant, bar In-room data ports. Cable TV. Laundry service. Pets allowed. | 1623 2nd Ave. W | 701/572–6321 or 800/433–8529 | fax 701/572–6321 | 91 rooms | AE, D, DC, MC, V | $

Lund's Landing Marina Resort. Cedar camping cabins have a knotty pine interior and camp furniture with bunk beds. The cabins have no running water; shower and toilets are in the main building. You can rent kayaks, pontoons, and fishing boats, and there's a kids' fishing dock. The restaurant serves breakfast, lunch, and dinner. This resort is 22 mi east in Ray on Highway 1804. Picnic area. Refrigerators. Lake. Dock, boating, fishing. No smoking. | 11350 Hwy. 1804, Ray, 58849 | 701/568–3474 | www.lundslanding.com | 6 cabins (shared shower only) | Closed Dec.–Apr. | MAP | MC, V | $

OUACHITA NATIONAL FOREST ALONG U.S. 59

TRAVELS INTO THE OLD CHOCTAW NATION

Distance: 140 mi
Overnight Break: Poteau

Time: 2–3 days

Drive along U.S. 59 to the pine-covered heart of the old Choctaw Nation and the Ouachita Forest. ("Ouachita" is the French spelling of two Choctaw words *owa* and *chito,* for "big hunt.") The highway weaves in and out of protected wilderness areas and advance planning is a must, since the few available overnight accommodations are booked months in advance. Campers have an easier time of it, since there are hundreds of both improved and unimproved campsites available. The most scenic times to travel are in the spring, when the dogwoods are in bloom, or in the fall: South-eastern Oklahoma's fall foliage is definitely the state's showiest.

❶ Begin at the **Overstreet-Kerr Living History Farm,** 10 mi south of **Sallisaw.** Life in Indian Territory is re-created here, and period demonstrations include the making of sorghum, soap, and brooms, as well as territorial farming and gardening.

❷ The attractions for the next five stops on this tour are in the environs of the cozy river valley town of **Poteau,** named for a nearby river. **Spiro Mounds Archaeological State Park** contains eleven earthen mounds used by the Spiro Mounds people from AD 600 to 1450. The mounds have yielded burial treasure, including engraved shells, embossed copper plates, stone tools, textiles, and prehistoric lace.

❸ A purported Viking rune stone measuring 12 ft high, 10 ft wide, and 2 ft thick and carved with eight runic letters can be seen at **Heavener Runestone State Park.** The park has a visitor information center, a nature trail, and picnic tables. Plan to stay the night in Poteau.

❹ The **Peter Conser Historic House Site** is the restored 19th-century residence of a prominent politician, businessman, and member of the Choctaw Lighthorsemen, an

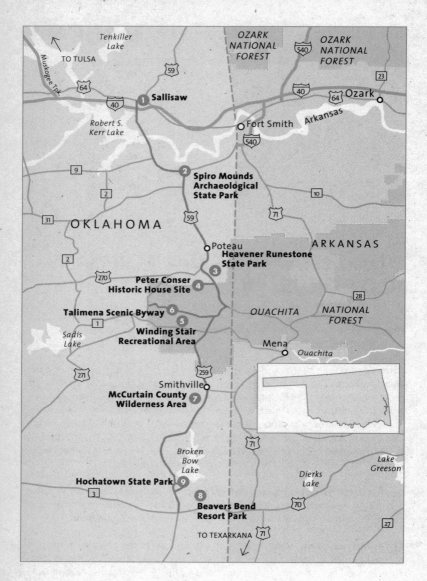

elite tribal law-enforcement corps that patrolled the Choctaw Nation during territorial days.

⑤ Bordering the Peter Conser Historic House Site is **Ouachita National Forest,** the South's oldest national forest and the largest shortleaf pine forest in the country. In addition to the pines, white and scrub oak, hickory, dogwood, and other varieties of trees blanket the blue-tinged faces of the Winding Stair Mountains. The 26,445-acre **Winding Stair Recreation Area** is home to numerous scenic lookouts and campgrounds, including **Cedar Lake Campground** and **Cedar Lake Equestrian Camp.** Cedar Lake Campground has an 84-acre lake, hiking trails, and RV and tent campsites, and is a trailhead for the 46-mi long Ouachita Trail. Cedar Lake Equestrian Camp is known as the "Cadillac of horse camps," as it provides individual corrals and hot showers for both horse and rider.

⑥ The **Talimena Scenic Byway** intersects U.S. 259 15 mi south of the northern edge of Ouachita National Forest. The byway proceeds westward, scaling the peaks of the Winding Stair and Rich mountains. The road, built purely for its scenic potential, runs from Mena, Arkansas, to Talihina, Oklahoma. There are numerous scenic turnouts and picnic stops along the 56-mi-long route. **The Robert S. Kerr Nature Center Arboretum** has a visitor information center, and two 1-mi trails are designed to educate hikers about tree species.

⑦ A 1-mi walking trail at the 14,000-acre **McCurtain County Wilderness Area** has markers designating prime wildlife viewing stops.

⑧ The pine-studded, 3,500-acre **Beavers Bend Resort Park** is built around the Mountain Fork River and Broken Bow Lake. It's Oklahoma's most-visited park, with miles of hiking trails. Inside the park, the **Forest Heritage Center** traces the history of the area back to prehistoric times with painted murals and artifacts. The center is built around an atrium with a hundred-year-old oak-log cabin moved to the park from the Kiamichi Mountains.

OKLAHOMA RULES OF THE ROAD

License Requirements: Home state licenses are honored for non-residents.

Right Turn on Red: Permitted throughout the state *after* a complete stop, unless otherwise posted.

Seat Belt and Helmet Laws: Seat belts are mandatory for drivers and front-seat passengers; child restraints are mandatory for children under four years of age. Children four and five years old must use child restraints or seat belts at all times. Safety helmets are required for motorcyclists under age 18; face shields, goggles, or windscreens are mandatory. Motorcyclists are required to use their headlights at all times, even during daylight hours.

Speed Limits: 70 mph on four-lane or divided highways; 75 mph on turnpikes; and 55 mph on county roads. Residential and business-district limits are set by local ordinance.

For More Information: Contact the **Oklahoma Department of Public Safety** | 405/425–2424.

◉ Beavers Bend Resort Park adjoins the McCurtain County Wilderness Area as well as **Hochatown State Park. Cedar Creek Golf Course**, at the Hochatown park, was carved out of the pine woods with chainsaws and machetes; it has a winding mountain stream and a revolving cast of wildlife, including wild turkeys and bald eagles.

Broken Bow

Attractions

Beavers Bend Resort Park. Oklahoma's most popular state park encompasses 3,500 densely forested acres. Park activities include fly-fishing, boating, scuba diving, swimming, horseback riding, and hiking. There are also a nature center, the Forest Heritage Center, a miniature train, canoe rentals, cabins, a lakefront lodge, and RV and tent campsites. | Rte. 259A | 580/494–6300 | www.touroklahoma.com | Daily.

The **Forest Heritage Center** has natural history exhibits, antique chainsaws, Choctaw artifacts, and a century-old cabin. | 580/494–6497 | Daily 8–8.

Hochatown State Park. Abutting Beavers Bend Resort Park and the McCurtain County Wilderness Area, this park has the 18-hole Cedar Creek Golf Course as its centerpiece. Wildlife is sometimes spied on the fairways. | U.S. 259 | 580/494–6451 | www.touroklahoma.com | Daily.

McCurtain County Wilderness Area. Flying squirrels, bobcats, red and gray foxes, and 100 species of birds have been spotted in the 14,000-acre wilderness area. A 1-mi walking trail has markers designating prime viewing spots. | Off U.S. 259 | 800/528–7337.

Poteau

Attractions

Cedar Lake Campground. An 84-acre lake, hiking trails, and RV and tent campsites can be found on this 200-acre campground. | Holson Valley Rd., 3 mi west of U.S. 59 S | 918/653–2991 | Daily.

Cedar Lake Equestrian Camp. Tent and RV campsites are equipped with individual corrals for horses and hot and cold showers for both horses and humans. | Holson Valley Rd., 3 mi west of U.S. 59 S | 918/653–2991.

Heavener Runestone State Park. A 12-ft by 10-ft granite slab bearing carved markings that some claim were left behind by Viking explorers in AD 900 is the centerpiece of this state park. Grounds include a hiking trail, a picnic area, a playground, and a gift shop. | U.S. 259, 12 mi east of Poteau | 918/653–2241 | www.touroklahoma.com | Daily.

Ouachita National Forest. More than 200,000 acres of the nation's largest shortleaf pine forest have been set aside for such activities as camping, hiking, mountain biking, horseback riding, hunting, and fishing. | Between U.S. 59 and Rte. 63 | 918/653–2991 weekdays; 918/567–2046 weekends | Daily.

The **Robert S. Kerr Nature Center Arboretum** is in the forest and includes two 1-mi-long marked trails and a visitor center that provides information about tree species, soil conditions, and Native American traditions. | Rte. 1 and U.S. 259 | 918/653–2991.

The **Winding Stair Recreation Area** includes a 20-acre primitive campground (no showers) at scenic Emerald Vista. | Rte. 1, 2 mi west of the U.S. 259 junction.

Peter Conser Historic House Site. In the 19th century, Conser patrolled the Choctaw Nation with his Lighthorsemen. His 1894 home has been restored and is open for tours. | Conser Rd., 3 mi west of U.S. 59 | 918/653–2493 | Wed.–Sat. 10–5, Sun. 1–5.

Spiro Mounds Archaeological State Park. A dozen earthen mounds have yielded many artifacts and ceremonial items, including jewelry, pottery, and sculpture. The mounds were plundered in the 1930s and few artifacts remain on site. A resident archaeologist gives guided tours. | Intersection of Rtes. 13 and 12, 25 mi north of Poteau | 918/962–2062 | www.touroklahoma.com | Wed.–Sat. 9–5, Sun. 12–5.

Talimena Scenic Byway. The 54-mi road links Talihina, Oklahoma, in the west to Mena, Arkansas, in the east. It's most popular when the fall foliage is at its peak, and in spring when the dogwood trees are in bloom. There are a number of scenic turnouts and picnic areas. | Starts in Talimena where it intersects with Rte. 1 | 918/567–3434 | Daily.

Dining

Chan's. Chinese. Known for egg rolls, sweet and sour pork, chow mein, and lemon chicken, the restaurant also serves American dishes. | 1008 N. Broadway St. | 918/647–2065 | No dinner Sun., Mon. | No credit cards | $–$$

Warehouse Willie's. American. In a converted warehouse, this restaurant has music playing in the background, and a toy train that runs around the second-floor dining room. The menu includes hamburgers, sandwiches, shrimp, and steaks. | 300 Dewey Ave. | 918/649–3400 | Closed Sun., Mon. | MC, V | $–$$

Lodging

Best Western Traders Inn. Within walking distance of restaurants and shops is this two-story mottled brick motel. Rooms have king-size or double beds. Complimentary Continental breakfast. In-room data ports. Cable TV. Pool. Hot tub. No pets. | 3111 North Broadway | 918/647–4001 | fax 918/647–9555 | www.bestwestern.com | 56 rooms | AE, D, DC, MC, V | $

Kerr Country Mansion Inn. The former home of Oklahoma statesman Robert S. Kerr has spectacular views of the river valley, a tiny museum, and a K-shaped swimming pool. Complimentary breakfast. Cable TV. Pool. | 1507 S. McKenna, 74953 | 918/647–8221 | 20 rooms | MC, V | $

Sallisaw

Attractions

Overstreet-Kerr Living History Farm. Once the residence of Indian Territory settlers, the grounds include a restored 1895 home and historic strains of grains, vegetables, and livestock that would have been used by the Choctaws in the late 19th century. | U.S. 59, Keota, 10 mi south of Sallisaw 74941 | 918/966–3396 | Fri.–Sat. 10–4.

Robert S. Kerr Lake. Boating, fishing, sailing, campsites, and a swimming beach are the highlights of this 42,000-acre lake. Boat rentals are available at the marina. | U.S. 59, 15 mi west of Sallisaw | 918/489–5541; 918/775–4522 marina | Daily.

Sequoyah's Home. The one-room cabin built by Cherokee linguist Sequoyah after he moved to Indian Territory from Tennessee in 1829 has exhibits about the Cherokee alphabet he invented. | Rte. 101, 10 mi northeast of Sallisaw | 918/775–2413 | Tues.–Sun.

Sequoyah National Wildlife Refuge. Migratory geese, ducks, and other waterfowl flock to this 28,000-acre reserve at the confluence of the Canadian and Arkansas rivers. Refuge facilities include a photo blind, hiking trails, and observation towers; fishing, hunting, and boating are permitted. | Rte. 1, 10 mi west of Sallisaw | 918/773–5251 | Daily.

OREGON

OREGON COAST
FROM ASTORIA TO BROOKINGS

Distance: Approximately 306 mi (without scenic byway detours) Time: 3–4 days
Overnight Breaks: Cannon Beach, Newport, Florence

A drive along the Oregon coast is at once dramatic and dazzling. Passing through small beach towns, fishing villages, and maritime resorts, U.S. 101—conveniently, the only roadway you'll need for this tour—dips, climbs, and curves through stretches of forest and along rocky headlands, windswept cliffs, and pristine white-sand beaches. Numerous state parks, overlooks, and scenic byways provide access to ocean vistas, historic lighthouses, and marine wildlife sanctuaries. Best of all, every amazing inch of the Oregon coast is accessible to the public.

The weather along the coast is generally mild, especially south of Gold Beach, but it is unpredictable. Pack a raincoat along with your swimsuit.

❶ **Astoria** is located where the mighty Columbia River empties into the Pacific, 96 mi west of Portland on Route 30. Maritime history buffs should stop in at the **Columbia River Maritime Museum** to see memorabilia salvaged from the almost 2,000 ships that have foundered in the treacherous waters; you can also explore a fully operational U.S. Coast Guard ship. Tour **Flavel House,** to see inside a restored mansion from the 1880s. The observation platform atop the 125-ft **Astoria Column** offers a view over Astoria, the Columbia River, and the Coast Range.

❷ Having finally reached the Pacific Ocean, the explorers Lewis and Clark spent the rainy winter of 1806 in a small wooden fort that has been faithfully replicated at **Fort Clatsop National Memorial,** 5 mi south of Astoria on Alt. U.S. 101.

❸ **Seaside** (12 mi south of Astoria on U.S. 101), one of the most tourist-oriented towns on the Oregon coast, has a long, sandy beach with a 2-mi boardwalk surrounded by hotels and restaurants.

❹ **Cannon Beach** (10 mi south of Seaside on U.S. 101), another popular tourist mecca, is named for a cannon that washed ashore from a schooner in 1846. There are plenty of places to shop in this hamlet—one of the more upscale resort towns on the

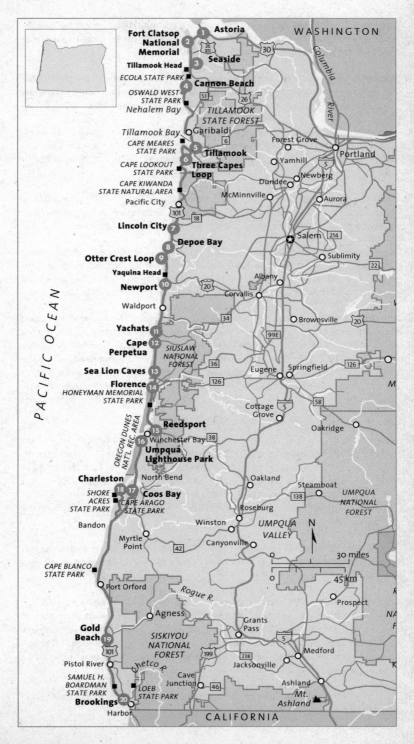

Oregon coast—but the real glory of the place is its broad beach, great for walking and kite flying, and presided over by a formidable offshore monolith known as **Haystack Rock.** Spend the night in Cannon Beach.

⑤ **Tillamook** (40 mi south of Cannon Beach on U.S. 101), surrounded by lush green fields, has long been known for its dairy industry. Stop in at the **Tillamook County Creamery** to sample the cheese and ice cream that have made this town famous.

⑥ From Tillamook, take the **Three Capes Loop** (marked turnoff in town), a 35-mi scenic byway that passes three magnificent headlands—**Cape Meares, Cape Lookout,** and **Cape Kiwanda**—as it winds along the coast, rejoining U.S. 101 just south of **Pacific City.**

⑦ What **Lincoln City** (16 mi south of Pacific City on U.S. 101) lacks in charm it more than makes up for in tourist amenities. The most popular destination on the Oregon coast sprawls along the Coast Highway and has plenty of shops and galleries.

⑧ From the tiny harbor at **Depoe Bay** (12 mi south of Lincoln City on U.S. 101), excursion boats run by **Tradewinds** head out on whale-watching cruises, conditions permitting. Some of the gigantic gray whales that annually migrate along the Oregon coast break away from the pod to linger year-round in Depoe Bay.

⑨ The **Otter Crest Loop** (5 mi south of Depoe Bay, off U.S. 101) scenic byway winds along the cliff tops to **Cape Foulweather,** a 500-ft headland, and down to a fascinating sea cave known as the **Devil's Punchbowl** before rejoining U.S. 101 north of Newport. Once you are back on U.S. 101, take the well-marked turnoff to **Yaquina Head,** where the gleaming white **Yaquina Bay Lighthouse,** activated in 1873, acts as the focal point for what has been designated an Outstanding Natural Area. On the rocky offshore islands you can often see harbor seals, sea lions, cormorants, murres, puffins, and guillemots.

⑩ **Newport** (12 mi south of Depoe Bay on U.S. 101) has an old **Bayfront** area where you'll find galleries, stores selling fresh crab and fish, and good seafood restaurants. It's also a good place to stay the night. A colorful fleet of fishing boats is docked in Yaquina Bay. As you leave Newport, signs on the south side of Yaquina Bay Bridge will direct you to the famous **Oregon Coast Aquarium,** a 4½-acre complex that provides a wonderful introduction to the various marine habitats found along the Oregon coast.

⑪ **Yachats** (pronounced YA-hots, 23 mi south of Newport on U.S. 101) is a small, attractive coastal hamlet with B&Bs, restaurants, and a rocky, surf-pounded beach with tidepools.

⑫ Towering 800 ft above the Pacific, **Cape Perpetua** (9 mi south of Yachats on U.S. 101) is the highest lookout point on the Oregon coast. For more information on this 2,700-acre scenic area, popular with hikers, naturalists, campers, and beachcombers, stop by the **Cape Perpetua Visitors Center.** A well-marked Auto Tour winds through Siuslaw National Forest to the ¼-mi **Whispering Spruce Trail,** where the views extend some 150 mi north and south and 37 mi out to sea.

⑬ On U.S. 101, 11 mi south of Cape Perpetua are the **Sea Lion Caves,** one of the Oregon Coast's premier attractions.

⑭ Just 13 mi south of the sea lions is the restored waterfront Old Town in **Florence,** a good source of seafood restaurants and places to spend the night. The town serves as the jumping-off point for the **Oregon Dunes National Recreation Area** (Visitor Center south side of Umpqua River Bridge), an awesome 41-mi-long stretch of dunes with forests, lakes, and camping facilities.

⑮ In **Reedsport** (20 mi south of Florence on U.S. 101) you may want to stop at the **Umpqua Discovery Center,** where the chief attraction is the *Hero,* the laboratory ship used by Admiral Byrd on his expeditions to the Antarctic.

⑯ Some of the highest sand dunes in the country are found in **Umpqua Lighthouse Park** (turnoff 6 mi south of Reedsport on U.S. 101). The **Umpqua River Lighthouse,** built in 1861, flashes its warning beacon from a bluff overlooking the south side of Winchester Bay.

⑰ **Coos Bay** (27 mi south of Reedsport on U.S. 101), a former lumber town, lies on the largest natural harbor between San Francisco and Seattle's Puget Sound. The town itself is not particularly attractive, but west of it there are three beautiful oceanfront parks.

⑱ Head first to **Charleston** (7 mi west of Coos Bay on Newmark Ave.), a small fishing village; the road becomes Cape Arago Highway as it loops into town. **Sunset Bay State**

OREGON RULES OF THE ROAD

License Requirements: To drive in Oregon, you must be at least 16 years old and hold a valid driver's license or be 15 years old with an instruction permit and accompanied by a licensed driver at least 21 years old. Residents of other states and countries may drive as long as they hold valid licenses from their home states or countries.

Speed Limit: The maximum speed limit in any city and on urban interstates and highways is 55 mph, while on rural interstate highways it is 65 mph. The maximum for trucks and passenger transport vehicles is 55 mph on all roads. The maximum speed allowed in residential districts and public parks is 25 mph. In school districts, fines for exceeding the limit of 20 mph can be doubled.

Right Turn on Red: A right turn may be made onto a two-way street *after* stopping at a red light and yielding as necessary, unless otherwise prohibited by a sign or police officer. When entering a one-way street, you may turn right or left with the movement of the traffic after stopping for the red light and yielding as necessary.

Seat Belt and Helmet Laws: Safety belt use is mandatory for all drivers and passengers in all available seating positions when the vehicle is in motion. Children under 4 who weigh 40 pounds or less are required to be in an approved child safety seat. Anyone under 16 riding a bicycle or being carried on a bicycle is required to wear approved protective headgear. All motorcycle operators and passengers and moped operators are required to wear motorcycle helmets at all times when operating motorcycles or mopeds on public streets.

For More Information: Contact **Oregon Driver and Motor Vehicles Services** at | 503/945–5000.

Park (2 mi south of Charleston off Cape Arago Highway) has a protected lagoon where you can actually swim (if you're brave enough for the cold waters) without worrying about currents and undertows. **Shore Acres State Park** (1 mi south of Sunset Bay State Park) is the setting for a beautifully landscaped garden—part of a former seaside estate—that incorporates formal English and Japanese design elements. **Cape Arago State Park** (1 mi south of Shore Acres State Park) overlooks the **Oregon Islands National Wildlife Refuge,** where offshore rocks, beaches, islands, and reefs provide breeding grounds for seabirds and marine mammals. From Cape Arago State Park you'll have to backtrack to Coos Bay to regain U.S. 101.

⑲ At **Gold Beach** (35 mi south of Cape Blanco on U.S. 101), the fabled **Rogue River,** one of the few U.S. rivers to merit Wild and Scenic status from the federal government, pours into the Pacific. The town's seasonal tourist industry is based largely on fishing and jet-boat trips up the Rogue. For more information, contact **Jerry's Rogue Boats** or **Rogue River Mail Boat Trips.**

⑳ Nearly 90 percent of the nation's potted Easter lilies are cultivated in **Brookings** (27 mi south of Gold Beach on U.S. 101). With its mild year-round climate, this southern part of the Oregon coast is sometimes referred to as Oregon's Banana Belt. The town, at the mouth of the Chetco River, is equally renowned as a commercial and sport-fishing port.

Astoria

Attractions

Astoria Column. Follow scenic drive signs to Coxcomb Hill to see this 125-ft monument, which is listed in the National Register of Historic Places. It was built in 1926 on the site of the first permanent U.S. settlement west of the Rockies. A spiral staircase leads up to a viewing platform where you get a panoramic view of the Astoria Bridge, the Pacific Ocean, and the mouth of the Columbia River. | Daily.

★ **Columbia River Maritime Museum.** The star of this downtown waterfront museum is the U.S. Coast Guard lightship *Columbia*. There are also exhibits and artifacts relating to lighthouses, shipwrecks, navigation, fishing, and naval history. | 1792 Marine Dr. | 503/325–2323 | www.crmm.org | Daily 9:30–5.

Flavel House. Built by Captain George Flavel, a Columbia River bar pilot, this 1885 Queen Anne Victorian home has six fireplaces with hand-carved mantels and tiles imported from Italy, Holland, Belgium, and Algeria. | 441 8th St. | 503/325–2203 | May–Sept., daily 10–5; Oct.–Apr., daily 11–4.

★ **Fort Clatsop National Memorial.** Capts. Meriwether Lewis and William Clark camped here during the winter of 1805–06. A replica of their fort is the highpoint of the 125-acre park, which is 5 mi southeast of Astoria. Demonstrations on making candles and clothing, smoking meat, building canoes, and firing flintlocks add life to the expedition displays. | 92343 Ft. Clatsop Rd., 97103 | 503/861–2471 | www.nps.gov/focl | Oct.–May 8–5; June–Sept. 8–6.

Fort Stevens State Park. Fort Stevens is the only military installation in the continental U.S. to have been fired upon since the War of 1812. The park, 6 mi southwest of Astoria, has a museum of U.S. military history, a blacksmith shop, guided tours, and daily Civil War-era cannon and rifle demonstrations. On Labor Day weekend a Civil War reenactment is staged. | Warrenton Hammond Rd., 97121 | 503/861–1671 or 800/551–6949 | www.prd.state.or.us | May–Oct., daily 10–6; Nov.–Apr., daily 10–4.

Josephson's. One of the Oregon coast's oldest commercial smokehouses, Josephson's uses alderwood for all its processing and specializes in Pacific Northwest chinook and coho salmon. You can also buy smoked sturgeon, tuna, oysters, mussels, scallops, and prawns by the pound or in sealed gift packs. An exhibit of photos and magazine articles provides a history of the smokehouse. | 106 Marine Dr., 97103 | 503/325–2190 | fax 503/325–4075 | www.josephsons.com | Weekdays 8–5:30; weekends 10–5:30.

Dining

Gunderson's Cannery Cafe. Seafood. Overlooking the Columbia River on Pier 6 in a century-old cannery, Gunderson's in-season seafood is prepared fresh and never fried. The lime prawns, halibut burger, or crab and shrimp cakes are good choices. Homemade soups, focaccia pizza, breads, and desserts are also available. | One 6th St. | 503/325–8642 | No supper Sun.–Mon. | D, DC, MC, V | $$–$$$

Home Spirit Bakery Café. Contemporary. In an 1891 Queen Anne house with a river view, this unique restaurant is filled with artifacts from the 1902–1912 Arts and Crafts period. It's known locally for its baked goods. The owners serve lunch five days a week. On Thurs.–Sat., there's a prix-fixe dinner with a choice of four entrées: seafood, chicken, red meat, and vegetarian. The price of the meal depends on the night; Saturday is highest. | 1585 Exchange St., 97103 | 503/325–6846 | Closed Sun.–Mon. No dinner Tues.–Wed. | No credit cards | $$–$$$

Ship Inn. Seafood. The Ship Inn is well known among locals and savvy tourists for its famous fish (halibut is used) and chips. But don't overlook the many other seafood dishes prepared with a Pacific Northwest flair. | 1 2nd St., 97103 | 503/325–0033 | Closed major holidays | AE, D, MC, V | $–$$$

Brookings

Attractions

Alfred A. Loeb State Park. In a fragrant myrtle forest on the Chetco River 10 mi from Brookings, this park offers some of the best salmon and steelhead fishing in southern Oregon. | Off U.S. 101 | 541/469–2021 or 800/551–6949 | www.prd.state.or.us | Daily.

Azalea City Park. Five varieties of the flower bloom at this park on the edge of town, which also includes a playground filled with imaginatively designed wooden equipment. | Off North Bank Chetco River Rd. | 800/535–9469 | Daily.

Chetco Valley Historical Museum. Two miles south of Brookings, this museum is inside a mid-19th-century stagecoach stop and trading post. An iron casting with a likeness of Queen Elizabeth I has led to speculation that it was left during a landing by Sir Francis Drake. On a nearby hill is the World Champion Cypress Tree, 99 ft tall with a 27-ft circumference. | 5461 Museum Rd., 97415 | 541/469–6651 | Memorial Day–Labor Day, Wed.–Sun. noon–5; Labor Day–Memorial Day, Fri.–Sun. noon–5.

Harris Beach State Park. You can watch the gray whales migrate in spring and winter. Bird Island, also called Goat Island, is a National Wildlife Sanctuary and a breeding site for rare birds. There is a campground with 34 full hookups, 52 electrical and 66 tent sites, and 4 yurts. | U.S. 101 | 541/469–2021 or 800/551–6949 | www.prd.state.or.us | Daily.

Samuel H. Boardman State Park. Four miles north of Brookings, this 12-mi-long linear park runs along the rugged, steep coast. Highlights include a view of Arch Rock and Natural Bridges, as well as a 27-mi-long Oregon Coast Trail, which packs a lot of appeal for hikers. | U.S. 101 | 541/469–2021 or 800/551–6949 | www.prd.state.or.us | Daily.

Dining

Smuggler's Cove. Seafood. Fishing vessels docked in the next boat basin and picture windows looking out to sea lend a salty ambience to this low-key restaurant. The daily seafood specials—usually halibut and salmon—are good bets; try the fish and chips or the crab melt for lunch. | 16011 Boat Basin Rd., 97415 | 541/469–6006 | MC, V | $$–$$$

City Grill. American. Inside the 1915 Historic Central Building, this downtown, Victorian-style place done in mauve and burgundy was formerly the California & Oregon Lumber Company. Try Uncle Hootie's special—prawns in Alfredo sauce over linguine with steak on the side—or if you're in the mood for something lighter, order the fish and chips. | 703 Chetco Ave., 97415 | 541/412–0375 | Closed Mon. | AE, D, DC, MC, V | $$

Cannon Beach

Attractions

Ecola State Park. A winding road along Tillamook Head will lead you to an extraordinary view of the Pacific Ocean. You might see elk and deer as you drive through the forest. The park is 2 mi north of Cannon Beach. | U.S. 101 | 503/436–2844 or 800/551–6949 | www.prd.state.or.us | Daily.

Neahkahnie Mountain. A road with some hair-raising curves climbs to 700 ft as it winds around the flank of this 1,661-ft mountain, south of Cannon Beach. The views are dramatic. Carvings on nearby beach rocks and Native American legends have given rise to a tale that a fortune in gold doubloons from a sunken Spanish galleon is buried somewhere on the mountainside. | U.S. 101.

Oswald West State Park. Several different trails wind through the park, leading to the beach and the Cape Falcon overlook. | Ecola Park Rd. | 503/436–2623 or 800/551–6949 | www.prd.state.or.us | Mar.–Nov., daily.

Dining

Stephanie Inn. Contemporary. The dining room of this handsome oceanfront hotel 1¼ mi south of town has a river-rock fireplace, an open kitchen, and views of mountain scenery. There are two seatings for the four-course prix-fixe meal, with entrées that might include shrimp-stuffed halibut or NY strip steak. Diners may request vegetarian meals. | 2740 S. Pacific, 97110 | 503/436–2221 or 800/633–3466 | fax 503/436–9711 | Reservations essential | AE, D, DC, MC, V | $$$$

Dooger's. Seafood. Like the original Dooger's in Seaside, the Cannon Beach branch serves superb seafood and steaks in a casual, contemporary setting. Don't pass up the clam chowder. No smoking. Kids' menu. | 1371 S. Hemlock St. | 503/436–2225 | Closed 2 wks in Jan. | AE, MC, V | $$$

★ **The Bistro.** Contemporary. Flowers, candlelight, and classical music enhance the three-course prix-fixe dinners at this 12-table restaurant. The menu includes imaginative Continental-influenced renditions of fresh local seafood and such specials as lamb, prawns, oysters, and Pacific seafood stew. | 263 N. Hemlock St., 97701 | 503/436–2661 | Reservations essential | Closed Tues., Nov.–Jan. No lunch | MC, V | $$–$$$

Lazy Susan Café. Café. A favorite for breakfast in Cannon Beach, this laid-back spot welcomes you with omelets, waffles, hot cereal, home fries, and fresh-baked scones. | Coaster Sq., 126 N. Hemlock St., 97110 | 503/436–2816 | Reservations not accepted | Closed Tues. No dinner Sun.–Mon., Wed.–Thurs. | No credit cards | $–$$

Lodging

Hallmark Resort. Large suites with fireplaces and great views make this triple-decker oceanfront resort a good choice for families, or for couples looking to splurge. The rooms, all with oak-tile baths, have soothing color schemes. The least expensive units do not have views. Some kitchenettes, refrigerators, some in-room hot tubs. Cable TV. Indoor pool, wading pool. Hot tub. Exercise equipment. Laundry facilities. Business services. Airport shuttle. Pets allowed (fee). | 1400 S. Hemlock, 97110 | 503/436–1566 or 888/448–4449 | fax 503/436–0324 | 131 rooms, 63 suites, 4 cottages | AE, D, DC, MC, V | $$$–$$$$

Cannon Beach Hotel. Walk to the beach and downtown shopping from this restored, turn-of-the-20th-century, European-style inn at the entrance to Haystack Rock. There's a cozy fireplace in the lobby, and some rooms have fireplaces, too. Restaurant, complimentary Continental breakfast. No air-conditioning, some in-room hot tubs. Cable TV. Hot tub. Business services. No smoking. | 1116 S. Hemlock | 503/436–1392 | fax 503/436–2101 | 9 rooms | AE, D, DC, MC, V | $–$$$

Grey Whale Inn. In operation since 1948, this charming inn is in a quiet residential neighborhood, just a 5-minute walk from the beach and a 20-minute walk from Haystack Rock. All the rooms are individually decorated with original artwork, done either by the owners or local artists. No air-conditioning, some kitchenettes. Cable TV, in-room VCRs. No smoking. | 164 Kenai St., 97110 | 503/436–2848 | 5 rooms (with shower only) | MC, V | $–$$

Coos Bay

Attractions

Cape Arago Lighthouse. Cape Arago Lighthouse is on a rock island just 12 mi south of Coos Bay. The first lighthouse was built here in 1866, but it was destroyed by storms and erosion. A second, built in 1908, suffered the same fate. The current one, built in 1934, is 44 ft tall. If you're here on a foggy day, listen for its unique foghorn. The lighthouse is connected to the mainland by a bridge. Neither are open to the public, but there's an excellent spot to view this lonely guardian and much of the coastline: from Highway 101, take Cape Arago Highway to Gregory Point, where it ends at a turnaround, and follow the short trail.

Cape Arago State Park. Fourteen miles southwest of Coos Bay, this park juts out into the Pacific Ocean. It's a good place to watch for whales. If you take the north cove trail, you might also spot seals and sea lions. | Cape Arago Hwy., off U.S. 101, 97420 | 541/888–8867 | Daily.

Charleston Marina Complex. The marina includes a launch ramp, a store where you can buy tackle and marine supplies, a 110-space RV park, a motel, restaurants, and gift shops. Fishing charters also set out from here. | 4535 Kingfisher Drive, Charleston, 97420 | 541/888–2548 | www.charlestonmarina.com | Daily.

Golden and Silver Falls State Park. Twenty-four miles north of Coos Bay on Highway 101, this park's old-growth forest, sprinkled with maidenhair ferns, hides two natural wonders. Silver Falls pours over a 200-ft-high semicircular rock ledge. One-quarter mi to the northwest, thundering Golden Falls is even more impressive, especially in the spring. | No phone | Daily dawn–dusk.

Shore Acres State Park and Botanical Gardens. Once the grand estate of a pioneer timber baron, Shore Acres, set on rugged sandstone cliffs high above the ocean, off U.S. 101, has lushly planted gardens with plants and flowers from around the world. | Cape Arago Hwy. | 541/888–3732 or 541/888–8867 | Daily 8–dusk.

Sunset Bay State Park. Two miles south of Charleston, the park includes cliffs and beaches, and a campground with 29 full hookups, 34 electrical and 72 tent sites, and 4 yurts. Its lagoon is protected from the sea, making it one of the few places on the Oregon coast where you can swim without worrying about currents or an undertow. You can also hike to Shore Acres and Cape Arago state parks from here. | Cape Arago Hwy., off U.S. 101 | 541/888–4902 or 800/551–6949 | www.prd.state.or.us | Daily.

Dining
Portside. Seafood. The view of the harbor through the restaurant's picture window, overlooking the Charleston boat basin off U.S. 101, is pretty and peaceful. Try the steamed Dungeness crab with drawn butter, bouillabaisse, or fresh salmon. On Friday nights there is an all-you-can-eat seafood buffet. If the weather cooperates, dine on the patio. Entertainment Wed.–Sun. Kids' menu. | 8001 Kingfisher Rd., Charleston | 541/888–5544 | AE, DC, MC, V | $$–$$$

★ **Blue Heron Bistro.** American. Subtle preparations of local seafood, chicken, and pasta are served up at this busy bistro. The innovative soups and desserts are excellent. The skylit tile-floor dining room is accented with natural wood and blue linen. Patio dining is also available. | 100 W. Commercial St. | 541/267–3933 | Closed Oct. and Sundays | AE, D, MC, V | $$

Kum-Yon's. Pan-Asian. On the main drag, this tiny spot serves up satisfying and inexpensive Asian food, including sushi, sashimi, and kung-pao shrimp. | 835 S. Broadway, 97420 | 541/269–2662 | fax 541/267–3821 | Closed Mon. | AE, D, MC, V | $–$$

Depoe Bay

Attractions
Depoe Bay Park. With its narrow channel and deep water, the park's tiny harbor is one of the most protected on the coast. It supports a thriving fleet of commercial- and charter-fishing boats. The Spouting Horn, a natural cleft in the basalt cliffs on the waterfront, blasts seawater skyward during heavy weather. | South on U.S. 101 | 541/765–2889 | www.stateoforegon.com/depoe_bay/chamber | Daily.

Tradewinds. Every year a few of the gigantic gray whales migrating along the coast decide to linger in Depoe Bay and, for more than six decades, Tradewinds has operated cruises to watch them. The skippers are all marine naturalists who give a running commentary, and the boats can accommodate from six to 40 passengers. Daylight hours only. The ticket office is on Highway 101 at the north end of Depoe Bay Bridge. | Hwy. 101 97341 | 541/765–2345 or 800/445–8730 | fax 541/765–2282 | www.tradewindscharters.com | Closed Christmas.

Florence

Attractions
Devil's Elbow State Park. Heceta Head Lighthouse is among the sights in this park 13 mi north of Florence. Also seek out the natural caves and tidepools. | U.S. 101 | 800/551–6949 or 541/997–3851 | www.prd.state.or.us | Daily.

The beacon that shines from **Heceta Head Lighthouse** in Devil's Elbow State Park, visible for more than 21 mi, is the most powerful on the Oregon coast. A trail leads from the lighthouse to Heceta House, a pristine white structure said to be haunted by the wife of a lighthouse keeper whose child fell to her death from the cliffs shortly after the beacon was lit in 1894. The house, which was once the light keeper's residence, is now one of Oregon's most remarkable B&Bs. The lighthouse is accessed via a half-mi-long trail from the parking lot in Devil's Elbow State Park. | U.S. 101 | 541/997–3851 | www.hecetalighthouse.com | Memorial Day–Labor Day, tours daily by appointment.

Jessie M. Honeyman Memorial. Two miles of sand dunes lie between the park and the ocean. Two natural freshwater lakes are within the 522-acre park, 3 mi south of Florence, which has the second-largest campground in the state. There are 50 full hookups, 91 electrical and 237 tent sites, and 10 yurts. | U.S. 101 | 541/997–3851 | www.prd.state.or.us | Daily.

Sea Lion Caves. An elevator near the ticket office at the cliff top, 11 mi north of Florence on U.S. 101, descends to the floor of the cavern, near sea level, where Stellar and California sea lions and their fuzzy pups can be viewed from behind a wire fence. In spring and summer the sea lions are on the rocky ledges outside the cave; during fall and winter they are usually inside the cave. You'll also see several species of sea birds, including migratory pigeons, guillemots, cormorants, and three varieties of gulls. Gray whales are visible during their northern and southern migrations, from October to December and from March to May. | U.S. 101 | 541/547–3111 | www.sealioncaves.com | Daily 9–sunset.

Dining

Bridgewater Seafood Restaurant. Seafood. Freshly caught seafood—25 to 30 choices nightly—is the mainstay of this creaky-floored Victorian-era restaurant in Florence's Old Town. | 1297 Bay St. | 541/997–9405 | MC, V | $$–$$$

Windward Inn. Seafood. One of the south coast's most elegant eateries, this tightly run ship prides itself on its vast menu, which includes fresh seafood and home-baked breads and desserts. Steak is also on the menu, but try the Chinook salmon fillets poached in Riesling or the shrimp and scallops sautéed in white wine. A pianist plays on weekends. Kids' menu. | 3757 U.S. 101 N | 541/997–8243 | Breakfast also available | AE, D, MC, V | $–$$$

Mo's. American. Mo's chain of family-style restaurants has been an institution on the Oregon coast for more than four decades. At this location, built right out over the water, bay-front views and down-home service complement the fresh seafood. Try the creamy clam chowder. | 1436 Bay St., 97439 | 541/997–2185 | fax 541/997–3504 | D, MC, V | $–$$

Lodging

Driftwood Shores Resort. The chief amenity of this resort is that it's directly above Heceta Beach, one of the longest sand beaches on the south coast. The simple rooms have ocean views, and the three-bedroom suites have fireplaces. Kitchenettes. | 88416 1st Ave., 97439 | 541/997–8263 or 800/422–5091 | fax 541/997–5857 | 107 rooms, 21 suites | AE, D, DC, MC, V | $$–$$$

Holiday Inn Express. Just 3 mi from the beach and close to restaurants and shopping, this Holiday Inn Express is both convenient and comfortable. Complimentary Continental breakfast. In-room data ports. Cable TV. Hot tub. Exercise equipment. | 2475 U.S. 101, 97439 | 541/997–7797 | fax 541/997–7895 | 51 rooms | AE, D, DC, MC, V | $$

Johnson House. The guest rooms in this 1892 Italianate Victorian in Old Town have lace curtains, crocheted doilies, and goose-down comforters. The house is carefully preserved and the period and antique furnishings are genuine. You can drive to the beach in 10 minutes, and it's a short walk from the antiques shops, crafts boutiques, and eateries on the bay dock. Complimentary breakfast. No air-conditioning. No kids under 12. No smoking. | 216 Maple St., 97439 | 541/997–8000 or 800/768–9488 | fax 541/997–2364 | 3 rooms, 1 suite, 1 cottage | D, MC, V | $$

Landmark Inn. The new Landmark, on a hilltop above the Siuslaw River, is surrounded by rhododendrons. It's near Dunes National Park and Old Town, and the grounds offer a great view of the Fourth of July fireworks. The rooms have vaulted ceilings and the owners pride themselves on their clean and quiet home. Complimentary Continental breakfast. No air-conditioning, in-room data ports, some kitchenettes, some microwaves, some refrigerators, some in-room hot tubs. Cable TV. Spa. No smoking. | 1551 4th St., 97439 | 541/997–9030 or 800/822–7811 | www.presys.com/~landmarkinn | 4 rooms, 6 suites | $–$$

Gold Beach

Attractions

Cape Sebastian State Park. The parking lots here are more than 200 ft above sea level. At the south parking vista you can see up to 43 mi north to Humbug Mountain. Looking south you can see nearly 50 mi toward Crescent City, California, and the Point Saint George Lighthouse. A deep forest of Sitka spruce covers most of the park. There's a 1½-mi walking trail. | U.S. 101 | 800/551–6949 | www.prd.state.or.us | Daily.

Cedar Bend Golf Course. Two tees at each hole of this 9-hole course 10 mi north of town allow you to golf 18 holes among the deer, elk, hawk, eagles, and other wildlife that inhabit the valley around Cedar Fork Creek. | 34391 Squaw Valley Rd., 97444 | 541/247–6911.

Curry County Historical Museum. Native American baskets and historic photos and documents are among the displays at this small museum on the Curry County Fairgrounds. | 920 S. Ellensburg | 541/247–6113 | June–Sept., Tues.–Sat. noon–4; Oct.–May, Sat. 10–4.

Jerry's Rogue River Jet Boat Trips. Take a 64-, 80-, or 104-mi round trip up the Wild and Scenic–designated section of the Rogue River. The trips last 6–8 hours and leave from the Rogue River Bridge at the port of Gold Beach Boat Basin. | 541/247–4571 or 800/451–3645 | fax 541/247–7601 | www.roguejets.com | May–Oct., daily; call for hours.

Official Rogue River Mail Boat Hydro-Jet Trips. Slightly upstream from the north end of Rogue River Bridge in Wedderburn, this company has provided the area with over 100 years of continuous postal service. You can ride along on 64-, 80-, or 104-mi trips along the Rogue River. Bring a picnic lunch, or have a reasonably priced meal at one of three lodges in Agness. Keep an eye out for bears. | Mail Boat Dock | 541/247–7033 or 800/458–3511 | www.mailboat.com | May–Oct., daily; call for hours.

Prehistoric Gardens. Colorful life-size replicas of dinosaurs are the artistic interpretations of the late sculptor E. V. Nelson. The "Dinopark" is 15 mi from Gold Beach in a rain forest filled with giant ferns. | U.S. 101, in Oregon's rain forest | 541/332–4463 | Daily, 8–dusk; call for hours in winter.

Dining

Tu Tu' Tun Lodge. Contemporary. Dinner in the Lodge's restaurant, 7 mi upriver from Gold Beach, is open to non-guests and consists of a five-course prix-fixe meal that changes nightly. Portions are memorably large. | 96550 N. Bank Rogue, 97444 | 541/247–6664 or 800/864–6357 | fax 541/247–0672 | Reservations essential | Closed Nov.–Apr. | D, MC, V | $$$$

Nor'wester Seafood. Continental. Overlooking the boat harbor and the Rogue River, this restaurant serves good seafood, steaks, and pasta. Kids' menu. | 29971 Harbor Way | 541/247–2333 | Closed Dec.–Jan. No lunch | AE, MC, V | $$–$$$

Newport

Attractions

Bayfront. With its tall-masted fishing fleet, well-worn buildings, seafood markets, and art galleries and shops, Newport's old Bayfront is an ideal place for an afternoon stroll. So many male sea lions in Yaquina Bay loiter near crab pots and bark from the piers that local people call the area the Bachelor Club.

Devil's Punch Bowl State Natural Area. A rocky shoreline separates this day-use park from the surf. It's a popular whale-watching site just 9 mi north of Newport and has excellent tidepools. | U.S. 101 | 541/265–9278 | Daily.

★ **Oregon Coast Aquarium.** One of the most popular attractions in the state, this complex contains re-creations of offshore and near-shore Pacific marine habitats, all teeming with life: playful sea otters, comical puffins, fragile jellyfish, and a 60-pound octopus. There's a hands-on interactive area for children, and North America's largest seabird aviary. For a few years the biggest attraction was Keiko, the 4-ton killer whale and star of the movie *Free Willy*. He was moved to Iceland in 1998, and the aquarium has developed some new attractions in the space he occupied. There is a new 35,000-gallon saltwater salmon and sturgeon exhibit. You should plan to spend at least 3 hours here. | 2820 S.E. Ferry Slip Rd. | 541/867–3474 | www.aquarium.org | July–Labor Day, daily 9–8; Labor Day–Memorial Day, daily 10–5; Memorial Day–June, daily 9–6.

Yaquina Bay State Park. At the north end of Yaquina Bay near its outlet to the Pacific, this park is home to a historic lighthouse that in more recent years was used as a Coast Guard Lifeboat Station. It's been restored and is now open to the public. | U.S. 101 S | 541/867–7451 | Daily.

Ninety-three-foot **Yaquina Head Lighthouse** is the tallest on the Oregon Coast. Guided morning tours are limited to 15 people. | 4 mi north of bridge in Newport | 541/574–3100 | Mid-June–mid-Sept., daily noon–4. In winter, call ahead.

Dining

Canyon Way Restaurant and Bookstore. Seafood. Cod, Dungeness crab cakes, bouillabaisse, and Yaquina Bay oysters are among the popular dishes at this Newport dining spot, which is up the hill from the center of the Bayfront. There's also a deli counter for take-out. At lunchtime the restaurant sets up patio tables that permit a great view of the bay. The patio is to one side of a well-stocked bookstore. | 1216 S.W. Canyon Way | 541/265–8319 | Closed Sun.–Mon. | AE, MC, V | $$–$$$

Whale's Tale. Seafood. Casual and family-oriented, this bay-front restaurant serves fresh local seafood, thick clam chowder, fish-and-chips, burgers, and sandwiches. Kids' menu. | 452 S.W. Bay Blvd., 97365 | 541/265–8660 | Breakfast also available. Closed Jan.–Feb. and Wed. until June | AE, D, DC, MC, V | $$–$$$

Tables of Content. Contemporary. In this restaurant at the literary-themed Sylvia Beach Hotel, the setting is unadorned, with family-size tables; the main plot is a prix-fixe menu that changes nightly; the central character might be local seafood, like grilled salmon fillet in a sauce Dijonnaise (but you can choose among four entrées, one of them vegetarian); and the conclusion will certainly be a decadent dessert, such as Chocolate Oblivion Torte. | 267 N.W. Cliff St., 97365 | 541/265–5428 | Reservations essential | No lunch | AE, MC, V | $$

Italian Food Co. Italian. The Italian Food Co. (formerly Don Petrie's) is a block from the beach in the increasingly trendy Nye Beach area. In a building that was once an electrical machine shop, it now has the look of a funky trattoria. You'll find such basics as spaghetti and meatballs or other pasta with a wide choice of sauces, and if you come early, before 5:30, you'll get 15% off the price of your dinner entrée. | 613 N.W. 3rd St., 97365 | 541/265–3663 | Closed Tues. No lunch | D, MC, V | $–$$

Lodging

Tyee Lodge. Tyee means "chinook salmon" in the Indian trading language. This 1940s house in Agate Beach is on a bluff and a nearby trail leads down to the beach. The guest rooms all have pine furniture and views of the ocean through towering Sitka Spruce trees. Breakfast is served family-style in a bay-windowed room facing the ocean. Composer Ernest Bloch lived nearby. Complimentary breakfast. No air-conditioning, no room phones. TV in common area. No kids under 16. No smoking. | 4925 N.W. Woody Way, 97365 | 541/265–8953 or 888/553–8933 | www.tyeelodge.com | 5 rooms | AE, D, MC, V | $$–$$$

★ **Sylvia Beach Hotel.** Antiques-filled rooms named for famous writers gives a fun twist to this 1913-vintage beachfront hotel. A pendulum swings over the bed in the Poe room. The Christie, Twain, and Colette rooms are the most luxurious; all have fireplaces, decks, and ocean views. A well-stocked split-level upstairs library has decks, a fireplace, slumbering cats, and too-comfortable chairs. Every night at 10, mulled wine is served. Restaurant, complimentary Continental breakfast. No room phones. TV in common area. Library. | 267 N.W. Cliff St., 97365 | 541/265–5428 | 20 rooms | AE, MC, V | $–$$$

Whaler. All rooms at this motel have ocean views; some have fireplaces. Set in a residential area across from the city park and the beach, it's a short walk from the Yaquina Bay Lighthouse. Complimentary Continental breakfast. Some microwaves, some refrigerators. Cable TV. Laundry facilities. Airport shuttle. Pets allowed. | 155 S.W. Elizabeth St., 97465 | 541/265–9261 or 800/433–9444 | fax 541/265–9515 | 73 rooms | AE, D, DC, MC, V | $$

Nye Beach Hotel. Despite its century-old appearance, suitable to the historic Nye Beach district, the Nye Beach Hotel was built in 1992. It stands on a cliff above the beach and all the guest rooms have balconies with ocean views, private baths, and fireplaces. The pastel colors and potted tropical plants in the lobby remind some guests of Key West. Keep an eye out for the macaw and the African love birds. Restaurant. Some in-room hot tubs. Cable TV. | 219 N.W. Cliff St., 97365 | 541/265–3334 | fax 541/265–3622 | www.nyebeach.com | 18 rooms | AE, D, MC, V | $–$$

Pacific City

Attractions

Cape Lookout State Park/Cape Kiwanda State Natural Area. The coastal bluffs make this a popular hang-gliding and kite-flying area. This park, 1 mi north of Pacific City, has views of the ocean and easy access to the beach. A campground has 54 full hookups, 1 electrical and 191 tent sites, and 4 yurts. The Cape Lookout Trail, 10 mi north of Pacific City, follows the headland for more than 2 mi. | Whiskey Creek Rd. | 800/551–6949 | www.prd.state.or.us.

Three Capes Scenic Route. The coastal drive begins in Tillamook and winds for about 25 mi through Oceanside and south to Pacific City. Highlights are Cape Lookout State Park (above) and the Cape Meares Lighthouse. | West of U.S. 101.

Reedsport

Attractions

Dean Creek Elk Viewing Area. A large herd of Roosevelt elk can be seen at this 1,000-acre site with pasture, woodlands, and wetlands. | Rte. 38 E | 541/756–0100 | Daily.

Oregon Dunes National Recreation Area. The Oregon Dunes stretch along the coast from Florence to North Bend. You'll find fine beaches, campgrounds, boat launch ramps, and picnic areas. Hiking trails pass through green areas that are home to many species of wildlife. All-terrain vehicles are permitted in some areas. | The Visitors Center, at U.S. 101 and OR 38 | 541/271–3611 | Daily.

Salmon Harbor. Located 2 mi south of Reedsport at the mouth of the Umpqua River, this is one of the largest marinas on the Oregon Coast. An RV park is near the county-operated facility. | U.S. 101 | 541/271–3407 | May–Sept., daily; Oct.–Apr., weekdays.

Umpqua Discovery Center. Exhibits about early settlers are the focus of this educational and cultural center. Other displays explain the history of Native Americans and early explorers. | 409 Riverfront Way | 541/271–4816 | Daily 10–4.

Umpqua Lighthouse State Park. At the entrance to Winchester Bay in the Oregon Dunes is this 65-ft lighthouse and museum. Just 4 mi from Reedsport, the campground has 20 full hookups, 42 tent sites, 2 yurts, and 2 cabins, and surrounds Lake Marie. Recreational activities include non-motorized boating and swimming. There is also a small beach. | Off U.S. 101 | 541/271–4118 or 800/551–6949 | www.prd.state.or.us | Daily.

William M. Tugman State Park. On Eel Lake near the town of Lakeside, this little-known park is surrounded by a dense forest of spruce, cedar, fir, and alder. Recreational activities include fishing, swimming, canoeing, and sailing. A campground has 115 electrical sites and 3 yurts. | U.S. 101 S | 541/888–4902 or 800/551–6949 | www.prd.state.or.us | Daily.

Seaside

Attractions

Ecola State Park. Ecola State Park, 5 mi south of Seaside, is a playground of sea sculpted rocks, sandy shoreline, green headlands, and panoramic views. The main beach can be crowded in summer, but Indian Beach has an often deserted cove and explorable tide pools. | Hwy. 101 97138 | 800/551–6949 | www.prd.state.or.us | Daily dawn–dusk.

Saddle Mountain State Park. It's a 2½-mi hike from the parking lot to the summit of Saddle Mountain. It's much cooler at that elevation. The campground, which is 14 mi north of Seaside, has 10 primitive sites. | Off U.S. 26 | 800/551–6949 or 503/436–2844 | Mar.–Nov., daily.

Seaside Aquarium. Jellyfish, giant king crab, octopus, moray eels, wolf eels, and other sea life swim in the tanks at this attraction on the 2-mi-long beachfront Promenade. You can feed the harbor seals. | 200 N. Promenade | 503/738–6211 | Wed.–Sun. 9–5.

Tillamook Head. Follow signs on Hwy. 101 south of Seaside until you reach a parking area; from there, a 2-mi hike will bring you to the 1,100-ft-high viewing point atop Tillamook Head. You'll be able to see the Tillamook Rock Light Station, a mile or so out to sea. The lonely beacon, built in 1881 on a straight-sided rock, towers 41 ft above the ocean. Decommissioned in 1957, it is now a columbarium, used to bury human remains. | Hwy. 101 97138 | 800/551–6949 | www.prd.state.or.us.

Dining

Stephanie Inn. Contemporary. The cozy dining room at this three-story oceanfront hotel serves four-course prix-fixe suppers of innovative Pacific Northwest cuisine. The menu changes daily but might include fresh Dungeness crab cakes, artichoke and pine nuts salad, salmon or lamb chops, and dessert. | 2740 S. Pacific St., 97110 | 503/436–2221 or 800/633–3466 | Reservations essential | AE, D, DC, MC, V | $$$$

Dooger's Seafood and Grill. Seafood. The sister restaurant of the original Dooger's in Cannon Beach, this branch serves the same superb seafood and steaks in a casual, contemporary setting. Don't pass up the famous clam chowder. Kids' menu. No smoking. | 505 Broadway, 97138 | 503/738–3773 | Closed first 2 weeks in Dec. | MC, V | $$–$$$

Premier Pasta Italian Dining Room. Italian. Dishes at this restaurant on the Necanicum River focus on pasta—it's owned by a pasta maker. There are several varieties of fettucine, linguine, and rotelle plus homemade sauces, which you can buy. Try the three-layered lasagna filled with sweet Italian sausage, red sauce, three cheeses, and black olives. | 1530 S. Holladay Dr. | 503/738–3692 | Closed Sun.–Mon. No lunch | D, MC, V | $$–$$$

Breakers Restaurant and Lounge. Contemporary. In a Best Western, this family restaurant serves steaks, chicken, seafood, and pastas. Try the Oregon crab cakes or be a rebel and have Alaskan salmon and halibut. Plan on having the Oregon blueberry white chocolate cheesecake for dessert. | 414 N. Promenade, 97138 | 503/738–3334 or 800/234–8439 | fax 503/738–5959 | No lunch | AE, D, DC, MC, V | $–$$$

Sam's Seaside Café. American/Casual. Half a block from the boardwalk and beach, this quiet, casual spot serves inexpensive burgers, salads, seafood dishes, and homemade cakes and pies at lunch and dinner. Sam's stays open late, too. | 104 Broadway, 97138 | 503/717–1725 | AE, MC, V | $–$$

Tillamook

Attractions

Blue Heron French Cheese Company. In business since 1979, Blue Heron specializes in Camembert, Brie, and other French-style cheeses. There's a petting zoo, a deli with seating, and a gift shop that carries Oregon wines, jams, mustards, and other products. You can eat outside at picnic tables. A popular addition is a tasting room where you can sample the products of Oregon wineries. | 2001 Blue Heron Dr., 97141 | 503/842–8281 or 800/275–0639 | fax 503/842–8530 | www.blueheronoregon.com | Memorial Day–Labor Day, daily 8–8; Labor Day–Memorial Day, daily 9–5.

Pioneer Museum. The displays in Tillamook's 1905 county courthouse include Native American, pioneer, logging, and natural history exhibits, plus antique vehicles and military artifacts. Most popular are the collections of dolls, quilts, and guns. | 2106 2nd St., 97141 | 503/842–4553 | fax 503/842–4553 | Mon.–Sat. 8–5, Sun. 11–5.

Tillamook County Creamery. The largest cheese-making plant on the West Coast, 2 mi north of Tillamook, draws more than 750,000 visitors each year. Here the milk from local Holstein and brown Swiss cows becomes ice cream, butter, and cheddar and Monterey Jack cheeses. You can see exhibits and get free samples. | 4175 Hwy. 101 N, 97141 | 503/842–4481 | fax 503/842–6039 | www.tillamookcheese.com | June–mid-Sept., daily 8–8; Mid-Sept.–May, daily 8–6.

Tillamook Naval Air Station Museum. During World War II, blimps patrolled the coast to watch for enemy submarines and were based at this site in massive hangars. Today, the remaining hangar is home to a museum that displays vintage aircraft. | 6030 Hangar Rd. | 503/842–1130 | www.tillamookair.com | Daily, 10–5, except Thanksgiving and Christmas Day.

Dining

Roseanna's. Seafood. Nine miles west of Tillamook in Oceanside, Roseanna's is in a rustic 1915 building on the beach opposite Three Arch Rock, so you might be able to watch sea lions and puffins while you eat. Amid a casual beach atmosphere, enhanced in the evening with candlelight and fresh flowers, you can have fresh halibut or salmon, poached baked oysters, or Gorgonzola seafood pasta. | 1490 Pacific Ave., Oceanside, 97134 | 503/842–7351 | Reservations not accepted | MC, V | $$–$$$

Artspace. Eclectic. Everything is homemade at Artspace in Bay City, 6 mi north of Tillamook. The menu may include garlic-grilled oysters, vegetarian dishes, and other specials, all beautifully presented, often with edible flowers. And if you reserve in advance, you'll get a complimentary appetizer for your thoughtfulness. | 9120 5th St., Bay City, 97107 | 503/377–2782 | fax 503/377–2010 | Closed Sun.–Wed. | No credit cards | $$

Cedar Bay. Steak. Steaks, prime rib, and seafood are the draws at this casual downtown restaurant. Kids' menu. | 2015 1st St., 97141 | 503/842–8288 | MC, V | $$

Yachats

Attractions

Cape Perpetua Campground. Just 3 mi south of Yachats, a group site here can accommodate 100 campers. There are 37 sites for RVs, tents, or trailers, picnic tables, fire grills, flush toilets, potable water, and a dump station. | U.S. 101 | 541/547–3289 | Mid-May–late Sept., weekends.

★ **Cape Perpetua Visitors Center.** The Interpretive Center is inside the Siuslaw National Forest and provides information about the cultural and natural history of the central Oregon Coast. But the big attraction here is the view. The 2,700-acre Cape Perpetua Scenic Area was created to protect the area's Sitka spruce rain forest. | U.S. 101 | 541/547–3289 | May, Wed.–Sun. 10–4; June–Labor Day, daily 9–5; Labor Day–Apr., weekends 10–4.

Neptune State Park. You can look for animals, watch the surf, or gaze at Cumming Creek from benches set on the cliff above the beach. It's also a great spot for whale watching. Low tide provides access to a natural cave and tidepools. | U.S. 101 S | 800/551–6949 | www.prd.state.or.us | Daily.

Sea Rose. Sea Rose, 6 mi south of Yachats, sells seashells from Oregon and around the world, plus gift items and souvenirs. A free museum displays shells and sealife. There's an exhibit of glass fishing floats, including a giant clam. | 95478 Hwy. 101, 97498 | 541/547–3005 | fax 541/547–5197 | Memorial Day–Labor Day, daily 9:30–6; Labor Day–Memorial Day, daily 10–5.

Strawberry Hill. Strawberry Hill, just south of Yachats, is one of the best spots on the Oregon coast to view harbor seals resting on rocky islets just offshore, and to see the starfish, anemones, and sea urchins exposed at low tide. | Hwy. 101.

Tillicum Beach Campground. Three and a half miles north of Yachats, this oceanside campground is so popular that there's a 10-day stay limit. Stairs provide access to the beach. Open year-round, there are 61 sites. | U.S. 101 | 541/563–3211 | Daily.

Yachats Ocean Road State Recreation Area. The Yachats River meets the Pacific Ocean here just 1 mi from Yachats. Whale watching is a popular activity. | U.S. 101 to Yachats Ocean Rd. | 541/997–3851 or 800/551–6949 | www.prd.state.or.us | Daily.

SOUTH DAKOTA

BLACK HILLS AND BADLANDS
*FROM BADLANDS NATIONAL PARK TO MOUNT RUSHMORE
NATIONAL MEMORIAL*

Distance: 250 mi   Time: 3 days
Overnight Breaks: Rapid City, Custer (or Custer State Park)

Stunning buttes, canyons, badlands, and hills will be your driving companions. You will pass through the exquisitely restored gold-rush town of Deadwood, then retreat to the vast wildlife preserve of Custer State Park. Along the way, you'll visit South Dakota's best-known memorials. Avoid this tour at the height of winter, when heavy snowfalls sometimes make roads impassable.

❶ **Badlands National Park** is a 244,000-acre geologic wonderland. Route 240 wiggles through this moonlike landscape on its 32-mi loop off I–90. The Ben Reifel Visitor Center at Cedar Pass, 9 mi south of the interstate, and the White River Visitor Center, in the southern Stronghold Unit off BIA 27, will help acquaint you with the remote area and its wildlife. The roadless 64,250-acre Sage Creek Wilderness Area inside the park is protected from development and is open only to hikers, backpackers, and other outdoor enthusiasts. The only trails within the wilderness area have been created by the hooves of bison.

❷ The town of **Wall** is home to the **Wall Drug Store**; just follow the signs. The internationally known emporium of galleries and unique attractions became famous during the Depression by offering free ice-water to road-weary travelers, a practice that continues today. It now stocks Black Hills gold jewelry, Native American pottery and moccasins, western clothing, books, art, postcards, curios, and thousands of pairs of cowboy boots. It also owns the **Western Art Gallery Restaurant,** with more than 200 original oil paintings and seating for 530 diners. Try the 5¢ coffee and homemade pies, rolls, and donuts.

❸ **Rapid City,** just 55 mi west of Wall on I–90, is the gateway to the Black Hills and a pleasant stop in its own right. From here it is possible to visit five national parks, memorials, and monuments on simple day trips, after which you'll want to spend the night. You can stop at the free **Dinosaur Park,** with its commanding views, **Story-**

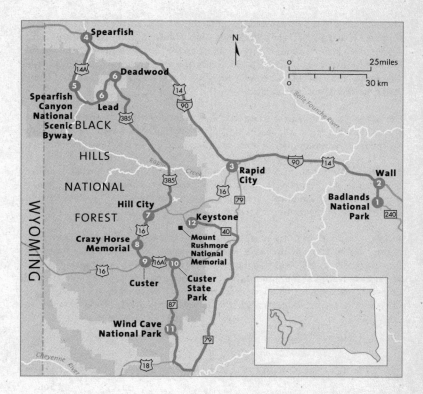

book Island, a free children's fantasyland park, and the **Stavkirke Chapel in the Hills,** a replica of the 850-year-old Borgund Church in Norway. You'll also discover numerous restaurants and a 13-mi bike and walking path through the center of town. The **Journey Museum** examines Black Hills history and culture. For outstanding shopping head downtown or visit the 12-store Rushmore Mall off I–90 on the city's north side.

④ Begin day two with the 46-mi drive west on I–90 to **Spearfish,** one of the state's prettiest towns. Set in a broad valley at the mouth of Spearfish Canyon, the town's main attractions are a convention center, historic sandstone buildings, the **Black Hills Passion Play,** presented on an outdoor stage since 1938, and the **Matthews Opera House,** a restored 1906 theater. You might also want to stop by the **D. C. Booth Historic Fish Hatchery,** which offers a century of history and free admission to its museum, historic home, fish ponds, and underwater viewing windows, or the **High Plains Heritage Center and Museum,** which has western art and artifacts, as well as cowboy music and poetry on certain nights.

⑤ **Spearfish Canyon National Scenic Byway** greets motorists with 1,000-ft-high limestone palisades that tower to the right and left of U.S. 14A as it winds through the 19-mi gorge. The actual entrance to the canyon is in town, on the southwest side of Spearfish. Spearfish Creek splashes along the canyon floor as towering Black Hills spruce scent the air. Several canyon waterfalls, including Bridal Veil and Roughlock, are popular roadside stops. Summertime hikers enjoy donning "creek shoes" and exploring the side canyons, including Squaw Creek, Iron Creek, and Eleventh Hour Gulch.

❻ The twin cities of **Lead/Deadwood,** a bit farther on U.S. 14A, provide the ideal spot to stretch your legs. Visit Lead's **Black Hills Mining Museum** or the Homestake Visitor Center to learn more about mining's impact on the hills. In Deadwood, the **Adams Memorial Museum** displays rare artifacts from the town's colorful past. The **Old Style Saloon No. 10** bills itself as "the only museum in the world with a bar" and offers music, blackjack, poker, and slots.

❼ **Hill City,** approximately 40 mi south on U.S. 385, is another mining town turned tourist mecca. Its Main Street has fascinating shops and galleries, as well as the **Mount Rushmore Brewing Company,** with good pub fare and a wide selection of microbrews.

❽ **Crazy Horse Memorial,** the colossal mountain carving of the legendary Lakota leader, is just south of Hill City on U.S. 16/385. The memorial's complex includes the **Indian Museum of North America,** which displays beautiful bead and quillwork representing many of the continent's Native nations.

❾ **Custer,** 5 mi south of Crazy Horse Memorial on U.S. 385, is a friendly community surrounded by some of the most incredible scenery in the Black Hills, including Custer State Park, the Needles Highway, Harney Peak, Wind Cave National Park, and **Jewel Cave National Monument.** Jewel Cave was named for the nailhead and dogtooth spar crystals that line its more than 100 mi of passageways. It is currently ranked as the second-longest cave in the United States (after Kentucky's Mammoth

SOUTH DAKOTA RULES OF THE ROAD

License Requirements: To drive in South Dakota, you must be at least 14 years old and have a valid driver's license. Residents of other states, Canada, and most other countries may drive as long as they possess a valid license.

Right Turn on Red: Everywhere in the state, unless otherwise posted, you may make a right turn on red *after* a full stop. Exceptions include one-way streets in downtown Rapid City, which are posted.

Seat Belt and Helmet Laws: All drivers and front-seat passengers under 18 years of age must wear a seat belt. Children under age 5 may only ride in a federally approved child safety seat, or if they exceed 40 pounds, the child may be secured with a seat belt. Motorcyclists 18 and older are not required to wear a helmet in South Dakota. Minors riding or driving a motorcycle must wear a helmet. Eye protection is required for all motorcyclists. It is recommended that all motorcyclists have headlights and taillights on at all times.

Speed Limits: In 1995, South Dakota raised its speed limit to 75 mph on its two interstates, except as noted near Rapid City and Sioux Falls. Posted limits on state and secondary highways are usually 65 mph, although most Black Hills scenic roadways are set at 55 mph.

For More Information: Contact the **South Dakota Highway Patrol.** | 500 E. Capitol Ave., Pierre, 57501 | 605/773–3105.

Cave). You can take an elevator down 234 ft, and various tours are offered at different times of the year.

⑩ **Custer State Park,** 5 mi east of Custer on U.S. 16A, has 73,000 acres of scenic beauty, exceptional drives, close-up views of wildlife, and fingerlike granite spires rising from the forest floor. Relax through a hayride and chuckwagon supper, or take a Jeep tour into the buffalo herds. Plan on spending the night in Custer or Custer State Park.

⑪ **Wind Cave National Park** is south of Custer State Park via Rte. 87 and U.S. 385. The park has 28,000 acres of wildlife habitat above ground and the world's seventh-longest cave below, with 76 mi of mapped passageways. Six miles farther south on U.S. 385 you come to **Hot Springs.** Here are still more historic sandstone buildings, the amazing **Mammoth Site,** where some 50 of the giant beasts have been unearthed, and **Evans Plunge,** with the world's largest naturally heated indoor swimming pool.

⑫ Take U.S. 18 east, then Route 79 north, then Route 40 west to **Keystone** to visit nearby **Mount Rushmore National Memorial.** Patiently awaiting you are the awesome carved busts of four U.S. presidents, Washington, Jefferson, Lincoln, and Theodore Roosevelt.
　　Return to Rapid City via U.S. 16A and 16, then follow I–90 east approximately 50 mi to Badlands National Park, your point of origin.

Badlands National Park

Attractions
Badlands National Park. The 244,000-acre park has 64,000 acres of wilderness, eight marked hiking trails that stretch over 11 mi, and two visitor centers (Ben Reifel Visitor Center at Cedar Pass and the White River Visitor Center). Towering spires, ragged ridgelines, and deep canyons are some of the memorable sights. | Hwy. 240, Interior, 57750 | 605/433–5361 | fax 605/433–5404 | www.nps.gov/badl | Daily.

White River Visitor Center Museum. Artifacts from the parklands and educational maps make this a worthy stop. | Off Hwy. 27 57750 | 605/455–2878 | Call for hours.

Dining
★ **Cedar Pass Lodge and Restaurant.** Southwestern. The atmosphere is rustic in this open-air full-service restaurant with its exposed beam ceiling and knotty pine walls. Enjoy steak and trout or Indian tacos and fried bread, accompanied by a cold beer or a glass of wine. | Badlands Loop Rd. | 605/433–5460 | Breakfast also available. Closed Nov.–Apr. 1 | AE, D, DC, MC, V | $–$$

Custer

Attractions
★ **Black Hills National Forest.** Custer is the headquarters for this forest, on the western edge of South Dakota. The forest covers more than 1 million acres and makes up almost half of the entire Black Hills region. Teeming with wildlife and natural beauty, it offers fishing, camping, hiking, mountain biking, and horseback riding. Other entry points are Deadwood, Hill City, Hot Springs, Lead, Rapid City, Spearfish, and Sturgis. | 605/343–8755 | www.fs.fed.us/r2/blackhills.

Cathedral Spires. Granite towers reach above the top of the trees toward the heavens. This registered National Landmark lies on Needles Highway in Custer State Park. | Custer Needles Hwy. 57730 | 605/255–4515 | www.state.sd.us/gfp/sdparks.

Centennial Trail. A 111-mi trail, Centennial crosses the prairie grasslands near Bear Butte State Park and climbs into the Black Hills high country, skirting lakes and streams, monuments, memorials, and campgrounds until it reaches Wind Cave National Park. Hikers are welcome on the entire trail, which is accessible from 22 trailheads. Portions are open to horseback riders and mountain bikers. | 605/347–5240.

★ **Crazy Horse Memorial.** The colossal mountain carving still in progress depicts Lakota leader Crazy Horse atop his steed. At the memorial's base are a restaurant and gift shop, as well as work by Crazy Horse sculptor Korczak Ziolkowski. | Ave. of the Chiefs | 605/673–4681.

At the base of the memorial is one of the most impressive collections of Plains Indian artifacts in the country. The collection is presented in an airy setting of ponderosa pine and skylights at the **Indian Museum of North America.**

Custer County Courthouse Museum. See three floors of artifacts and the region's premier exhibit on General George A. Custer's 1874 Black Hills expedition. Also here is an 1875 log cabin, the first built in the Black Hills. | 411 Mt. Rushmore Rd., 57730 | 605/673–2443 | June–Aug., Mon.–Sat. 9–9, Sun. 1–9; Sept., call for hours.

★ **Custer State Park.** You'll find 83 square mi of preserve alternating between alpine meadows, rolling foothills, pine forests, and fingerlike granite spires that jut up from the surrounding landscape. The park is also home to the nation's largest bison herds. There's camping, summer theater, and four rustic mountain retreats. | HC 83 57730 | 605/255–4515 | www.state.sd.us | Daily.

The **Peter Norbeck Visitor Center Museum** includes park history exhibits in a rugged granite and wood structure. | 605/255–4464 | Mid-May–Memorial Day, daily 9–5; Memorial Day–Labor Day, daily 8–8; Labor Day–Oct., daily 9–5.

Flintstones Bedrock City. Step into Bedrock at this Stone Age fun park with rides on the Flintmobile and the Iron Horse train. Play areas, a theater, camping, gifts, and bronto-burgers and dinodogs at the drive-in round out the Flintstones experience. | U.S. 16/385 | 605/673–4079 | Mid-May–mid-Sept., daily 8:30–8.

Jewel Cave National Monument. The cave, the world's third-longest, has over 120 mi of known passages. It was formed by water dissolving minerals out of the limestone, and exploration is hampered by occasional flooding. You'll see unusual boxwork, frostwork, and popcorn formations, as well as stalactites, stalagmites, and crystals. An elevator takes you 234 ft underground to view this incredible maze. Tours are available. | 605/673–2288 | Memorial Day–Labor Day, daily 8–7:30; Labor Day–Memorial Day, daily 8–4; call for tour hours.

National Museum of Woodcarving. The works of an original Disney animator, prominent caricature carvers, and more than 70 other artists are displayed here. | 605/673–4404 | May–Oct., daily; call for hours.

Dining

Bavarian Restaurant. German. In a dining room with murals of German country scenes, this family-style restaurant and lounge offers buffets, as well as German and American meals at reasonable prices. The popular dish here is *rouladen* (thinly sliced sirloin wrapped with mustard, bacon, and a dill pickle and seared, then baked for several hours until wonderfully tender). Buffet dining is available, as is a fine selection of German beers and liqueurs. Kids' menu. | U.S. 16/385 N | 605/673–4412 | Breakfast also available (May–Sept.). Closed Feb. | D, MC, V | $$

Blue Bell Lodge and Resort. American. After feasting in a rustic log dining room, try a hayride. Blue Bell is known for fresh trout and buffalo, which you can have as a steak or as stew. Kids' menu. | Rte. 87 S | 605/255–4531 or 800/658–3530 | Breakfast also available. Closed mid-Oct.–Mother's Day | AE, D, MC, V | $$

Chief Restaurant. American. One of Custer's 30 restaurants, the Chief has family-style dining and a broad menu. Choices include buffalo steaks and burgers, a Philly steak sandwich, or the "Cochise buffalo steak" (a tender sirloin fillet with herb butter), as well as prime rib. Many of the tables are set up around a large indoor fountain. There is a salad bar and the service is family-style. Kids' menu. | 140 Mt. Rushmore Rd. | 605/673–4402 | Breakfast also available. Closed Nov.–mid-Apr. | AE, D, MC, V | $$

Laughing Water Restaurant. Native American. With windows facing the Crazy Horse Memorial, this airy pine restaurant is noted for its fry bread and buffalo burgers. There's a soup and salad bar, but you'd do well to stick to the Native American offerings— try the Indian taco and Buffaloski (a Polish sausage made with Dakota buffalo). Kids' menu. | Ave. of the Chiefs | 605/673–4681 | Closed Nov.–Apr. | AE, D, MC, V | $–$$

Lodging

Blue Bell Lodge and Resort. The modern hand-crafted log cabins at this hideaway in Custer State Park have fireplaces, a lodge, and a conference center. There is a campground on the premises, and hayrides and cookouts are part of the entertainment. A stable offers trail rides and overnight pack trips on old Indian trails. Restaurant, bar, picnic area. No air-conditioning, some kitchenettes, some refrigerators. Cable TV, some room phones. Hiking, horseback riding. Playground. Laundry facilities. Pets allowed. | 605/255–4531 or 800/658–3530 | fax 605/255–4706 | www.custerresorts.com | 29 cabins | Closed Oct.–Mother's Day | AE, D, MC, V | $$–$$$

Strutton Inn B&B. Sitting on 4 acres, this luxurious three-story Victorian home has king-size rooms. It's in the heart of the Black Hills, which can be enjoyed from the 140 ft veranda with a gazebo on each corner looking out over a lovely garden. Inside this well-furnished retreat are an antique doll and crystal collection and a 46-inch big screen TV. The inn is within 20 mi of Mt. Rushmore and Crazy Horse Monument; Custer Park is 2 mi from downtown. Complimentary breakfast. Microwaves, refrigerators. Airport shuttle. No pets. No smoking. | 605/673–4808 or 800/226–2611 | fax 605/673–2395 | www.strutton-inn.cc | 9 rooms | MC, V | $–$$$

Bavarian Inn. Nestled in pines, this resort has some rooms with views of the Black Hills, and all upstairs rooms open onto balconies with seating areas. The inn is less than 1 mi from downtown. Special rates are available for families with children under 12. Restaurant, bar. Cable TV. 2 pools (1 indoor). Hot tub, sauna. Tennis courts. Video games. Playground. Pets allowed. | U.S. 16/385 N, 57730 | 605/673–2802 or 800/657–4312 | fax 605/673–4777 | www.custer-sd.com/bavariansd.com/bavarian | 64 rooms | AE, D, DC, MC, V | $$

French Creek Guest Ranch B&B. You can soak up views of the Needles formation while porch-sitting at this luxurious "bed-and-barn" on a 25-acre working horse ranch. French Creek is designed to meet the needs of the traveling horse owner: the stable has eight wooden box stalls each with its own run, and four large corrals with wooden fencing. Horses may be boarded for an additional fee. Facilities are also available for a horse trailer or camper hook-up. The ranch is 1½ mi from Custer State Park. Restaurant, complimentary Continental breakfast. Refrigerators. Sauna. Tennis court. Basketball, hiking, horseback riding, volleyball. Fishing. No kids under 13. | 605/673–4790 or 877/673–4790 | fax 605/673–4767 | www.frenchcreekranch.com | 2 rooms | MC, V | $$

American President's Resort (Cabins and Camp). Family reunions are the specialty of this resort. The individual cabins have kitchens. Camping with full hookups is also available. Picnic areas. Some kitchenettes. Pool. Spa. Miniature golf. Horseback riding. Playground. Laundry facilities. | U.S. 16A, 57730 | 605/673–3373 | www.presidentsresort.com | 45 cabins, 15 rooms, 70 campsites | D, MC, V | $–$$

Deadwood

Attractions

Adams Memorial Museum. The oldest history museum in the Black Hills is an exceptional repository of historic Deadwood memorabilia. There are frequent special exhibits and events. | 54 Sherman St. | 605/578–1714 | May–Sept., Mon.–Sat. 9–6, Sun. noon–5; Oct.–Apr., Mon.–Sat. 10–5.

Broken Boot Gold Mine. Join guides on a journey into an authentic underground gold mine and pan for gold. If nothing else, you'll receive a souvenir stock certificate. | Upper Main St., Hwy. 14A | 605/578–9997 | May–Aug., daily 8–5:30; Sept., daily 9–4:30.

Casino Gambling. Deadwood has offered casino-style gaming for more than a decade; just don't expect the glitz of Las Vegas or Atlantic City. In Deadwood, you can check out nearly 80 small gaming halls in the downtown area, many with elaborate century-old Victorian facades. Each gaming hall has its own charm and ambience, but check out the **Franklin Hotel** (700 Main St., 605/578–2241 or 800/688–1876), the town's oldest building and gaming hall, and the **Midnight Star** (677 Main St., 605/578–1555), the town's tallest building and owned by none other than actor Kevin Costner.

Mickelson Trail. Named for the late Governor George S. Mickelson, this 114-mi trail has 13 trailheads, most with parking, toilets, and tables; many provide access to the rails-to-trails project extending across the back-country from Deadwood to Edgemont. Bicycles and horses are allowed on the trail. A trail pass (required for users aged 12 and up) can be purchased at self-service trail stations at most trailheads. | HC 37, Lead, 57754-9801 | 605/584–3896.

Old Style Saloon #10. The Saloon is billed as the only museum in the world with a bar. Thousands of artifacts, vintage photos, and a two-headed calf are among this hangout's decorations. You'll find live entertainment nightly, gaming, and excellent food upstairs at the Deadwood Social Club. A reenactment of "The Shooting of Wild Bill Hickok" is featured four times a day during the summer. | 657 Main St. | 605/578–3346 | Memorial Day–Labor Day, Sun.–Mon. 8 AM–2 AM, Tues.–Sat. 8 AM–3 AM; Labor Day–Memorial Day, daily 8 AM–2 AM.

Dining

Jake's. Contemporary. Owned by actor Kevin Costner, this may well be South Dakota's premier restaurant experience. Enjoy elegant dining in an atrium setting, with cherry wood, fireplaces, and special lighting. Try buffalo roulade, Cajun seafood tortellini, filet mignon, or fresh fish. | Midnight Star Casino, 677 Main St. | 605/578–1555 | Closed Sun. No lunch | Reservations essential | AE, D, DC, MC, V | $$–$$$

Creekside Restaurant. American. Part of the Deadwood Gulch Resort, this restaurant resembles an old saloon, complete with a bar from the 1880s. You'll find yourself greeted with hearty breakfasts and plate-size steaks. The rib-eye is considered by some to be the best steak in town, and the apple-almond chicken is also a crowd pleaser. | Hwy. 85 S | 605/578–1294 or 800/695–1876 | Breakfast also available | AE, D, MC, V | $$

★ **Deadwood Social Club.** Italian. Homey and relaxed, with light jazz and blues playing in the background, the restaurant is known for Black Angus beef and chicken, seafood, and pasta dishes. The cellar stocks one of South Dakota's best wine selections. | 657 Main St. | 605/578–3346 or 800/952–9398 | Closed Mon. | AE, MC, V | $–$$

Franklin Hotel Dining Room. American. Charbroiled steaks, buffalo, pasta, and vegetarian dishes are served in a Victorian dining room with a bar. | 700 Main St. | 605/578–2241 | AE, DC, MC, V | $–$$

Hill City

Attractions

Pactola Reservoir. Surrounded by ponderosa pine forests, this reservoir in the Black Hills National Forest has a public beach, three picnic areas, two scenic overlooks, two campgrounds, two boat-launch facilities, hiking trails, and the Pactola Pines Marina, a full-service facility with pontoon rentals, gasoline, and a convenience store with supplies. | Hwy. 385, 15 mi north of Hill City | 605/343–8755 | www.fs.fed.us/bhnf | Mid-May–Oct. 1, daily 8:30–6.

Sheridan Lake. The lake has 400 surface acres and is surrounded by ponderosa pine forests, picnic areas, and hiking trails. The facilities include two public beaches and a full-service marina with slip rental, boat rental, convenience store, gasoline, and supplies. Group and individual campsites are available. You will need to purchase a National Forest Service day-use permit. The marina is closed when ice is too thick to boat or too thin to ice fish. | 16451 Sheridan Lake Rd., 9 mi north of Hill City | 605/574–2169 | www.sheridanlakemarina.com.

Sylvan Rocks Climbing Lessons and Adventures. You can try rock climbing at Sylvan Rocks. Classes range from beginner to advanced and the maximum number of climbers per guide is three. | 301 Main St., Hill City, 57745 | 605/574–2425 | fax 605/342–1487 | Call ahead for hours.

Dining

Alpine Inn. American. Find European charm in the Old West. The lunchtime menu changes daily but always includes an array of healthy selections from sandwiches to salads (with no fried food). The dinner menu has only one item: filet mignon. Lunch is offered on the veranda overlooking Main St. Beer and wine only are served. | 225 Main St. | 605/574–2749 | Reservations not accepted | Closed Sun. | No credit cards | $–$$

Mount Rushmore Brewing Company. American. Spacious dining is on tap in this Black Hills' microbrewery, in a building listed on the National Historic Register. Exposed brick and prominent equipment remind you that something is always brewing, and there is a large selection of microbeers and imports. Specialties are steaks, seafood, pizza, and hearty pub fare, including the popular "white chili" made from great northern beans and chicken and spices. Beer and wine only are served. | 349 Main St. | 605/574–2400 | May 1–Labor Day | D, MC, V | $–$$

Hot Springs

Attractions

Evans Plunge. Get ready to splash in the world's largest natural warm-water indoor swimming pool. The Plunge also has indoor-outdoor pools, waterslides, a sauna, a steam room, and a fitness center. | 1145 N. River St. | 605/745–5165 | Memorial Day–Labor Day, weekdays 5:30 AM–10 PM, weekends 8 AM–10 PM.

★ **Mammoth Site of Hot Springs.** Nearly 50 giant mammoths have already been unearthed from a prehistoric sinkhole where they came to drink 26,000 years ago. You can watch the excavation in progress and take guided tours of this unique discovery. | Southern city limits on U.S. 18 truck bypass | 605/745–6017 or 800/325–6991 | www.mammothsite.com | Daily, call for hours.

Wind Cave National Park. The park is about 7 mi north of Hot Springs. This is the world's seventh-longest cave, and you can explore 92 mi of known passageways. Above ground, discover a 28,000-acre wildlife preserve that is home to bison, pronghorns, and prairie dogs. | Hwy. 385 | 605/745–4600 | Daily 8–6.

Dining

Elk Horn Cafe. American. Your choices include burgers and steaks that are hand cut on the premises. Eat breakfast on one of two outdoor decks with a view of town. | 310 S. Chicago St., 57747 | 605/745–6556 | Breakfast also available | AE, MC, V | $–$$

Keystone

Attractions

Beautiful Rushmore Cave. Stalagmites, stalactites, helectites, flowstone, ribbons, columns, and the "Big Room" are all part of a worthwhile tour into the depths of the Black Hills. In 1876, miners found the opening to the cave while digging a flume into the mountainside to carry water to the gold mines below. The cave was opened to the public in 1927, just before the carving of Mount Rushmore began. | 13622 Hwy. 40 | 605/255–4384 or 605/255–4634 | www.beautifulrushmorecave.com | May 1–Memorial Day and Labor Day–Oct. 31, daily 9–5; Memorial Day–Labor Day, daily 8–8.

Big Thunder Gold Mine. Tour an underground gold mine, pick up some free gold ore samples, and do a little gold panning. | Rte. 40 | 605/666–4847 or 800/314–3917 | May–mid-Oct., daily 9–5.

Borglum Historical Center. Study paintings and sculptures by Gutzon Borglum, the creator of Mount Rushmore, and see a collection of the artist's mementos. | 342 Winter St. | 605/666–4448 | May and Oct., daily 8:30–4; June–Aug., daily 8–7.

Cosmos Mystery Area. No one stands up straight and balls roll uphill at this unusual and entertaining attraction. | Hwy. 16, 4 mi north of Keystone | 605/343–9802 | Apr.–Oct., daily 9:45–4.

Keystone Historical Society Museum. There's a celebration each August 3rd for Carrie Ingalls Day in the old Keystone School Building, with an open house and birthday cake. | Main St., 57751 | 605/666–4494 | June 1–Labor Day, Mon.–Sat. 10–4.

★ **Mount Rushmore National Memorial.** One of the nation's most popular attractions is just 3 mi from Keystone. Ample visitor facilities complement the giant likenesses of Washington, Jefferson, Lincoln, and Theodore Roosevelt. | Hwy. 244 | 605/574–2523 | www.nps.gov/moru.

Wildcat Valley Resort and Campground. Attractions include an exotic wildcat exhibit, a camp store, animal prints, and a chance to pan for gold. | 999 Front St., 57751 | 605/255–4059 | Call for hours.

Dining

Ruby House Restaurant and Red Garter Saloon. American. A quiet hideaway with Victorian decor, Ruby House is just a few miles from Mount Rushmore. Popular menu items include buffalo steak, prime rib, and a homemade bread pudding with caramel sauce. | Main St. | 605/666–4404 | Breakfast also available. Closed Nov.–Apr. | Reservations essential | D, MC, V | $$

Buffalo Dining Room. American. The building is made of glass and has views of Mount Rushmore; the menu offers a wide range of choices for breakfast, lunch, and dinner, including such standard fare as burgers and pasta but also the very popular buffalo stew. You can choose to end your meal with a "monumental bowl of ice cream." | Hwy. 24 | 605/574–2515 | Breakfast also available. No dinner mid-Oct.–early Mar. | AE, D, MC, V | $–$$

Spokcane Creek Resort. American. Eat pizza and subs for lunch and dinner and try the homemade biscuits and gravy for breakfast. | Box 927, Hwy. 16A, Keystone, 57751 | 605/666–4430 | Closed Labor Day–Memorial Day | DC, MC, V | $

Lead

Attractions

Andy's Trail Rides. Adventures in the Black Hills include buggy and wagon rides, cattle drives, overnight camping, and fishing trips. | 5 mi southwest of Lead on Hwy. 14 57754 | 605/584–1100.

Black Hills Mining Museum. Displays explore the history of mining in the Black Hills. There are guided tours through simulated tunnels and stopes (underground steps), a video theater, and gold panning. | 323 W. Main St. | 605/584–1605 or 888/410–3337 | May–Sept., daily 9–5; Oct.–Apr., Tues.–Sat. 9–4.

Deer Mountain. Ski lessons, rentals, and cross-country trails are available here, as well as three lifts and 32 downhill trails with a 700-ft vertical drop. | 1000 Deer Mt. Rd. | 605/584–3230 | www.skideermountain.com | Nov.–Mar., Wed.–Thurs., Sun. 9–4, Fri.–Sat. 9–9.

Terry Peak. A 1,100-ft vertical drop, 20 trails, and loads of snow account for the popularity of this 400-acre ski area in the Black Hills. The peak has five chairlifts, a rental shop, lessons, and day lodge facilities. | Hwy. 85, 3 mi west of Lead | 605/584–2165 or 800/456–0524 | www.terrypeak.com | Nov.–Mar., daily 9–4.

Dining

Stampmill Restaurant and Saloon. American. The dark-wood and brickwork interior give this 1892 building an intimate feel. Photos trace the history of Lead and the mines. Two suites are available for overnight accommodations. Food is available in the saloon. You might try the Black Angus steaks or the French onion soup. | 305 W. Main St. | 605/584–1984 | D, MC, V | $–$$

Rapid City

Attractions

Bear Country U.S.A. Bears, wolves, elk, bighorns, and other North American wildlife roam free in their natural habitat. Bear cubs, wolf pups, and other park offspring are housed in a walk-through area. Allow at least 1½ hrs for your visit. | 13820 Hwy. 16 S | 605/343–2290 | www.bearcountryusa.com | May–Oct., daily 8–6, or during daylight hours.

Black Hills Caverns. Frost crystal, amethyst, logomites, calcite crystals, and other specimens fill the cave, first discovered by pioneers in the late 1800s. Half-hour and hour tours are available. | 2600 Cavern Rd. | 605/343–0542 | May 1–Oct. 15, daily 8:30–5:30.

Black Hills National Forest. Hundreds of miles of hiking, mountain biking, and horseback riding trails crisscross this million-acre forest on the western edge of the state. Other entry points are Custer, Deadwood, Hill City, Hot Springs, Lead, Spearfish, and Sturgis. | Black Hills National Forest Visitor Center, 803 Soo San Dr., 57702 | 605/343–8755 | www.fs.fed.us/bhnf | Daily, visitor center mid-May–Sept.

Children's Science Center. A great rainy-day choice if you have young children, the Center offers interactive learning programs about wild animals and the universe. Programs change with the season. Call ahead for information. | 515 West Blvd., 57701 | 605/394–6996 | www.hpcnet.org/sdsmt/childrens_science_center | Tues.–Fri. 9–5, Sat. 10–4.

Crystal Cave Park. A trout pond and the bones of a hapless explorer are two of the sights on the 45-minute, non-strenuous tours of this crystal-lined cavern. | 7770 Nameless Cave Rd. | 605/342–8008 | May 1–Oct. 15, daily 9–6.

Dinosaur Park. Seven life-size replicas of colossal prehistoric reptiles guard the crest of Skyline Drive, where you have a view of the entire city. | 940 Skyline Dr. | 605/348–0462.

The Journey Museum. Interactive exhibits explore the history of the Black Hills from the age of the dinosaurs through Native American history to the days of the pioneers. | 222 New York St. | 605/394–6923 | www.journeymuseum.com | Memorial Day–Labor Day, daily 8–7; Labor Day–Memorial Day, Mon.–Sat. 1–4, Sun. 11–5.

Stavkirke Chapel in the Hills. Norse dragon heads mix with Christian symbols in this chapel, held together with pegs. Scandinavian immigrant artifacts are displayed in a log-cabin museum next door. | 3788 Chapel La., 57702 | 605/342–3880 | May 1–Sept. 30, 7 AM–sunset.

Storybook Island. Nursery rhymes come to life in animated and real-life scenes at this children's fantasy theme park, which has summer children's theater. | 1301 Sheridan Lake Rd. | 605/342–6357 | Memorial Day–Labor Day, daily 8–8.

Thunderhead Underground Falls. Six hundred feet within a mountain, along a deserted mineshaft, you'll find a spectacular waterfall, first discovered by miners while blasting for gold. | 10940 W. Hwy. 44 | 605/343–0081 | May–Oct., daily 9:30–6:30, or during daylight hours.

Dining

Landmark Restaurant and Lounge. American. Popular for its lunch buffet, this hotel–restaurant also serves dinner specialties that include prime rib, beef Wellington, freshwater fish, and wild game. | 523 6th St., 57702 | 605/342–1210 | AE, D, DC, MC, V | $$$–$$$$

Firehouse Brewing Co. American. Occupying a historic 1915 firehouse, the state's first brewpub is ornamented throughout with brass fixtures and fire-fighting equipment. The five house-brewed beers are the highlight of the menu, which also includes pastas, salads, and gumbo. Thursday nights buffalo prime rib is the specialty. Kids' menu. | 610 Main St. | 605/348–1915 | Reservations not accepted | No lunch Sun. | AE, D, DC, MC, V | $$–$$$

Circle B Ranch Chuck Wagon Supper & Music Show. American. Chuckwagon suppers include tender roast beef and chicken, biscuits, and all the trimmings. The ranch also offers western music shows, miniature golf, gold panning, and trail and wagon rides. | 22735 Hwy. 385, 57702 | 605/348–7358 | Reservations essential | Closed Oct.–Apr. No lunch | MC, V | $$

Fireside Inn. Steak. A warm fireside setting complements some of the best beef in the Dakotas. A spacious patio is ideal for cocktails before dinner. Try the bean soup, New York steak, or the 20-ounce Cattlemen's Cut. | Hwy. 44 W | 605/342–3900 | No lunch | AE, D, MC, V | $$

Flying T Chuckwagon. Barbecue. Ranch-style meals of barbecued beef, potatoes, and baked beans are served on tin plates in this converted barn. Dinner is followed by a western show with music and cowboy comedy, and there's now a western breakfast show from 7–9 AM. | 8971 Hwy. 16 S, 57702 | 605/342–1905 | Reservations essential | Closed mid-Sept.–late May. No lunch | D, MC, V | $$

Lodging

★ **Alex Johnson Hotel.** Period furnishings recreate the air of the '20s in this nine-floor 1928 hotel surrounded by shops and restaurants in downtown Rapid City. Restaurant, bar (with entertainment). Some refrigerators, some in-room hot tubs. Cable TV. Airport shuttle. No pets. | 523 6th St., 57701 | 605/342–1210 or 800/888–2539 | fax 605/342–7436 | www.alexjohnson.com | 141 rooms, 2 suites | AE, D, DC, MC, V | $$–$$$

Best Western Town 'N Country Inn. The five, two-story buildings of this chain motel sit 1 mi from downtown on the road to Mount Rushmore and near Rapid City Regional Hospital. Restaurant. Some refrigerators. Cable TV. 2 pools. Playground. Airport shuttle. No pets. | 2505 Mt. Rushmore Rd., 57701 | 605/343–5383 or 877/666–5383 | fax 605/343–9670 | www.bestwestern.com | 100 rooms | AE, D, DC, MC, V | $$

Hayloft Bed & Breakfast. Antique furnishings and gingham and floral print linens accent this Victorian farmhouse. Some rooms have private baths and entrances, and young children are welcome. Complimentary breakfast. Some in-room hot tubs. Cable TV. | 9356 Neck Yoke Rd., 57701 | 605/343–5351 or 800/317–6784 | 8 rooms | MC, V | $$

Holiday Inn–Rushmore Plaza. Within the eight-story atrium of this hotel, glass elevators ascend and descend beside a waterfall and lush trees. Restaurant, bar. In-room data ports, in-room safes, some refrigerators. Cable TV. Indoor pool. Hot tub. Exercise equipment. Laundry facilities. Business services, airport shuttle. No pets. | 505 N. 5th St., 57701 | 605/348–4000 | fax 605/348–9777 | www.basshotels.com | 205 rooms, 48 suites | AE, D, DC, MC, V | $$

Spearfish

Attractions

Black Hills State University. Founded in 1883, this four-year, state-sponsored university commands a near-idyllic small-town setting, with 3,600 students, and courses offered in 42 majors and 40 minors. Call for campus tour information. | 1200 University Ave. | 605/642–6343 | www.bhsu.edu | Mon.–Fri. 7–4.

D. C. Booth Historic Fish Hatchery. Once owned by Dewitt Clinton Booth, the facility's first superintendent, the century-old hatchery contains a museum, a historic home, fish ponds, and underwater viewing windows. | 423 Hatchery Circle | 605/642–7730 | www.fws.gov/r6dcbth/dcbooth.html | Museum and Home, Memorial Day–Labor Day, daily 9–6; Grounds open year-round, daily dawn to dusk.

High Plains Heritage Center and Museum. Western art and artifacts, including bronze sculptures and paintings, are displayed in this modern facility. Outdoors, you can view antique implements, a sod dugout, a 1-room school, a log cabin, live buffalo, longhorns, and mini-horses. Cowboy poetry and music are performed in the theater on Wednesday evenings from Memorial Day to Labor Day. | 825 Heritage Dr. | 605/642–9378 | Memorial Day–Labor Day, daily 9–8; Labor Day–Memorial Day, daily 9–5.

Matthews Opera House. When it was opened in 1906, this opera house was the only cultural establishment in this part of the country. Refurbished and reopened in the late 1980s, the opera house continues its tradition with a mix of music, vaudeville, comedy, and drama. | 614½ Main St. | 605/642–7973.

Spearfish Canyon. Southwest of Spearfish, this canyon is home to more than 1,000 species of plants. The road that winds through the canyon is designated a National Scenic Byway, and meanders along the banks of Spearfish Creek past waterfalls and towering trees. The upper reaches of the canyon provided the backdrop for the closing scenes of Kevin Costner's epic *Dances With Wolves*. | U.S. 14A | 605/642–2626 or 800/626–8013 | Daily.

Dining

Mad Mary's. Steak. Guns, saddles, and ropes scattered throughout this eatery combine to give it a Western feel. Popular dishes include the filet mignon and prime rib. Kids' menu. | 539 W. Jackson Blvd. | 605/642–2848 | No lunch | AE, D, DC, MC, V | $$–$$$

Eleventh Hour Bistro. American. Flowers and linen tablecloths adorn the tables at this casual spot. You can try one of the wild game items, such as pheasant, or a sirloin steak. Outdoor dining is available on a covered patio. Kids' menu. | 447 Main St. | 605/642–5701 | D, MC, V | $$

Latchstring Restaurant. American. A wonderful view of Spearfish Canyon will accompany your meal at this casual spot. For breakfast try the sourdough pancakes. Popular dinner entrées include the fresh trout and steaks. Kids' menu. | Spearfish Canyon, U.S. 14A | 605/584–3333 | Breakfast also available | D, MC, V | $$

Wall

Attractions

National Grasslands Visitor Center. Managed by the U.S. Forest Service, this visitor center focuses on interpreting and providing information about the national grasslands with more than 20 exhibits highlighting a variety of subjects, including prairie plants and animals, recreation opportunities, and management activities. Three national grasslands are in western South Dakota: Grand River, Fort Pierre, and Buffalo Gap. | 708 Main St. | 605/279–2125 | Jun.–Aug., daily 7 AM–8 PM; Sept.–May, daily 8–4:30.

Wall Drug Store. The store's claim to fame during the Depression—offering free icewater to road-weary travelers—is still appreciated by drivers today. Wall Drug has grown to accommodate four art gallery–dining rooms that seat 520 visitors; its Western Mall has 14 shops. The store also has a life-size mechanical Cowboy Band and Chuckwagon Quartet. | 510 Main St. | 605/279–2175 | Memorial Day–Labor Day, daily 6 AM–10 PM; Labor Day–Memorial Day, daily 6:30 AM–6 PM.

Dining

Cactus Family Restaurant and Lounge. American. Hotcakes and made-from-scratch pies are the specialties of this restaurant in downtown Wall. A roast-beef buffet is offered in summer. | 519 Main St., 57790 | 605/279–2561 | D, MC, V | $–$$

★ **Elkton House Restaurant.** American. Wood paneling and a sunroom set the tone for this comfortable restaurant, which has fast service. Try the terrific hot roast-beef sandwich, served on white bread with gravy and mashed potatoes. | 203 South Blvd., 57790 | 605/279–2152 | D, MC, V | $–$$

Western Art Gallery Restaurant. American. In the Wall Drug Store and capable of seating more than 500 patrons, this restaurant displays more than 200 original oil paintings, all with a Western theme. Try a hot beef sandwich or a buffalo burger. Kids' menu. | 510 Main St. | 605/279–2175 | Breakfast also available | $–$$

BANDERA TO NEW BRAUNFELS

A GERMAN HERITAGE TOUR

Distance: 110 miles   Time: 3 days
Overnight Breaks: Fredericksburg, Austin

Hill Country, a scenic area tucked north of San Antonio and west of I–35, is the setting for this drive. Created by an earthquake more than 30 million years ago, the region spans 23 counties and is chock full of small towns, picturesque lakes, dramatic caves, and countless historic attractions. Be wary of this tour during heavy rains, however, as many roads are subject to flash-flooding.

1. Begin your tour in **Bandera.** This community, known as the "Cowboy Capital of the World," is surrounded by numerous dude ranches that offer you a chance to take to the saddle for a few days of cowboy fun. Rodeos, country and western music, and horse racing are regular pastimes.

2. From Bandera, head north on Route 173 for approximately 25 mi to **Kerrville.** Attractions in the area include the **Y.O. Ranch,** one of the most famous ranches in the nation. At one time, the ranch covered 80 mi; today it offers guided tours as well as hunting. The **Cowboy Artists of America Museum** exhibits Western-theme paintings and sculpture.

3. Leaving Kerrville, proceed north on Route 16 for approximately 25 mi into **Fredericksburg.** This quaint German community is a longtime favorite with shoppers and bed-and-breakfast lovers (plan on spending the night here). Downtown, the **Admiral Nimitz Museum and State Historical Center** honors Fredericksburg native Admiral Chester Nimitz, World War II Commander-in-Chief of the Pacific. Hikers enjoy **Enchanted Rock State Natural Area,** site of the largest stone formation in the West; both easy and challenging climbs are available. In summer, climbers should start the hike early to avoid midday heat.

4. From Fredericksburg, head east on U.S. 290 for about 10 mi to **Stonewall,** the birth and burial place of Lyndon B. Johnson. Visit the **Lyndon B. Johnson State Historical Park,** where you can catch a guided tour of the LBJ Ranch. You can also visit the **Sauer-**

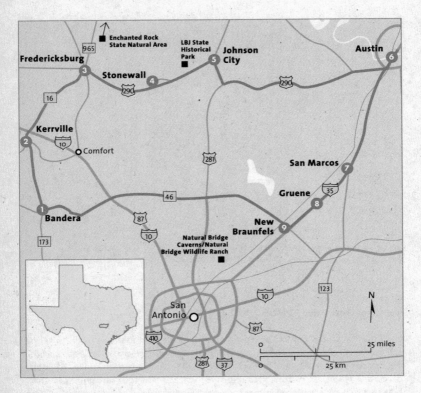

Beckmann Farmstead, a farm that recalls the early 1900s. During the spring, this portion of the drive is lined with blooming peach trees.

❺ Approximately 10 mi east of Stonewall on U.S. 290 is **Johnson City,** named for Sam Ealy Johnson, Sr., LBJ's grandfather. LBJ moved here from Stonewall when he was 5 years old. Headquarters for the **Lyndon B. Johnson National Historic Park** are here, as is the simply titled **Boyhood Home** of LBJ.

❻ From Johnson City, head east on U.S. 290 for about 40 mi, then north on I–35 into **Austin.** The centerpiece of the city as well as the state government is the **State Capitol.** Guided tours of the building are offered daily.

   South of the Capitol is the **Governor's Mansion,** with historic reminders of the many governors of the Lone Star State. You're taken past the main staircase, through the formal parlor, and finally into the dining room. On the north side of the Capitol is the **University of Texas at Austin,** the largest university in the nation. On its campus, the **Lyndon Baines Johnson Library and Museum** traces the history of Johnson's presidency through exhibits and films. On the eighth floor you can tour a model of the Oval Office as it looked during LBJ's administration. Spend the night in Austin.

❼ Approximately 40 mi south of Austin at Exit 206 off I–35 is **San Marcos,** a favorite with shoppers, who come to browse its two massive outlet malls. Summer visitors find recreation along the banks of the San Marcos River, popular with snorkelers for its clear waters. The waters form the focal point for **Aquarena Center for Continuing**

Education, a historic park that dates back to 1928 when A. B. Rogers purchased 125 acres at the headwaters of the San Marcos River to create a grand hotel.

8 When you've finished shopping, head to **Gruene** (pronounced Green), a former town and now actually a neighborhood in New Braunfels. From its founding in the 1870s, Gruene was a happening place with a swinging dance hall and busy cotton gin. But when the boll weevil arrived in Texas with the Great Depression, Gruene became a ghost town. Today that former ghost town is alive with small shops and restaurants as well as Texas's oldest dance hall. **Gruene Hall** is as lively today as it was in the late 1800s. Burlap bags draped from the ceiling dampen the sound, 1930s advertisements plaster the walls, and a U.S. flag with 46 stars still hangs over the dance floor.

9 From Gruene, reach **New Braunfels** by returning to I-35 and continuing south, or by traveling south on Gruene Rd. The self-proclaimed "Antique Capital of Texas" is home to numerous antiques shops, most in the downtown region. New Braunfels recalls its German heritage with many festivals and the name of its waterpark, **Schlitterbahn,** which means "slippery road" in German. Summer visitors will have the chance to canoe, raft, or inner-tube down the city's Guadalupe and Comal rivers. Outside of New Braunfels, you'll find cool conditions year-round in **Natural Bridge Caverns**; families also enjoy visiting adjacent **Natural Bridge Wildlife Ranch.**

From New Braunfels, take Route 46 W for about 50 mi back to Bandera.

TEXAS RULES OF THE ROAD

License requirements: To drive in Texas you must be at least 16 years old and have a valid driver's license. Residents of most other countries may drive as long as they have valid licenses from their home countries.

Right Turn on Red: You may make a right turn on red *after* a full stop anywhere in the state, unless otherwise posted.

Seat Belts and Helmet Laws: All drivers and front-seat passengers must wear seat belts. Children under age four must wear a seat belt, whether seated in the front or back. Children under age two must only ride in a federally approved child safety seat. Motorcyclists under age 21 must wear a helmet; motorcyclists age 21 and over are not required to wear helmets if they have proof of insurance valued over $10,000 or have proof of completion of a motorcycle operations course.

Speed Limits: The speed limit in Texas is 70 mph. In heavily traveled corridors, though, the limit is 55. Be sure to check speed limit signs carefully.

For More Information: Contact the **Texas Department of Transportation** at | 800/687-7846.

Austin

Attractions

Austin Museum of Art at Laguna Gloria. Stephen F. Austin, who had founded the Tejas province's first Anglo-American colony a decade earlier, purchased the 12-acre museum site in 1832, but died before he could build on it. The museum has become nationally known for its art exhibits, sculpture gardens, and educational programs. | 3809 W. 35th St. | 512/458–8191 | Tues.–Wed., Fri.–Sat. 10–5, Thurs. 10–8, Sun. 12–5.

Governor's Mansion. For more than 130 years, Texas governors have lived in this grand, modified Greek Revival home. The mansion has an impressive collection of 19th-century American antiques and furnishings. Tours (scheduled every 20 minutes) are conducted weekdays from 10 AM to 12 PM. Call to check the status of tours; the home is sometimes closed because of incoming dignitaries. | 1010 Colorado St. | 512/463–5516 | Weekdays 10–5.

Guadalupe Street. Also known as "the Drag," this thoroughfare bordering the west side of the University of Texas campus is lined with restaurants and trendy boutiques. | 512/474–5171 | Daily.

Lady Bird Johnson Wildflower Center. Founded in the early 1980s, this 43-acre complex has extensive plantings of wildflowers that bloom year-round. The grounds include a visitor center, nature trail, observation tower, elaborate stone terraces, and flower-filled meadows. | 4801 LaCrosse Ave. | 512/292–4200 | www.wildflower.org | Tues.–Sun. 9–5:30.

State Capitol. Pink granite quarried from Granite Mountain, near the town of Marble Falls, was used to construct the state capitol building (the nation's largest), which houses the governor's office, the Texas legislature, and several other executive state agencies. From 1892 to 1898, hundreds of stonecutters from Scotland along with gangs of Texas convicts cut the stone. | 11th St. and Congress Ave. | 512/463–0063 | Weekdays 8:30–4:30, Sat.–Sun. 9:30–4:30.

On the east side of the State Capitol is the **Lorenzo de Zavala State Archives and Library Building,** with archives of the Texas State Library. A genealogical collection is on the first floor. | 1201 Brazos St. | 512/463–5480 | Library: Weekdays 8–5; Archives: Tues.–Sat. 8–5.

University of Texas at Austin. Founded in 1883, UT–Austin is home to the largest member of the University of Texas system. Its student population is approximately 48,000. | Guadalupe between 22nd and 23rd Sts. | www.utexas.edu | 512/471–3434.

Considered one of the top 10 university art galleries in the country, the **Jack S. Blanton Art Gallery** is in two separate facilities on the university campus—including the Harry Ransom Humanities Research Center. The galleries contain 20th-century artwork as well as popular culture items from the late 19th and early 20th centuries. Works from Mexican artists are also on display. | 23rd and San Jacinto Sts. | 512/471–7324 | Mon.–Wed., Fri. 9–5, Thurs. 9–9, weekends 1–5.

The largest presidential library in the nation, the **Lyndon Baines Johnson Library and Museum** is in an eight-story building made of travertine marble. The building is the repository for all 35 million documents produced during the LBJ administration and has many exhibits on Johnson's life, family, and presidential years. | 2313 Red River | 512/916–5136 | Daily 9–5.

Zilker Park. The site of temporary Franciscan missions in 1730 and a former Native American gathering place is now a popular park. The 351 acres along the shores of Lake Austin include Barton Springs Pool, whose clear springs produce from 12 million to 90 million gallons in any 24-hour period; the swimming pool is more than 300 yards long, and the water varies from 66° to 70°. The park also has numerous gardens, a meditation trail, and a Swedish log cabin dating from the 1840s. Plays are held in the park's theater during the summer. | 2201 Barton Springs Rd. | 512/397–1463; 512/476–9044 (pool) | Daily.

Dining

Shoreline Grill. Seafood. Right on the shoreline of Town Lake, this spot is popular for power lunches, as well as romantic dinners. Floor-to-ceiling windows provide wonderful views of the lake, and candlelight and hardwood floors add to the elegant feel. Popular items are shark, prime rib, and crème brûlée. Open-air dining is available on an enclosed patio with a view of the lake. Kids' menu. | 98 San Jacinto Blvd. | 512/477–3300 | No lunch Sat., Sun. | AE, D, DC, MC, V | $$–$$$$

Louie's 106. Mediterranean. Although best known for its tapas, this downtown eatery also serves up duck confit and pork chops. A large wine selection awaits. Kids' menu. | 106 E. 6th St. | 512/476–1997 | No lunch Sat., Sun. | AE, D, DC, MC, V | $$–$$$

Güeros. Tex-Mex. A former feed store, this spacious and popular restaurant has high ceilings and tall windows, a rustic bar, and live music. After President Clinton ordered the Numero Dos (a Mexican plate including a tamale, a marinated chicken taco, a beef taco, guacamole, beans, and rice) during a visit, the dish was renamed El Presidente. The little *tacos al pastor* (marinated rotisserie-roasted pork with pineapple, cilantro, and onions) are stellar, and the fresh-lime margaritas are justly famous. | 1412 S. Congress Ave., 78704 | 512/447–7688 | Reservations not accepted | Breakfast also available weekends | AE, D, DC, MC, V | $–$$

Threadgill's. Southern. Janis Joplin was drawn to this local legend for its massive chicken-fried steak. Don't overlook the homemade cobbler or the free seconds on extensive vegetable side orders—butter beans, okra and tomatoes, black-eyed peas, and squash casserole are but a few. | 6416 N. Lamar Blvd., 78752 | 512/451–5440 | Reservations not accepted | MC, V | $–$$

Scholz Garten. American. Established in 1866, this beer garden and dining room is a venerable local favorite. In addition to standard American fare, the menu includes Tex-Mex barbecue and German dishes. Sides might include German potato salad, red cabbage sauerkraut, creamed corn, and green beans. | 1607 San Jacinto Blvd., 78701 | 512/474–1958 | Closed Sun. | AE, D, DC, MC, V | $

Lodging

Driskill. Built in 1888, the lobby of this downtown hotel has a stained-glass dome and 30-ft high ceilings. Restaurant, bar (with entertainment), room service. Cable TV. Business services, free parking. | 604 Brazos St., 78701 | 512/474–5911 | fax 512/474–2214 | 188 rooms | AE, D, DC, MC, V | $$$–$$$$

Embassy Suites. Shopping and entertainment are four blocks from this nine-story hotel in the heart of downtown. Restaurant, bar, complimentary breakfast. In-room data ports, microwaves, refrigerators. Cable TV. Pool. Hot tub. Exercise equipment. Laundry facilities. Business services, free parking. | 300 S. Congress St., 78704 | 512/469–9000 | fax 512/480–9164 | www.embassysuites.com | 262 suites | AE, D, DC, MC, V | $$$

Days Inn University/Downtown. Its downtown location puts this two-story motel just blocks from the University of Texas. Complimentary Continental breakfast. Microwaves, refrigerators. Cable TV. Pool. Pets allowed. | 3105 I–35N, 78722 | 512/478–1631 or 800/725–7666 | fax 512/236–0058 | 61 rooms | AE, D, DC, MC, V | $–$$

La Quinta–Capitol. Restaurants and the State Capitol building are two blocks from this four-story hotel. In-room data ports. Cable TV. Pool. Business services, free parking. Pets allowed. | 300 E. 11th St., 78701 | 512/476–1166 or 800/687–6667 | fax 512/476–6044 | www.laquinta.com | 145 rooms | AE, D, DC, MC, V | $–$$

Bandera

Attractions

Bandera County Historic Tours. A walking or driving tour of the county can bring you to the original town jail and county courthouse, historic 11th Street, present-day blacksmiths and saddle makers, and a working ranch. Information on self-guided tours is available at the Bandera Convention and Visitors Bureau. | 606 Rte. 16S, 78003 | 830/796–3045 or 800/364–3833 | Daily.

Frontier Times Museum. Cowboy paraphernalia, Indian arrowheads, Western show posters, Buffalo Bill memorabilia, and prehistoric artifacts are on display in this museum, established in 1927. | 506 13th St. | 830/796–3864 | Mon.–Sat. 10–4:30, Sun. 1–4:30.

Dining

Busbee's Barbecue. Barbecue. On the town's main drag, this popular spot serves chicken, brisket, and ribs. As a variation on the usual ultra-heavy barbecue meal, the chef will slice your grilled chicken or beef and toss it onto a bed of fresh greens. | 319 Main St., 78003 | 830/796–3153 | No credit cards | $–$$

Cabaret Cafe and Dance Hall. Continental. The dance hall of this all-wood ranch-style restaurant is the second-oldest in Texas, circa 1936. The wait on weekends is worthwhile for a taste of the mesquite-grilled prime rib or mahimahi, embellished with lemon wine salsa, garlic shrimp cream, or other sauces. Judge for yourself whether the big brownie with ice cream handles the pressure of being the only dessert on the menu. | 801 Main St., 78003 | 830/796–8166 | Reservations not accepted | Closed Mon. | AE, MC, V | $–$$

O.S.T. Restaurant. American. An institution for over 75 years, the acronym stands for Old Spanish Trail, which once passed through Bandera. Expect such down-home country-style American food as chicken-fried steak with cream gravy. Come early before the homemade biscuits run out, or if you're there for lunch, try the all-you-can-eat buffet. Mexican dishes are also available, and breakfast is served all day. | 305 Main St., 78003 | 830/796–3836 | Breakfast also available | D, DC, MC, V | $–$$

Fredericksburg

Attractions

Admiral Nimitz Museum and State Historical Center. World War II Pacific Commander Adm. Chester Nimitz, the town's most famous resident, is honored at the site of this former hotel, built by Nimitz's grandfather. Three-stories of exhibits focus on Nimitz, World War II, and the Pacific campaign. Several hotel rooms, the hotel kitchen, and the bathhouse have been restored. Behind the museum is the Garden of Peace, a gift from the people of Japan. | 340 E. Main St. | 830/997–4379 | fax 830/997–8220 | www.nimitz-museum.org | Daily 10–5.

Enchanted Rock State Natural Area. The 640-acre granite outcropping here is the largest stone formation in the West; it places second nationally to Georgia's Stone Mountain. Experienced climbers can scale the smaller formations next to the main dome. Picnic facilities and a 60-site primitive campground at the base of the rock round out the offerings. No vehicular camping is permitted. Entry into the park is limited during busy weekends. | Off Rte. 965, 18 mi north of Fredericksburg | 915/247–3903 | www.tpwd.state.tx.us/park/enchantd/enchantd.html | Daily 8 AM–10 PM.

Dining

George's Old German Bakery and Cafe. German. You might find such solid German fare as schnitzels and rouladen at this casual storefront café. The rye wheat bread and rich strudels are popular. | 225 W. Main St. | 830/997–9084 | Breakfast also available. No supper | No credit cards | $–$$

Mamacita's. Tex-Mex. Traditional Mexican tile and Tex-Mex favorites help create a satisfying experience. Kids' menu. | 506 E. Main St. | 830/997–9546 | AE, D, DC, MC, V | $–$$

Lodging

Fredericksburg Bed and Brew. Note the second "B" of this unusual B&B: included in the room rate is a sampler of the Fredericksburg Brewing Co.'s four current beers. Each room is decorated by a different store in town, and everything is for sale. It's right on Main St., convenient to shopping and local sightseeing. No pets. No kids. No smoking. | 245 E. Main St., 78624 | 830/997–1646 | fax 830/997–8026 | www.yourbrewery.com | 12 rooms | MC, V | $$

Herb House. On the Fredericksburg Herb Farm, this 1940s frame guest house is on a four-acre plot of organic herb and flower gardens just six blocks off Main St. At breakfast, guests can sample the farm's homemade herb breads, spiced butter, and fresh fruit. Restaurant, complimentary breakfast. Kitchenettes. Cable TV. No pets. No kids. No smoking. | 402 Whitney St., 78624 | 830/997–8615 or 800/259–4372 | fax 830/997–5069 | www.fredericksburgherbfarm.com | 1 two-bedroom guest house | AE, D, MC, V | $$

Schmidt Barn. One of the first guest houses in Fredericksburg, this B&B is a restored century-old barn behind the 1860s Schmidt farmhouse. The sunken brick tub and wood-burning stove provide a truly authentic setting. Expect a German-style breakfast of meats, cheeses, and pastries. Complimentary breakfast. Microwaves, refrigerators. No smoking. | 231 W. Main St., 78624 | 830/997–5612 | fax 830/997–8282 | www.fbglodging.com | 1 one-bedroom guest house | AE, D, MC, V | $$

Peach Tree Inn. A grassy courtyard with a waterfall and large pecan trees provide a pretty setting for this motel within walking distance of the Nimitz museum, restaurants, and shopping. Picnic area, complimentary Continental breakfast. Some microwaves, refrigerators. Cable TV. Pool. Playground. Business services. No pets. | 401 S. Washington, (U.S. 87S) 78624 | 830/997–2117 or 800/843–4666 | fax 830/997–0827 | www.thepeachtreeinn.com | 34 rooms, 10 suites | AE, D, MC, V | $–$$

Comfort Inn. Within walking distance of shopping and restaurants, this standard motel is nine blocks from downtown. Picnic area, complimentary Continental breakfast. Cable TV. Pool. Tennis courts. No pets. | 908 S. Adams, 78624 | 830/997–9811 | fax 830/997–2068 | 46 rooms | AE, D, DC, MC, V | $

Johnson City

Attractions

Lyndon B. Johnson National Historical Park. Headquarters for this park are in downtown Johnson City. The former U.S. president moved here from Stonewall, approximately 10 mi west of Johnson City, when he was 5 years old. | Visitor Center, off Main St. | 830/868–7128 | Daily, 8:45–5.

From 1913 to 1934 Lyndon Johnson lived in a simple white frame house. Johnson's father, Sam Ealy Johnson, Jr., was a state representative, and the **Boyhood Home** often echoed with political debate. At the same time, a future statesman was being tutored on the front porch at the knee of his mother, Rebekah Baines Johnson. | Daily 9–5, by guided tour only.

The **Johnson Settlement** consists of a restored cabin and other buildings that belonged to Sam Ealy Johnson, Sr., LBJ's grandfather. Photos, farm implements, and clothing from the 1800s are displayed in a visitors center. An old cypress cistern serves as a mini-auditorium with recorded readings of letters written by original settlers of this rugged land. | Daily 9:30–4:30, self-guided tour.

In Stonewall, this reconstructed **Birthplace** is best seen on a guided tour that begins at the visitor center in the state park. | About 10 mi from the visitor center on U.S. 290, Rte. 49.

Lyndon B. Johnson State Historical Park. In Stonewall, this park is where Lyndon Johnson lived until he was 5 years old. It's the boarding point for the guided tours of the LBJ ranch. The park also has interpretive exhibits about the Hill Country and the Johnson family.

A large white home sprawling under shady oaks, the LBJ Ranch hosted many national and international visitors during LBJ's presidency. For this reason it was dubbed the "Texas White House." The home is not open to the public and is seen only as a drive-by attraction on guided tours operated from the visitor center. | From Johnson City, 14 mi west on U.S. 290, enter on Rte. 52 | 830/644–2252 | Daily; tours available 10–4.

Costumed docents carry on farm chores typical of the early 1900s and children can see farm animals at the **Sauer-Beckmann Farmstead** living history farm on the park grounds. | 830/644–2455 | Daily 8–4:30.

Dining

Uncle Kunkel's Bar-B-Q. Barbecue. Stop here if you're in the mood for brisket, pork, ribs, or sausage; this joint has won blue ribbons at four state fairs and runs a successful mail-order business. If you want chicken, be sure to call ahead. | 210 U.S. 290, (281S) 78636 | 830/868–0251 or 888/814–5900 | fax 830/868–9122 | No supper. Closed Mon., Tues. | MC, V | $

Kerrville

Attractions

Cowboy Artists of America Museum. Filled with Western-theme paintings and sculpture, this hilltop museum has work by members of the Cowboy Artists of America. | 1550 Bandera Hwy., (Rte. 173) 78028 | 830/896–2553 | fax 830/896–2556 | Mon.–Sat. 9–5, Sun. 1–5.

Hill Country Museum (Capt. Charles Schreiner Mansion). The town's development and the story of Texas Ranger Charles Schreiner are the focus of this local history museum. Schreiner came to Kerrville as a young man in the 1850s, and after the Civil War he opened a dry goods store and began acquiring land. Schreiner's company was the first business in America to recognize the value of mohair, a prelude to Kerrville becoming the mohair capital of the world. | 226 Earl Garrett St., 78028 | 830/896–8633 | Mon.–Sat. 10–4:30.

Kerrville-Schreiner State Park. Seven miles of hiking trails, as well as fishing and swimming in the Guadalupe River are among the attractions. Screened shelters and campsites are available. | 2485 Bandera Hwy., 78028 | 830/257–5392 | fax 830/896–7275 | www.tpwd.state.tx.us | Daily.

Scott Schreiner Municipal Golf Course. Green hills and clusters of trees accent this gorgeous 18-hole course. Reservations are essential on weekends. | Country Club Rd. at Sidney Baker St. | 830/257–4982 | Year-round, Tues.–Sun. 7–dusk.

Y. O. Ranch. The ranch once sprawled over more than 600,000 acres in Mountain Home, covering a distance of 80 mi.; today it spans a mere 40,000 acres. Tour the ranch and view its famous Texas longhorns and many exotic animal species. | Rte. 41 W, Exit 490 (Mountain Home) | 830/640–3222 | fax 830/640–3227 | www.yoranch.com | Daily, tours at 10 and 1.

Dining

Bill's Barbecue. Barbecue. A local fixture for over 30 years, this rustic dining spot serves up such hearty comfort food as brisket, sausage, chicken, and ribs. | 1909 Junction Hwy., 78028 | 830/895–5733 | Closed Sun., Mon. No supper | No credit cards | $–$$

Joe's Jefferson Street Cafe. Southern. In an 1890 Victorian mansion, this casual eatery has such traditional Texas dishes as steak, Gulf shrimp, catfish, and chicken-fried steak. | 1001 Jefferson St., 78028 | 830/257–2929 | Closed Sun. | MC, V | $–$$

Rich's Hill Country Cafe. American. A longtime breakfast and lunch café, Rich's is popular with local residents for its down-home cooking. American breakfasts, huevos rancheros, breakfast tacos, baked chicken, and chicken-fried steak are among the choices. | 806 Main St., 78028 | 830/257–6665 | Breakfast also available. Closed Sun. No supper weekdays | No credit cards | $–$$

Del Norte Restaurant. Southern. Casual dining in a family atmosphere with good down-home cooking is the recipe here. Offerings include catfish, chicken-fried steak, and breakfast tacos. | 710 Junction Hwy., 78028 | 830/257–3337 | Breakfast also available. Closed Sun. No supper | D, MC, V | $

New Braunfels

Attractions

Canyon Lake. You can boat, picnic, and camp at the public parks that line this lake. It is a popular destination with anglers in search of catfish, largemouth bass, and, below the dam, rainbow and brown trout. | 601 Coe Rd., Headquarters is on Rte. 306 | 830/964–3341 or 800/528–2104 | fax 830/964–2215 | www.swf.usace.army-mil.com | Daily 7 AM to dusk.

Museum of Texas Handmade Furniture. Furniture hand-crafted in Texas during the 1800s is on display. There is an extensive Biedermeier collection. | 1370 Church Hill Dr., 78130 | 830/629–6504 | Tues.–Sun. 1–4. Closed Mon.

Hummel Museum. Sister Maria Innocentia Hummel's extensive collection is on display, including 350 original paintings and early sketches that inspired the popular figurines, plates, and other collectibles. | 199 Main Plaza | 830/625–5636 or 800/456–4866 | www.bigmac.bullcreek.austin.tx.us/hummel/index.htm | Mon.–Sat. 10–5, Sun. noon–5.

Natural Bridge Caverns. Named for the rock arch over the entrance, this cave is one of the most spectacular in the area. Guided tours are available. | 26495 Natural Bridge Caverns | 830/651–6101 | fax 830/438–7432 | www.naturalbridgetexas.com/cavern | Late May–Aug., daily 9–6; Sept.–late May, daily 9–4.

Natural Bridge Wildlife Park. See zebras, gazelles, antelopes, and ostriches, and even feed them, at this drive-through wildlife ranch. There's a petting zoo with pygmy goats at the entrance. | 26515 Natural Bridge Caverns Rd. | 830/438–7400 | www.naturalbridgetexas.com/cavern | Daily 9–6:30.

Schlitterbahn Water Park. Come enjoy the largest tubing park in the world. The Comal River supplies cool springwater at the rate of 24,000 gallons a minute and replicates the look and feel of river rapids. Brave the 60-ft Schlittercoaster and the mile-long Raging River tube chute or go for a dip in the 50,000-gallon hot tub with a swim-up bar. For the less adventurous there's a gentle wave pool. Picnic sites. | 305 W. Austin | 830/625–2351 | fax 830/620–4873 | www.schlitterbahn.com | Late Apr.–mid-May, weekends Sat. 10–7, Sun. 10–6; mid-May–late Aug., daily 10–8; late Aug.–late Sept., weekends 10–6.

Dining

New Braunfels Smokehouse. Barbecue. There's plenty of barbecue and hickory-smoked meat at this casual restaurant that seats nearly 300. In addition to barbecue are such tasty dishes as sausage, chicken and dumplings, apple dumplings, and bread pudding. The all-you-can-eat buffet is served on the wooden patio. Kids' menu. Beer and wine only. | 146 Rte. 46 E | 830/625–2416 | Breakfast also available | AE, D, MC, V | $$–$$$

Huisache Grill. Contemporary. Formerly a train station, the grill's downtown location, parklike setting, and recycled glass and wood interior attract crowds, as do the seafood, steak, and salads. There are live music and jazz on the weekends. Open-air dining is available on the patio, which has a stone fireplace. Kids' menu. | 303 W. San Antonio | 830/620–9001 | AE, D, DC, MC, V | $–$$

Oma's House. German. Authentic German cuisine rules at this family-owned restaurant, where the Wiener schnitzel is a standout. | 541 Hwy. 46 | 830/625–3280 | fax 830/625–9681 | AE, D, DC, MC, V | $–$$

Granzin Bar-B-Q. Barbecue. Take-out only, this family-owned restaurant dishes up a tasty and portable sliced beef sandwich. Ribs are also popular. | 954 W. San Antonio St. | 830/629–6615 | Closed Sun. | AE, D, MC, V | $

San Marcos

Attractions

Aquarena Center for Continuing Education. The resort dates back to 1928, when A. B. Rogers purchased 125 acres at the headwaters of the San Marcos River to build a hotel. He provided glass-bottom boats to cruise Spring Lake, home to many fish (including some white albino catfish) and various types of plant life. Today you can still enjoy a cruise on a glass-bottom boat and even see the site of an underwater archaeological dig. Visible is the spot that yielded the remains of Clovis Man, a hunter-gatherer who lived on the San Marcos River 13,000 years ago. The park has an educational focus with many ecotourism displays. | 921 Aquarena Springs Dr. | 512/245–7575 or 800/999–9767 | Daily 9:30–7:30.

Calaboose African-American History Museum. Photos and memorabilia document the history and experiences of African-Americans in southwest Texas. Docents guide you through permanent exhibits on the Tuskeegee Airmen, the Buffalo Soldiers, and the Cotton era in the San Marcos area. The museum is in the original Hays County Jail building, built in 1873. | 200 Martin Luther King Dr. | 512/393–8421 or 512/353–0124 | By appointment.

Lockhart State Park. The 263-acre park has a nine-hole golf course, fishing on Plum Creek, picnic areas, a swimming pool, and campsites for both tents and trailers. Many of the facilities were built by the Civilian Conservation Corps in the 1930s. | 4179 State Park Rd. | 512/398–3479 | fax 512/396–7175 | Daily.

Prime Outlets. One of Texas's largest collections of outlet stores includes the Gap, Calvin Klein, Guess, J. Crew, Polo, Bass, and Nike. | 3939 I-35S | 512/396–2200 | Daily.

Southwestern Writers Collection and Wittliff Gallery of Southwestern and Mexican Photography. The archival repository contains the works of writers and photographers with links to the Southwest. Exhibits, which change three times a year, have explored Texan music, Mexican women photographers, and Larry McMurtry's *Lonesome Dove*. | Albert B. Alkek Library, Southwest Texas State University, 601 University Blvd., 7th floor | 512/245–2313 | www.library.swt.edu/swwc/index.html | Weekdays 8–5, except Tues. 8 AM–9 PM, Sat. 1–5, Sun. 2–6.

Wonder World. A guided tour lasting nearly 2 hours covers the entire park, including the 7½-acre Texas Wildlife Park, Texas's largest petting zoo. A miniature train chugs through the animal enclosure, stopping to allow riders to pet and feed white-tail deer, wild turkeys, and many exotic species. One stop on the tour is Wonder Cave, created during the earthquake that produced the Balcones Fault, an 1,800-mi line separating the western Hill Country from the flat eastern farmland. Visitors can also go to the top of the 110-ft Tejas Tower, which allows a spectacular view of the fault. | 1000 Prospect St. | 512/392–3760 | June–Aug., daily 8–8; Sept.–Oct., daily 9–6; Nov.–Feb., weekdays 9–5, weekends 9–6; Mar.–May, weekdays 9–6, weekends 9–6.

Dining

Joe's Crab Shack. Cajun/Creole. Enjoy the crab claws, fried shrimp, and the gumbo. Great music and dancing create a festive mood. | 100 Sessums Dr. | 512/396–5255 | AE, D, DC, MC, V | $–$$$

Café on the Square and Brew Pub. Tex-Mex. The Café and pub is in a historic building with a pressed-tin ceiling and southwestern artwork. It's known for migas (a mixture of eggs, tortilla, and other ingredients), enchiladas, fajitas, venison, and buffalo burgers. | 126 N. LBJ St. | 512/396–9999 | AE, D, MC, V | $–$$

Gordo's Grill. American. In a former movie theater, the stage is still used for live entertainment. Burgers, chili, sandwiches, and steak are popular. | 120 E. San Antonio St. | 512/392–1874 | AE, D, DC, MC, V | $–$$

Centerpoint Station. American. Antique memorabilia, from jewelry and clothes to furniture, toys and candles fill this family restaurant that serves good burgers, tacos, enchiladas, and shakes. | 3946 I–35, Exit 200 | 512/392–1103 | AE, D, MC, V | $

KINGSVILLE TO ARANSAS NATIONAL WILDLIFE REFUGE

SOUTH TEXAS TOUR

Distance: 117 mi   Time: 2 days
Overnight Break: Corpus Christi

Cruise through the Coastal Bend, a region spanning Rockport, Aransas Pass, Port Aransas, Corpus Christi, and Kingsville. Once a magnet for travelers in the days of buccaneers and Spanish conquistadors, the region today is one of the top ecotourism destinations in the nation. Besides drawing visitors to its relaxed atmosphere and coastal beauty, the area attracts bird-watchers from around the globe who come for a chance to view more than 400 species. The area is dotted with birding and hiking trails, guided tour boats, and other attractions that lend themselves to copious picture-taking.

❶ Begin your tour at **King Ranch.** Most guests make their first stop at the visitor center for a guided tour of the expansive ranch, which was founded in 1853 by Capt. Richard

King. It ranks as one of the largest spreads in the world, spanning 825,000 acres, larger than Rhode Island. Today it's home to more than 60,000 cattle and 300 quarter horses and welcomes visitors from around the world.

② Next, stop in **Kingsville,** at the intersection of Route 141 and I–77. The town named for the nearby ranch also offers several ranching attractions. The **King Ranch Museum** centers on the history of the ranch, including a photo essay on life on the ranch in the 1940s. Nearby, the **King Ranch Saddle Shop,** opened after the Civil War to supply the ranch with saddles, today produces purses, belts, and, of course, saddles.

③ From Kingsville, head north on I–77 for about 25 mi, then east on Route 44 for about 10 mi into **Corpus Christi.** One of America's 10 busiest ports, Corpus Christi has a bustling waterfront with tour boats, shrimp boats, and deep sea fishing charters. The **Corpus Christi Museum of Science and History** has some of the state's top exhibits, including life-size replicas of the Niña, Pinta, and Santa María. Across the Harbor Bridge, the **Texas State Aquarium** showcases the aquatic animals and habitats indigenous to the Gulf of Mexico. Next door, the **U.S.S. Lexington Museum on the Bay** is set in the most decorated aircraft carrier in U.S. Naval history. Spend the night in Corpus Christi.

④ Visitors to Corpus Christi shouldn't miss a stop at **Padre Island National Seashore,** open year-round for beachcombing, fishing, and swimming. Its visitor center contains exhibits on the region. Surfers will find wave action created by a surf pier at the **J. P. Luby Surf Park** on Route 361, while campers can enjoy covered picnic areas and overnight hookups at **Padre Balli Park** on Park Road 22.

⑤ When you've finished exploring Padre Island, head north on Route 22, then right on Route 53 into **Mustang Island State Park.** The park offers a mile and a half of beach camping, and horseback riding is popular along the island's beaches.

⑥ When you've finished exploring the park, head north on Route 53/361 out of Mustang Island and into **Port Aransas.** Known as "Port A" among Texans, it's perched on the northern tip of Mustang Island. Spend an afternoon out in the Gulf aboard a deep sea fishing cruise. Large group trips, taking as many as 100 passengers, provide bait and tackle; serious anglers looking for big game fish such as marlin and shark can book charters. For a chance to see dolphins, stop by the Roberts Point Park on Route 361. Dolphins often chase the ferries as they make their way across the ship channel. If you'd like to learn more about marine life, stop by the small aquarium at the **University of Texas Marine Science Institute.**

⑦ Route 53 becomes Route 361 beyond Port Aransas. Stay on Route 361 to **Aransas Pass,** which is more a genuine fishing village and less a tourist destination than many other coastal communities. (Most of its 7,000 residents are employed in the fishing industry.) The **Seamen's Memorial Tower,** a monument to the fishermen lost at sea, marks the entrance to the working harbor.

⑧ Ten miles north of Aransas Pass on Route 35L is **Rockport.** The town is considered a bird-watching paradise, with more than 500 species on record. Rockport's position on a major bird flyway (the Central Flyway) has made it an international birding destination. It's particularly known for migrating passerines, shorebirds, waterfowl, birds of prey, and hummingbirds. History buffs will also find plenty of activities in Rockport–Fulton. The **Fulton Mansion State Historic Structure,** refurbished by the Texas Parks and Wildlife Department, was somewhat of a futuristic home when first built in 1876.

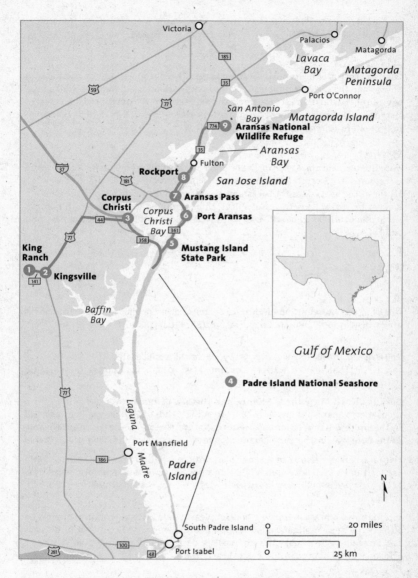

For an even earlier look at coastal life, stop by the **Texas Maritime Museum,** which traces maritime history from the Spanish shipwrecks off the Gulf coast to the offshore oil industry.

9 **Aransas National Wildlife Refuge** is the winter nesting ground of the endangered whooping crane, a statuesque bird with a 7-ft wingspan. A self-guided drive allows you the opportunity to spot several species of birds and mammals (as well as alligators); a visitor center explains more about the delicate ecology of the region.

To return to Kingsville, take Route 35N from the Aransas National Wildlife Refuge to Route 239W and proceed for about 10 mi to U.S. 77. Proceed south on U.S. 77 for about 90 mi into Kingsville.

Aransas Pass

Attractions

Conn Brown Harbor. The nexus of Aransas Pass, this harbor is home to fish-packing houses and the site of commercial shrimp boats docking and departing. Rent a boat to visit the coastal islands of Mustang and St. Joseph, picnic, or visit the memorial to lost seamen. From downtown, take Business 35N to Stapp Ave., turn right and continue to the water. | 361/758–2750 | Daily.

Dining

Nopalitos Restaurant. Mexican. The brightly painted dining area of this local favorite is festooned with sombreros, serapes, and neon signs (one in the shape of Mexico). Try the grilled beef fajitas, the beef shank–and–vegetable soup, or the popular menudo (beef tripe seasoned with secret spices, chilis, and oregano), served with hominy. Homemade tortillas come with every dish. | 306 E. Goodnight St., 78336 | 361/758–1080 | AE, D, DC, MC, V | $

Corpus Christi

Attractions

Asian Cultures Museum and Educational Center. Asian art ranging from dolls to pagodas are on display here. | 1809 N. Chaparral | 361/882–2641 | fax 361/882–5718 | Tues.–Sat. 10–5.

Bob Hall Pier. The fishing pier extends beyond the third sand bar into the Gulf of Mexico; rod, reel, and bait may be purchased or rented. | 15820 Park Rd. 22, Corpus Christi, 78418 | 361/949–8121 | 24 hrs.

Corpus Christi Museum of Science and History. Exhibits cover everything from dinosaurs to Spanish shipwrecks. Don't miss the "Seeds of Change" exhibit, designed by the Smithsonian's National Museum of Natural History for the 500th anniversary of the European discovery of America. | 1900 N. Chaparral St. | 361/883–2862 | Daily.

Heritage Park. Here you can see nine historic homes dating from 1851. Each has been restored and is used occasionally by civic groups for concerts and performances. | 1581 N. Chaparral, 78401 | 361/883–0639 | Mon.–Sat. 10–2; tours: Wed.–Thurs. 10:30, Fri.–Sat. 10:30, 12:45.

International Kite Museum. Two thousand years of kite history—from Imperial China to modern-day scientific and military applications—are charted here. Colorful displays and engaging videos make this an excellent destination for families with children. The museum is housed inside a local beach resort complex. | 3200 Surfside Dr. | 361/883–7456 | Daily 10–6.

South Texas Institute for the Arts. Traditional and contemporary work by artists associated with Texas is displayed here. | 1902 N. Shoreline Blvd. | 361/980–3500 | Tues.–Wed., Fri.–Sat. 10–5, Thurs. 10–9, Sun. 1–5.

Texas State Aquarium. Aquatic animals and habitats indigenous to the Gulf of Mexico are showcased through exhibits and outdoor touch tanks. The Flower Gardens Coral Reef exhibit focuses on the coral gardens 115 mi off the coast, which attract such marine animals as moray eels, tarpon, and rays. In the Octopus's Garden, a 20-ft tall purple octopus invites young visitors to enjoy a marine-inspired playground. The interpretive center is entered from beneath a cascading waterfall. | 2710 N. Shoreline Dr. | 361/881–1200 or 800/477–4853 | fax 361/881–1257 | Mon.–Sat. 9–5, Sun. 10–5.

U.S.S. *Lexington* Museum on the Bay. In the most decorated aircraft carrier in U.S. Naval history, this museum offers five self-guided tour routes that give you a close look at the ship termed "The Blue Ghost." | 2914 N. Shoreline Blvd. | 361/888–4873 or 800/523–9539 | fax 361/883–8361 | www.usslexington.com | Daily 9–5.

Dining

Lighthouse. Seafood. Enjoy a spectacular view of the bay and downtown Corpus Christi from this restaurant built in the shape of a lighthouse. Dine inside or out on a menu with fresh Gulf fare. Steak, chicken, and pasta specialties are popular. Kids' menu. | 444 N. Shoreline Blvd. | 361/882–2837 | AE, D, DC, MC, V | $$–$$$

The Astor. American. Known far and wide for its savory mesquite-grilled steaks and fresh seafood, the Astor has been a Corpus Christi institution since 1957. Banquet rooms are available. | 5533 Leopard St. | 361/289–0101 | Breakfast also available | AE, D, DC, MC, V | $–$$$

Blackbeard's on the Beach. American. Very laid-back and meant to appeal to beach-combing vacationers, Blackbeard's is popular for its mounds of fried shrimp and fierce margaritas. It's down the beach from the U.S.S. *Lexington* Museum on the Bay and the Texas State Aquarium. | 3117 Surfside Blvd. | 361/884–1030 | AE, D, DC, MC, V | $–$$

Crawdaddy's. Cajun/Creole. Specializing in tear-inducing Cajun fare, Crawdaddy's makes up for its roadhouse amenities with some of the best swamp food in the downtown area. The restaurant's claim to fame is its "Cajun Boil," a dish of shrimp, crawdad, crab claws, sausage, corn on the cob, and new potatoes, all boiled together in a powerfully spicy broth. For the less adventurous, there are such relatively tame dishes as red beans and rice. | 414 Starr St. | 361/883–5432 | AE, D, MC, V | $–$$

La Bahia. Mexican. A satisfying blend of authentic Mexican and Tex-Mex fare awaits you here. The hip, stylish interior has exposed brick, high ceilings, arched doors and windows, and richly textured wall treatments. The flour and corn tortillas are homemade, the breakfast taquitos are available all day, and the full bar is open late. | 224 S. Mesquite | 361/888–6555 | No supper Sun. | AE, D, DC, MC, V | $–$$

Lodging

Villa del Sol. Perched on the Gulf's edge, this condominium hotel has breathtaking views of the bay. Each unit has a full kitchen, a living room, and a private balcony. It's a 3-minute walk from downtown Corpus Christi, and the U.S.S. *Lexington* Museum on the Bay is ½ mi away. Kitchenettes. Cable TV. 2 pools. Hot tub. No pets. | 3938 Surfside Blvd. | 800/242–3291 | 238 apartments | AE, D, DC, MC, V | $$–$$$

Days Inn Corpus Christi Beach. One block from the beach, this three-story motel is within walking distance of the Texas State Aquarium and the U.S.S. *Lexington* Museum on the Bay. Complimentary Continental breakfast. Cable TV, in-room VCRs (and movies). Business services. | 4302 Surfside Blvd., 78402 | 361/882–3297 | fax 361/882–6865 | www.daysinn.com | 56 rooms | AE, D, DC, MC, V | $–$$

Drury Inn. The Corpus Christi International Airport is 3 mi from this motel, and popular attractions such as the Texas State Aquarium and the U.S.S. *Lexington* Museum on the Bay are just 5 mi away. Complimentary Continental breakfast. In-room data ports, some refrigerators. Cable TV. Pool. Business services, airport shuttle. Pets allowed. | 2021 N. Padre Island Dr., 78408 | 361/289–8200 | www.drury-inn.com | fax 361/289–8200 | 105 rooms | AE, D, DC, MC, V | $–$$

Monterrey Motel. Across the street from the Bob Hall Pier, this is the closest motel to the Padre Island National Seashore. There are a few restaurants less than 2 mi away. Some kitchenettes, some refrigerators. Cable TV. Pets allowed. | 15705 South Padre Island Dr., Corpus Christi, 78418 | 361/949–8137 | fax 361/949–8137 | 24 rooms | AE, D, MC, V | $–$$

Ramada Hotel Bayfront. In the downtown business district, this 10-story hotel is one block from the bay and marina. Restaurant, bar, room service. In-room data ports. Cable TV. Pool. Exercise equipment. Laundry facilities. Business services, airport shuttle. | 601 N. Water St., 78401 | 361/882–8100 | fax 512/888–6540 | www.ramada.com | 200 rooms | AE, D, DC, MC, V | $–$$

Kingsville

Attractions

King Ranch. Sprawling across 825,000 acres, the King Ranch traces its history to 1853 when it was founded by Capt. Richard King, who made his fortune on Rio Grande riverboats. Visitors can enjoy a guided tour of the working ranch in air-conditioned buses. Still one of the largest in the world, the ranch developed the Santa Gertrudis and King Ranch Santa Cruz breeds of cattle as well as the first registered American quarter horse. | Santa Gertrudis Ave. or Hwy. 141, 1½ mi west of town | 361/592–8055 or 800/333–5032 | fax 361/595–1344 | www.king-ranch.com | Mon.–Sat. 9–4, Sun. noon–5.

King Ranch Museum. The history of the King Ranch is conveyed through exhibits that include a collection of saddles, antique carriages, and antique cars. | 405 N. 6th St. | 361/595–1881 | www.king-ranch.com | Mon.–Sat. 10–4, Sun. 1–5.

King Ranch Saddle Shop. The King Ranch Saddle Shop carries on the tradition of saddle making and also produces fine purses and belts. | 201 E. Kleberg | 361/595–1881 | www.king-ranch.com | Mon.–Sat. 10–6.

Port Aransas

Attractions

Mustang Island State Park. The 3,500-acre park has 5 mi of open beaches and such facilities as freshwater showers, picnic tables, and tent and RV camping. | Rte. 361, 14 mi south of Port Aransas | 361/749–5246 | www.tpwd.state.tx.us/park/mustang/mustang.htm | Daily.

San Jose Island. Pirate Jean Lafitte is said to have camped here. Large iron rings, thought to have been used to tie up his group's small boats, were discovered at the site. Even today, the island is accessible only by boat, and there are no public facilities. It is a quiet getaway for fishing, beachcombing, swimming, or shelling. Ferries leave throughout the day year-round from Woody's Sport Center. | 136 W. Cotter St. | 361/749–5252 | www.gulfcoastfishing.com/jetty.htm | Daily.

University of Texas Marine Science Institute. Students of oceanography, ecology, marine chemistry, and botany train at this branch of the University of Texas, located on 82 beachfront acres. Stop by the visitor center for a self-guided tour or to view exhibits and films on Texas Gulf life. | 750 Channel View Dr. | 361/749–5246 | www.utmsi.utexas.edu | Weekdays 8–5.

Dining

Crazy Cajun. Cajun. Butcher paper covers the wooden tables, and you'll see why if you or your neighbors order the Hungry Cajun, a heap of Cajun-spiced shrimp, crawfish, crab, sausage, corn, and potatoes that waiters deposit directly onto the paper. On weekends, live Cajun-style music keeps the joint jumping. | 303 Beach St. | 361/749–5069 | No lunch weekdays | AE, D, MC, V | $–$$

Pelican's Landing Restaurant. Seafood. Serving island cuisine before a magnificent waterfront view of Lake Texoma, this bustling eatery specializes in locally caught fish, fresh-cut steaks, and crab-cakes. Dine inside the windowed, covered deck or out on the breezy patio. A kids' menu and a seniors' menu are also available. | 337 Alister St. | 361/749–6405 | fax 361/749–6485 | AE, D, DC, MC, V | $–$$

Rockport

Attractions

Aransas National Wildlife Refuge. The National Park Service set aside this 54,829-acre refuge as the prime wintering ground for the endangered whooping crane and 300 other bird species. A chartered boat can take you out to the birds' protected area, or you can hike or drive the paved, 15-mi loop to see some of the area's other critters, including bats, armadillos, bobcats, feral hogs, and alligators. Be sure to visit the observation tower and the Wildlife Interpretive Center. | 25 mi north of Rockport on Rte. 35, then east on Rte. 774 to Rte. 2040 | 361/286–3559 | fax 361/286–3722 | www.southwest. fws.gov/refuges/texas/aransas.html | Daily dawn to dusk.

Connie Hagar Cottage Sanctuary. More than 6 acres of bayside trails run through this historical sight, named after the woman who helped put Rockport on the birding map. The bay is ideal for sighting many shore bird species. Just follow signs along Broadway until you see bird-watching platforms across the street from the bay. | Church and 1st. St. | 361/729–6445 or 800/242–0071 | Daily.

Copano Bay Causeway State Park. A lighted fishing pier, public boat ramp, picnic area, and bait shop are among the attractions at this 5 9/10-acre facility. | Rte. 35, 5 mi north of Rockport | 361/729–8519 | www.tpwd.state.tx.us/park/copano/copano.htm | Daily.

Fulton Mansion State Historic Structure. Col. George Fulton's regal 1874 home overlooks Aransas Bay. The French-Second-Empire mansion was built with surprisingly modern conveniences, including central forced-air heating, hot and cold running water, and a gas plant at the back of the house to fuel the chandeliers. | 317 Fulton Beach Rd. | 361/729–0386 | fax 361/729–6581 | www.tpwd.state.tx.us/park/fulton/fulton.htm | Daily, call for tour times.

Goose Island State Park. "Big Tree," considered one of the largest oak trees in the world, sits in this 314-acre park. It is said to be more than 1,000 years old, and is 35 ft in circumference and 44 ft in height. | Rte. 35 to Park Rd. 13, 12 mi north of Rockport | 361/729–2858 | fax 361/729–1041 | www.tpwd.state.tx.us | Daily 8 AM–10 PM.

Rockport Center for the Arts. The center's galleries, classrooms, pottery studio, and sculpture garden are used to exhibit local and theme-based artwork. The landscaped grounds are a tranquil place to unwind. | 902 Navigation Circle | 361/729–5519 | Tues.–Sun. 10–4, Sat. 1–4.

Texas Maritime Museum. Displays at this two-story complex in Rockport Harbor highlight shipbuilding, prominent seafaring Texans, shipwrecks through the ages, and the development of the offshore oil industry. | 1202 Navigation Blvd. | 361/729–1271 | fax 361/729–9938 | Tues.–Sat. 10–4, Sun. 1–4.

South Padre Island

Attractions

Padre Island National Seashore. First established in 1962, this 70-mi stretch of unblemished seashore is a haven for beachcombers, boaters, and swimmers. Go in spring to enjoy wildflowers, bird watching, and windsurfing; in summer to view nesting sea turtles. You can drive along parts of the island, but a four-wheel drive vehicle is required to explore most areas. Hiking trails abound and swimming is permitted on all beaches, though lifeguards are on duty only at Malaquite Beach Memorial Day–Labor Day. Camping facilities are available at Malaquite Beach and Bird Island Basin. The Malaquite Beach visitor center, open year-round, has educational programs, brochures, a small museum, and a concession stand. | 20301 Park Rd. | 361/949–8173 | www.nps.gov/pais | Daily.

★ **Sea Turtle, Inc.** Ila Loetscher, a.k.a. the "Turtle Lady," passed away in 2000 at the age of 95, but her lifelong conservation efforts—which focused the world's attention on Kemp's Ridley sea turtles—are continued at the site of her former home. Volunteers run shows on Tuesday and Saturday at 10 AM. | 5805 Gulf Blvd. | 956/761–2544 | Tues. and Sat. 10 AM.

University of Texas Pan American Coastal Studies Laboratory. Just south of town, the University of Texas Coastal Studies Laboratory offers a chance to learn more about Gulf marine life. Research focuses on coastal ecosystems, including a study of the sea turtles and dolphins that live in the area. You can stop by the lab Sunday through Friday for a look at the aquariums. | Isla Blanca Park at south end of island | 956/761–2644 | Sun.–Fri. 1:30–4:30.

Dining

Amberjacks. Seafood. Colorful and low-key, this spot is known for its tropical Caribbean flavor and fanciful fish decorations. Try the rasta shrimp, snapper Rockefeller, and sautéed amberjack. Entertainment on weekends. Kids' menu. | 209 W. Amberjack St. | 956/761–6500 | Closed Mon. | AE, D, DC, MC, V | $$–$$$

Blackbeard's. Seafood. A 12-ft alligator and other large fish mounted on the walls add to the nautical theme at this casual family restaurant with two levels of seating. Try the fried shrimp plate or the flounder sandwich with onion rings. | 103 E. Saturn St. | 956/761–2962 | AE, D, DC, MC, V | $$–$$$

Lantern Grill. Contemporary. The gas lanterns in the entranceway give this upscale restaurant its name. The chef pairs seafood and meat with inventive sauces, and gives each dish a little southwestern kick. The grilled beef tenderloin comes with potato flautas and a Portobello mushroom glaze; the sautéed red snapper is served with saffron rice and a shrimp-Chardonnay sauce. | 3109 Padre Blvd. | 956/761–4460 | fax 956/761–4460 | Closed Mon. No lunch | AE, D, DC, MC, V | $$–$$$

Scampi's. Seafood. Casual and family-friendly, this waterfront restaurant is one of South Padre's busiest; expect crowds. Fresh seafood and homemade pasta are among the offerings. Open-air dining overlooks the bay. | 206 W. Aries St. | 956/761–1755 | Closed Dec. 12–25. No lunch | AE, D, MC, V | $$–$$$

FROM SALT LAKE INTO THE MOUNTAINS

PARK CITY TO THE MIRROR LAKE HIGHWAY THROUGH
THE WASATCH-CACHE NATIONAL FOREST ON ROUTE 150

Distance: 90 mi   Time: 2 days
Overnight Break: Park City

Your drive will take you from Salt Lake City to Park City, northern Utah's premier year-round resort town. From there the tour leads to the Heber Valley and into the pristine beauty of the Wasatch-Cache National Forest. Don't do this drive in winter: Route 150 may be closed due to snow, and some of Park City's dining and lodging rates double during ski season.

❶ From **Salt Lake,** I–80 runs through Parley's Canyon toward Park City. This is Utah's original toll road, devised by enterprising Mormon settler Parley P. Pratt; he stationed his home midway and charged settlers a fee to pass through the canyon, the easiest route into the Salt Lake valley.

❷ Proceed 20 mi east on I–80, then south for approximately 5 mi on Route 224 into Park City. Main Street in **Park City** is an easy up-and-down walk of less than a mile. Window shopping is its chief interest, but take time to enjoy the art galleries on both sides of the street and settle on a good place for dinner. Spend the night in Park City.

❸ Leaving Park City, head east on Route 248 approximately 7 mi to the **Kamas** Ranger District Office to determine the road conditions and gather interpretive information before heading into the **Wasatch-Cache National Forest.**
　　The **Uinta Mountains** will be visible to the east for the remainder of this tour. They are one of only a few mountain ranges in North America running on an east–west axis.

❹ The Provo River parallels the road along much of this drive. **Upper Provo River Falls** (22 mi east of Kamas on Rte. 150) is a lovely place to stretch your legs. Walkways near the road follow the river past a series of small cascades.

⑤ As the highway continues to climb in elevation, there are several signed turnoffs leading to small lakes. Some of these roads may be suitable only for high-clearance vehicles, but a couple are maintained gravel with developed picnic and camping areas, and others permit short hikes to lakes nestled in thick pine forest. **Washington Lake** (approximately 27 mi northeast of Kamas on the west side of Rte. 150) is particularly beautiful in summer when wildflowers are in bloom.

⑥ Continue along Route 150 for another 5 mi or so to **Bald Mountain Pass,** where the road climbs to 10,687 ft, an elevation close to the timberline. Watch during the climb as tree stands begin to thin out and meadow areas are strewn with boulders.

⑦ Another mile on Route 150 will take you to **Mirror Lake,** on the northeastern descent from Bald Mountain, about 1 mi from the top of the pass. This alpine lake's tranquil waters beautifully reflect the sky and the ring of pine trees surrounding the shore.

⑧ To finish this drive, you can either continue north to **Evanston,** Wyoming (32 mi north on Rte. 150), then take I–80 back into the Heber Valley (approximately 40 mi southwest), or go back the way you came (33 mi southwest to Kamas).

Park City

Attractions
Alpine Slide, Gorgoza Skate Park, and Little Miners' Park. In summer, the resort center at Park City Mountain Resort transforms ski operations into facilities for other sports.

The Alpine Slide begins with a chairlift ride about halfway up the mountain, then special "sleighs" carry sliders down 3,000 ft of winding concrete and fiberglass track at a breath-taking pace. In winter, the Gorgoza Skate Park is the snow tubing course. The Little Miners' Park has children's rides: a mini Ferris wheel, a slow-moving train, and an airplane ride. There's also a miniature golf course. | Park City Mountain Resort | 435/647–5333 | www.parkcitymountain.com | June–Sept., weekdays 2–9, weekends 11–9.

The Canyons. Now the fifth-largest ski resort in the country, this establishment is also open year-round for hiking, biking, and horseback riding. In winter, snowboarders remain loyal to the place, one of the first in Utah open to them. With 3,625 acres, though, the mountain has plenty of room for everyone to co-exist peacefully. The vertical drop is 3,190 ft, and there are 13 lifts, including an eight-passenger gondola and five high-speed quads. | 4000 The Canyons Dr., north on Rte. 224 | 435/649–5400 or 888/226–9667 | fax 435/649–7374 | www.thecanyons.com.

Deer Valley Resort. Deer Valley is considered Utah's most upscale resort—and is proud of it. Now year-round, the resort has lift-assisted mountain biking in summer, as well as hiking and riding. The vertical drop is 3,000 ft, serviced by 18 lifts including a gondola, and six high-speed quads. The 84 runs and six powder bowls yield a total of 50% intermediate terrain. | 2250 Deer Valley Dr. S | 435/649–1000; 435/649–2000 snow report | www.deervalley.com.

Factory Stores at Park City. The 50 factory outlet stores on hand include Nike, Brooks Brothers, and Carter's. | 6699 N. Landmark Dr. | 435/645–7078 | www.shopparkcity.com | Mon.–Sat. 10–9, Sun. 11–6.

UTAH RULES OF THE ROAD

License Requirements: The minimum driving age in Utah is 16. All drivers must have a valid driver's license. Visitors from other states or countries may drive in Utah as long as they have a current driver's license and are at least 16 years old.

Speed Limits: On major highways the speed limit is 55 miles per hour, particularly in urban areas. Speed limits increase to 65 or 75 miles per hour on interstate highways in rural areas, but watch out: "Rural areas" are determined by census boundaries, so their delineation may seem arbitrary to the casual driver. Transition zones from one speed limit to another are indicated with pavement markings and additional signs. Fines are automatically doubled for speeding in highway work zones.

Right Turn on Red: Generally, right turns are allowed on a red light *after* the vehicle has come to a complete stop, unless otherwise posted.

Seat Belt and Helmet Laws: Utah law requires seat belt use for drivers, front-seat passengers, and all children under 10. Children under the age of two are required to be in federally approved safety seats. Helmet use is mandatory for motorcyclists and passengers under the age of 18.

For More Information: Contact the **Utah Department of Motor Vehicles** | 801/965–4518, or the **Utah Highway Patrol** | 801/297–7780.

Utah Winter Sports Park. Take a 2-hour ski-jumping lesson at the official training site for the U.S. Nordic and free-style ski teams. Choose the 18- or 38-m hill, and use your own equipment or rent it from the park. There are public recreational rides on the bobsled–luge track. After the snow melts, you can watch the free-style skiers train on an artificial slope, landing in a huge splash pool. | 3000 Bear Hollow Dr., off Rte. 224 | 435/658–4200 | fax 435/647–9650 | www.saltlake2002.com | Daily.

Dining

★ **Glitretind.** Continental. Self-described as "a European mountain bistro," it's really more of a grand lodge. The menu highlights such wild game dishes as grilled buffalo and venison, but also offers lunch sandwiches on thick, crusty bread, dinners of Asian duck, baked salmon, or tender steaks. In warm weather, you can eat on the deck, with a view of the Heber and Deer valleys. Kids' menu. | 7700 Stein Way, in the Stein Eriksen Lodge | 435/649–3700 | AE, D, DC, MC, V | $$$–$$$$

Claimjumper. American. In the center of historic Old Town, this lively restaurant is pure Americana, from its hardwood floors, green drapes, and grand stone fireplace to its emphasis on steaks, prime rib, and burgers. All the beef is aged, and cooked to your request. | 573 Main St. | 435/649–8051 | AE, D, DC, MC, V | $$–$$$

Texas Red's Pit Barbecue and Chili Parlor. Barbecue. Tables are crowded together in a friendly way in the southwestern-style dining room of this downtown eatery. Try catfish filets or barbecued anything—ribs, beef brisket, pork, turkey, or chicken. Kids' menu. | 440 Main St. | 435/649–7337 | AE, D, MC, V | $$

Eating Establishment. American. Near the top of Main Street, this affordable local favorite is known for its hearty keep-you-skiing-all-morning breakfasts and its barbecue dinner specials. Dine on the patio in summer; the glass roof, atrium, fireplaces, and plants make winter seem warm and bright. | 317 Main St. | 435/649–8284 | AE, D, MC, V | $–$$

Morning Ray Café & Bakery. American. The Continental crowd favors this bakery café that serves specialty breads, bagels, pastries, and substantial omelettes, pancakes, and quiches. Wooden chairs and tables and yellow-toned walls with local art make the space inviting. | 268 Main St. | 435/649–5686 | AE, MC, V | No dinner | $–$$

Lodging

1904 Imperial Hotel. Built in 1904 as a boarding house for miners and travelers, the hotel has been restored to a more upscale turn-of-the-century Western Victorian style. Complimentary breakfast. No air-conditioning. Cable TV. Hot tub. | 221 Main St. | 435/649–1904 or 800/669–8824 | fax 435/645–7421 | www.1904imperial.com | 10 rooms, 2 suites | AE, D, MC, V | $$$–$$$$

Silver King Hotel. Minutes from the ski lifts, this modern, luxurious condominium hotel has an expansive atrium lobby with fireplace and plush sofas, huge windows, and exposed beams. Units vary in size, from studio to three bedrooms, and are made cozy with handmade furniture, pastel colors, and woven rugs. In-room VCRs. Pool. Laundry facilities. | 1485 Empire Ave. | 435/649–5500 or 800/331–8652 | fax 435/649–6647 | www.silverkinghotel.com | 62 rooms | AE, D, MC, V | $$$–$$$$

Park City Marriott. The contemporary condos come in various sizes, each individually decorated. Restaurant, bar, room service. In-room data ports. Cable TV. Indoor pool. Hot tub. Exercise equipment. Business services. | 1895 Sidewinder Dr. | 435/649–2900 or 800/234–9003 | fax 435/649–4852 | www.parkcityutah.com | 199 units | AE, D, DC, MC, V | $$–$$$$

Shadow Ridge. The basic hotel rooms here have the same amenities as the lavish suites, making them a good value for a modest price. The hotel is at the base of the Park City

Mountain Village. Restaurant. Some microwaves. Cable TV. Pool. Hot tub. Exercise equipment. Laundry facilities. Business services. | 50 Shadow Ridge Dr. | 435/649–4300 or 800/451–3031 | fax 435/649–5951 | www.davidholland.com | 150 rooms, 50 suites | AE, D, DC, MC, V | $$–$$$$

Best Western Landmark Inn. Right off I-80, near a cluster of popular factory outlet stores, this inn is a little less pricey than most Park City hotels. Pleasantly furnished rooms, a relaxing poolside area, and a recreation area make this a good bet for stopovers and families. Restaurant, complimentary Continental breakfast. In-room data ports, refrigerators. Cable TV. Indoor pool. Hot tub. Gym. Laundry facilities. Pets allowed (fee). | 6560 N. Landmark Dr. | 435/649–7300 or 800/548–8824 | fax 435/649–1760 | 92 rooms, 14 suites | AE, D, DC, MC, V | $$$

Salt Lake City

Attractions

★ **Alta Ski Area.** Alta is the perennial favorite of serious local skiers. There's no glitz, no fancy cuisine, and no fashion show on the slopes, just an excellent ski school, incredible powder snow, and a mountain that some consider a sort of monument to the sanctity of skiing. Alta limits the uphill capacity of its lifts per hour, thus limiting the number of skiers on the mountain so as to "protect the skiing experience." | Big Cottonwood Canyon, east on Rte. 152 | 801/359–1078 or 801/742–3333 | www.altaskiarea.com | Mid-Nov.–mid-Apr.

Beehive House and Lion House. The Beehive House was Brigham Young's home when he was Utah's territorial governor from 1850–57, and the Lion House next door was built in 1855 to accommodate his large family. The Lion House is used for wedding receptions and other group gatherings. No formal tours are offered, but the Pantry Restaurant on the lower level is open to the public weekdays for lunch and dinner and Saturday for brunch. | 63 and 67 E. South Temple | 801/363–5466 (Lion House); 801/240–2671 (Beehive House) | Daily.

State Capitol. On a hill at the north end of State Street, the capitol building, completed in 1915, is built in Renaissance Revival style. Depression-era murals in the rotunda depict events from Utah's past. Knowledgeable volunteer guides lead free hourly tours. | 300 N. State St. | 801/538–1563 or 801/538–3000 | Weekdays, hours vary.

Delta Center. The arena is home to both the NBA's Utah Jazz, the Western Conference champions, and the upstart WNBA's Utah Starzz. | 301 South Temple | 801/355–3865 | www.utahjazz.com | Jazz: Nov.–Apr.; Starzz: June–Aug.

★ **Snowbird Ski and Summer Resort.** When it opened in the 1970s, Snowbird was on the cutting edge of ski trends, and it has managed to stay there. Snowbird has the highest elevations, the greatest vertical drop, and black diamond runs all over the mountain. A gondola that holds 125 people takes you to deep powder bowls. At the base, several angular buildings provide upscale lodging, fine dining, and such amenities as swimming pools, tennis courts, and a full-service spa, all of which are open throughout the year. | Little Cottonwood Canyon, east on Rte. 210 | 801/742–2222 or 800/385–2002 | fax 801/947–8227 | www.snowbird.com | Mid-Nov.–late Apr.

★ **Temple Square.** The 10-acre plot is the very center of Mormonism. The square blooms with bright gardens in spring, summer, and fall. Thousands of colored lights illuminate the buildings and trees during the holiday season. Two visitor centers house exhibits and art with religious themes. Bordered by Main Street and North, South, and West Temple streets. | North Visitors' Center, 50 W. North Temple | 801/240–2534 | www.saltlake.org/slc | Daily.

The Mormon Tabernacle Choir performs on Thursdays and Sundays in the squat, oval-shape, domed **Tabernacle.** You can also attend the extra rehearsals scheduled weekly. | Temple Square | 801/240–4872 | Thurs. evening, Sun. morning.

The **Utah Museum of Natural History**'s largest hall holds the skeletons of dinosaurs and other prehistoric creatures. An exhibit on rocks and minerals includes information on mining in Utah. The many hands-on science adventures for children change often. Also on display is a collection of more than 1,000 pieces of Indian art, including jewelry and elaborate masks. | 200 S. 1390 E. President's Circle | 801/581–4303 | www. umnh.utah.edu | Daily.

Dining

★ **The Aerie.** Continental. Elegant dining and breathtaking views unite here on the 10th floor of the Cliff Lodge at Snowbird, at the base of the mountain. The dining room is decorated with Chinese art from the owner's collection. The specialties include rabbit ravioli and duck breast with fresh seasonal fruit sauce. There's a sushi bar in winter. Kids' menu. Sun. brunch. No smoking. | Rte. 210 | 801/742–2222 ext. 550 | www. snowbird.com | Reservations essential | AE, D, DC, MC, V | No lunch. Breakfast in winter only | $$–$$$

Cuchina. Continental. Part bakery, part Italian deli, part coffee shop, and part candy store, this popular eatery bakes famous breakfast scones. Lunch and dinner yield such entrées as meat loaf with garlic potatoes, chicken orzo salad with feta cheese and raisins, or salmon filets stuffed with cheeses and herbs. Dine on the porch with a view of the garden. | 1026 E. 2nd Ave. | 801/322–3055 | www.cuchina.com | MC, V | $$–$$$

Lamb's Restaurant. American. Claiming to be Utah's oldest restaurant (in operation since 1919), this historic building in the heart of downtown draws locals and tourists alike. The original interior and furniture from 1939 remain. Specials include beef tenderloin Stroganoff, baby beef liver, fresh trout and halibut, and a variety of lamb dishes. | 169 S. Main St. | 801/364–7166 | AE, D, DC, MC, V | Closed Sun. | $$–$$$

Porcupine Pub and Grille. Eclectic. The decor is modern southwestern chic, but the menu really gets around; cherry-barbecue salmon, Thai chicken, a Portobello mushroom sandwich, and tequila-lime pasta. Dessert lovers go wild for the Chocolate Porcupine: a small chocolate cake (shaped like a porcupine) filled with German chocolate mousse then dipped in milk chocolate, with vanilla-bean ice cream on the side. | 3698 E. Fort Union Blvd., south of downtown at the mouth of Big Cottonwood Canyon | 801/942–5555 | AE, D, MC, V | $–$$$

The Sugar House Barbeque Company. Barbecue. You'll place and pick up your own orders and dine with plastic utensils, but be happy that the focus is on the food. Try the Memphis-style dry-rubbed ribs or the wide array of smoked meats, including pulled pork, beef brisket, and turkey breast. Eat outside at the picnic tables on the patio in nice weather. No smoking. | 2207 S. 700 E | 801/463–4800 | www.redbones.com | AE, D, DC, MC, V | $–$$

UTAH COLOR COUNTRY
ZION, BRYCE, AND GRAND STAIRCASE–ESCALANTE NATIONAL MONUMENTS

Distance: Approximately 140 miles   Time: 3 days
Overnight Breaks: Springdale, Bryce Canyon National Park, Escalante

The beauty of red-rock terrain awaits you on this drive through southern Utah. The tour takes in vastly different landscapes and incorporates pieces of three designated scenic byways.

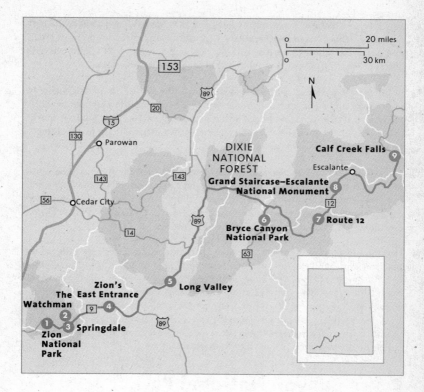

① It's easy to spend a full day in the western portion of **Zion National Park.** A stop at the visitor center should be the first thing on your agenda. A sign lists any ranger-guided hikes or lectures for the day and indicates trails that may be closed due to weather or poor trail conditions. Three-dimensional topographic maps help orient visitors and get them ready for the scope of Zion Canyon. For example, note how deeply the Virgin River has cut through the rock.

② The first thing you'll notice as you enter Zion Canyon is **The Watchman,** a formation carved, like the canyon's other dramatic features, from layers of the Markagunt Plateau—Navajo sandstone and sedimentary rock cemented by iron, silica, and lime. There are many other soaring formations in the park, and a variety of walks and hikes.

③ Spend the night in **Springdale** (just south of the park on Rte. 9), where there are numerous hotels, motels, restaurants, and bed-and-breakfasts.

④ After breakfast, head east on gradual switchbacks and pass through two tunnels cut through the massive canyon walls in the late 1920s. East of the tunnels, petrified sand dunes roll along the roadside to **Zion's East Entrance.** From Springdale east to the park entrance is approximately 12 mi on Route 9.

⑤ Turn north onto U.S. 89 at Mt. Carmel Junction and drive through verdant **Long Valley,** which is naturally irrigated by the Virgin River and bordered by yellow-, red-, and white-banded cliffs. After 44 mi, turn east on Route 12 toward Bryce Canyon.

⑥ Drive 15 mi on Route 12 to reach the junction with Route 63, which leads to the park boundary of **Bryce Canyon National Park.** Tour the canyon's rim or amphitheater trails and enjoy the **Scenic Drive** (the Park Service road running south from the park entrance for 37 mi). Stay the night at one of the park's rustic lodgings.

⑦ In the morning, watch how the rising sun makes the formations of Bryce seem to shift shape and color. Spend a couple of hours exploring the park. When you're ready, return to **Route 12** and head east. *Car and Driver* has called Route 12 one of the country's most enjoyable drives. So, enjoy as you travel through the towns of Tropic, Boulder, Cannonville, and Henrieville.

⑧ Enter **Grand Staircase–Escalante National Monument.** Everything you can see is part of this enormous park. Many of the monument's most incredible landscapes and features—slot canyons, rock-art panels, ancient ruins, twisted river courses—are deep inside these formidable mesas. Continue to the town of **Escalante** (30 mi northeast on Route 12) to eat, gas up, and fill your water bottles.

⑨ From Escalante, travel north to the signed parking area for **Calf Creek Falls** (20 mi north on Route 12). If you're so inclined, take the 2½-mi hike to the falls. (Don't forget to carry plenty of water.) A brochure at the trailhead locates more than 20 points of interest along this level path, including Anasazi ruins, interesting petroglyphs, some abandoned late 19th-century farming equipment, and wildlife. At the canyon's end, an impressive waterfall plunges from the top of a high sandstone cliff.

After hiking back to the trailhead, take a moment to rest and replenish your water supply before returning to Escalante to spend the night.

Bryce Canyon National Park

Attractions

Bristlecone Loop. At the southernmost edge of the park, right off Rainbow Point, this short 1½-mi trail enters briefly into Bryce Canyon's conifer forest, and, in places, offers spectacular 270° views of the surrounding canyon country. | Daily, most of year.

Navajo Loop Trail. The Navajo Loop is actually a "down, and then back up the way you came." It is short, only 1½ mi round-trip, but from the trail's beginning at Sunset Point to the turnaround deep in the canyon, it's a drop of 520 ft. You get the best view of many of Bryce's most famous formations—Thor's Hammer, The Pope, and Temple of Osiris among them—from this trail. Rangers lead guided trips on the Navajo Loop at least twice a day. | Daily, except when icy or snow-packed.

Queen's Garden Trail. Considered the "easiest" trail into Bryce Canyon, the Queen's Garden hike begins at Sunrise Point. Round-trip, this jaunt is 1½ mi, and its 320-ft descent is more gradual than that of most of the park's other trails. The route is marked with signs offering geological information on the pillars, hoodoos, balanced rocks, and spires on every side. Stories of the origin of formation names, like Gulliver's Castle and Queen Victoria, also make interesting reading. | Daily, except when icy or snow-packed.

Rim Trail. Skirting the edge of Bryce Canyon for 5½ mi, this trail is probably the most complete way to see and enjoy the bizarre and beautiful geology of Bryce. Though the distance may sound a bit daunting (particularly if you don't arrange for a shuttle or someone with a car to meet you at the trail's end), the path is fairly level and rated easy to moderate. The ½-mi stretch between Sunrise and Sunset Points sees the most traffic, but there are amazing vistas along the way. Plenty of benches are nicely positioned for resting and enjoying the views. | Daily, most of year.

Sunrise and Sunset Points. The 1/2-mi stretch between these two overlooks is paved and level, well adapted for wheelchairs or strollers. These viewpoints are two of the park's most impressive, with sweeping panoramas of the colors, erosional forms, and mysterious landscapes for which Bryce Canyon is known. | Daily.

Dining

Bryce Canyon Lodge. American. In the middle of the historic lodge built in 1924, this restaurant is a long room with native stone fireplaces. The specialties are mountain red trout and wagon-wheel pasta with marinara sauce. | 1 Bryce Canyon | 435/834–5361 | www.amfac.com | AE, D, DC, MC, V | Closed Nov.–Mar. | $–$$

Bryce Canyon Pines Restaurant. American. Known for homemade soups like tomato broccoli and corn chowder, and for fresh berry and cream pies, this homey, antiques-filled restaurant 6 mi northwest of the park entrance dishes up quality comfort food. | Rte. 12 | 435/834–5441 | AE, D, DC, MC, V | $–$$

Lodging

★ **Bryce Canyon Lodge.** Built in 1925, this lodge has been named a National Historic Landmark. With no television, it's a great place to come for peace and quiet. You can stay in the spacious motel rooms or the cabins, which have southwestern furnishings, and walk to the canyon rim. Restaurant. Room phones. Laundry facilities. Business services. | 1 Bryce Canyon | 435/834–5361; 303/297–2757 (reservations) | fax 435/834–5464 | www.amfac.com | 40 cabins, 70 motel units, 3 suites, 1 studio | Closed Nov.–mid-Apr. | AE, D, DC, MC, V | $$

Bryce Canyon Pines. Some of the pine-paneled rooms in this motel have fireplaces and kitchens. Six miles from Bryce Canyon, the establishment has a campground, too, and horseback riding. Restaurant. Cable TV. Pool. Business services. | Highway 12, Milepost 10 Bryce, 84764 | 435/834–5441 or 800/892–7623 | fax 435/834–5330 | www.brycecanyonmotel.com | 50 rooms | D, DC, MC, V | $$

Bryce Canyon Resort. Renovated and remodeled, this rustic lodge is across from the local airport and 3 mi from the park entrance. Restaurant. In-room data ports. Cable TV. Indoor pool. Laundry facilities. | 13500 E. Rte. 12 | 435/834–5351 or 800/834–0043 | fax 435/834–5256 | 57 rooms, 2 suites | MC, V | $$

Best Western Ruby's Inn. The closest accommodation outside the park, this large two-story inn has spacious rooms and a comfortable lobby. It's a good place to stay if you like such organized activities as chuckwagon cookouts, trail rides, and helicopter and ATV tours. Restaurant, picnic area. Cable TV, in-room VCRs (and movies). 2 indoor pools. Cross-country skiing. Laundry facilities. Business services. Pets allowed (fee). | Rte. 63, 1 mi off Rte. 12 | 435/834–5341 or 800/468–8660 | fax 435/834–5265 | www.rubysinn.com | 368 rooms | AE, D, DC, MC, V | $–$$

Bryce View Lodge. Next to the Bryce Canyon National Park entrance, this motel has reasonable rates, and you can use the pool and other amenities at the mammoth Ruby's Inn next door. 2 restaurants. Cable TV. Laundry facilities. Pets allowed. | Rte. 63 | 435/834–5180 or 888/279–2304 | fax 435/834–5181 | 160 rooms | AE, D, DC, MC, V | $

Escalante

Attractions

Escalante State Park. The park was created to protect a huge repository of fossilized wood and dinosaur bones. It takes very little time on either of the two brief interpretive trails before you start to feel like an expert on things that are petrified. You'll see twisted and partially buried pieces of wood, and entire fallen forests. Another feature of the park is Wide Hollow Reservoir, with its associated wetlands. You can fish for trout in the reservoir, and go birding at the wetlands, one of the few bird-watching sites in southern Utah. | 710 N. Reservoir Rd. | 435/826–4466 | www.utah.com | Daily.

Grand Staircase–Escalante National Monument. At 1⁷⁄₁₀ million acres, the national monument dominates any map of southern Utah, stretching west from Glen Canyon National Recreation Area and Capitol Reef National Park to Bryce Canyon. Its southern boundary is U.S. 89 and the Utah–Arizona border. Route 12 and a block of the Dixie National Forest serve as a rough northern boundary. There are three major sections: the Escalante Canyons, the Kaiparowits Plateau, and the Paria River. Only a few roads go into the depths of the monument, none of which you should try to negotiate in a standard passenger car. Nevertheless, you can still experience and enjoy these fabulous landscapes; guided tours, including bicycle, four-wheel-drive, and backcountry hiking trips, are readily available in Escalante and other monument border towns. The Bureau of Land Management (BLM) maintains a list of guides and outfitters permitted to operate inside the monument. Advance reservations are suggested. | 337 S. Main St., Suite 10, Cedar City, 84720 | 435/865–5100 | fax 435/865–5170 | www.ut.blm.gov/monument | Daily.

Kodachrome Basin State Park. Within a single day, the sandstone chimney formations of Kodachrome Basin may appear gray, buff, or any of a huge palette of reds and oranges, all depending on the sunlight and weather. | 9 mi SE of Cannonville | 435/679–8562 | www.utah.com | Daily.

Lower Escalante River. Some of the best backcountry hiking in the area lies 15 mi east of Escalante on Route 12, where the river carves through striking sandstone canyons and gulches. You can camp at numerous sites along the river for extended trips, or you can spend a little time in the small park where the highway crosses the river. | 435/865–5100 | Daily.

Lodging

Escalante's Grand Staircase Bed & Breakfast Inn. Rooms in this in-town inn have skylights, tile floors, log furniture, and murals reproducing area petroglyphs. You can relax on the outdoor porches or in the library, or make use of the on-premises bike-rental shop and explore the adjacent national monument. Dining room, complimentary breakfast. Cable TV. Hot tub. | 280 W. Main St. | 435/826–4890 | fax 435/826–4889 | 5 rooms | MC, V | $$

Escalante Outfitters. If you're on a budget and not fussy about amenities, this might be a fine place to stay. The seven log bunkhouses–cabins have a common bath house. Barbecues. | 310 W. Main St. | 435/826–4266 | fax 435/826–4388 | www.arof.net/~slickroc/escout | 7 double-occupancy cabins (3 with double beds, 4 with bunk beds) | MC, V | $

Prospector Inn. A large, square, three-story brick building on Main Street, this is the largest hotel in town, and the rates are reasonable. Restaurant. Cable TV. Business services. | 380 W. Main St. | 435/826–4653 | fax 435/826–4285 | 50 rooms | AE, MC, V | $

Springdale

Attractions

O. C. Tanner Amphitheater. The performance venue is set amid huge sandstone boulders at the base of the enormous red cliffs spilling south from Zion National Park. *The Grand Circle* is a multimedia presentation on the Southwest that shows nightly at dusk from Memorial Day to Labor Day. In summer, live concerts are held at the amphitheater each weekend, and acts range from local country-music bands to the

Utah Symphony Orchestra. | Lion Blvd. | 435/652–7994 | www.dixie.edu/community | May–Oct., daily.

Springdale Fruit Company. Surrounded by apple orchards, this small market is an interesting and healthy stop. The store carries freshly squeezed juices, organic fruit and vegetables, a huge variety of trail mix concoctions, and bakery items. A picnic area is behind the market. | 2491 Zion Park Blvd. | 435/772–3222 | Daily 8–dusk.

Zion Canyon Theatre. A 37-minute film, *Zion, Treasure of the Gods*, is shown once an hour in a 500-seat auditorium on a screen 80 ft wide and 6 stories high. | 145 Zion Park Blvd. (Rte. 9) | 435/772–2400 or 888/256–3456 | www.ziontheatre.com | Apr.–Oct., daily 9–9; Nov.–Mar., daily 11–7.

Dining

The Switchback Grille and Trading Company. Contemporary. Crowds swarm Switchback for wood-fired pizzas, ribs, and vegetarian dishes, but the vaulted ceilings make the dining room open and comfortable. Try the excellent Portobello sandwich for lunch, and don't miss the smoothies, which are rare in Utah. | 1149 S. Zion Park Blvd. | 435/772–3777 | AE, D, MC, V | $$–$$$

Bumbleberry Inn. American. Famous for its homemade, one-of-a-kind bumbleberry pie (a combination of "burple" and "binkel" berries) and bumbleberry specials like pancakes and stuffed French toast, this local favorite is convenient to the park and area lodging. The salmon fish-and-chips, burgers, marinated chicken breast, fresh trout, and steak specials are also popular. | 897 Zion Park Blvd. | 435/772–3611 | D, MC, V | $$

Pioneer Lodge and Restaurant. American. A good place to take the family, this rustic country diner with log walls and a fireplace serves meat and potato dishes, fish, and pasta, and has a full salad bar and homemade rolls. Try the ice-cream pie for dessert. | 828 Zion Park Blvd. | 435/772–3009 | AE, D, MC, V | $–$$

Zion Pizza and Noodle Company. Italian. In the former Springdale Mormon church, this eatery serves salads, calzones, and crispy pizzas baked in slate ovens. Eat on the patio or on the front apron overlooking Zion Park Blvd. Beer and ale are on tap. | 868 Zion Park Blvd. | 435/772–3815 | AE, D, MC, V | Closed Dec. | $–$$

Lodging

Flanigan's Inn. Close to the park with canyon views, this rustic country inn has contemporary furnishings. You can catch a shuttle to Zion on the property and walk to the visitor center. Restaurant, complimentary Continental breakfast. Cable TV. Pool. Business services. | 428 Zion Park Blvd. | 435/772–3244 or 800/765–7787 | fax 435/772–3396 | www.flanigans.com | 33 rooms | AE, D, MC, V | $–$$$

The Harvest House. A half-mile from the park entrance, this attractive pioneer-house inn with large wraparound porch caters to hikers and peace-and-quiet seekers. You can relax on the deck overlooking the koi pond or in the hot tub, which has a view of Watchman Peak, or spend time in the quiet, tasteful rooms, none of which has a telephone or television. Complimentary breakfast. Hot tub. | 29 Canyon View Dr. | 435/772–3880 | fax 435/772–3327 | 4 rooms | MC, V | $$

Snow Family Guest Ranch. On 12 acres of pastureland adjacent to Zion National Park, this working horse ranch has comfortable ranch-style guest rooms with log furniture and inviting common areas. You can take trail rides on the property for an extra fee. Complimentary breakfast. TV in common area. Pool. Hot tub. | 633 E. Rte. 9, Virgin | 435/635–2500 or 877/655–7669 | fax 435/635–2758 | 9 rooms | AE, D, MC, V | $$

Canyon Ranch Motel. These small cottage facilities tucked away from the highway are peaceful and well appointed. Rooms are basic and bright, and the pleasant lawn area has large shade trees, picnic tables, and swings. Picnic area. Pool. Hot tub. | 668 Zion Park Blvd. | 435/772–3357 | fax 435/772–3057 | 22 rooms in cottages | AE, D, MC, V | $–$$

Zion Park Inn. Springdale's largest property has some sophisticated amenities, including a liquor store. Restaurant, picnic area. Cable TV. Pool. Hot tub. Playground. | 1215 Zion Park Blvd. | 435/772–3200 | www.zionparkinn.com | 120 rooms | AE, D, MC, V | $–$$

Zion National Park

Attractions

Bicycling. The paved, 3½-mi Pa'rus Trail winds along the Virgin River in Zion Canyon. You can take guided tours both in the park and on land south of the park. Electric bikes, tandem bikes, mountain bikes, children's bikes, and helmets for all ages can be rented by the hour, the half day, or all day in Springdale, just south of Zion Canyon. | Bike Zion, 1458 Zion Park Blvd. (Rte. 9) | Scenic Cycles, 205 Zion Park Blvd. (Rte. 9) | 435/772–3929 Bike Zion; 435/772–2453 Scenic Cycles.

Emerald Pools Trail. The trailhead for an easy to moderate hike to this series of pools and waterfalls lies across the street from the Zion Park Lodge, about 6 mi north of the park's main south entrance. You can walk to the Lower Emerald Pools in about an hour to see waterfalls cascading off the red cliffs into a series of pools. Getting to the Upper Pools is a bit more difficult, and takes about an hour longer, but the 1,000-ft sheer sandstone cliffs harboring other pools are worth the hike. | Zion Canyon Rd. | 435/772–3256 | Daily.

Hiking. Zion has hikes for every ability, and hiking is highly recommended if you want to better appreciate the size and complexion of the park. You can get hiking brochures and sound advice at the visitor center or at Zion Lodge. | 435/772–3256.

Kolob Canyons. The Kolob Canyons are the northern primitive section of Zion National Park. A scenic drive enters the area, but backcountry exploration requires a permit issued at the Kolob Canyons visitors center.

Zion Nature Center. The Zion Nature Center has a program geared toward children under 12. It focuses on the geology, flora, and fauna of the park. | Next to South Campground | 435/772–3256 | Daily, but activities may not be scheduled every day.

Dining

Zion Lodge Restaurant. American. Photographs of the early days of this national park make interesting study while waiting for a table in the dining room. The casual lunch fare includes sandwiches, burgers, and sack lunches for hikers. Dinner choices include pastas, chicken-fried steak, and some seafood. You can eat on the porch for a grand view. Buffet breakfast. No smoking. Reservations essential June–Aug. | Zion Canyon Rd., off Rte. 9 | 435/772–3213 | MC, V | $$–$$$

The Golden Hills Restaurant. American. A funky little pink-and-blue roadside diner 12 mi east of the park's east entrance serves such good, basic country-style fare as chicken-fried steak, liver and onions, and homemade breads and pies. It's quieter and less crowded than many other Zion-area establishments. | Mt. Carmel Junction, U.S. 89 and Rte. 9 | 435/648–2602 | AE, MC, V | $–$$

WASHINGTON WATERFRONT
ISLAND HOPPING BY CAR AND FERRY

Distance: approximately 175 mi
Overnight Break: Port Townsend

Time: 4 hrs actual driving time,
but allow 1 to 2 days with stops

From Seattle's downtown area, you'll travel to peninsulas, islands, and waterfront towns during a tour that should especially please drivers who are prone to feeling landlocked.

❶ Today **Seattle** has a busy port, but it has moved south beyond Pioneer Square to the shores of the lower Duwamish and to Harbor Island. The wharves of the downtown waterfront now are home to shops, restaurants, a waterfront park on Pier 57, **Odyssey,** the Maritime Discovery Center on Pier 66, and the **Seattle Aquarium** on Pier 59.

Almost all ship traffic is gone, except for the harbor tours leaving from Pier 55 and Pier 57, the Victoria Clipper passenger ferry leaving from Pier 69 at the northern end of the downtown waterfront, and the Washington State Ferry terminal at Colman Dock on Pier 52. The latter dock has been busy since the days when the small steamers of the **Mosquito Fleet** docked here and puttered their way to towns up and down the Sound.

❷ Early in the morning, drive to the **Colman Dock on Pier 52** to board the ferry for **Bremerton.** The crossing should take about an hour, but give yourself an extra half hour to buy your ticket and get in line. Once you're on the ferry you can leave your car and go upstairs for a grand view of saltwater and the mountains. If you haven't had breakfast, this is a good time to get it. You won't find a better window seat at any restaurant in the city.

After leaving the Colman Dock, the ferry crosses **Elliott Bay** and rounds **Duwamish Head,** turns southwest across **Puget Sound,** and heads west into **Rich Passage,** which separates Bainbridge Island from the Kitsap Peninsula. If you look closely at the headlands to either side of the inlet, you'll notice the gun emplacements of turn-of-the-20th-century forts that guarded the entrance to the Bremerton Navy Base.

❸ The Naval Shipyard and Navy docks loom ahead of you after the ferry turns into **Port Orchard,** which is the name both of an inlet and the county seat on its southern shore.

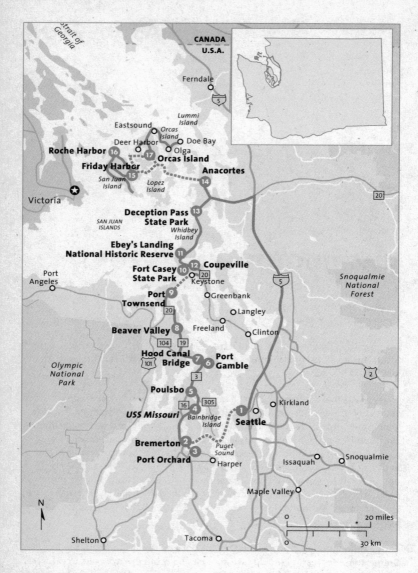

(If you had a boat and were to turn right, up the inlet, you'd come to Liberty Bay, and your next stop, Poulsbo.)

④ After returning from Port Orchard to Bremerton by ferry, you can turn left and drive along the waterfront of Bremerton Navy Base, one of the largest in the country. Until she was moved to Pearl Harbor in 1998, the **U.S.S. *Missouri,*** on whose deck the Japanese surrendered in World War II, was docked here. Continue driving west until you get to Route 3; turn right (north). Take Route 3 north. Shortly after this road ceases to be a freeway, you should see Liberty Bay to your right (east). To the west, out of sight on the east shore of the Hood Canal is Bangor with its Trident submarine base. Since these huge subs are the modern replacements for battleships like the *Missouri,* they are named after states.

⑤ Take Route 305 north for about 17 mi into **Poulsbo** and follow signs to the waterfront. Poulsbo was founded in the 19th century by Norwegian immigrants as a fishing port. It still has an old-country bakery and other Scandinavian touches. But yachts have taken over the fishing boat slips, and modern-day Poulsbo looks a lot more like a marina city than a grungy fishing port where cod once dried on racks. Have lunch in Poulsbo or buy the fixings for a picnic and eat at **Kitsap Memorial State Park** north of Lofall.

⑥ After lunch, drive north on Route 3 to its junction with Route 104 and continue north for about 8 mi to **Port Gamble,** a well-restored New England–style village that gives little indication that only a hundred years ago it had one of the largest lumber mills in the world, as well as several shipyards. Today, it's a great place for a stroll.

⑦ After Port Gamble, return on Route 104 to the junction with Route 3 and turn right across the **Hood Canal Bridge.** The predecessor of this floating bridge was sunk by a storm gusting up to 150 mph. Today, the bridge's draw-span opens for the huge Trident submarines to pass through.

⑧ West of the bridge turn north on Route 19 toward Port Townsend. You'll pass through **Beaver Valley,** where Betty MacDonald lived in the 1920s and wrote the best-seller *The Egg and I.* The locals claim they were unhappy with the way she wrote about the region, but there is an Egg and I Road, named after the book. (Look for the street sign on Route 19 north of Beaver Valley.)

⑨ Shortly after you pass through small and rustic Chimakum, you'll get to Route 20. Turn right to **Port Townsend,** a well-preserved holdover from the Victorian age. Stroll through the port area, the lower "water town," and explore the shops, cafés, and taverns. Also take in the more stately upper town, reached by steps climbing the bluff, where the former mansions of local merchants have been turned into comfortable inns.

⑩ Port Townsend is a great place for spending the night and having dinner, but if you arrive early, you could take the ferry across Admiralty Inlet to **Keystone** on **Whidbey Island.** (Crossing time: 30 minutes.) Look to the left as you approach the ferry landing. The grassy bluffs hide the gun emplacements of former Fort Casey. The lighthouse towering above the fort was built in 1899; it is now part of **Fort Casey State Park.**

When you land at Keystone and look around, it seems hard to believe that a city named "Chicago" stood here a hundred years ago with aspirations of outdoing its "rival" in the Midwest. Today, not even the foundations remain.

⑪ When leaving the ferry at Keystone, ignore the direction signs and turn *left,* not right (Rte. 20). Drive past the fort (or turn left into the grounds and take a walk through the old batteries and on the grassy bluffs) and continue north on Fort Casey Road to Hill/Ebey's Landing Road. Turn left. After passing a pretty bluff topped by pines, the road drops to the beach at **Ebey's Landing National Historic Reserve.** A Tlinkit raiding party landed its canoes here on August 11, 1857, and attacked the cabin of Colonel Isaac Ebey, which stood on the embankment south of Ebey Road. The Alaska natives shot Ebey and took his head, in retaliation for the death of a Tlinkit chief killed by gunfire from the U.S.S. *Massachusetts.* You can take a walk up the peaceful beach, or hike a narrow trail up the bluff, covered with wildflowers in spring. Both walks will take you to a vantage point from which you can look straight down Juan de Fuca Strait.

To leave the beach take Ebey Road to Route 20 and proceed south about 4 mi; turn right, then left at Main Street (the next traffic light). This will take you to Coupeville's waterfront on Penn Cove.

⑫ **Coupeville,** founded in 1853, has more historic buildings than any other town in Washington and enjoys an incredible scenic setting. The shops on the cove side of narrow Front Street stand above the sandy beach on pilings. Streets rise from the waterfront to the residential district, which has great views of the water and, on clear days, of Mt. Baker and the North Cascades. Coupeville is a very comfortable town made for strolling.

Leave Coupeville via Coveland Street to Madrona Way, which winds along the southern shore of Penn Cove past the historic Captain Whidbey Inn to Route 20. The road takes its name from the gnarled, red-trunked madrona trees that line the bluff on the waterside.

Turn right on Route 20 and drive north for 10 mi through Oak Harbor to **Deception Pass,** a narrow rock-bound inlet separating Whidbey Island from Fidalgo Island to the north. The rocks you see are the only bedrock on Whidbey Island, which is a glacial moraine almost 40 mi long. Deception Pass has Washington's most popular and perhaps most scenic state park.

⑬ If you're planning to camp in **Deception Pass State Park,** you need to make a reservation well ahead of time.

⑭ Route 20 takes you north to Route 20: the roads are a bit confusing here, because the state highway running north from Keystone and the highway running east from Anacortes have the same number. After the merger, the road continues east to I–5 and eventually becomes the North Cascades Highway. But you want to turn left at the merger and drive to **Anacortes,** a waterfront town with a ferry landing for San Juan Island.

⑮ Take the ferry to **San Juan Island,** the most developed and second largest of hundreds of islands that comprise the San Juan Islands. Crossing time is about an hour and a half to two hours, depending on how many stops the ferry makes. (Consult the schedule.) Park your car and walk around **Friday Harbor,** the county seat.

⑯ Head north on San Juan Island Road for 5⁴/₁₀ mi to **Roche Harbor,** a former industrial town. The limestone mined here helped build towns throughout the Salish Sea region. You can still see the old lime kilns, but all other traces of the village's industrial past are gone. Roche Harbor today is a pleasant waterfront community with a 19th-century hotel and modern condominiums. It is very popular with visiting yachtsmen and in summer the docks are quite lively. The road along the island's western shore is scenic and is a good vantage point for whale watching.

⑰ Leave San Juan Island by taking the ferry from Friday Harbor to **Orcas Island.** You'll arrive at the tiny harbor of Orcas, its streets lined with shops in the shadows of big trees and an old clapboard hotel. Orcas is the biggest of the San Juans and you'll need a car to get around. You'll want to drive north on the main road to **Eastsound,** a relaxing waterfront village with a sandy beach at the head of East Sound, the inlet that almost cuts the island in two. Drive to the top of Turtleback Mountain for a magnificent view of the other islands.

From Orcas Island, take the ferry back to Anacortes. You can reverse this tour back to Seattle or, if you want to return by land, drive east on Route 20 and pick up I–5 south for about 60 mi back to Seattle.

NOTE: For up-to-date ferry information, call the following numbers for schedule information: 888/808–7977 or 800/84–FERRY (in WA); 206/464–6400 (outside WA); for fares, 888/808–7977 (the rates are listed in a separate *Passenger and Vehicle Fares* brochure). For schedule information on the Internet: www.wsdot.wa.gov/ferries. Please note that the schedule changes with the seasons; fewer ferries run in fall, winter, and spring.

Anacortes

Attractions

Anacortes Historical Museum. The changing exhibits of this museum focus on the history and culture of Fidalgo and Guemes Islands. Past installations have covered boat building and the history of Commercial Avenue in Anacortes. | 1305 8th St., 98222 | 360/293–1915 | www.anacorteshistoricalmuseum.org | Mon., Thurs.–Sun. 1–5.

Deception Pass State Park. Explore this beautiful park on the southern tip of Fidalgo and the northern tip of Whidbey Island, with a rocky chasm in the center separating the two sections. Canoe Island in the center of the pass can be reached by the Route 20 highway bridge, which crosses the gorge. There are campsites, picnic areas, sandy beaches (although the water is too cold and turbulent for swimming), shaded trails in the woods, and sunny trails on the headlands. Watch for the wildflowers in spring. | Rte. 20S | 360/675–2417 | fax 360/675–3288 | www.prd.state.or.us | Daily.

Washington Park. West of Anacortes, this gorgeous park has dense forests and sunny meadows. Overlooks with views of islands and saltwater can be reached by a narrow loop road that winds through woods and over cliffs. | 12th St. (Oakes Ave.) | 360/293–1927 | fax 360/293–1928 | Daily.

WASHINGTON RULES OF THE ROAD

License Requirements: Washington drivers must be at least 16 years old, possess a valid driver's license, and carry proof of insurance. (Uninsured cars may be impounded.)

Right Turn on Red: Permitted throughout the state unless posted signs state otherwise.

Seat Belt and Helmet Laws: Seat belts are mandatory for the driver and for all passengers. Children under 40 pounds must be strapped into approved safety seats. Motorcyclists must wear helmets.

Speed Limit: Speed limits on highways and interstates vary from 60 to 70 mph. Follow posted signs.

For More Information: Call the **Traffic Safety Commission** at | 360/753–6197.

Dining

La Petite. French. The menu is petite—only six dishes are offered at a time—but the quality, from chops to desserts, is anything but small. | 3401 Commercial Ave., 98221 | 360/293–4644 | No lunch, no supper Mon. | AE, D, DC, MC, V | $$–$$$

Randy's Pier 61. Seafood. The only waterfront restaurant in Anacortes, Randy's provides a generic nautical decor and nice views across the Guemes Channel to Guemes and the San Juan Islands. Steak, lobster, and fresh seafood are specialties. There is a patio for alfresco dining. Kids' menu. | 209 T Ave., 98221 | 360/293–5108 | AE, D, MC, V | $$–$$$

Bella Isola. Italian. In a turn-of-the-20th-century structure, this restaurant has three intimate dining rooms, two of which overlook the downtown area. The menu has many Italian specialties, including pizzas, pastas, lasagnas, grilled fish, and chicken entrées. Daily specials, usually fresh fish and seafood, might include halibut or salmon. | 619 Commercial Ave., 98221 | 360/299–8398 | No lunch Sun. | AE, D, MC, V | $–$$$

Bremerton

Attractions

Belfair State Park. Three miles from Belfair, this small park is on a sheltered water-front on the lower part of the Hood Canal, where the canal hooks north for a few miles. It's great for canoeing and kayaking and, in very warm summers, the water may even be warm enough for swimming. | Hwy. 300 | 360/275–0668 or 800/452–5687 | fax 360/275–8734 | Daily.

Bremerton Marina. You can walk or picnic here while watching the boats and ferries come and go. You might also see a host of birds and wildlife. | Off Washington Ave.

Bremerton Naval Museum. In the ferry terminal, this museum's displays include ship models and American and Japanese war artifacts. | 130 Washington Ave. | 360/479–7447 | fax 360/377–4186 | Tues.–Sat 10–5, Sun. 1–5; Summer also open Mon. 10–5.

Illahee State Park. On the shore of Port Orchard (with 25 campsites), this park is mainly for day use, providing beach access for nearby urban areas. | Rte. 306 | 360/478–6460 or 800/223–0321 | fax 360/792–6067 | www.parks.wa.gov | Daily 8–dusk.

Kitsap County Historical Society Museum. Pioneers' artifacts, nautical items of local historical interest, and a collection of old photographs are among the offerings in this small museum. | 280 4th St. | 360/479–6226 | www.waynes.net/kchsm | Tues.–Sat. 9–5.

Naval Undersea Museum. The museum has the country's largest collection of undersea artifacts, including submarines, torpedoes, diving equipment, and undersea mines. Exhibits also examine the ocean environment and undersea naval technology. The museum is located in Key Port, approximately 10 mi north of Bremerton. | Downtown Key Port | 360/396–4148 | num.kpt.nuwc.navy.mil | Oct.–May, daily 10–4, closed Tues; June–Sept, daily 10–4.

Scenic Beach State Park. On the eastern shore of the Hood Canal, this small park has campsites, oyster beds, and great views of the Olympic Mountains mirrored in the waters of the "canal." | Rte. 3 to Newberry Hill exit, 1½ mi to Seabeck Hwy. | 360/830–5079 or 800/233–0321 | www.parks.wa.gov | Daily.

U.S.S. *Turner Joy*. Now that the U.S.S. *Missouri* has been towed to Pearl Harbor, this Navy destroyer is currently the only vessel open for regular visiting. Check for roadside sandwich boards announcing other tourable ships. | 300 Washington Beach Ave. | 360/792–2457 | Daily 10–4.

Dining

Illahee Manor Restaurant. Contemporary. When you dine here on a clear night, the moon shimmers off Port Orchard Bay and, together with the candlelight, plants, and purling fountain, creates an inimitable dining experience. The prix-fixe dinner consists of five to six courses, with entrées that might include salmon, crab cakes, or stuffed Cornish game hen. | 6680 Illahee Rd. NE | 360/698–7555 or 800/693–6680 | fax 360/698–0688 | www.illaheemanor.com | No lunch | AE, D, MC, V | $$$

Boat Shed. Contemporary. Some of the best seafood in Bremerton comes from the kitchen of this rough-sided, rustic, waterfront restaurant. In warm weather, there's outside seating on the deck. Clam chowder, steamed clams, and mussels are among the highlights. There is boat moorage available. No smoking. Sunday brunch. | 101 Shore Dr., 98310 | 360/377–2600 | AE, MC, V | $$–$$$

Yacht Club Broiler. Contemporary. Ten miles north of Bremerton, this simple but elegant restaurant overlooks Dyes Inlet. The seafood dishes are uncommonly fresh and prepared with flair. This restaurant is also known for Nebraska corn-fed prime steak. There is open-air dining on the deck. Kids' menu. Sun. brunch. | 9226 Bayshore Dr., Silverdale, 98383 | 360/698–1601 | AE, D, MC, V | $$–$$$

Oyster Bay Inn Restaurant. Contemporary. The large picture windows of this restaurant offer tremendous panoramic views of the bay and the tree-lined coast. The menu favors seafood but also includes steaks and pasta. | 4412 Kitsap Way, 98312 | 360/377–5510 | www.oysterbaymotel.com | AE, D, DC, MC, V | $–$$$

Coupeville

Attractions

Alexander Blockhouse. Built in 1855, the blockhouse now stands near the waterfront, next to the historical museum. Note the squared logs and dove-tailed joints of the corners—no overlapping log ends. Several native canoes are exhibited in an open, roofed shelter. | 902 N.W. Alexander St. | 360/678–3310 | Oct.–Apr., Fri.–Mon. 10–4; May–Sept., daily 10–5.

Ft. Casey State Park. Four miles outside Coupeville above the Keystone ferry landing is this turn-of-the-20th-century army fort whose concrete gun emplacement has a couple of "disappearing" guns. The park is named after the last U.S. Army chief of engineers, Brigadier General Thomas Lincoln Casey. The Admiralty Head Lighthouse Interpretive Center is north of the gunnery emplacement. | Hwy. 20 | 360/678–4519 or 800/233–0321 | www.parks.wa.gov | Daily 8 AM–dusk.

Ft. Ebey State Park. West of Coupeville on Point Partridge, this park has campsites in the woods, trails to the headlands, World War II gun emplacements, wildflower meadows, a boggy pond, and large stands of native rhododendrons, which bloom around Memorial Day. | Whidbey Island | 360/678–4636 or 800/233–0321 | www.parks.wa.gov | Daily.

Dining

Rosi's. Italian. Inside a Victorian home, this restaurant has three candlelit dining rooms serving Italian and Pacific Northwest cuisine. Among the entrées are chicken mascarpone, osso buco, lamb chops, and Penn Cove mussels. | 602 N. Main St. | 360/678–3989 | No lunch | AE, MC, V | $$–$$$

Christopher's. Mediterranean. The ambience is warm and casual at this eclectically furnished restaurant whose tables are set with linens, fresh flowers, and candles. It is known for seafood and pasta dishes, as well as salads and soups. | 23 Front St., 98239 | 360/678–5480 | AE, D, DC, MC, V | $$

Orcas Island

Attractions

Emmanuel Church. Built in 1886 to resemble an English countryside church, this house of worship sits directly on the sound and is a favorite place for weddings. Concerts are held each summer Thursday at noon. | Main St., Eastsound Village.

Moran State Park. Wooded 5,000-acre Moran State Park is part of the former estate of shipbuilder and former Seattle mayor Robert Moran. The mountainous park includes lakes, trails, campsites, and 2,409-ft-high Mt. Constitution, with a road leading to the top. There are great views across the islands and the Salish Sea. The park is *very* popular; you may have to make campsite reservations a year in advance. | 3572 Olga Rd., Eastsound | 360/376–2326 or 800/452–5687 | fax 360/376–2360 | www. parks.wa.gov | Daily.

Dining

★ **Christina's.** Contemporary. The food may surpass the serene interior and the stunning views; the chef handles the local seafood—salmon and oysters are standouts—and game adeptly. You'll be able to consider an ample wine list, too. There is open-air dining on a rooftop deck overlooking Eastsound. Full bar. Kids' menu, no smoking. | 310 Main St., 98245 | 360/376–4904 | Closed Nov. 1–day before Thanksgiving. No lunch | AE, D, DC, MC, V | $$$

Inn at Ship Bay. Seafood. Oysters—raw, baked, stewed, or pan-fried—are the mainstay of this farmhouse restaurant. Fresh fish and the occasional meat dish may also be available. | 326 Olga Rd., 98245 | 360/376–5886 | Call for hrs | AE, D, MC, V | $$–$$$

Bilbo's Festivo. Mexican. Weavings from New Mexico hang from stucco walls, and wooden benches await the road weary hankering for enchiladas, burritos, and other south-of-the-border favorites. Specialties include fresh Northwest seafood and marinated meats cooked on a mesquite grill. The courtyard is a perfect place to enjoy a fresh-squeezed lime margarita in the summer. | N. Beach Rd., Eastsound | 360/376–4728 | No lunch Oct.–May | MC, V | $–$$

Port Gamble

Attractions

Heronswood. One of the great gardens and nurseries of the Pacific Northwest and of America, Heronswood's gardens and plant collection attract visitors from around the world. Garden "Open Days" in late May, mid-July, and early September have docents on hand to explain the gardens, which are not generally open to the public. | 7530 N.E. 288th St., Kingston, 98346 | 360/297–4172 | fax 360/297–8321 | www. heronswood.com | Mid-May–Jan., by appointment.

Kitsap Memorial State Park. The waterfront park 4 mi south of Port Gamble on Hood Canal has boating, fishing, hiking, picnicking, and camping. You can also dig clams and gather oysters as long as you have a license. | Rte. 3 | 360/779–3205 | fax 360/779–3161 | Daily dawn–dusk.

Of Sea and Shore Museum. An amazing array of shells are displayed in the General Store, whose deli is locally famous for its sandwiches. | 1 Rainier St. | 360/297–2426 | fax 360/297–2426 | www.ofseaandshore.com | Daily 9–5.

Port Gamble Historic Museum. Exhibits spotlight the heyday of the Pope and Talbot Timber Co., which built the town. Period rooms from houses and hotels are also on display. | 1 Rainier Ave. | 360/297–8074 | fax 360/297–7455 | www.ptgamble.com | Daily May–Oct., 10:30–5; Mar., Apr., and Nov., weekdays by appointment only.

Dining

General Store. American. Pick up picnic fixings or delectable deli sandwiches from this turn-of-the-20th-century general store. | 1 Rainier Ave., 98364 | 360/297–7636 | No supper | AE, D, DC, MC, V | $

Port Townsend

Attractions

Ft. Flagler State Park. Atop a headland at the northern tip of Marrowstone Island 20 mi southeast of Port Townsend, the park has campsites and a picnic area. | North end of Marrowstone Island | 360/385–1259 | fax 360/379–1746 | www.parks.wa.gov | Daily dawn–dusk.

Ft. Worden State Park. Designed to guard the approaches to Admiralty Inlet, the fort anchors a pleasant, tree-shaded park. The turn-of-the-20th-century officers' quarters and barracks are now a conference center. Point Wilson Lighthouse, at the tip of a sandy spit, still serves as an aid to navigation. There are campsites and picnic areas. | 200 Battery Way | 360/344–4400 or 800/233–0321 | fax 360/385–7248 | www.olympus.net/ftworden | Daily.

Jefferson County Historical Museum. In the 1898 City Hall building, the museum contains four floors of Native American artifacts, photos of the region, and exhibits on the history of Port Townsend. | 210 Madison St. | 360/385–1003 | Mon.–Sat. 11–4, Sun. 1–4.

Old Ft. Townsend (Historical) State Park. Only a gazebo remains from the original fort, but the bluff-top meadows, picnic area, campground, and miles of hiking trails make this a very popular park. Built in 1856 to help suppress a possible Indian attack, the fort was built too late to be of any use in the Puget Sound Indian War (besides, the local natives remained friendly). | 1370 Old Fort Townsend Rd. | 360/385–3595 or 800/233–0321 | fax 360/385–7248 | www.olympus.net/ftworden | Mid-Apr.–Sept., daily 6:30–dusk.

Rothschild House. Built in 1858 by D. C. H. Rothschild, a local merchant, this simple home is furnished with 19th-century household goods and surrounded by herb and flower gardens. | Jefferson and Taylor Sts. | 360/385–2722 | www.ptguide.com | May–Sept., daily 10–5; Nov. weekends only 10–5.

Dining

The Belmont. American/Casual. Dine in this historical 1880s building and enjoy the serene view of ships sailing in and out of the harbor. The menu includes a variety of pasta, chicken, steak, and seafood dishes; most popular are the clam chowder, the Dungeness crab sandwich, and the clams and mussels with a pesto cream sauce. | 925 Water St., 98368 | 360/385–3007 | AE, D, DC, MC, V | $–$$$

Ajax Café. Seafood. Wonderful harbor views are afforded from all the tables at this unique eatery. You'll check in with a hostess at a 1965 Cadillac front desk. Then, if you so choose, try on a hat or tie from the collection of vintage accessories. The menu includes wild salmon, mahimahi, snapper, and halibut as well as a selection of pastas and steaks. Live music is hosted here Thursday through Sunday. | 271 Water St., Port Hadlock | 360/385–3450 | No lunch. Closed Mon. | MC, V | $$

Fountain Cafe. Contemporary. Locals and visitors frequent this tiny storefront café for its vegetarian pasta with artichokes, olives, and feta; seafood pastas; and oysters Dorado. | 920 Washington St., 98368 | 360/385–1364 | Reservations not accepted | Closed Thurs. | MC, V | $$

Salal Cafe. Contemporary. Informal and bright, Salal is popular for its healthy menu items, especially the breakfast omelettes. Lunch tends to run to Mexican dishes; dinner entrées can be ambitious, with such dishes as tofu Stroganoff, mushroom risotto with oysters, or pan-seared sea scallops. Try for a table in the glassed-in back room facing a plant-filled courtyard. | 634 Water St., 98368 | 360/385–6532 | Reservations not accepted | No supper Tues., Wed. | MC, V | $$

Silverwater Cafe. Contemporary. On the first floor of the historic Elks Club building, this warm, comfortable restaurant dishes up great food on plates handmade by one of the owners. The lemon poppy seed cake has become a local legend. Try artichoke pâté, the sautéed fresh oysters, or the seafood pasta. Kids' menu. No smoking. | 237 Taylor St., 98368 | 360/385–6448 | MC, V | $$

Lodging

James House. When it was first built in 1891, this large Queen Anne Victorian served as the home of a sea captain. It is now a comfortable inn with antiques and blessed with a great seaside garden. Some of the rooms can get quite chilly when a nor'easter blows across the water, making you want to snuggle up near a parlor fireplace with a good book. Complimentary breakfast. No air-conditioning, in-room data ports. No smoking. | 1238 Washington St. | 360/385–1238 or 800/385–1238 | fax 360/379–5551 | www.jameshouse.com | 12 rooms (2 with shared bath) | AE, D, MC, V | $$–$$$

Tides Inn. Directly on the beach, this inn also has views of the surrounding Olympic and Cascade mountains. The rooms have contemporary furniture, which complement the pine walls and ceilings. Some rooms have decks that stretch over the water; the suites all have fireplaces, hot tubs, and views of the bay and mountains. The inn is close to the historic downtown area, restaurants, and shopping. Complimentary Continental breakfast. Some kitchenettes, some microwaves, some refrigerators, in-room hot tubs. Cable TV, in-room VCRs. Hot tub. Pets allowed. | 1807 Water St., 98368 | 360/385–0595 or 800/822–8696 | fax 360/379–1115 | www.tides-inn.com | 21 rooms, 21 suites | AE, D, MC, V | $$–$$$

Manresa Castle. Built as a home for an immigrant businessman and his wife in the 1890s, the castle has served as a comfortable inn since 1968. Many of the rooms have distant views of the bay and mountains. Restaurant, bar, complimentary Continental breakfast. No air-conditioning. Cable TV. Business services. | Seventh and Sheridan Sts., 98368 | 360/385–5750 or 800/732–1281 | fax 360/385–5883 | www.manresacastle.com | 40 rooms | D, MC, V | $–$$$

Palace Hotel. In the heart of downtown Port Townsend, this 1889 watertown inn is in an old brick building that was once a sailors' bordello. Complimentary Continental breakfast. No air-conditioning, some refrigerators. No room phones. Cable TV. Laundry facilities. Pets allowed (fee). | 1004 Water St., 98368 | 360/385–0773 or 800/962–0741 | fax 360/385–0780 | www.olympus.net/palace | 17 rooms | AE, D, MC, V | $–$$$

The Belmont. Built in the 1880s as a restaurant and saloon, this waterfront hotel has high ceilings and beautiful views of the harbor. The guest rooms have exposed brick walls and floral, Victorian wallpaper; windows overlook the water. Restaurant, bar. No air-conditioning. TV in common area. No pets. No smoking. | 925 Water St., 98368 | 360/385–3007 | www.the-belmont.com | 4 rooms, 3 suites | AE, D, DC, MC, V | $–$$

Poulsbo

Attractions

Poulsbo Marine Science Center. "Please touch the animals" could be the motto for this unique science museum that encourages you to "get personal" with over 100 species of marine life typical of the Puget Sound region, including sea stars, tube worms, and crabs. | 18743 Front St. NE | 360/779–5549 | www.poulsbomsc.org | Daily 11–5.

Dining

Christopher's at the Inn. Contemporary. Part of the Manor Farm Inn, this dining room underscores the inn's clean, simple aesthetic: white walls, exposed beams, gleaming hardwood floors, and plenty of windows. The menu changes seasonally but may include such dishes as Jamaican jerk chicken and Argentinian flank steaks. | 26069 Big Valley Rd. NE | 360/779–4628 | Breakfast also available. No lunch. No supper Mon., Tues. | AE, MC, V | $–$$$

Seattle

Attractions

Monorail. A survivor of the 1962 Seattle World's Fair and a city favorite, this elevated train runs between Seattle Center and the Westlake mall downtown at 5th and Pine. | 305 Harrison St. | 206/441–6038 | www.seattlemonorail.com | Daily.

★ **Museum of Flight.** One of the best aviation museums in the world includes Bill Boeing's red barn, where the Seattle pioneer built his first airplane in 1916; it now houses an exhibit on the history of human flight. Other attractions include World War I planes, and modern jets. Best of all, you can clamber around in many of them, including JFK's Air Force One. | 9404 E. Marginal Way S | 206/764–5720 | fax 206/764–5707 | www.museumofflight.org | Fri.–Wed. 10–5, Thurs. 10–9.

Odyssey: The Maritime Discovery Center. Farther north along the waterfront at Pier 66, the discovery center has exhibits on Puget Sound, its fisheries, and its maritime trade. There's also a transient boat moorage, a conference center, a fish processor and market, and a restaurant. | Pier 66, 2205 Alaskan Way | 206/374–4000 | fax 206/374–4002 | www.ody.org | Daily 10–5.

★ **Pike Place Market.** One of the great public markets in the country, this bluff-top collection of shops and restaurants still has a few tables where local farmers sell their (often organic) produce. Most farmers come on set days; weekends are especially good but very crowded. The Hillclimb steps connect the market to the waterfront and the Seattle Aquarium. | First Ave. and Pike St. | 206/682–7453 | www.ci.seattle.wa.us/html/visitor | Daily.

Seattle Aquarium. Northwest marine life is the star of this waterfront attraction that includes a spectacular domed walk-through aquarium. Puget Sound habitats have been recreated, and you can watch seals and sea otters dive and play. | 1483 Alaskan Way | 206/386–4300 (recording) | fax 206/386–4328 | www.seattleaquarium.org | Day after Labor Day–day before Memorial Day, daily 10–5; Memorial Day–Labor Day, daily 10–7.

Seattle Art Museum. The museum's extensive collection surveys Asian, Native American, African, Oceanic, and pre-Columbian art. Among the highlights are the anonymous 14th-century Buddhist masterwork *Monk at the Moment of Enlightenment* and Jackson Pollock's *Sea Change*. | 100 University St. | 206/654–3100 | www.seattleartmuseum.org | Fri.–Sun. and Tues.–Wed. 10–5, Thurs. 10–9.

Seattle Asian Art Museum. In the old Art Deco Seattle Art Museum building, this museum has one of the country's best collections of Japanese art, including the famed Crow Screen. | 1400 E. Prospect St., Volunteer Park | 206/654–3100 | www.seattleartmuseum. org | Fri.–Sun. and Tues.–Wed. 10–5, Thurs. 10–9.

★ **Space Needle.** The distinctive exterior of the 520-ft-high Space Needle can be seen from almost any Downtown spot. The view (especially at sunset) from the inside out is even better. The observation deck, a 42-second elevator ride from street level, yields vistas of the entire region. Have a drink at the Space Needle Lounge or a latte at the adjacent coffee bar and take in Elliott Bay, Queen Anne Hill, and on a clear day, the peaks of the Cascade Range. | 305 Harrison St. | 206/443–2100 or 800/937–9582 | fax 206/684–7342 | www.spaceneedle.com | Daily.

★ **Washington Park Arboretum.** South of the U-District and the Ship Canal at the Montlake Cut, the 200-acre arboretum has over 40,000 native and exotic trees, shrubs, and vines, belonging to some 4,800 different species and cultivars. More than 130 endangered plants are preserved in the arboretum. A small store sells an excellent selection of garden books and objets d'art. Pick up a self-guided walking tour brochure, or dispense with maps and take a carefree amble. | 2300 Arboretum Dr. E, (visitor center) | 206/543–8800 | www.ci.seattle.wa.us/parks | Daily 7 AM–dusk.

★ **Woodland Park Zoo.** Many of the 300 species of animals in this 92-acre botanical garden roam freely in habitat areas that have won several design awards. The African Savanna, the Asian Elephant Forest, and the Northern Trail, which shelters brown bears, wolves, mountain goats, and otters, are of particular interest. Wheelchairs and strollers can be rented. A memorial to musician Jimi Hendrix, a Seattle native, overlooks the African Savanna exhibit; appropriately, it's a big rock. | 5500 Phinney Ave. N | 206/684–4800 (recording) | fax 206/615–1070 | www.zoo.org | Daily 9:30–6.

Dining

★ **Lampreia.** Italian. The beige-and-gold interior of this Belltown restaurant is the perfect backdrop for the sophisticated food. Try one of the seasonal menu's intermezzi or light main courses—perhaps squid-and-salmon-filled cannelloni—or a full entrée such as pheasant with apple-champagne sauerkraut or lamb with pesto and whipped potatoes. The clear flavors of such desserts as lemon mousse with strawberry sauce are a soothing conclusion to an exciting experience. No smoking. | 2400 1st Ave., 98121 | 206/443–3301 | Closed Sun., Mon. No lunch | AE, MC, V | $$$–$$$$

★ **Ray's Boathouse.** Seafood. The view of Puget Sound might be the big draw here, but the seafood is also impeccably fresh and well prepared. Perennial favorites include broiled salmon, Kasu sake–marinated cod, Dungeness crab, and regional oysters on the half shell. Ray's has a split personality: a fancy dining room downstairs and a casual café and bar upstairs. In warm weather you can sit on the deck outside the café and watch the parade of fishing boats, tugs, and pleasure craft floating past, almost right below your table. Kids' menu. | 6049 Seaview Ave. NW, 98107 | 206/789–3770 | AE, D, DC, MC, V | $$–$$$$

★ **Saigon Gourmet.** Vietnamese. The small café in the International District is about as plain as they get, but the food is superb and inexpensive. Aficionados make special trips for the Cambodian soup and the shrimp rolls, but consider the unusual papaya with beef jerky. Parking can be a problem, but the food rewards your patience. | 502 S. King St. | 206/624–2611 | Reservations not accepted | Closed Sun. | MC, V | $

FROM THE POWDER RIVER TO THE PARKS

SUNDANCE TO JACKSON HOLE

Distance: 488 mi   Time: Minimum 5 days
Overnight Breaks: Buffalo, Sheridan, Cody, Yellowstone National Park, Jackson

On this drive you'll see Wyoming's premier attractions, including Devils Tower, the first national monument; Yellowstone, the first national park; and other outstanding sites, from Grand Teton National Park to the world-class Buffalo Bill Historical Center, the Medicine Wheel, an ancient Native American ruin, and spectacular mountains, basins, and plains. You can't make this entire tour by automobile in winter as some of the roads close, particularly those in Yellowstone. For the best conditions, travel either in September and early October or late May and early June, when you'll encounter fewer cars and people.

1. Begin at **Sundance**, (I–90, Exit 187 or 189, 19 mi east of South Dakota) which introduces you to the region's Native American culture; the town is named not for the robber-bandit of movie fame, but for the Indian ritual held each summer. However, the Sundance Kid did spend time in jail in the town, which is where he earned his nickname.

2. Take I–90 north for approximately 21 mi to **Devils Tower** (Exit 185 off I–90 onto U.S. 14 and Route 24), which rises from the Belle Fourche River valley and is a sacred site for Native Americans. Popular with climbers, the tower has 7 mi of hiking trails, camping, picnicking, and a visitor center.

3. Following U.S. 14 south to I–90, proceed west approximately 60 mi into **Gillette** (Exit 132). This is a coal-mining town with a high tax base, so it has great public facilities, from a recreation center to the Cam-Plex, where the town holds anything from craft shows to rodeos. Explore Devils Tower for the morning, then eat lunch in Gillette. Continue your drive across the rolling grasslands of the Powder River Basin.

④ Nearly 70 mi west of Gillette at the intersection of I–90 and I–25 is **Buffalo,** which became nationally known in 1892 when cattlemen raised an "army" and invaded Johnson County in an attempt to eliminate rustlers. The cattlemen killed two cowboys before Buffalo townspeople surrounded the invaders, who were subsequently rescued by the U.S. Army. Visit the Jim Gatchell Museum for an interpretation of the invasion. Spend the night in Buffalo.

⑤ When you're finished exploring Buffalo, continue on I–90 for about 12 mi to **Fort Phil Kearny** (Exit 44), a military post on the Bozeman Trail from 1864 to 1866. Nearby are the sites of the 1866 Fetterman Massacre and the 1867 Wagon Box battle. The fort has an interpretive center, and guides can direct you to the battle sites on Route 193 and U.S. 87. Take the latter to Big Horn and the Bradford Britton Memorial, which displays works by Charles Russell and Frederic Remington.

⑥ From the battle sites, continue on U.S. 87 along the east face of the Bighorn Mountains for about 23 mi to **Sheridan** (I–90, Exit 20). Visit the King Museum and enjoy walking around the historic town center. Stay overnight in Sheridan.

⑦ From Sheridan, head north on I–90 to Exit 14. Get onto U.S. 14 and cross the Bighorn Mountains through the **Bighorn National Forest.** At Burgess Junction continue west on U.S. 14A to **Medicine Wheel,** where a short hike takes you to the Native American site. Then follow U.S. 14A down into the Bighorn Basin. The road is steep and curvy,

WYOMING RULES OF THE ROAD

License Requirements: To drive in Wyoming you must be at least age 16 and have a valid driver's license, unless you are 15 with a valid learner's permit and a licensed driver over 18 is in the front passenger seat. Youth under age 15 can obtain "hardship permits" that allow them to drive to work or to school.

Speed Limit: Wyoming was one of the first states to adopt higher speed limits when federal authorities allowed it in 1995. Limits are 65 mph on state highways and 75 mph on interstate highways for all vehicles.

Right Turn on Red: Allowed throughout the state unless posted otherwise.

Seat Belt and Helmet Laws: Drivers must wear seat belts; carseats are required for infants and young, small children.

Road and Travel Reports: Available from WYDOT October–April, the regularly updated reports provide the most up-to-date road conditions. Call 800/996–7623.

For More Information: Contact the **Wyoming Department of Transportation** | 307/777–4484 or wydot@missc.state.wy.us.

so take it slow and enjoy the incredible view. **Bighorn Canyon National Recreation Area** is at the bottom of the mountain; there you can boat and fish, or take drives and hikes on which you may see wild mustangs in the Pryor Mountain herd.

8 Continue west on U.S. 14A for approximately 40 mi to **Cody** (U.S. 14A and U.S. 14/16/20). Cody is named for Wild West scout and showman Buffalo Bill Cody. One of the four major museums at the **Buffalo Bill Historical Center** focuses on his life. The four museums—the Plains Indian Museum, the Buffalo Bill Museum, the Cody Firearms Museum, and the Whitney Gallery of Western Art—are in the same complex and have outstanding collections and diverse activities. Consider an overnight in Cody.

The rest of this tour will take you through Yellowstone National Park and Grand Teton National Park and into the town of Jackson. The drive is approximately 177 mi.

9 **Yellowstone National Park** (52 mi west of Cody on U.S. 14/16/20 or Rtes. 120 and 296) was America's first national park and has a deserved reputation as one of the best, with its boiling mud pots, steaming and spouting geysers, spectacular waterfalls, and diverse wildlife. The Yellowstone roads range from very good, with new pavement, to poor, with potholes. Plan to travel slowly on the basic figure-eight system. Key places to stop include Grand Canyon of the Yellowstone, Old Faithful, Mammoth Hot Springs, and Yellowstone Lake. If you travel early in the morning or late in the evening, you may see black or grizzly bears or wolves. Remember that all the animals in Yellowstone are wild; keep your distance. Find lodging in the park and spend the night.

10 **Grand Teton National Park** (south of Yellowstone National Park, north of Jackson on Rte. 26/89/191) encompasses the spectacular Grand Teton Mountain range and much of broad Jackson Hole. From any of the roads crossing the valley you can see the majestic Tetons, and you will often catch glimpses of the Snake River. You can hike, bike, fish, boat, ride horses, camp, and picnic. You may want to climb these mountains, but such excursions are only for skilled climbers. Companies in Jackson Hole can teach you the ropes—literally.

11 Continue south on Route 26/81/191 to **Jackson** (U.S. 189 and Rte. 22), a small Western town of about 4,000 people who play host to some 3 million visitors annually. It's compact, so you can park and walk to most hotels, motels, restaurants, and downtown attractions. The town has a western flair and manages to maintain a folksy feeling most of the time. Consider taking a walking tour of historic sites led by the **Jackson Hole Museum.** Art galleries abound, and the **National Wildlife Art Museum** has an impressive collection of sculpture and paintings. In the winter, you might spy elk, coyotes, bald eagles, or a wolf on a sleigh ride through the **National Elk Refuge.** Stay overnight in Jackson.

The quickest way back to Sundance is to retrace your route.

Buffalo

Attractions

Bighorn National Forest. The Bighorn Mountains—roughly between Buffalo and Tensleep in the south and Sheridan and Lovell in the north—are one of the many huge areas of public land in north-central Wyoming. You can camp (at 19 managed campgrounds and uncounted backcountry sites) hike, ride horseback, fish, and in winter, snowmobile. The Cloud Peak Wilderness Area, with 189,000 acres, has enough room for backpacking and horsepacking. Elevations range from 8,500 to 13,165 ft. | Buffalo Ranger District, 1425 Fort St., Buffalo | 307/684–1100 | www.fs.fed.us/r2/bighorn | Daily.

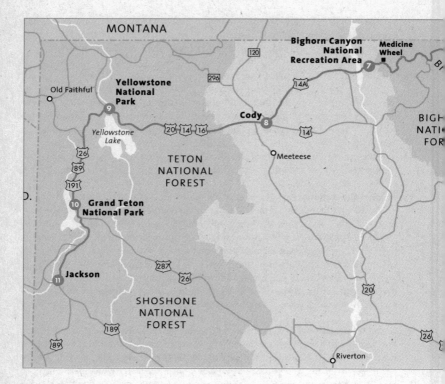

Clear Creek Trail. Signs bearing a buffalo symbol mark the Clear Creek Trail, which includes about 11 mi of trails following Clear Creek through Buffalo and past historic areas. The trail has both paved and unpaved sections. Along the way you'll see the Occidental Hotel (made famous by novelist Owen Wister in *The Virginian*), a brewery and mill, and the site of Fort McKinney, now the Veterans' Home of Wyoming. You can walk, cycle, or skateboard on the trail. | 307/684–5544 or 800/227–5122.

Fort Phil Kearny Site. In 1866 the army established several forts along the Bozeman trail from central Wyoming to Montana's gold fields. Fort Phil Kearny was one of the posts established along the trail to protect travelers from skirmishes between the U.S. military and the Northern Plains Indians. The Native Americans opposed it fiercely, raided routinely, and won several decisive battles before forcing the military to withdraw from the region in 1868. Although the Indians promptly burned the fort, the site is now marked and the original foundations are still visible. | 528 Wagon Box Rd. | 307/684–7629 | Mid-May–Sept., daily 8–6.

Jim Gatchell Museum of the West. You'll see detailed dioramas of the Powder River Basin Indian conflicts and the Johnson County Invasion of 1892 at this museum, which started as the private collection of a local resident. | 100 Fort St. | 307/684–9331 | www.jimgatchell.com | Mid-Apr.–Dec.; call for hrs.

Dining

Wagon Box Restaurant. American. Bright and spacious, this cabin in the Bighorn Mountains is surrounded by ponderosa pines. It serves well-prepared steak, seafood, burgers, and sandwiches. Prime rib is the specialty, and the huge wine selection is unmatched in the area. It's 15 mi northwest of Buffalo on I–90. | 108 N. Piney Rd., Story | 307/683–2444 | AE, D, DC, MC, V | $$

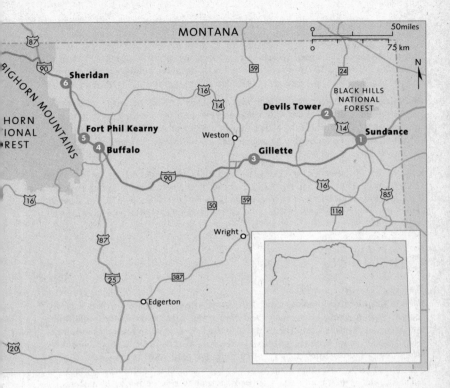

Art Works Too & Cowgirl Coffee Cafe. American. In an 1890s stone-front building in historic downtown Buffalo, this funky coffee house–café is a local hangout with a backyard sitting area and sculpture garden. Try the organic coffee or tea, bagel sandwiches, biscotti, and brownies for a quick lunch; weekend barbecues include homemade meals and live folk music. | 94 S. Main St. | 307/684–1299 | D, MC, V | $–$$

Colonel Bozeman's. Southwestern. On the Bozeman Trail, Colonel Bozeman's serves good food amid Western memorabilia. Local favorites include buffalo steak and prime rib. You can also dine out on the deck. Kids' menu. | 675 E. Hart St. | 307/684–5555 | AE, D, MC, V | $–$$

Deerfield Boutique and Espresso Bar. Contemporary. For a change from steak and potatoes, try this deli-style café next to Clear Creek, on a quiet side street in downtown Buffalo. In a renovated historic theater, with high ceilings and old wallpaper, Deerfield offers a wide range of tortilla wraps and specialty sandwiches like lemon-ginger chicken pita and turkey and Swiss on foccacia. Chilled summer soups might be tomato wine, cream of canteloupe, or spinach cucumber. The Polynesian and mandarin orange salads are equally refreshing. | 7 N. Main St. | 307/684–2788 | MC, V | $–$$

Stagecoach Inn. American. On the edge of town, this restaurant specializes in prime rib, steak, and seafood dishes, and is filled with Western antiques and memorabilia. | 845 Fort St. | 307/684–0713 | MC, V | $–$$

Lodging

Crossroads HoJo Inn. Near the Bighorn Mountains and I–25, this large, modern hotel has spacious rooms and convenient access to the interstate. Restaurant, bar, complimentary breakfast. Pool. Hot tub. Pets allowed (fee). | 75 N. Bypass | 307/684–2256 | fax 307/684–2256 | 60 rooms | AE, D, DC, MC, V | $$

Blue Gables Motel. Clustered like a small group of cabins, this U-shape motel is a homey place with Old West collectibles and cozy quilts. No-smoking rooms. No room phones. Pool. | 662 N. Main St. | 307/684–2574 or 800/684–2574 | 17 rooms | D, MC, V | $

Wyoming Motel. Some extra-large rooms, and some with kitchenettes, make this a good stopping place for families on the road. The motel is near the intersection of I–90, I–25, and U.S. 16. Restaurant, picnic area. Cable TV. Pool. Hot tub. Pets allowed. | 610 E. Hart St. | 800/666–5505 | fax 307/684–5442 | 27 rooms, 5 with kitchenettes | AE, D, DC, MC, V | $

Z-Bar Motel. At the base of the Bighorn Mountains, these quiet cabins are in a huge shaded yard with tables and barbecue grills. Some kitchenettes are available—ideal if you are traveling with pets or children. Picnic area. Refrigerators. Cable TV. Pets allowed. | 626 Fort St. | 307/684–5535 or 888/313–1227 | fax 307/684–5538 | 4 rooms, 22 cabins | AE, D, DC, MC, V | $

Cody

Attractions

Buffalo Bill Historical Center. One of the West's finest museums, this is actually several museums rolled into one, showcasing art, firearms, the Wild West of Buffalo Bill Cody, and Plains Indians. The center also has educational courses and presentations. | 720 Sheridan Ave. | 307/587–4771 | www.TrueWest.com/BBHC | Apr., daily 10–5; May, daily 8–8; June–Sept., daily 7–8; Oct., daily 8–5; Nov.–Mar., Thurs.–Mon. 10–2.

The **Buffalo Bill Museum** is dedicated to the incredible life of William F. "Buffalo Bill" Cody. Shortly after Cody's death, some of his friends took mementos of the famous scout, Indian fighter, and Wild West showman and opened the museum in a small log building. It is now in the historical center and includes huge posters from the original Buffalo Bill Wild West and Congress of Rough Riders shows.

Started as the Winchester Museum, the **Cody Firearms Museum** was rededicated in 1991; it is comprehensive, tracing the history of firearms through thousands of models on display, from European blunderbusses to Gatling guns and modern weapons. Included are examples of Winchester and Browning arms, as well as a replica of an arms manufacturing plant.

The West's greatest artists are a part of the historical center's **Whitney Gallery of Western Art.** The wing has art by Frederic Remington, Charles M. Russell, Albert Bierstadt, George Catlin, and Thomas Moran, and contemporary artists, including Harry Jackson, James Bama, and Peter Fillerup.

The history of the Plains Indians is highlighted in the **Plains Indian Museum,** with information about the Sioux, Blackfeet, Cheyenne, Crow, Shoshone, and Nez Percé tribes.

Buffalo Bill State Park. The Buffalo Bill Reservoir is the focus of the park, and you can indulge in all sorts of water sports here, as well as hike and camp and picnic nearby. | 47 Lakeside Rd. | 307/587–9227 | commerce.state.wy.us | Daily (campground May–Sept.).

Bricks with the names of local residents form the sidewalk in front of the **Buffalo Bill Dam and Visitor Center.** You can walk across the actual dam, peering over to see the lake to the west or the outflow to the east. | East end of reservoir | 307/527–6076 | May–Sept., daily 8–8.

Cody Nite Rodeo. Some towns have intermittent rodeos; Cody has had one every night since 1938. It's a training ground for tomorrow's world-champion cowboys and a competition arena for some of today's best rodeo hands. | Stampede Park, 1143 Sheridan Ave. | 307/587–5155 | www.comp-unltd.com/~rodeo/rodeo.html | Memorial Day–Labor Day.

Shoshone National Forest. The first national forest, Shoshone is a catch-all for various outdoor activities, including hunting, fishing, hiking, and mountain biking. You can ride horses in non-snowy weather and snowmobile and cross-country ski the trails after snow falls. There are picnic areas and campgrounds. | U.S. 14/16/20 | 307/527–6241 | www.fs.fed.us/r2/shoshone | Daily.

Tecumseh's Wyoming Territory Old West Miniature Village and Museum. Dioramas depict early Wyoming Territorial and Native American history and Western events. | 140 W. Yellowstone Hwy. | 307/587–5362 | June–Aug., daily 8–9; May and Sept., daily 10–6.

Trail Town and the Museum of the Old West. Started by a local archaeologist, Trail Town is a collection of historic cabins, homes, and buildings, including one that served as a hideout for Butch Cassidy and the Sundance Kid. There is a cemetery with seven relocated graves, including that of Jeremiah "liver-eatin'" Johnson. | 1831 Demaris Dr. | 307/587–5302 | Mid-May–Sept., daily 8–7.

Dining

Stephan's. Contemporary. A Cody favorite, this intimate restaurant is adorned with palm plants, tablecloths, and earth-toned Western art. Specialties include filet mignon stuffed with Gorgonzola, sun-dried tomatoes, and Portobello mushrooms, Southwest shrimp kebab grilled and scored with jalapeños and pepper jack cheese, and a penne with artichoke hearts and prosciutto in a lemon caper sauce. Save room for the homemade chocolate cake or strawberries Napoleon. | 1367 Sheridan Ave. | 307/587–8511 | AE, MC, V | $$–$$$

Cassie's Supper Club. American. Steaks, prime rib, and hamburgers are the mainstays—along with seafood and chicken. The hometown favorite is stuffed mushrooms. Early in the evening the atmosphere is low-key, but at about 9 the band warms up and the dancing begins. Cassie's, a former house of prostitution just a mile from the rodeo, gets downright rowdy; it's certainly the best place in Cody to do some boot-scooting. Entertainment nightly. | 214 Yellowstone Ave. | 307/527–5500 | www.cassies.com | AE, MC, V | $–$$$

Hong Kong Restaurant. Chinese. Authentic homemade Mandarin- and Cantonese-style dishes are served at this popular restaurant. Silkscreens, plants, and Chinese portraits add a traditional touch to the contemporary building. | 1201 17th St. | 307/527–6420 | D, MC, V | Closed Sun. Oct.–Apr. | $–$$

Cody Coffee Company and Eatery. American. Cozy and laid-back, this sandwich and coffee shop serves excellent Italian grilled sandwiches such as the chicken pesto and turkey artichoke, and prepares its own muffins, cinnamon rolls, freshly squeezed juices, smoothies, and coffee drinks. In downtown Cody but off the main tourist strip, this is a great place to grab lunch, relax, and take in the views of Spirit and Rattlesnake mountains. | 1702 Sheridan Ave. | 307/527–7879 | No credit cards | Closed Sun. No dinner | $

Lodging

Days Inn. Southwestern in style both inside and out, the motel is modern and comfortable. Complimentary Continental breakfast. Cable TV. Indoor pool. Hot tub. Laundry facilities. | 524 Yellowstone Ave. | 307/527–6604 | fax 307/527–7341 | 52 rooms | AE, D, DC, MC, V | $$

Holiday Inn. The hotel has perhaps the longest hallway of rooms in the state. In the same building are the Bottoms Up Lounge and QT's Restaurant. Amenities include an outdoor courtyard with a pool, and a convention center. Restaurant, bar, room service. In-room data ports. Cable TV. Pool. Business services, airport shuttle. | 1701 Sheridan Ave. | 307/587–5555 | fax 307/527–7757 | 184 rooms | AE, D, DC, MC, V | $$

Shoshone Lodge. The cabins are basic, but the location is scenic, on Grinnell Creek about 5 mi east of Yellowstone National Park. Restaurant. No air-conditioning, no room phones. Cross-country skiing, downhill skiing. Laundry facilities. Pets allowed. | 349 Yellowstone Hwy. | 307/587–4044 | fax 307/587–2681 | 16 cabins, 3 kitchenettes (no equipment) | AE, D, MC, V | $$

Irma Hotel. An ornate cherry-wood bar sent by the Queen of England in 1904 is one of the highlights of this hostelry, which is named for Buffalo Bill's daughter. The hotel was built in 1902, and some rooms have an early 20th-century Western style, with brass beds and period furniture. During the summer, locals stage a gunfight on the porch Tuesday–Saturday at 7 PM (using blank bullets, of course). Restaurant, bar. | 1192 Sheridan Ave. | 307/587–4221 | fax 307/587–4221 | www.irmahotel.com | 40 rooms | AE, D, DC, MC, V | $–$$

Gateway Motel and Campground. Reasonable rates, friendly service, and a large shaded yard with mountain vistas keep people coming back. Accommodations are basic—cabins are smaller than the hotel rooms, but are separate. Gateway is convenient to Cody attractions, and good for those wanting to get an early start for Yellowstone. No room phones. Cable TV. Playground. Laundry facilities. | 203 Yellowstone Ave. | 307/587–2561 | fax 307/587–4862 | 6 rooms, 4 cabins, 37 campsites | AE, MC, V | $

Gillette

Attractions

Campbell County Recreation Center and Pool. An indoor track, gymnasium, five racquetball–handball courts, squash court, free-weight room, golf driving range, locker rooms, and steam rooms are part of this facility that also includes a junior Olympic pool with a water slide (summer only). You can also try the Campbell County ice arena, the Bell Nob golf course, and the Cam-Plex picnic area. | 1000 Douglas Hwy. | 307/682–7406 | fax 307/682–7050 | ccg.co.campbell.wy.us/parkrec | Daily 5 AM–9 PM.

Cam-Plex. It's worth investigating what's on at this multi-use facility; it could be anything from a rodeo to a concert to a craft show. | 1635 Reata Dr. | 307/682–0552; 307/682–8802 (tickets) | fax 307/682–8418 | www.cam-plex.com.

Devils Tower National Monument. Native American legend has it that the corrugated Devils Tower was formed when a tree stump turned into granite and grew taller to protect some stranded children from a clawing bear. Geologists say that the rock tower, rising 1,280 ft above the Belle Fourche River, is the core of a defunct volcano. Seventy miles northeast of Gillette (I–90 east, then U.S. 14 and Rte. 24 north), it was a tourist magnet long before a spaceship landed on it in the movie *Close Encounters of the Third Kind.* During June, rock climbers respectfully keep their distance so that Natives Americans may conduct spiritual rites. You'll find 7 mi of hiking trails, a campground, a picnic area, and a visitor center. Hulett, a few miles northeast of the monument, is the closest town with services. | Rte. 24 | 307/467–5430 (Hulett Chamber of Commerce) | www.nps.gov/deto | Daily (visitor center Apr.–Sept., daily 8–7:30; Oct.–March, daily 8:30–4:30); Campground open Apr.–Oct.

Keyhole State Park. You can fish, boat, and swim at this state park. Camping and picnic areas are available, and the marina has a shower house and restaurant. | 353 McKean Rd. | 307/756–3596; 307/756–9529 marina info | fax 307/756–3534 | www.state.wy.us | Daily.

Rockpile Museum. Local historical artifacts, from bits and brands to rifles and sheep wagons, make up the collection at this county museum. | 900 W. 2nd St. | 307/682–5723 | June–Aug., Mon.–Sat. 9–8, Sun. 12:30–6:30; Sept.–May, Mon.–Sat. 9–5.

Dining

Bailey's Bar and Grill. Eclectic. With an interior that evokes an English pub, this handsome restaurant in an old brick building serves delicious sandwiches at lunch and has some Mexican dishes at dinner. | 301 S. Gillette Ave. | 307/686–7678 | AE, MC, V | $–$$

Packard's Grill. American. Families are drawn to this large, airy, casual, no-smoking establishment. The favorites include prime rib and Southern-style dishes. Kids' menu. | 408 S. Douglas Hwy. | 307/686–5149 | AE, D, DC, MC, V | No dinner Sun. | $–$$

Grand Teton National Park

Attractions

Chapel of the Transfiguration. Scenes for the movie *Spencer's Mountain* were shot at this tiny mountain chapel—still a functioning house of worship. The chapel attracts couples who want to exchange vows with the Tetons as a backdrop.

Hiking Trails. Hiking is one of the best ways to see the park. You can get trail maps and information about hiking conditions from rangers at the park visitor centers at Moose or Colter Bay. Popular trails are those in the Jenny Lake area, the Leigh and String lakes area, and the Taggart Lake Trail, with views of Avalanche Canyon. You may see moose, but keep your distance.

Jackson Lake. The biggest of the Grand Teton Park's glacier-scooped lakes, Jackson Lake, in the northern reaches of the park, was enlarged by construction of the Jackson Lake Dam in 1909. You can fish, sail, and windsurf and stay at the campgrounds and lodges that dot the shoreline. | U.S. 89/191/287 and Teton Park Rd.

Jenny Lake. Named for the Indian wife of mountain man Beaver Dick Leigh, this pristine mountain lake south of Jackson Lake draws boaters and hikers. You can use the trails surrounding the lake. | Teton Park Rd.

Menor's Ferry. The ferry on display is not the original, but it is an accurate re-creation of the craft built by Bill Menor in the 1890s, and it demonstrates how people crossed the Snake River before bridges were built. Several cabins, including the home and store used by Bill Menor, who also operated the ferry, remain at the site. You can see a historic photo collection in one of the cabins. | Signal Mountain Summit Rd.

Moose Visitors Center. At the park's south entrance, this is a good place to start any visit to Grand Teton National Park. You'll find information about all activities, a decent resource room where you can purchase maps and books, and knowledgeable people who can tell you what to expect on trails and lakes.

★ **Signal Mountain.** North of Moose and midway between Moose and Moran, Signal Mountain got its name when a valley resident was overdue and a search party agreed that whoever found him would light a signal fire atop the mountain, which would be visible throughout Jackson Hole. Though the missing man was dead by the time he was found, searchers burned the signal fire anyway. The narrow road (not suitable for RVs) leads to an overlook with spectacular views of Jackson Hole. | Teton Park Rd.

Dining

Jenny Lake Lodge Dining Room. Continental. Elegant yet rustic, this is Grand Teton National Park's finest dining establishment. The breakfast and dinner menus are offered prix-fixe; lunch is à la carte. The wine list is extensive. House favorites are prime rib and steaks. Kids' menu. No smoking. Dinner reservations essential. | Jenny Lake Rd. | 307/733–4647 | Jacket required | AE, DC, MC, V | Closed Oct.–May | $$$$

Dornan's. Barbecue. Hearty portions of beef, beans, potatoes, stew, and hot coffee or lemonade are the standbys at Dornan's, which is easily identified by its tepees. Locals know it for the beef and barbecue cooked over wood fires. You can eat inside the tepees if it happens to be raining or windy; otherwise, enjoy your meal at outdoor picnic tables with views of the Snake River and the Tetons. Buffet dinner. | 10 Moose Rd. | 307/733–2415 | MC, V | $$$

Jackson Lake Lodge Pioneer Grill. American. Seat yourself at the 86-person continuous, winding counter at this homey luncheonette. They serve great comfort dishes like bacon and eggs, vegetable lasagna, and rotisserie chicken. Huckleberry pancakes and anything from the old-fashioned soda fountain are real treats. | U.S. 89 N | 307/543–2811 ext. 1911 | AE, DC, MC, V | Closed early Oct.–late May | $–$$

Jackson

Attractions

Bridger-Teton National Forest. In the hundreds of thousands of acres of forest, some wilderness, you'll find both developed and back-country campsites, and can hike, fish, hunt, and study nature. | 340 N. Cache St. | 307/739–5500 | fax 307/739–5010 | www.fs.fed.us/btnf | Daily.

Grand Targhee Ski and Summer Resort. Just one hour from Jackson, Grand Targhee gets more than 500 inches of snow annually. The mountain village has five restaurants, shopping, lodging, and skiing. You can get there on the Targhee Express, daily round-trip coaches, from Jackson and Teton Village mid-December through late March. The vertical rise is 2,200 ft and there are two quads; 10% beginner, 70% intermediate, 20% advanced. | Follow Rte. 22 over Teton Pass and turn right onto Rte. 33; in Driggs, ID, turn right and follow Little Ave. 6 blocks to a fork; bear left onto Ski Hill Rd. and follow to Grand Targhee | 307/353–2300; 800/827–4433 snow reports | www.grandtarghee.com | Dec.–early Apr., daily 9:30–4.

Granite Hot Springs. You can soak in the small pools of the hot springs or go hiking and mountain biking in non-snowy months, staying at shady creekside campgrounds. There's a changing room if you just want to stop in for a soak. In winter you might get there via snowmobile or dogsled. | U.S. 189/191 south to Granite Creek Rd., then east | 307/739–5500 | Daily.

Jackson Hole Museum. Learn how Deadwood Bar got its name, or the story of Jackson's all-female town government. Historic photos, artifacts, and displays are part of the museum exhibits. You can also take walking tours of downtown and historic sites. | 105 N. Glenwood St. | 307/733–2414 (summer only); 307/733–9605 | fax 307/739–9019 | Late May–early Sept., Mon.–Sat. 9:30–6, Sun. 10–5.

National Elk Refuge. More than 7,000 elk spend the winter in the National Elk Refuge, which was established in 1912 to save starving herds. The animals migrate to the refuge grounds in late fall and remain until early spring. The bulls tend to congregate while the cows and calves remain in their own groups. Trumpeter swans live here, too, as do bald eagles, coyotes, and wolves. In winter, you can take one of the regular wagon and sleigh rides through the herd; the sleigh rides leave from the National Wildlife Art Museum. | Visitors Center, 532 N. Cash St. | 307/733–9212 | www.r6.fws.gov/REFUGES/natlelk | Visitors Center, daily 8–5; National Wildlife Art Museum, 2820 Rungius Rd., mid-Dec.–early Apr., daily 10–4 (reservations not accepted).

National Wildlife Art Museum. A collection of wildlife art—most of it devoted to North American species—is displayed in the 12 galleries that have both permanent and traveling exhibits. Among the artists represented are Karl Bodmer, Albert Bierstadt,

Charles Russell, John Clymer, Robert Bateman, and Carl Rungius. You can also look outward, using one of the spotting scopes set up in areas overlooking the National Elk Refuge to watch wildlife in its native habitat. | 2820 Rungius Rd. | 307/733–5771 | fax 307/733–5787 | www.wildlifeart.org | Summer and winter, daily 9–5; spring and fall, Mon.–Sat. 9–5, Sun. 1–5.

Snow King Resort. At the western edge of Jackson, Snow King Resort has 400 acres of ski runs in the daytime and 110 acres for night skiing, plus an extensive snowmaking system. | 400 E. Snow King Ave. | 307/733–5200 or 800/522–5464 | Dec.–Apr., daily; snowtubing park weekdays 4–8, weekends noon–8.

Dining

The Range. Continental. The menu at one of Jackson's finest restaurants varies seasonally but always has nightly fish and game specials. Try linguine with roma tomatoes and the fresh artichoke pâté. Kids' menu. | 225 N. Cache St. | 307/733–5481 | AE, MC, V | No lunch | $$$–$$$$

Bar J. Barbecue. Perhaps one of Jackson Hole's best values is Bar J's full ranch-style meal, served outdoors, plus a complete Western show with singing, stories, and cowboy poetry. The Bar J Wranglers not only serve your food, they also sing to you. The dinner and show take place inside if necessary, so don't let the weather keep you away. Reservations recommended. | Teton Village Rd. | 307/733–3370 or 800/905–2275 | AE, MC, V | Closed Oct.–Memorial Day | $$

Jedediah's. American. Friendly, noisy, and elbow-knocking, this restaurant a block east of the town square in a historic Jackson home caters to the big appetite. Try the sourdough pancakes, called sourjacks, or Teton taters and eggs. Kids' menu. | 135 E. Broadway | 307/733–5671 | AE, D, MC, V | $$

★ **The Bunnery.** American. Tucked into a tiny spot in the Hole-in-the-Wall Mall, this is where locals go for breakfast. It's usually busy, so there may be a short wait, but the food's worth it. All the breads are made here, mostly of a combined grain known as OSM (oats, sunflower, millet), and the owners have been known to ship the bread to customers throughout the world. Open-air dining. Kids' menu. | 130 N. Cache St. | 307/733–5474 | MC, V | $–$$

Lodging

★ **Wort Hotel.** The locals have been gathering at this Jackson landmark half a block from the town square since the early 1940s, and you can view the history of Jackson through the photos and clippings posted in the lobby. Completely renovated after a fire in the 1980s, the spacious rooms now have lodgepole furniture and comfortable armchairs. Junior suites have large sitting areas. Restaurant, bar, room service. Cable TV. Hot tubs. Exercise equipment. Business services. | 50 N. Glenwood | 307/733–2190 or 800/322–2727 | fax 307/733–2067 | www.worthotel.com | 60 rooms | AE, D, DC, MC, V | $$$–$$$$

Anvil Motel. The two-story motor inn with a red wood exterior is steps from Old Town, and is one of the nicer mid-priced inns in the central Jackson area. Old West porches and banisters and family-friendly innkeepers contribute to the casual tone. Comfortable rooms have Western-style pine furniture. Microwaves, refrigerators. Cable TV. Hot tub. No pets. | 215 N. Cache St. | 307/733–3668 or 800/234–4507 | fax 307/733–3957 | www.anvilmotel.com | 27 rooms, 2 suites | MC, V | $$

Buckrail Lodge. At the base of Snow King mountain, these beautifully appointed, spacious cedar log rooms have cathedral ceilings and Western-style furnishings. Although the town square is just a short walk away, this is a quiet place to stay. Picnic area. No air-conditioning, no room phones. Cable TV. Hot tub. No smoking. | 110 E. Karns Ave. | 307/733–2079 | fax 307/734–1663 | www.buckraillodge.com | 12 rooms | AE, D, MC, V | Closed winter | $$

4 Winds. The hotel is 1½ blocks from the downtown square, where you can see the elk-horn arches and the longest-running Western shoot-out. The rooms are contemporary and quiet. Basketball and tennis courts are a nice extra. Picnic area. Cable TV. Playground. | 150 N. Millward St. | 307/733-2474 or 800/228-6461 | www.jacksonholefourwinds.com | 21 rooms | AE, D, MC, V | Closed winter | $$

Sheridan

Attractions

Big Horn Equestrian Center. In the 1880s, aristocratic cattle barons built Wyoming's first polo field. You can watch polo games on Sunday afternoon from May through September, and other occasional equestrian events include dressage competitions, steeplechase races, and steer roping. | 800/453-3650.

Bighorn National Forest. No region in Wyoming has a more diverse landscape—lush grasslands, alpine meadows, rugged mountaintops, canyons, and deserts. | 307/684-1100 | www.fs.fed.us/r2/bighorn | Daily.

Bradford Brinton Memorial. Once the Quarter Circle A Ranch, owned by Bradford Brinton, this is now a memorial to a family known for fine art collections and an elegant home. The displays include art by Charles M. Russell, Frederic Remington, and John James Audubon, among others. You'll also see antique furnishings, quilts, rare books, and other memorabilia. | 239 Brinton Rd., Big Horn | 307/672-3173 | May 15-Labor Day, daily 9:30-5.

King's Saddlery and Museum. Don King started making saddles decades ago, and he's been collecting them for just as long. His craft is on full display in this small downtown museum, along with other cowboy gear. The Saddlery itself is still in business, run by King's sons, and it has a tradition for making some of the finest saddles in the world, even crafting them for royalty. The Kings also make King Ropes, used by professional rodeo cowboys and ranchers. Hundreds of ropes (some of them in neon colors) fill racks at the back of the store, and you'll likely find one or more cowboys there trying them out. | 184 N. Main St. | 307/672-2702 or 800/443-8919 | Mon.-Sat. 8-5.

Main Street Historic District. Historic buildings, most still used by businesses, line Main Street. You can get a map from the Chamber of Commerce or many of the businesses. | 307/672-8881.

Trail End Historic Center. When John B. Kendrick brought the first cattle into this area, he established himself as one of the "elite" citizens. Kendrick became Wyoming's governor and a senator, and he lived in this elegant Flemish Revival home completed in 1913. The furnishings at the state historic site are authentic Kendrick items. | 400 Clarendon Ave. | 307/674-4589 | commerce.state.wy.us | June-Aug., daily 9-6; Sept.-May, call for hours.

Dining

Sugarland Restaurant at the Holiday Inn. American. Quiet atmosphere and a diverse menu make this a good choice for dining out. Menu favorites are the beef, seafood, and pasta dishes. Salad bar. Kids' menu | 1809 Sugarland Dr. | 307/672-8931 | AE, D, DC, MC, V | $$-$$$

Sanford's Grub, Pub, Brewery. American. The name pretty much says it all. This is a noisy place that caters to the college crowd, but the burgers and sandwiches are good and the brews equally so. Particularly popular is the Big Horn Wheat brew. | 1 E. Alger Ave. | 307/674-1722 | $$

Gourmet Galley. American. Despite the name, this restaurant in a large log building is best known for basics: steak, chicken, and seafood. You can eat on the large deck that overlooks nearby mountains. Entertainment. Kids' menu. | 850 Sibley Circle | 307/674–5049 | AE, D, DC, MC, V | Closed Sun. | $–$$

Silver Spur. American. You might have to look twice: first to find this downtown breakfast-and-lunch place, and then to decide to go in. It's small and undistinguished, but the helpings are cowboy-size, and the omelettes are well prepared. | 832 N. Main St. | 307/672–2749 | No credit cards | $–$$

Lodging

Best Western Sheridan Center Motor Inn. Just two blocks from the main downtown area—and with a covered walkway over the main street—this is a convenient place to stay. The indoor pool is welcome in winter. Restaurant, bar. Cable TV. 2 pools (1 indoor). Hot tub. Airport shuttle. | 612 N. Main St. | 307/674–7421 | fax 307/672–3018 | 138 rooms | AE, D, DC, MC, V | $$

Holiday Inn. Five minutes from downtown Sheridan, this hotel is decorated in Western style throughout. The lobby has a four-story atrium with a waterfall and plants. Raquetball courts are a nice extra. Restaurant, bar, picnic area, room service. In-room data ports, some refrigerators. Cable TV. Indoor pool. Beauty salon, hot tub. Putting green. Exercise equipment. Laundry facilities. Business services, airport shuttle. Pets allowed. | 1809 Sugarland Dr. | 307/672–8931 | fax 307/672–6388 | 212 rooms | AE, D, DC, MC, V | $$

Ranch Willow Bed & Breakfast. Built in 1901, this lovely all-stone guest ranch is on 550 acres of rolling farm land, and is surrounded by huge cottonwood and apple trees. Your hosts include an internationally known furniture-maker who appoints the elegant but homey Western-style rooms and common areas with her unique pieces, and a third-generation Basque sheep farmer, who knows the area inside and out. There's a 3-night minimum stay, and the entire guest house is available for larger groups. Some shared bathrooms. Dining room, complimentary Continental breakfast. No room phones. TV in common area. Hot tub. | 501 U.S. 14E | 307/674–1510 or 800/354–2830 | fax 307/674–1502 | 4 rooms | MC, V | $$

Mill Inn Motel. An old mill by a bridge is incorporated into this motel, which has large guest rooms with pastel spreads, drapes, and rugs. The offices of *American Cowboy* magazine are upstairs, and the walls in the lobby and breakfast room are decorated with Western art prints, boots, and saddles. Complimentary Continental breakfast. Gym. Pets allowed. | 2161 Coffeen Ave. | 307/672–6401 | 45 rooms | AE, D, MC, V | $–$$

Big Horn Mountain KOA Campground. The pleasant, shady, and relatively peaceful campground 3½ mi from Sheridan makes roughing it easy with numerous amenities and extras such as mini-golf, basketball courts, fishing, and an on-site snack bar. A convenient stopover point for those going on to Yellowstone, it also has five cabins that sleep four or five and a bunkhouse that sleeps up to eight. Pool. Hot tub, sauna. Playground. Laundry facilities. | 63 Decker Rd. | 307/674–8766 or 800/562–7621 | www.koa.com | 40 tent sites, 100 trailer slots, 5 cabins, 1 bunkhouse | D, MC, V | Closed early Oct.–Mar. | $

Sundance

Attractions

Vore Buffalo Jump. Thousands of buffalo bones are piled atop each other at the Vore Buffalo Jump on Frontage Rd., where Native Americans forced buffalo to fall to their deaths in the era when hunting was done with spears rather than fast horses and guns. | 307/283–1000.

Dining

Aro Restaurant and Lounge. American. In downtown Sundance, this large family diner has a cowboys-and-Indians theme and an extensive, well-priced menu. Standards include burgers, prime rib, southwestern smothered burritos, Reuben sandwiches, and a huge Devils Tower brownie sundae dessert. | 205 Cleveland St. | 307/283–2000 | D, MC, V | $–$$

Country Cottage. American. Flowers, gifts, and simple meals, including submarine sandwiches, are sold at this one-stop shop. | 423 Cleveland St. | 307/283–2450 | MC, V | $–$$

Log Cabin Cafe. American. Locals crowd this small log-cabin restaurant for its burgers, steaks, and seafood. It's 3 mi from town. | U.S. 14 | 307/283–3393 | MC, V | $–$$

Yellowstone National Park

Attractions

Yellowstone Highlights. You can't run out of "firsts," "mosts," or "lasts" when it comes to describing Yellowstone National Park—it was the world's first national park; it is the largest national park in the lower 48; and it is, with surrounding wildlands, the center of the last truly intact temperate ecosystem. | Box 168, Mammoth, WY 82190 | 307/344–7381; 307/344–2386 TDD | fax 307/344–2014 | www.nps.gov/yell.

A cascading waterfall and rushing river carved the **Grand Canyon of the Yellowstone,** which is 24 mi long and 1,200 ft deep. The red and ochre canyon walls are topped with emerald-green forest.

At **Mammoth Hot Springs**—multicolored travertine terraces formed by slowly flowing hot mineral water—elk who graze nearby are frequent visitors.

★**Norris Geyser Basin,** the hottest and oldest such basin in Yellowstone, is constantly changing. Some geysers or hot springs might suddenly stop flowing, but others blow and hiss into life. Among the features at Norris are Whirligig Geyser, Whale's Mouth, Emerald Spring, and Arch Steam Vent.

You can learn the history of Yellowstone's watchdogs, from turn-of-the-last-century army troops to today's rangers, at the **Norris Museum,** a small log-cabin museum.

The huge, though unpredictable, Steamboat Geyser is one of the attractions at **Back Basin,** a big geyser area. Though Steamboat only performs about once a year, when it does, it shoots 300 ft into the air.

The **Porcelain Basin** is a small geyser area that has a 1 mi boardwalk often crammed with people, but it's a good place to watch the ground bulge and push from underground pressure.

The long-standing centerpiece of Yellowstone is **Old Faithful–Upper Geyser Basin.** The mysterious plumbing of Yellowstone has lengthened Old Faithful's eruption cycle somewhat in recent years, but the geyser still spouts the same amount of water—sometimes reaching to 140 ft—and pleases spectators every 80 minutes or so. Sometimes it doesn't shoot so high, but in those cases the eruption lasts longer. To find out when Old Faithful is next expected to erupt, check at the visitor center. Marked trails and bridges lead to Geyser Hill, and you can visit Castle Geyser and Morning Glory Pool as well as the Giantess Geyser and Giant Geyser. Elk and buffalo commonly share the area. In winter, cross-country ski trails converge at Old Faithful.

The Grand Prismatic Spring and Excelsior Geyser Crater are at **Midway Geyser Basin,** which has some beautiful, richly colored, bottomless pools.

The Great Fountain Geyser is the most spectacular of the attractions at **Lower Geyser Basin.** But you'll find bubbling mudpots, blue pools, fumaroles, pink mud pots, and the mini-geysers at Fountain Paint Pots here as well.

A small geyser basin and views of Lake Yellowstone are worth stopping for at **West Thumb,** which also has a visitor center and a warming hut if you're here in winter.

You can use the riding trails and have cookouts in the **Tower-Roosevelt** area, check out the Petrified Tree, and hike on trails through the Lamar Valley or to Specimen Ridge with its unusual fossils.

Yellowstone Lake, North America's largest mountain lake, was formed by glaciers. You can boat and fish or simply sit along the shore and watch the waves. In the winter you might see otters and coyotes.

Dining

Roosevelt Lodge. American. At this rustic log cabin in a pine forest, the menu ranges from barbecued ribs and Roosevelt beans to hamburgers and steak. Chuckwagon cookouts involve one- or two-hour trail rides or stagecoach rides. Kids' menu. Reservations essential for chuckwagon cookouts. | Tower at Roosevelt | 307/344–7901 | AE, D, DC, MC, V | Closed Sept.–early June | $$–$$$$

Mammoth Hot Springs Hotel. American. After exploring Yellowstone during the day, you'll welcome the quiet of the Mammoth Hot Springs Hotel dining room. The service is low-key, and the menu varied, with beef, chicken, and pasta dishes. Dinner reservations essential. | Mammoth Hot Springs | 307/344–7901 | AE, D, DC, MC, V | $$–$$$

Old Faithful Snow Lodge. American. From the wood and leather chairs, complete with etched figures of park animals, to the intricate lighting that resembles snow-capped trees and whimsical figures, you'll appreciate the atmosphere of the Old Faithful Snow Lodge. This is the only place in the park, aside from Mammoth, where you can enjoy a relaxing, sit-down lunch or dinner during the winter season. The huge windows give you a view of the Old Faithful area, and you can sometimes see the famous geyser as it erupts. Try the French onion soup. The menu also includes beef, chicken, and pasta. | 307/344–7901 | AE, D, DC, MC, V | Open Dec.–Mar. and May–Oct., daily 7:30–10:30, 11:30–2:30, 5:30–10 | $$–$$$

Lake Yellowstone Dining Room. American. Huge windows give you a view of Lake Yellowstone, and there is usually a musical interlude during the dinner hour. The menu is strong on steaks, prime rib, and trout. Kids' menu. No smoking. Dinner reservations essential. | Lake Village | 307/344–7901 | AE, D, DC, MC, V | Closed Oct.–May | $$

Lodging

★ **Lake Yellowstone Hotel.** Relax on the lawn or view the lake from the restaurant. Some rooms have lake views. Restaurant, bar. No air-conditioning. | Lake Village | 307/344–7311 | fax 307/344–7456 | www.amfac.com | 194 rooms | AE, D, DC, MC, V | Closed Oct.–mid-May | $$–$$$

Old Faithful Inn. An architectural wonder built in 1903 and later expanded, the log building has a six-story lobby with huge rock fireplaces. Some rooms have views of Old Faithful. Restaurant, bar. No air-conditioning, some refrigerators. Some room phones. | Old Faithful | 307/344–7311 | fax 307/344–7456 | www.amfac.com | 325 rooms, 246 with bath | AE, D, DC, MC, V | Closed mid-Oct.–Apr. | $$–$$$

Canyon Lodge. Yellowstone's largest lodging facility, this property is central, busy, and basic, and probably where you'll stay if you don't make reservations elsewhere. Pine-frame cabins have modest furnishings, and surround the somewhat ungainly 1970s-style main lodge, which has a gift shop and snack bar. Close to the Yellowstone River, this is a good spot if you opt for convenience over luxury. 3 restaurants, bar, cafeteria. Laundry facilities. | North Rim Dr. | 307/344–7311 | fax 307/344–7456 | www.travelyellowstone.com | 572 cabins, 80 annex rooms | AE, D, MC, V | Closed early Sept.–early June | $–$$$

Grant Village. You get the southernmost accommodations in the park at this complex on the shore of Yellowstone Lake. The rooms are spread throughout six buildings. Sightseeing tours of the area begin from here. Restaurant, bar. No air-conditioning. Laundry facilities. | 307/344–7311 | fax 307/344–7456 | www.amfac.com | 300 rooms | AE, D, DC, MC, V | Closed Oct.–late May | $$

Lake Lodge. The main lodge, a part of which dates to the 1920s, has views of Yellowstone Lake and is nestled among pine groves. Although the basic cabin-style accommodations are similar to other facilities in the park, the cozy lodge and semi-secluded site at the far end of Lake Village Road make this a better choice if you want something more homey. Bar, cafeteria. | 307/344–7311 | fax 307/344–7456 | www.travelyellowstone. com/ | 186 cabins | AE, D, MC, V | Closed mid-Sept.–mid-June | $–$$

HISTORIC TRAILS TREK
TORRINGTON TO EVANSTON

Distance: 390 mi   Time: Minimum of 4 days
Overnight Breaks: Casper, Lander, Rawlins

On this drive you can cross the same ground pioneers did when they traveled to Oregon, Utah, and California 150 years ago. In many ways the landscape has changed little in the intervening years. You can make this trip at any time, but spring, summer, and fall are best because all the visitor centers are open and you'll be less likely to run into a snowstorm on South Pass. Bear in mind, though, that the pass is 7,550 ft high, so you could hit snow even in July or August.

❶ Begin at **Fort Laramie National Historic Site** (U.S. 26, 20 mi west of Torrington), which became the most important site on the Oregon-California-Mormon trail route because it was a provisioning point and, after 1849, a U.S. Army post. Many of the fort's original buildings remain, and during the summer costumed interpreters illustrate life there. Actual ruts of the historic emigrant trails cross the fort grounds.

❷ Continuing west on U.S. 26, you'll come to Register Cliff and the Guernsey Ruts, both near **Guernsey,** where 1840s pioneers would congregate to bathe. A mile northeast of town is Guernsey State Park, where you can swim and boat. The Depression-era Civilian Conservation Corps built the museum on the grounds.

❸ From Guernsey continue west on U.S. 20/26 for 15 mi to I–25, then head north on I–25 to **Ayres Natural Bridge,** off the interstate between Douglas and Glenrock. Overland emigrants sometimes visited this rock outcrop that spans LaPrele Creek, and now it's a popular small picnic area and campsite where you can wade in the creek or simply enjoy the quiet.

❹ After taking in the beauty of the bridge and its surroundings, head west on I–25 for approximately 40 mi to **Casper** (I–25, U.S. 20/26, and Rte. 220). Several major trails converged here as emigrants crossed the North Platte River and continued west along the Oregon-California-Mormon routes to the Sweetwater River valley or headed north to Montana's gold fields over the Bozeman or Bridger trails. No community existed here during the migration period, but **Fort Caspar,** which originally went by the name Platte Bridge Station, was a military installation during the later years of overland travel. Indoor activities in Casper might include visits to the **Nicolaysen Art Museum & Discovery Center** and the **Casper Planetarium.** Spend the night in Casper.

⑤ **Independence Rock State Historic Site** (60 mi west of Casper on Rte. 220) is one of the best-known of all trail sites along the entire 2,000-mi corridor from Missouri to Oregon or California, and pioneers almost always mentioned it in their journals. You can stretch your legs at a rest area, perhaps by climbing to the top of the rock, where you'll see some of the emigrant names carved in the granite. Then continue west on Route 220 to the **Mormon Trail–Martin's Cove Visitors Center** at the Sun Ranch, a site that interprets the Mormon migration to Utah and other emigrant stories as well. You can pick up a handcart and pull it along the trail route.

⑥ Leaving Independence Rock, continue west on Route 220/U.S. 287 to **Lander** (U.S. 287). Lander is off the main emigrant trail route, but it is a good place to hang your hat for the night and learn about the Shoshone and Arapaho Indian tribes, who have a reservation just to the northeast.

⑦ Head south out of Lander on U.S. 287 to Route 28. **South Pass City State Historic Site** (off Rte. 28 between Lander and Farson) is only a few miles from the most important site of the entire route—South Pass—the long, low pass over the Rocky Mountains used by early travelers to cross the Continental Divide. South Pass City was a gold town established in 1869 and is the birthplace of women's suffrage in Wyoming. A collection of historic buildings still marks the town site, where you can sometimes pan for gold or hike trails used by miners of yesteryear.

⑧ From South Pass City, backtrack to U.S. 287 and head southeast for approximately 125 mi to **Rawlins** (I–80 Exit 220 and U.S. 287), in the Great Divide Basin, a depression between two branches of the Continental Divide. Visit the **Carbon County Museum** to see artifacts from outlaw George Parrott, or take a tour of the Wyoming Frontier Prison. The Overland and Cherokee trails crossed southern Wyoming from near Laramie to Evanston. The Cherokees made their route in 1849 as they headed to California's gold fields; the Overland Route became the main stagecoach road across the region after 1865. I–80 parallels the two, which are generally south of today's highway. Spend a night in Rawlins.

⑨ From Rawlins proceed west on I–80 for about 110 mi to **Rock Springs** (Exit 104), a historic coal-mining town. **Green River** (I–80, Exits 89 and 91) also owes its prosperity to mining. At the **Flaming Gorge National Historic Area** (south on U.S. 191 or Rte. 530) you can boat, fish, camp, bike, and hike.

⑩ After you've explored Rock Springs, head west on I–80 for approximately 60 mi to the **Fort Bridger State Historic Site** (I–80, Exit 48 westbound or Exit 34 eastbound), the emigrants' major trading and provisioning point—the first they had seen since leaving Fort Laramie. Mountain man Jim Bridger and his partner Louis Vasquez established Fort Bridger "in the path of the emigrants" in 1841. It later became a military fort, and many original buildings remain.

⑪ Continue west out of the Fort on I–80 to **Evanston** (Exit 3), a town that got its start as a Union Pacific hell-on-wheels town.

To return to Fort Laramie, head east on I–80 to Rawlins, north on U.S. 287/Route 789 to Route 220, then east into Casper. From Casper, follow I–25 east and south back to U.S. 26, which leads east into Fort Laramie.

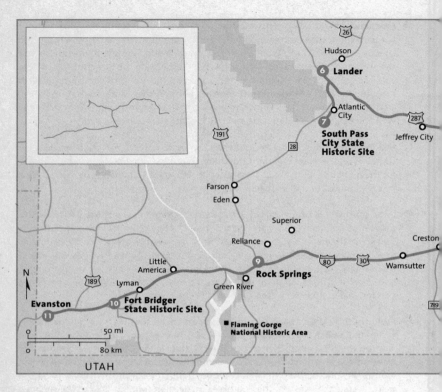

Casper

Attractions

Casper Mountain and Beartrap Meadow Parks. Rising to the east of the city, Casper Mountain is a recreational paradise where you can hike and fish in summer and cross-country and downhill ski in winter. The Crimson Dawn Museum is the original log-cabin home of Neal and Jim Forsling, who settled in the area with their daughters in 1915. Neal held her first Midsummer Night's Eve Celebration on June 21, 1929, and the event continues. She and her daughters and their friends built the first trails in the woods around Crimson Dawn Park. Today those same trails are marked with shrines and plaques commemorating the mythical "Enchanted Witches and Elves of Casper Mountain." | Casper Mountain Rd. | 307/235–9325 | Daily; museum, mid-June–mid-Oct., Sat.–Thurs. 11–7.

In Skunk Hollow along Elkhorn Creek, 8 mi south of Route 251, the **Lee McCune Braille Trail** is a $\frac{1}{3}$-mi route with rope handrails and 37 stops with print and Braille markers describing the scenery. Built in 1975 by the Casper Mountain Lions Club and Casper Field Services students, the Braille Trail is part of the National Trails System. | Casper Mountain Rd. | 307/235–9325 | June–Sept., depending on snowfall.

Casper Mountain is rated a premier **bird-watching** area, and the local Murie Audubon Society offers both a hot line and guides to 13 local birding areas. | 307/265–2473.

Casper Planetarium. Watch multimedia programs on astronomy and space subjects. | 904 N. Poplar St. | 307/577–0310 | fax 307/235–9611 | www.trib.com/WYOMING/NCSD/planetarium.html | Sept.–May, Thurs. at 7 PM, and 1st and 2nd Sat. of each month; June–Aug., daily at 4, 7, 8 PM.

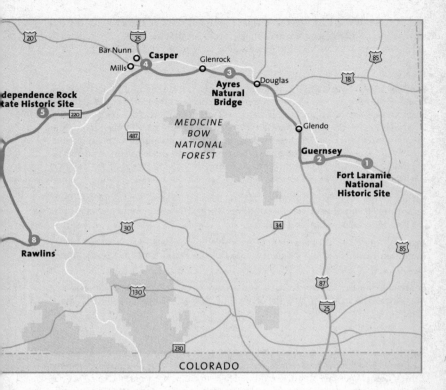

Fort Caspar Museum. A small museum re-creates the post at Platte Bridge, which became Fort Caspar after the July 1865 battle that claimed the lives of several soldiers, including Lt. Caspar Collins. A post depicts life at a frontier station in the 1860s. Museum exhibits show the migration trails. | 4001 Fort Caspar Rd. | 307/235–8462 | Closed Sat.

Independence Rock. The turtle-shape granite outcrop became an important site on the Oregon-California-Mormon trails. Pioneers carved their names in the rock, and many are still legible 150 years later. The rock, midway between Casper and Rawlins, is now a state historic site. A state rest area here has rest rooms and picnic tables. | Rte. 220 | 307/577–5150 | commerce.state.wy.us | Daily.

Mormon Trail Handcart Visitor Center. Opened for the 1997 sesquicentennial of the Mormon Trail, this visitor center at the Sun Ranch interprets general trail travel, and particularly the plight of the handcart pioneers in the Willie and Martin Companies, who became stranded in this area in 1856. You can walk the Mormon Trail, and handcarts are available. There's a picnic area, but no food is sold. | 50 mi southwest of Casper on Rte. 220 | 307/324–5218 | Daily.

Nicolaysen Art Museum and Discovery Center. Known locally as The Nic, this art museum has a permanent collection with works by Conrad Schweiring, as well as traveling exhibits. The Discovery Center is an interactive arts and crafts area for children. | 400 E. Collins Dr. | 307/235–5247 | www.thenic.org | Tues.–Sun. 9–5.

Platte River Parkway. The natural beauty and historic significance of the North Platte River are preserved along this 4-mi paved trail with access points at Amoco Park at 1st and Poplar streets, at the Historic Trails Overlook east of the Casper Events Center, and between Morad Park and Fort Caspar. Eventually the trail will cover 11½ mi. You can use it for walking, jogging, and wheeled-vehicles that are "user-powered," such as roller blades, bicycles, and skateboards. | Rte. 220 | 307/577–1206 | Daily.

Dining

Poor Boy's Steakhouse. American. Reminiscent of a frontier mining camp, this steak house at the Parkway Plaza has blue-and-white-checked tablecloths and chair backs, quick service, and large portions of steak, seafood, or chicken, plus bread and salad. Local favorites are the Moonshine Mama (grilled chicken breast with mushrooms and Monterey Jack and cheddar cheeses) and the filet mignon and shrimp. For dessert, try Ashley's Avalanche—a huge plate of ice cream, white-chocolate brownie, cherry-pie filling, chocolate sauce, and whipped cream. | 123 W. E St. | 307/235–1777 | fax 307/235–8068 | AE, D, DC, MC, V | $$–$$$$

Paisley Shawl. American. Specialties at this spot in the Hotel Higgins include steak and prime rib. You can also eat out on the deck. | 416 W. Birch, Glenrock | 307/436–9212 | DC, MC, V | Closed Sun.–Mon. | $$–$$$

Armor's. American. Quiet, with cozy booths, this place also has views of Casper Mountain. Favorite dishes include spare ribs and steaks. Kids' menu. | 3422 S. Energy La. | 307/235–3000 | AE, D, DC, MC, V | $–$$

El Jarro. Mexican. Usually crowded and always noisy, El Jarro has good food and margaritas. The local favorite is the green chili. | 500 W. F St. | 307/577–0538 | D, MC, V | $–$$

Lodging

Hampton Inn. Business travelers will appreciate the in-room data ports and other business services at this modern and comfortable hotel near I–25 and the Casper Events Center. Complimentary Continental breakfast. In-room data ports. Cable TV. Pool. Sauna. Business services, airport shuttle. Pets allowed (fee). | 400 W. F St. | 307/235–6668 | fax 307/235–2027 | 122 rooms | AE, D, DC, MC, V | $$

Holiday Inn. On the river, next to I–25 and several blocks from downtown Casper, this circular hotel has a lot of greenery in the public spaces. Restaurant, bar, picnic area, room service. In-room data ports. Cable TV. Indoor pool. Hot tub. Exercise equipment. Video games. Laundry facilities. Business services, airport shuttle. Pets allowed. | 300 W. F St. | 307/235–2531 | fax 307/473–3400 | 200 rooms | AE, D, DC, MC, V | $$

Radisson. The rooms are large and done in muted blue, green, and mauve. You'll find many amenities under one roof. Restaurant, bar, coffee shop, room service. Some in-room hot tubs. Cable TV. Indoor pool. Beauty salon, hot tub. Cross-country skiing, downhill skiing. Airport shuttle. Pets allowed. | 800 N. Poplar St. | 307/266–6000 | fax 307/473–1010 | 228 rooms | AE, D, DC, MC, V | $–$$

Hotel Higgins. The 1916 building looks a little questionable on the outside, but the interior is a delight. Rooms are furnished in Victorian style. Restaurant, bar, complimentary breakfast. No air-conditioning in some rooms. | 416 W. Birch, Glenrock, I–25 Exit 165 | 307/436–9212; 800/458–0144 (outside WY) | fax 307/436–9213 | 8 rooms | D, DC, MC, V | $

Parkway Plaza. Guest rooms are large and quiet, with double vanities, one inside the bathroom and one outside. The public areas have Western furnishings. Convention center. Restaurant, bar. Pool. Hot tub. Business services. | 123 W. E St. | 307/235–1777 | fax 307/235–8068 | 272 rooms | AE, D, MC, V | $

Evanston

Attractions

Bear River State Park. Wildlife, from ducks and Canada geese to herds of bison and elk, is abundant in the park, and you can hike and ski on the trails, which have picnic shelters. The park connects to Evanston's Bear Pathway, a paved trail that for much of its length is fully accessible to people with disabilities. | 601 Bear River Dr. | 307/789–6547 | www.state.wy.us | Daily; closed evenings.

Fort Bridger State Historic Site. Started in 1842 as a trading post by mountain man Jim Bridger, Fort Bridger was owned by Bridger and his partner Louis Vasquez until 1853, when Mormons took control of it. The Mormons deserted the area and burned the original Bridger post as the U.S. Army approached during the so-called Mormon War of 1857. The site then became a frontier military post until it was abandoned in 1890. It is now a state historic site. Many of the original military-era buildings remain and have been restored; you can attend interpretive programs and living-history presentations in the summer. The largest mountain-man rendezvous in the intermountain West occurs annually at Fort Bridger over Labor Day weekend, attracting hundreds of buckskinners and Native Americans and thousands of visitors. | 37000 Business Loop I–80 | 307/782–3842 | fax 307/782–7181 | www.state.wy.us | Mar.–Apr., weekends 9–4:30; May–Sept., daily 9–5:30; Oct.–Nov., daily 9–4:30; closed Dec.–Feb.; Bridger/Vasquez Trading Co.: May–Sept., daily 9–5:30.

Uinta County Historical Museum. Local history displays include antique photographs, historic books, and artifacts related to Chinese settlement in the area. | 36 10th St. | 307/783–0370 | Memorial Day–Labor Day, weekdays 9–5, weekends 10–4; Labor Day–Memorial Day, weekdays 9–5.

Dining

Legal Tender. American. In the Best Western Dunmar Inn, this restaurant is quiet, with good service. Salad bar. Kids' menu. Sun. brunch. | 1601 Harrison Dr. | 307/789–3770 | AE, D, DC, MC, V | $$–$$$

Don Pedro's Last Outpost. Mexican. You can't get more authentic than this small, family-owned and -operated restaurant that's always packed. Try the sizzling fajitas, or the special *molcajete* (a stew of beef and chicken). | 205 Bear River Dr. | 307/789–3322 | MC, V | $–$$

Main Street Artisans Cafe & Gallery. Contemporary. Recharge with an espresso at this cozy eatery and art gallery. The homemade muffins and cakes are favorites, as are the pasta salad, mesquite chicken sandwich, and fresh tomato-basil soup. | 927 Main St. | 307/789–4991 | MC, V | Closed Sun. and Oct.–May. No dinner | $–$$

Lander

Attractions

Arapaho Cultural Center Museum and Heritage Center. Art and artifacts related to the Arapaho tribe are included in the collection of this museum, which is off Route 137. The center is also the site of the historic St. Michael's Episcopal Mission. The Heritage Center has displays of beadwork, crafts, and clothing. | St. Stephens | 307/332–3040 | Weekdays 9–5.

Shoshone National Forest, Washakie District (Wind River Mountains). Known simply as the Winds, this is Wyoming's most rugged mountain range. It's a great place for mountain biking, hiking, climbing, dog sledding, cross-country skiing, and snowmobiling. The Continental Divide National Scenic Trail crosses the backbone of these mountains, and is a popular snowmobile trail in the winter. Lander is one of the gateway communities to this vast area that includes national forest and wilderness lands. A number of outfitters can help make your trip enjoyable; some specialize in guided hikes, others in horsepacking and treks with goats or llamas. Contact the Wind River Visitors Council or Shoshone National Forest for information. | Wind River Visitors Council, 337 E. Main St., Riverton, 82501 | 307/856–7566 or 800/645–6233 | www.wind-river.org | Shoshone National Forest, Lander District Office | 307/332–5460 | Daily.

Shoshone Tribal Cultural Center. Shoshone art and artifacts are part of the collections at this center that also has information about the two most famous Shoshones: Chief Washakie and Sacajawea, guide to Lewis and Clark. A small gift shop sells authentic Shoshone crafts and beadwork. | 31 Black Cove Rd., Fort Washakie | 307/332–9106 or 307/332–3040 | Weekdays 9–5.

South Pass City State Historic Site. Established during the South Pass Gold Rush of 1868, South Pass City was the birthplace of women's suffrage in Wyoming. Julia Bright and Esther Hobart Morris are two of the women from the community who fought for the vote. They no doubt expressed their opinions to Horace Bright, Julia's husband, who ultimately—and successfully—introduced the bill in the Wyoming Territorial Legislature. But South Pass City is also a model mining community. Many of the original buildings survive and have been restored. The small museum gives an overview of the South Pass gold district, and at certain times during the summer season you can try your hand at panning for gold in the cold stream that runs through town, which is off Highway 137. | South Pass City Rd. | 307/332–3684 | www.state.wy.us/sphs/south1.htm | Mid-May–early Sept., daily 9–5:30.

Dining

Svilars. American. Inside this small, family-owned restaurant you'll find what many natives say is the best food in all of Wyoming. A meal might begin with *sarma* (cabbage rolls) or other appetizers, and ought to be followed by a tremendous and tasty steak. | 175 S. Main St., Hudson | 307/332–4516 | No credit cards | Closed Sun. and every other Mon. No lunch | $$$–$$$$

Atlantic City Mercantile. American. You'll feel as if you've stepped directly into an old western when you enter this downtown building, with its long mirrored back bar and collection of mismatched tables and chairs. At times a honky-tonk piano player is on hand. In summer, steaks are cooked on an open-flame grill in the back of the building. The menu also includes chicken, seafood, and sandwiches. | 100 E. Main St., Atlantic City | 307/332–5143 | fax 307/332–9376 | D, MC, V | $$–$$$$

Lodging

Blue Spruce Inn. Named after the five enormous spruce trees on the property, this 1920s brick home has a huge front porch with a swing, and beautiful gardens. Theme rooms are cozy and individually decorated. In a residential area within walking distance of downtown, this is a quiet and convenient choice. Recreation room. Complimentary breakfast. No TV in some rooms. Library. No pets. No smoking. | 677 S. 3rd St. | 307/332–8253 or 888/503–3311 | fax 307/332–1386 | www.bluespruceinn.com | 4 rooms | AE, D, MC, V | $–$$

Budget Host Pronghorn. The sculpture garden that spreads through Lander starts at this downtown motel. Some rooms have kitchens. Restaurant, complimentary Continental breakfast. Some refrigerators. Cable TV. Hot tub. Laundry facilities. Pets allowed. | 150 E. Main St. | 307/332–3940 | fax 307/332–2651 | www.wyoming.com/~thepronghorn | 54 rooms | AE, D, DC, MC, V | $–$$

Best Western Inn at Lander. The cabin-style motel sits on the hill overlooking Lander. Some rooms have refrigerators, and the small outdoor area has picnic tables. Complimentary Continental breakfast. Some refrigerators. Cable TV. Pool. Hot tub. Exercise equipment. Airport shuttle. | 260 Grandview Dr. | 307/332–2847 | fax 307/332–2760 | 46 rooms | AE, D, MC, V | $

Rawlins

Attractions

Carbon County Museum. See a pair of shoes reportedly made from the skin of Big Nose George Parrott, an outlaw lynched in 1881 after he attempted to escape from the county jail. He was awaiting execution for his role in the murder of two lawmen, the first officers to die in the line of duty in Wyoming. After his death, Parrott's body was used for "medical study," and he was ultimately skinned. Other more traditional articles illuminate the area's settlement. | 9th and Walnut Sts. | 307/328–2740 | Oct. 1–Apr. 30, Mon., Wed., and Sat. 1–5; May–Oct., weekdays 10–12 and 1–5; tours by appointment.

Independence Rock. Called the "Register of the Desert" by pioneer travelers, this turtle-shape granite outcrop on Route 220 became an important landmark on the Oregon-California-Mormon trails. Emigrants carved their names in the rock, and many remain legible more than 150 years later. The rock is now a state historic site, midway between Casper and Rawlins. Stop to stretch your legs by climbing the rock face, which looks steep but is actually easy to manage. A state rest area has rest rooms and picnic tables. | 307/577–5150 | www.state.wy.us | Daily.

Seminoe State Park. The Seminoe Reservoir is the primary attraction here, and you can fish, boat, and water-ski, as well as camp and picnic. It's on a Bureau of Land Management backcountry byway, County Road 351, linking Sinclair with Alcova. | 307/320–3013 | www.state.wy.us | Daily.

Wyoming Frontier Prison. Cold steel and concrete, the Death House, and the Yard are all part of the tour of the Wyoming Frontier Prison, which remained in use as the state's penitentiary until about two decades ago. Now you can tour it, perhaps on a special midnight or Halloween tour. | 5th and Walnut Sts. | 307/324–4422 | Apr.–Sept., daily 8:30–5:30; other months by appt.

Dining

The Pantry. American. The original rooms of this historic house provide a quiet setting for your meal, which may include homemade soup and bread. | 221 W. Cedar St. | 307/324–7860 | D, MC, V | $$

Rose's Lariat. Mexican. A tiny place serving authentic fare, Rose's dishes lean toward the hot and spicy; if you can't take the heat, stick with a sandwich, hamburger, or one of the Italian selections. | 410 E. Cedar St. | 307/324–5261 | No credit cards | Closed Sun.–Mon. | $–$$

Su Casa. Mexican. Shrimp, beef, and chicken fajitas, green chili, and Navajo tacos are among the choices. Try the enchiladas or the chiles rellenos. Take out available. | 705 E. Lincoln Ave., Sinclair | 307/328–1745 | Closed Mon. | No credit cards | $–$$

Lodging

Cottontree Inn. Rawlins's finest motel, Cottontree has spacious guest rooms and inviting public areas with easy chairs. Restaurant, bar. In-room data ports. Cable TV. Indoor pool. Hot tub, sauna. Business services. Pets allowed. | 23rd and Spruce | 307/324–2737 | fax 307/324–5011 | 122 rooms | AE, D, DC, MC, V | $

Sleep Inn. Next to I–80 at the Rip Griffin Truck Stop, this is a basic modern motel with some nice amenities and good rates. Complimentary Continental breakfast. In-room data ports. Cable TV. Sauna. Business services. | 1400 Higley Blvd. | 307/328–1732 | fax 307/328–0412 | 81 rooms, many with shower only | AE, D, DC, MC, V | $

Index